The psychology of facial expression

This reference work provides broad and up-to-date coverage of the major perspectives on facial expression – ethological, neurobehavioral, developmental, dynamic systems, and componential. It reviews Darwin's legacy in the theories of Izard and Tomkins and in Fridlund's recently proposed Behavioral Ecology Theory. It explores continuing controversies on universality and innateness. It also updates the research guidelines of Ekman, Friesen, and Ellsworth.

This book anticipates emerging research questions: What are the roles of evolution and culture in children's understanding of faces? In what precise ways do faces depend on the immediate context? What is the ecology of facial expression? When do different expressions occur, and in what frequency?

STUDIES IN EMOTION AND SOCIAL INTERACTION
Second Series

Series Editors

Keith Oatley
University of Toronto

Antony Manstead
University of Amsterdam

This series is jointly published by the Cambridge University Press and the Editions de la Maison des Sciences de l'Homme, as part of the joint publishing agreement established in 1977 between the Fondation de la Maison des Sciences de l'Homme and the Syndics of the Cambridge University Press.

Cette collection est publiée co-édition par Cambridge University Press et les Editions de la Maison des Sciences de l'Homme. Elle s´intègre dans le programme de co-édition établi en 1977 par la Fondation de la Maison des Sciences de l'Homme et les Syndics de Cambridge University Press.

For a list of titles in the First Series of Studies in Emotion and Social Interaction, see the page following the index.

The psychology of facial expression

Edited by

James A. Russell
University of British Columbia

José Miguel Fernández-Dols
Universidad Autónoma de Madrid

 **CAMBRIDGE**
UNIVERSITY PRESS

& Editions de la Maison des Sciences de l'Homme
Paris

PUBLISHED BY THE PRESS SYNDICATE OF THE UNIVERSITY OF CAMBRIDGE
The Pitt Building, Trumpington Street, Cambridge, CB2 1RP, United Kingdom
and
EDITIONS DE LA MAISON DES SCIENCES DE L'HOMME
54 Boulevard Raspail, 75270 Paris Cedex 06, France

CAMBRIDGE UNIVERSITY PRESS
The Edinburgh Building, Cambridge CB2 2RU, United Kingdom
40 West 20th Street, New York, NY 10011–4211, USA
10 Stamford Road, Oakleigh, Melbourne 3166, Australia

First published 1997

Printed in the United States of America

Typeset in Palatino

Library of Congress Cataloging-in-Publication Data
The psychology of facial expression / edited by James A. Russell, José
Miguel Fernández-Dols.
    p.   cm. – (Studies in emotion and social interaction, second series)
ISBN 0-521-49667-5. – ISBN 0-521-58796-4 (pbk.)
1. Facial expression.   2. Nonverbal communication (Psychology)
I. Russell, James A.   II. Fernández-Dols, José Miguel.   III. Series.
BF592.F33P78   1997   96–36250
153.6'9 – DC20   CIP

*A catalog record for this book is available from
the British Library*

ISBN 0 521 49667 5 hardback
ISBN 0 521 58796 4 paperback
ISBN 2-7351-0726-4 hardback France only
ISBN 2-7351-0727-2 paperback France only

Contents

Part IV   With a psychological and social focus

Part V   Integrative summary

Foreword

The chapters in this collection represent the best thought on the role and function of human facial behavior, and many of them address what has become central to most contemporary accounts – the link between facial expression and emotion. The arguments for and against such a link between emotion and facial behavior are represented in the following pages. It is in part a theme of this book that the belief in such a link was not always thus in the past and that it need not be thus in the future.

The current predominance of the Tomkins–Izard–Ekman account of the meaning of facial expressions and their strong dependence on emotions started some 30 years ago, and 30 years is generally the lifetime of regnant psychological theories. In recent years, a new wave of thought has emerged and the debate has been joined between those who see facial expression as a necessary accompaniment or precursor of emotional experience, and those who see facial expression as communicative, expressive, and mimetic devices, possibly remnants of an early preverbal language but not necessarily tied to emotion. I joined the wave some 20 years ago and have been delighted by the momentum and the contributors it has gathered in the intervening period – most all of them represented here.

In retrospect, it seems strange that something as palpable and measurable as facial expression should be seen to be immersed in something as vague and intellectually slippery as emotion. Since I have been in the past accused of "not believing in emotion," let me briefly expand on this theme. In the common natural languages, we all know without much doubt what feeling emotions and being emotional is all about. It is about involuntary, strong, sometimes irrational feelings and commitments and mental and bodily reactions to significant or at least significant-seeming situations and people.

But when we come to the psychologists' and physiologists' emotions, no such easy agreement is available. One of the reasons that it is difficult to decide unequivocally among the multitude of theories of emotion is that most of them are invulnerable because the phenomena they address vary from theory to theory, and the various approaches may therefore – from the outset – be incommensurable. Definitions of emotion range from seeing them as of a piece among all animals and therefore only behaviorally diagnosable, to those that concentrate on autonomic physiology and its perception exclusively, to those that combine autonomic reactions with cognitive disposition, to theories that see peripheral autonomic reactions as optional, and those that simply talk about the natural language concept of affect alone (i.e., without any necessary autonomic accompaniment at all). The theories that map into those and intermediate positions are therefore theories about very different ranges of phenomena – dealing with observable "rage" and "fear" at one end to those that seem to encompass practically all of human actions and experience (i.e., a sine qua non of human experience). At one extreme, we are faced with an inadequate inclusion criterion that seems to forget about common human experience, and at the other extreme, the absence of an exclusion criterion does not give us an answer to "what is not an emotion?" One then comes to ask: Which of these "emotions" are facial movements supposed to express? Granted that it might be possible to find some (small) commonality among all of these positions, facial expressions still seem to claim much more than a reference to such a common denominator.

The question then is what the function of expressive facial and other movements might be. It is unlikely to be, as Darwin already noted, the sheer conversational communication of personal feelings. There is little argument that evolutionary pressures would produce a need – outside of such intimate situations as the therapeutic couch – to know how other people "feel." Is it likely that our prehistoric ancestors anticipated a contemporary Californian view that one needs to "get in touch with one's (or another's) feelings"? If such a need existed, then we would not be faced with the perplexing fact that neither facial expression nor basic emotion theorists have included either love or lust in their catalogs of emotions expressed or felt. It is more likely that expressive movements have a long history as communicative instruments, as several authors in this volume argue. I have argued that they are likely to be leftovers of a preverbal gestural language.

The virtual abandonment in the literature (but not in this volume) of a discussion of gesture language is an embarrassment for both the psychology of language and the psychology of emotion. The former, in its "miracle" Chomskian and neo-Chomskian mode, yields no place for any extensive communication skills in humans prior to the emergence of spoken language; the latter has, until recently, ignored the communicative functions of expressive movements (consisting of facial, bodily, and vocal expression and gestures). Again, this approach has a long history. Nearly 100 years ago, Wilhelm Wundt in the first volume of his monumental *Völkerpsychologie* noted that "language presumably developed out of the simpler forms of expressive movements." Among the expressive skills that surely contributed to the early communicative behaviors of preverbal *H. sapiens* were facial, gestural, vocal, and "body language" expressions. Even today, other primates communicate not too badly by the use of these devices. Should early humans have been expressively mute by comparison? And if not, is it unlikely that some of these devices survived into the present, just as so many other aspects of our bodily equipment did?

What has produced the contemporary fascination of the apparent link between emotion (however defined) and facial expression? And the question goes deeper than that since the conventional contemporary view of faces expressing emotion is based on a folk view that has been around for a long time. Either there is in fact some opaque emotion-signaling function of the face, or there are some behavioral contingencies that produce an illusory correlation between facial signals and "emotions" – commonly understood. If the latter, why should such a common understanding have arisen?

One possibility is that an older and still serviceable interpretation of facial expressions lies at the basis of the common understanding. I refer here to the work done more than 50 years ago by Schlosberg and Woodworth that led them to conclude that facial expressions can be ordered on a major axis of Pleasantness–Unpleasantness and a minor one of Attention–Rejection. It might be the case that Good and Bad on the one hand and Approach and Withdrawal on the other order some basic natural understanding of emotions that are then related to the facial expressions. Alternatively, if we see facial expressions as devices that communicate important messages (i.e., that are value-laden), then these expressions may well be *one* way of imparting valuation to emotional experiences. Under that view, facial expression may well be a sufficient but not a necessary component of emotional experience.

The chapters to follow convey the sense in which a much broader view of facial expression has replaced the conventional one that has dominated psychology for the past quarter of a century. Together with a presentation of the current state of the art, the volume opens new ways of looking at the biology and development of facial expression with a strong emphasis on the social function of expressive movements. In the process, much work is being done to loosen a strong association between expression and emotion. Such a step can only be helpful toward understanding what a realistic account of the relation between emotion and facial expression might be, and how best to analyze that most expressive of human characteristics – the face.

George Mandler
University of California, San Diego,
and University College London

Preface

The phrase *facial expression* is not a neutral description of a class of behavior but an assumption. The assumption, with us since Homer and now part of our folklore, is that human faces express something, presumably from our inner selves, presumably emotions.

Put in more modern terms, certain facial movements are said to signal emotions. By the 1980s, psychologists had largely accepted as a "fundamental axiom of behavioral science" the link between faces and emotions. Emotion therefore explains facial behavior, and facial behavior is an objective index of emotion. On one major theory, facial expressions determine the emotion we feel. Encouraged by the writings of Charles Darwin, eminent researchers such as Carroll Izard and Paul Ekman had developed a closely related set of theories, methods, and evidence that together form a "Facial Expression Program." This program stimulated a tremendous amount of valuable research on the face and revitalized the study of emotion in general. It provided the textbook account of facial behavior and guided the conduct of most available research on facial behavior.

In the last several years, there have appeared doubts about the program's fundamental assumptions, its methods, and its evidentiary base. Counterevidence has surfaced. Lack of evidence on some of its assumptions has become increasingly noticeable. As alternative views have appeared, advocates of the Facial Expression Program have revised some parts of it and vigorously defended others. This unprecedented turmoil has reopened questions once thought settled: Are emotions the cause of facial behavior? Do specific facial expressions express specific emotions? At all ages? In all societies and cultures? If not, what *do* faces express? How did facial expressions emerge over the course of human evolution? What is the evolutionary legacy to the newborn, and how does culture affect the development of facial behavior? Are *expression* and *emotion* even the right concepts, or has our everyday language frozen in place ideas that were only half baked and prescientific?

Clearly it was time to gather together some of the leading players, take a fresh look at the Facial Expression Program, and scrutinize the alternatives. Our book aims to summarize key areas of research and thinking on the psychology of human facial behavior. We sought a balance between defenders and detractors of the Facial Expression Program, with an eye toward charting future directions in theory, method, and research.

Three of the most important and influential figures in the field were invited to provide an overview of their research, a history of the evolution of their ideas, and their reaction to the current controversies: Carroll Izard, the leading theorist and respected proponent of the Facial Expression Program and an expert on infants' faces; Nico Frijda, who has provided insight, conceptual clarity, and telling data on faces for over 40 years; and Alan Fridlund, whose Behavioral Ecology account of faces has been conceded by its critics to be the most challenging and controversial since Darwin's. (Another important advocate of the Facial Expression Program, Paul Ekman, was also invited but unfortunately could not participate.)

Other chapters summarize how facial behavior can be clarified from Dynamic Systems, Componential, Ethological, and Social Communicative approaches. On the way, contributors review highly relevant research on such topics as spontaneous versus posed expressions, the ontogeny of recognition of facial expression, infants' smiles, animal signals, neurology of facial behavior, the role of context in the interpretation of the face, and facial behavior during dialogue. Methods of research relied on most heavily over the last 30 years are critically examined and new guidelines proposed.

Despite this breadth and diversity, the reader will not hear the usual collective monologue found in edited books. Gerald Ginsburg provides an integrative summary. The authors shared and reviewed each other's chapters before finalizing their own. It was stimulating and fascinating to watch authors review their own thinking so interactively and constructively. We thank each and every one, on behalf of each and every other!

We also thank our series editors, Tony Manstead and Keith Oatley, who gave generously of their time, Julia Hough of Cambridge University Press, who was always there with a steady and helping hand, and Lorraine, who provided the roast beef and Yorkshire pudding that fueled our collaboration.

James A. Russell
José Miguel Fernández-Dols

Contributors

Janet Beavin Bavelas   University of Victoria
James M. Carroll   University of British Columbia
Nicole Chovil   University of British Columbia
Michelle de Haan   University of Minnesota
K. Laurie Dickson   Northern Arizona University
Christopher Evans   Macquarie University
José Miguel Fernández-Dols   Universidad Autónoma de Madrid
Alan Fogel   University of Utah
Alan J. Fridlund   University of California, Santa Barbara
Nico H. Frijda   University of Amsterdam
G. P. Ginsburg   University of Nevada, Reno
Carroll E. Izard   University of Delaware
Peter Marler   University of California, Davis
Daniel S. Messinger   University of Miami and University of Utah
Charles A. Nelson   University of Minnesota
Robert R. Provine   University of Maryland, Baltimore County
María-Angeles Ruiz-Belda   Universidad Autónoma de Madrid
James A. Russell   University of British Columbia
Heather S. Scott   Vanderbilt University
Craig A. Smith   Vanderbilt University
Anna Tcherkassof   Université de Paris X Nanterre
Hugh L. Wagner   University of Manchester

PART I

Introduction

1. What does a facial expression mean?

JAMES A. RUSSELL AND
JOSÉ MIGUEL FERNÁNDEZ-DOLS

> The human face – in repose and in movement, at the moment of
> death as in life, in silence and in speech, when seen or sensed
> from within, in actuality or as represented in art or recorded by
> the camera – is a commanding, complicated, and at times confus-
> ing source of information.
>
> P. Ekman, W. Friesen, and P. Ellsworth, 1972, p. 1

Tradition, common sense, and science converge in seeing the face as a
window with a view opening onto our emotions. The Bible quotes God
as saying, "My fury shall come up in my face" (Ezekiel 39:18). Aristotle
(nd/1913, p. 808) wrote, "There are characteristic facial expressions
which are observed to accompany anger, fear, erotic excitement, and all
the other passions." When we turn our eyes to the face of another human
being, we often seek and usually find a meaning in all that it does or
fails to do. Grins, sneers, grimaces, and frowns, fleeting smiles and lin-
gering stares, animated faces and poker faces are not merely utilitarian
contractions and relaxations of the muscles, but glimpses into the heart
of the other – or so it seems.

Do such ideas contain a truth in plain sight, or are they just another
in a line of myths that will ultimately fall before scientific analysis? Common sense has been wrong before. And Aristotle believed that the coarse-
ness of one's hair revealed one's courage.

By the 1980s, psychology's answer was nearly unanimous: The face is
the key to understanding emotion, and emotion is the key to understanding the face. Over the past 30 years, psychologists as different as Maurice
Merleau-Ponty and Carroll Izard have linked faces to emotions extremely closely: "Anger, shame, hate, and love are not psychic facts hidden at the bottom of another's consciousness: they . . . exist *on* this face
or *in* those gestures, not hidden behind them" (Merleau-Ponty, 1961/

3

1964, pp. 52–53). Izard captured the idea with an aphorism, "Emotion at one level of analysis *is* neuromuscular activity of the face" (1971, p. 188).

Linking faces to emotions may be common sense, but it has turned out to be the single most important idea in the psychology of emotion. It is central to a research program that claims Darwin as its originator, Tomkins as its modern theorist, and Izard, Ekman, and dozens of other scientists as its practitioners. Facial expression is taken to be a universally understood signal, a visible outcropping of an otherwise hidden event, the triggering of a discrete categorical "basic" emotion. Through the face, the Facial Expression Program offered to make of emotion something measurable and understandable within an evolutionary framework and with implications for medicine, the criminal justice system, education, business, and psychotherapy (Ekman & Friesen, 1975).

The Facial Expression Program is presupposed in much work done on facial movements – although not all. Ethologists (e.g., Smith, 1977) have generally taken a different view of facial signals and communicative behavior more generally. Psychologists Mandler (1975) and Zajonc, Murphy, and Inglehart (1989) raised fundamental questions about the link between emotion and facial behavior. By the 1990s, empirical findings and theoretical considerations increasingly questioned the nature of facial expression, its precise link to emotion, and even whether "expression" is the right concept (Zajonc, 1994). Research on the face has recently introduced new conceptualizations, new findings, and new methods. Accepted assumptions are being questioned. Alternative accounts are being formulated, and older accounts are receiving renewed interest. Theorists within the Facial Expression Program are very actively revising some specific hypotheses and defending others.

The chapters of the book to which we now introduce you pursue this discussion. Our introduction is necessarily personal, rather than detached, and partial, rather than complete. Each chapter stands on its own but can perhaps be better appreciated after a discussion of our common historical context. We sketch that history here, outline in more detail one version of the Facial Expression Program, highlight the fundamental questions that have guided recent research, and suggest some guidelines for future research.

A brief history

A full history of the study of facial expressions has yet to be written. In writing this brief sketch, we noticed not only unsung heroes (e.g.,

Hjortsjö, 1969) but also ignored data (e.g., Kraut & Johnston, 1979) and forgotten ideas (e.g., Landis, 1934). Our view of the history of this area is thus somewhat different than that usually presented. It is also not clear where such a history should begin. Observations about emotions appearing on the face can be found in various ancient and medieval writers, West and East. (See Shweder, 1992, for a fascinating discussion of Indian literature on the facial expression of emotion.) We begin our story with Charles Darwin, the earliest writer whose work is still exerting an important influence on scientific work.

Darwin

Everyone knows that Darwin wrote about facial expressions, but not everyone agrees on what he meant. A frank assessment of Darwin's contribution to the study of facial expression is made difficult by his status as one of the greatest scientists of all time and by his indirect influence through what we *now* know of phylogenetic evolution. Vagueness in his conceptualization of emotion and of expression allows Darwin's 1872/ 1965 book to be read in different ways. His name has undoubtedly lent prestige to the study of the face, but the adjective *Darwinian* has been used for specific theories that are not exactly Darwin's, for ideas that Darwin did not originate, and occasionally for ideas that Darwin seemed to deny. Other equally legitimate theories have been branded *anti-Darwinian* – which might unintentionally seem to put them in a class with creation science and the flat-earth society.

We have yet to understand how to bring the great Darwinian principles – evolution, natural selection, and adaptation – to bear on human psychology, and so it is not surprising that Darwin's own attempt was not the final word. If you assumed that Darwin's (1872/1965) own account of faces centered on natural selection and adaptation, you would not be alone, but you would still be mistaken. Nor, as Darwin himself made clear, was he the first to think of facial expressions as universal – the thesis, he wrote, "has often been asserted" (p. 15). Nor did Darwin propose that expressions evolved in order to communicate – "there are no grounds, as far as I can discover, for believing that any muscle has been developed or even modified exclusively for the sake of expression" (p. 354).

Darwin's writings are best understood in terms of what Darwin meant to accomplish and against the background assumptions of his time, when facial expression was thought of as a universal, God-given language created for the expression of emotion (Bell, 1806; Duchenne, 1862/1990). Darwin's goal was not to create a psychological theory but to undermine creationist views of humans in general and emotional expressions in particular (Fridlund, 1992). His specific mechanism of inheritance (Lamarckian transmission of acquired characteristics) and his first principle of facial expression (useless vestiges of ancestral habits) play no role in any current account of facial behavior.

Darwin's ideas of "expression" and "emotion" were also far removed from any current approach to these topics. For Darwin (1872/1965), the notion of "expression" was extremely general. Instead of a small set of facial "signals," expressions were "actions of all kinds, [which] if regularly accompanying any state of mind, are at once recognized as expressive. . . . Even insects express anger, terror, jealousy, and love by their stridulation" (p. 349). What did these actions of all kinds express? Instead of a short list of basic emotions, Darwin worked with a loose, unconstrained set of "states of mind." Darwin described these "states of mind" in terms not only of emotion (such as anger, terror, jealousy, and love) but also of motivational, behavioral, or personality traits (e.g., determination, defiance, ambition, helplessness, impotence, modesty, shyness, pp. 233, 247, 261, 263, 325, 333), sensations (e.g., bodily pain, hunger, p. 69), and cognitive processes (e.g., abstraction, meditation, p. 226).

According to Darwin, among the best recognized expressions are those of "low spirits" (p. 176) and those of "high spirits" (p. 196). Darwin's rather vague notions of "state of mind" and of "high" versus "low" spirits could be taken to prefigure a dimensional at least as much as a categorical approach to emotion. Indeed, both his second principle, "Antithesis" (opposite states of mind are expressed through behaviors opposite in appearance), and his third, Direct Action of the Nervous System (the effects of over- and under-activation of the nervous system), would seem to require a dimensional understanding of "states of mind."

The concept of "state of mind" is vague enough to fit any model of emotion, including those approaches that deny the scientific value of the concept itself, translating it into cognitive (Mandler, 1975) or behavioral terms (Duffy, 1957; Fridlund, 1994). William James (1890/1950) drew an entirely different lesson from Darwin than did Tomkins, Izard, or Ekman. For biology in general, one of Darwin's great achievements was to view species not as fixed immutable categories but as groups within which is great diversity. Looking backward in geological time, we see not eternal species but streams that merge. As we discuss shortly, James suggested a view of emotions as similarly flexible.

One of Darwin's less fortunate influences was methodological. Darwin's methods were merely exploratory. For example, when Darwin wrote that a smiling person (or a dog with a wagging tail) is happy, he offered no systematic way to verify that happiness. At best, he relied on an informal and common-sense judgment that the person's (or dog's) situation was a happy one, and occasionally he provided no evidence other than the expression (smile or wagging tail) itself. For example, Darwin showed photographs of posed facial expressions to observers "without a word of explanation," asking them what emotion could be "agitating" the model. Those expressions on which people agreed were considered to be "true." Darwin's methods of cross-cultural research contained the same problem. His method became the method of choice in the Facial Expression Program, in which consensual attribution of a specific "basic" emotion to a particular facial expression was taken to establish that that emotion did indeed cause the facial expression. However, unfortunately, even when human observers agree with one another, they are not necessarily correct – as when everyone once agreed that the earth is flat, and most laypeople still agree that the singing bird is expressing joy or the howling wolf melancholy.

Darwin's legacy

Darwin's influence took two different courses, one in ethology and another in psychology. Ethologists moved from Darwin's specific analysis described in his 1872 book on expression to the implications of the modern synthesis of evolutionary theory with genetics. Early ethologists conceptualized facial "displays" in ways similar to Darwin's (Tinbergen, 1939, 1952; see Lorenz, 1970). Later ethologists, however, moved steadily away from explanations of behavior in terms of internal states and focused instead on the consequences of facial displays for interaction (Hinde, 1985a, b; Smith, 1977, 1985). They assembled evidence on how communicative behavior in general is dramatically shaped by the interactive context in which it occurs. For example, Marler and Evans (chapter 6, this volume) showed that bird calls vary as a function of the audience. Eibl-Eibesfeldt (e.g., 1972) explored the universality and regional/cultural variation of facial behavior (rather than "states of mind"). Andrew (1963) and van Hooff (1976) attempted to apply modern evolutionary theory to human facial displays, asking about what the original behaviors might have been, the selection pressures that fashioned facial displays, their genetic and epigenetic control, their relations to language, how they serve inclusive fitness, and the like. Kraut and Johnston (1979) and Provine (chapter 7, this volume) applied ethological methods to the study of human facial behavior, with startling results.

Psychologists were less influenced by Darwin's book initially but embraced it with fervor around the time of its centennial (Ekman, 1973). Ethological and psychological streams of thought continued their separate development until meeting head-on in Fridlund's (1994; chapter 5, this volume) critique of the Facial Expression Program. Here we trace only the psychological stream.

Experimental psychology, 1900–1930

Early experimental psychologists did not always cite Darwin but attributed to common knowledge the idea that faces express emotions. Like Darwin, researchers were conceptually open-minded and methodologically innovative. Recognition of emotion meant the recognition of the states of mind or particular circumstances accompanying facial actions (Buzby, 1924; Landis, 1929). One of their goals was to discover precisely what observers could infer from faces. They therefore tried to bring facial expression into the laboratory. Some tried to elicit genuine emotions or other states under controlled conditions (Landis, 1924; Sherman, 1927) and to record the ensuing facial movements. Others examined films of naturally occurring facial expressions (Lewin, 1927).

Although the methods of the early experimentalists were primitive, they accumulated evidence that collectively challenged traditional notions about facial expressions. When actual rather than simulated emotions were studied, faces did not seem to reveal that emotion (Landis, 1924). Observers not only failed to agree on precisely what emotion was conveyed even by simulated faces but were subject to the experimenter's suggestion (Fernberger, 1928) and to training (Allport, 1924). Researchers took up an issue ignored by Darwin: When an observer sees a facial expression, what is the role of the context in which the face is embedded? Overall, this era raised questions and challenged preconceptions – questions and challenges that remain relevant today.

Experimental psychology, 1930–1960

Just as relevant today is the very active conceptual and empirical work of the period broadly surrounding World War II (see reviews by Woodworth & Schlosberg, 1954; Bruner & Tagiuri, 1954; Taguiri, 1969). In addition to interesting individual studies (Coleman, 1949; Munn, 1940; Turhan, 1960; Landis & Hunt, 1939), three related schools of thought arose that sought to reconcile the traditional views of a face–emotion link with the doubts raised by experimental evidence gathered earlier. Woodworth (1938) and his students were especially active. Woodworth (1938) reanalyzed judgment data and found them not so damning after all. He proposed that although faces do not convey specific emotions, they do convey families of emotion. Schlosberg (1941, 1952, 1954) proposed that what holds these families together are underlying components, such as pleasantness or unpleasantness, arousal or relaxation, attention or rejection. Schlosberg's model was later upheld cross-culturally (Triandis & Lambert, 1958). Woodworth's students, Klineberg (1938, 1940) and Vinacke (1949; Vinacke & Fong, 1955) also observed both a universal aspect to facial expression and a role for culture as well; Klineberg (1938, 1940) proposed what later came to be called *display rules*. Culture's influence was reinforced by anthropological reports (LaBarre, 1947; and later Birdwhistell, 1963, 1970).

A second school began with Osgood (1955, 1966), who emphasized the meaning of a facial display as the observer's response to it. Osgood's dimensions of meaning (evaluation, potency, and activity) and his semantic differential technique were taken up in later studies of nonverbal communication (Mehrabian, 1972). Osgood (1955, 1966) also provided evidence on the cross-cultural generality of facial meaning.

A third school consisted of Frijda (1953, 1958, 1969) and his colleagues. Frijda proposed an information-processing model of the perception of emotion in the face and a multicomponent model of emotion that provided a link between facial expressions and emotion and that stressed action preparation in both emotion and the face. Frijda and Tcherkassof (chapter 4, this volume) describe the current version of this theory.

Psychology, 1960–today

The modern era of psychology's study of facial expression began in 1962 with the publication of books on emotion by Tomkins and by Plutchik. Stimulated by these books, the pace of research on facial expression accelerated through the 1970s. By 1980, research on the face was dominated by the Facial Expression Program, centered on a list of specific "basic" emotions as the cause of and the signal received from facial expressions. In this program, Darwin's (1872/1965) book was rediscovered, the issue of universality was made central, the history of the study of facial expression was reinterpreted (as if it were a clash between those who accepted Darwin and those who rejected him), previous research was severely criticized on theoretical (Izard, 1971) and technical (Ekman et al., 1972) grounds, new conceptual and methodological guidelines were offered, and much new research was undertaken. Indeed, this program has generated more research than any other in the psychology of emotion.

The influence of this program is very great. Its assumptions appear in important theories of emotion (Damasio, 1994; Oatley, 1992). Its language is implicit in psychologists' discourse. Facial expressions are named by the specific "basic" emotion allegedly expressed (a "surprise face" or the "facial expression of anger"). When experimental participants select the predicted name, they are said to have "recognized" the facial expression; they are "accurate" or "correct"; those who select a qualitatively different term are said to have made an "error." In studies on the important question of autonomic differentiation of the emotions, Levenson (1992) used the directed facial action task in which discrete emotions were claimed to be induced by the creation of the corresponding facial expression. When Cacioppo, Berntson, and Klein (1992) proposed the Somatovisceral Afference Model of Emotion – which combines the tradition of James (1890/1950) and Schachter and Singer (1962) with that of Tomkins, Ekman, and Izard – they relied on the Facial Expression Program. To test their model, they needed unambiguous bodily manifestations of single discrete emotions; they turned to facial expressions: "Research spearheaded by Tomkins (1962), Ekman (1972), and Izard (1971, 1977) . . . [identified] the prototypical facial configurations associated with discrete emotions" (p. 88). The Facial Expression Program has been equally important in inspiring and guiding research on the development of facial expression and its recognition (Camras, Malatesta, & Izard, 1991; see Izard and Nelson & de Haan, chapters 3 and 8, respectively, this volume).

Although alternative conceptualizations of the link between emotion and faces exist, by the 1980s, it was the work and conclusions of the Facial Expression Program that were presented to undergraduates in their textbooks. Advocates found that psychologists had accepted their conclusions: "Ekman and other psychologists have uncovered compelling evidence that six basic emotions are expressed in much the same way in all cultures" (Carlson & Hatfield (1992, p. 221). Even critics of the kind of emotion theory offered by Tomkins, Izard, and Ekman stated: "We do not (and did not) dispute the fact that there are universal facial expressions associated with certain emotions" (Turner & Ortony, 1992, p. 566). We next elaborate on that program.

The Facial Expression Program

The Facial Expression Program consists of a network of assumptions, theories, and methods, but it is surprisingly difficult to find a complete statement of that set. Each investigator (indeed, each article) presents a somewhat different version of the program, and the program is evolving rapidly. Rather than a history of who said what when, it may be more useful to make explicit a prototypical version, capturing the program in its clearest, most heuristic, interesting, and stimulating form. Some of that prototype's key assumptions, premises, and implications would be these:

1. There are a small number (seven plus or minus two) of basic emotions.
2. Each basic emotion is genetically determined, universal, and discrete. Each is a highly coherent pattern consisting of characteristic facial behavior, distinctive conscious experience (a feeling), physiological underpinnings, and other characteristic expressive and instrumental actions. (Note that in this definition, cognition is not *part* of an emotion, although cognition might be one of the possible *causes* of an emotion.)
3. The production (encoding) and recognition (decoding) of distinct facial expressions constitute a signaling system, which is an evolutionary adaptation to some of life's major problems. This premise predicts and relies upon similarity in facial configurations across species.
4. Any state lacking its own facial signal is not a basic emotion. Therefore, discovering which facial expressions signal the same emotion universally provides a list of candidate basic emotions. The seven candidates found so far are happiness, surprise, fear, anger, contempt, disgust, and sadness. There is some uncertainty over contempt and over the distinction between surprise and fear. Interest

and shame might be added to the list. Candidates could then be tested against the criteria outlined in premise number 2.

5. All emotions other than the basic ones are subcategories or mixtures (patterns, blends, combinations) of the basic emotions. For example, anger includes fury and annoyance as subcategories (which should therefore share anger's facial signal). Anxiety is a mixture of fear, sadness, anger, shame, and interest (and should therefore result in a facial blend).

6. Voluntary facial expressions can simulate spontaneous ones. Voluntary expressions are deceptive in nature and culturally conditioned. Different cultures establish different display rules, which dictate when an expression can be displayed freely, and when it must be inhibited, exaggerated, or masked with a different expression. The true emotion "leaks" through the camouflage and can be detected through facial measurement.

7. Any facial expression that deviates from the universal signals – either in an individual or in a cultural group – is a mixture of the basic signals or stems from the operations of culture-specific display rules.

8. Emotional state is revealed by facial measurement. Thus, the emotions of newborns and of others unable or unwilling to speak truthfully become accessible. Verbal report can be bypassed. Great effort has gone into the development of scoring systems for facial movements. These systems objectively describe and quantify all visually discriminable units of facial action seen in adults or in babies. Scoring keys are available to translate the observed facial action units into emotion categories. Subtle or inhibited emotions can be revealed through facial electromyography. Expressions too brief to be seen by the unaided eye can be detected through high-speed photography.

9. The subjective feelings associated with an emotion are due, at least in part, to proprioceptive feedback from facial movements. This "facial feedback hypothesis" has been offered as one means by which an individual "knows" which emotion he or she is feeling (and thus answers a question that has been central in the psychology of emotion since William James). The existence of these highly differentiated internal "cues" to an ongoing emotion would refute Schachter and Singer's theory that emotion consists of cognition plus undifferentiated arousal.

10. Deliberately manipulating the face into the appropriate configuration creates the neurological pattern of the corresponding emotion. For instance, wrinkling the nose creates the neurological pattern of dis-

gust. Facial manipulation can then be used in the laboratory to reveal the physiological signature of each emotion.

11. The seven (plus or minus two) facial signals are easily recognized by all human beings regardless of their culture.

12. The ability to recognize the emotion in a facial expression is innate rather than culturally determined. The ability is present very early, possibly at birth. In "social referencing," for example, young children use the emotion in their caregiver's face to decide how to handle ambiguous and potentially dangerous situations. The information obtained is more specific than simply whether the caregiver feels positively or negatively about the situation. For instance, anger and fear expressions send very different messages to the child.

13. The mental categories by means of which recognition occurs (in the self as facial feedback or in others through facial signaling) are genetically rather than culturally determined. The words *happiness, surprise, fear, anger, disgust, contempt,* and *sadness* thus designate innate and universal categories. Other languages may use other names, but the categories named are the same. These categories are natural kinds and semantic primitives. Like the emotions themselves, additional emotion labels designate mixtures or subcategories of the basic categories.

14. Like encoding and decoding, the meaning ("signal value") of a facial expression is fixed by nature and invariant across changes in the context in which it occurs. Observers can thus recognize the emotion in another's facial expression, even when the other's context and behavior provide conflicting information. Observers can recognize the same emotion in the same facial expression across a range of modes of presenting the facial expression.

No one now suggests that all of these corollaries are supported unequivocally, especially when stated so starkly. Still, textbooks (Carlson & Hatfield, 1992), popular science books (Ingram, 1994), and other secondary sources (Behavioral Science Task Force of the National Advisory Mental Health Council, 1995) present similarly stark and unconditional versions of the Facial Expression Program. In contrast, both Ekman and Izard have cautioned against some of the corollaries. There are also arguments about details, such as whether children actually engage in social referencing and about whether newborns can recognize emotions from facial expressions. Five rather than seven emotion words might be the semantic primitives. The ability to recognize facial expressions might not be innate. Conceivably, they might be so common and so obviously associated with the corresponding emotion that they are easily learned. Such arguments are within the program. Current theories and summaries of the evidence from this perspective are readily available (Izard, chapter 3, this volume; see also Ekman, 1992, 1994; Izard, 1992, 1994).

Evidence supporting any of these corollaries would be taken as strong support for the program, but no one pillar of support is necessary for the program to survive. Of course, if enough difficulties surface in enough domains, they may constitute the kind of anomalies that stimulate the questioning of the program itself. And this kind of questioning has begun. We consider here two questions that recently resulted in lively debate: first, the universality of facial expressions and, second, the nature of emotion and its link to faces.

Universality

For many, the most convincing and exciting accomplishment of the Facial Expression Program was dramatic evidence for the universality of the facial expression of emotion. To establish this conclusion would require the establishment of three related propositions:

1. The same patterns of facial movement occur in all human groups.
2. Observers in different societies attribute the same specific emotions to those universal facial patterns.
3. Those same facial patterns are, indeed, manifestations of those very emotions in all human societies.

Writers have not always distinguished among these three. For instance, Ekman (1980) published photographs of aboriginal people in New Guinea smiling, frowning, weeping, and so on. Ekman then concluded in favor of universality – "Ultimately, however, the best argument for universality is made by the faces of the New Guineans" (p. 12) – without specifying which aspect of universality was actually established. Of course, the existence of facial patterns per se addresses only Proposition 1.

Proposition 1 has been largely assumed true, although its empirical examination might be highly revealing. Proposition 2 has received great attention. Proposition 3 has been curiously ignored; independent evidence on 3 is much needed, since 3 would not necessarily be true even if 1 and 2 were established. (This last point might be dismissed by in-

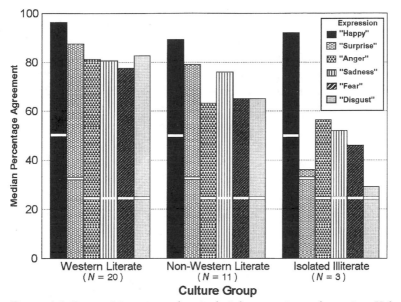

Figure 1.1. Recognition scores for six facial expressions of emotion. Values taken from Russell (1994). White horizontal bars represent level expected by chance alone. N is number of groups.

credulous readers, and so let us be clear: There is now no evidence showing that, in a number of different societies, happy people smile, angry people frown, disgusted people wrinkle their noses, and so on. See Fernández-Dols & Ruiz-Belda and Frijda & Tcherkassof, chapters 11 and 4, respectively, this volume, for discussions of this topic.)

Now consider the evidence on Proposition 2. Figure 1.1 provides a summary of relevant results from cross-cultural judgment studies using a standard method. The figures given are "recognition scores" (the percentage of observers who pick the predicted label). The first set of bars comes from Western literate societies (largely college students). The numbers are impressive (far above chance, represented in Figure 1.1 by white horizontal lines). The second set of bars comes from non-Western societies (although still largely college students). This second set of scores is reliably lower than the first but still high. Now turn to the third set, which comes from more isolated samples of non-Western observers (uneducated, indeed illiterate). These observers agreed on attributing happiness to the smiles but yielded noticeably lower recognition scores with all other photographs.

Clearly, both Western and non-Western observers conform to prediction to a greater degree than would be expected by chance. At the same time, the recognition scores are proportional to the amount of Western influence and may have been inflated by a series of method factors: exaggerated posed expressions, within-subject design, and a forced-choice response format (not to mention experimenter influence, Sorenson, 1975, 1976). (For example, in Russell's 1994 data, the within-subject design resulted in an 11-percentage-point increase in average recognition score over that achieved in a between-subjects design.)

So, return to the third set of bars, and picture each bar falling even a small amount each time an inflationary method factor is removed. It remains to be seen which if any of the bars would remain above chance. Whatever the answer to that question, there also remains the matter of their interpretation.

Suppose that all recognition scores remain above chance even when technical problems are overcome. There would still be various alternative explanations for the nonrandom associations, including that of the Facial Expression Program (Izard, chapter 3, this volume) but also including alternatives to it (e.g., Fernández-Dols & Carroll, Frijda & Tcherkassof, Russell, Smith & Scott, chapters 12, 4, 13, and 10, respectively, this volume).

The most parsimonious account of all evidence we now have on how facial expressions are produced and interpreted is something called *Minimal Universality*. It is outlined in Table 1.1. The phrase may sound like an oxymoron, but the paradox may stem from the presupposition that we face an either–or choice: either randomness (the null hypothesis used in the statistical tests carried out in the cross-cultural studies) or full universality. Like the nature–nurture dichotomy, this choice is simplistic. Minimal Universality predicts a certain amount of cross-cultural similarity in interpreting facial expressions without postulating an innate emotion signaling system. Calling this position *minimal* is meant to emphasize that at least this much universality appears to exist. The question for the future, then, is: What can be established beyond Minimal Universality?

Needless to say, the topic of universality remains controversial. See Russell (1994, 1995) for an elaboration of the analysis just presented. See Izard (1994) and Ekman (1944) for an alternative analysis. See van Brakel (1994), Cornelius (1996), Oatley and Jenkins (1996), and Parkinson (1995) for independent reviews.

Table 1.1. *Minimal universality*

Assumptions
1. Certain patterns of facial muscle movement occur in all human beings.
2. Facial movements are coordinated with psychological states (actions, preparation for actions, physical states, emotional states, cognitive states, and other psychological conditions).
3. Most people everywhere can infer something of another's psychological state from facial movement, just as they can from anything else that other person does.
4. People in Western cultures have a set of beliefs in which specific types of facial actions are expressions of specific types of emotion.

Some caveats
1. Facial actions are not necessarily signals.
2. Facial action is not necessary or sufficient for emotion. Facial action is not necessarily more associated with emotions than with other psychological states.
3. What inferences are made in one culture, or by one individual, need not coincide exactly with inferences made in another culture or by another individual.
4. People in all cultures need not share Western beliefs about the specific associations of emotions and facial actions.
5. Western beliefs about the association between facial expressions and emotions are not necessarily valid.

Predictions
1. Photographs of facial movements will be associated with psychological state with agreement that is greater than chance.
2. People are sometimes accurate in the inferences that they make on the basis of facial movements.
3. There will be similarities across cultures in what is inferred from facial movements.

Emotion and its link to the face

A second set of still deeper questions faces any theory explaining facial behavior in terms of emotion. How exactly is facial behavior linked to emotion? If facial behavior is linked to basic emotions, what are they, and how would their "basicness" be established? And what is an emotion, anyway?

How exactly is emotion linked to faces? That certain "facial expressions" actually "express" emotions presupposes that they are caused by emotion. This assumption remains untested. Casual observation suggests a link between faces and emotions (just as casual observation suggests that flu symptoms are linked to cold weather, wet feet, bad luck, and being around others with the flu). It remains for scientific analysis to establish which links are intrinsic and which merely correlational. So, just as influenza is intrinsically linked to the spread of germs and only accidentally linked to cold weather (in cold weather, people congregate closer together more often and therefore spread germs more effectively), facial behavior might be intrinsically linked to something correlated with emotion.

This question arises in an interesting form for those who think of emotion as consisting of components, no one of which is necessary. Is it the full emotion that is necessary and sufficient for facial action, or is it perhaps one of emotion's components: preparation for action (Frijda & Tcherkassof, chapter 4, this volume) or cognitive appraisal (Smith & Scott, chapter 10, this volume)? This same question arises in a more extreme form when Fridlund (chapter 5, this volume) argues that facial behavior can be accounted for in terms of social motives, which are only modestly correlated with emotion.

Are some emotions basic? Any account of emotion needs a description of the different categories of emotion. Izard (chapter 3, this volume) and most other proponents of the Facial Expression Program assume a fixed number of "basic" categories. Indeed, Tomkins and Izard saw the face as a tool in their more general aim, which was the understanding of basic emotions. Others, however, question the evidentiary and conceptual basis of the claim that some categories of emotion are basic (Ortony & Turner, 1990). Some writers emphasize the plasticity of emotion over fixed categories. Drawing on Darwin, William James inspired this perspective:

> So long as [categories of emotion] are set down as so many eternal and sacred psychic entities, like the old immutable species in natural history, all that *can* be done with them is reverently to catalogue their separate characters, points, and effects. But if we regard them as products of more general causes (as "species" are now regarded as products of heredity and variation), the mere distinguishing and cataloguing becomes of subsidiary importance. (James, 1890/1950, p. 449)

Following in James's footsteps are theories such as those of Averill (1980), Harré (1985), Hochschild (1983), Lutz (1982), Schachter and Singer (1962), and Wierzbicka (1992), who see social forces as influencing the particular categories of emotion found in each society.

What is an emotion? To account for facial behavior through emotions, basic or not, we would need a scientifically acceptable definition of emotion. After all, to test such an account requires that we know what counts as an emotion and what does not. Izard (1977, 1991) suggested defining emotion as consisting of neurophysiological, behavioral, and subjective components. Fehr and Russell (1984), however, pointed out that such a definition fails to distinguish emotion from wishes, intentions, motives, and, indeed, many psychological concepts. (Consider squinting on a sunny day or moving a pawn in a game of chess. These events have neurological, behavioral, and subjective components. Therefore, it is not clear why these would not count as emotions on Izard's definition. If squinting and chess moves express emotions, then it is hard to imagine what would not.)

Definitions of emotion proposed so far face a dilemma: Either they fail to capture what the word *emotion* means, or they fail to be precise enough to serve as a scientific concept. This dilemma should not surprise us. "Emotion" is an ordinary, everyday word understood by all rather than a precise concept honed through scientific analysis. Perhaps "emotion" is a concept that could be dispensed with in scientific discourse (except as a folk concept requiring rather than providing explanation), and therefore it would have no role to play in the analysis of facial behavior. Doubts about the scientific viability of the concept of "emotion" have been expressed by Duffy (1957), Kagan (1978), and Mandler (1975). Some everyday concepts survive scientific scrutiny (e.g., water), but others do not (witches). Many survive in name only (force, weight). In any case, we have probably reached the point where further usefulness of thinking of facial expressions in terms of emotion requires a clarification of the concept of emotion itself.

Some broad guidelines for future research

Everyone produces facial expressions, and everyone reacts to the facial expressions of others. Whatever one's answer to the foregoing perplexing theoretical questions, such happenings raise their own, more general questions:

1. [Description of The Face] Which facial movements and patterns occur? (e.g., How can facial behavior be described and assessed?)
2. [Production] What causes facial movement? (e.g., Of what state or

process or the like, if any, in the expresser is the facial movement a sign?)

3. [Reaction] How do others react to a facial movement? (e.g., What meaning does an observer find in the facial movements of the expresser? What is the process – direct perception, inference, attribution – whereby meaning is found or constructed?)

Further questions must also be raised about the neural mechanisms, the ontogeny, and the phylogeny of facial behavior and others' reactions to it. In the view of the field we have just outlined, there are many questions, few answers, many theories, few facts. There are few greater clichés in psychology than calling for more research, but what else can we do? One surprising fact about the psychology of facial expression is how little basic information on the topic we have. There's no question about the need. But how to conduct the research – that's the question.

Ekman et al. (1972) provided researchers with guidelines that have been of historic importance. Much of what they advocated was standard: objectivity, generality, and so on. We certainly don't quibble with such points, but their guidelines – as any guidelines would – also mix such consensual concerns with their own particular conceptual framework. As a consequence, each researcher might want to think carefully before accepting their advice in detail, and it is probably time to reconsider their guidelines in general. In chapter 2, Wagner reviews methodological issues in facial research. Here we provide general guidelines – similarly guided by our own assumptions – on conceptual issues that the researcher might want to consider.

Production of versus reaction to faces

"What does a facial expression mean?" – this question has two distinct meanings. It could be translated as "what about the expresser causes facial behavior?" But it could also be translated as "what does an observer see in the face?" This ambiguity is potentially dangerous, as when an answer to one question is taken to be an answer to the other. Past confusion urges us to emphasize our distinction between studies on the production of facial behavior versus studies on reactions to (including perception of) facial behavior.

Production of faces. Here the face is the *dependent* variable. The questions asked center on the conditions that influence facial behavior – conditions internal or external to the expresser (his or her emotion, social motives, intention, internalized display rules, current situation, developmental trajectory, evolutionary history, etc.). Such studies include what have been called *component* or *encoding studies*. Wagner calls them *measurement studies*. (See Ekman & Rosenberg, in press, for a compendium of such studies.)

Reaction to faces. Here the face is the *independent* variable. The questions asked concern an observer's reaction to the face. What influences the observer? Through what process does the observer "see" an emotion in a face – labeling? perceiving? Is it direct or mediated? More generally, what are the observers' emotional and behavioral reactions to the facial behavior of others? (For example, reactions to others' yawns, smiles, and laughs include yawning, smiling, and laughing, respectively; Provine, chapter 7, this volume.) Such studies include "judgment" or decoding studies, but the topic is really any reaction by an observer (including self-observation), not just judgments, and that reaction could be assessed in a variety of ways. For example, clever studies of babies examine how often the baby looks at a given face, or whether the baby habituates to kinds of faces, in order to explore the baby's processing of facial information (see Nelson & de Haan, chapter 8, this volume). These babies might not be making judgments at all, but they are processing information from the face they observe.

Maintenance of this distinction is needed in sorting what is known from what is not. For example, just because a face is caused by the expresser's anger would not necessarily imply that observers will know this. After all, human beings – even collectively – are not infallible. Scientists might detect information in the face previously misunderstood or never before exploited – just as geologists can extract from rocks information previously ignored or misunderstood. Conversely, just because lay observers infer anger from a face does not necessarily imply that the expresser is truly angry. Folk judgments of faces are not necessarily true – any more than owls are wise or camels proud just because they seem that way to observers. This distinction remains relevant even in the study of the full process of communication or of facial feedback. The relation between what causes the face to move and what an observer thinks causes the face to move should be an empirical question rather than an implicit assumption.

Faces are associated with more than emotion

The relation of the face to emotion will remain an important topic. But whatever the resolution of that question, the relation of facial behavior to other psychological events merits more study. States other than emotion (pain, fatigue, boredom, interest, sleepiness, alertness) can entail facial movements, and observers infer more than emotion from the face of others (again pain, fatigue, boredom etc.). Smith and Scott (chapter 10, this volume) discuss how the face might be used as an index of cognitive processes (attention, pre– or post–problem solving). Frijda and Tcherkassof (chapter 4, this volume) show that observers infer a full range of action tendencies from faces. Fridlund (chapter 5, this volume) considers the social intentions of the expresser as the message expressed by the face and received by the observer.

More to faces than seven prototypes

Every psychologist is familiar with the seven prototypical "facial expressions of emotion." The sets of photographs developed by Ekman and Friesen (1976) and by Matsumoto and Ekman (1988) have played a large role in the accumulated body of data about faces. But facial patterns and movements are not restricted to this small set, and very much work remains to be done in exploring other facial movements. Izard (chapter 3, this volume) emphasizes that even the basic emotions can be expressed through a range of facial patterns, not just the prototypes. Again, we mean this advice to apply both to the study of the production of faces and to the study of reactions to faces.

Spontaneous and posed faces

Common sense and scientific writing sharply distinguish spontaneous facial expressions from posed ones. This distinction is clearly important, with sometimes dramatic differences between the two (Fernández-Dols & Ruiz-Belda, chapter 11, this volume). It is also troubling that so very much of the research on facial expression employs posed faces. And yet the distinction as usually formulated is unclear and probably too simple. Spontaneous expressions are assumed to be natural, involuntary, undirected outbursts. Poses, in contrast, are assumed to be artificial, symbolic, produced on demand, deceptive in nature, and aimed at an audience.

And yet we spontaneously pretend, we naturally strike poses. As part of our dialogues, we spontaneously mime in comment on the stories told us or to illustrate our own stories (Bavelas & Chovil, chapter 15, this volume). Spontaneous, involuntary, undirected facial expressions, on the one hand, and artificial, posed behavior produced on demand, on the other hand, may each be extreme and rarely occurring end points on a continuum. Much naturally occurring facial behavior may be spontaneous and symbolic and communicative in nature and directed toward a specific audience.

Ecological questions

At least since Bell (1806), scientists have tried to bring the study of the face into the laboratory. Obviously, much is to be gained by doing so, and much more laboratory work remains to be done. At the same time, ecological questions have been terribly neglected. We do not know when or in what circumstances various types of facial behavior occur or in what frequency. For example, return to the seven highly researched prototype facial expressions published by Matsumoto and Ekman (1988). In what natural situations do such configurations occur? How frequently? When they occur, how often are they part of the emotion they are said to express? More importantly, we must ask the same set of questions about facial behavior other than the seven prototypes.

Ecological questions are relevant both to the study of the production of facial behavior and to the study of reactions to faces. Studying production, Provine (chapter 7, this volume) found that smiling and laughing occur much more frequently in social than in nonsocial situations. Similarly, when the topic is another's reaction to a face, such reactions may vary with how common or unusual that facial expression is, especially given the context. Reactions to commonly encountered expressions might differ from reactions to unusual ones. We also need to ask much more about observers' naturally occurring, spontaneous reactions to faces. Are they well represented by the kinds of judgment scales often used in studies of facial expressions?

Taking culture seriously

Some of the most widely cited cross-cultural studies ever carried out have concerned facial expressions. Available evidence arises from a rather narrow perspective on cultural studies. Typically, a hypothesis is formulated in our "Western" culture, and then its generality across cultural settings is tested. The information obtained from the resulting studies is thus restrained to a single quantitative dimension of degree of generality.

Much more interesting cultural studies are possible. We have very little information on what facial behavior is seen in a given society, on what influences that behavior, and how that behavior is interpreted by its members. Those who propose that observers infer emotions from faces might want to ask what observers understand by emotion. Culture includes a theory of human nature and of emotion (Shweder, 1992). A real understanding of how people of different cultures understand the link between faces and emotion (and anything else) has barely begun.

Testing among rival hypotheses

Much research on the face has pitted the experimenter's plausible hypothesis against an implausible null hypothesis. The null hypothesis might, for example, be that observers choose an emotion label completely at random for every facial stimulus shown. When human beings are given a task such as figuring out which emotion label goes with which face, completely random behavior is highly unlikely. Rejecting this null hypothesis (finding that the results are "statistically significant"), the experimenter then concludes – and here's the problematic step – that the experiment has established his or her hypothesis (or even has strongly supported his or her entire theory). The experimenter's hypothesis can be accepted as *the* explanation of the data only if no alternative rival explanation exists. Ruling out the null hypothesis in any particular study lends support not only to the experimenter's favorite account but to every possible account of the data other than sheer chance. The experimenter's own favorite enjoys no privileged position in the logic of experimental design.

Testing a null hypothesis such as random choice has its uses, but more useful and interesting research and analysis of the data will come from comparisons among more plausible rival hypotheses. Often a simple account (such as Minimal Universality, Table 1.1) could be constructed to serve as a more plausible rival to the experimenter's. In this book, nearly every question about the face has generated rival accounts. Nearly every hypothesis offered by one author can be contrasted with an alternative offered by another. We have deliberately sought a range of perspectives, on the belief that our field is ready for research that seeks to test among these rival hypotheses.

The remaining chapters

A second half of the introductory section of this book is a chapter by Wagner on methods. Wagner provides guidelines on how methods can be tailored more closely to the specific question being investigated.

Part Two presents three broad theoretical perspectives on the face. Izard writes from the perspective of his Differential Emotions Theory, Frijda from his multicomponent theory of emotion, and Fridlund from his Behavioral Ecology perspective.

Part Three pursues more specific topics, all from a broadly biological perspective. Marler and Evans reexamine the implications of work on animal signaling, once thought to be paradigm cases of eruptions of emotion. They find that emotions are not enough to account for signaling. Provine applies an ethological approach to human laughing, smiling, and tickling. Such an approach has been so neglected in the past that naturalistic observation can still yield surprising findings. (An ethological approach also yields a perspective on facial behavior that nicely complements the conclusions reached in later chapters by Bavelas and Chovil from a social-communications perspective.) The last two chapters in this part take up important developmental issues. Nelson and de Haan examine the recognition of facial expressions in infants from a neurobehavioral perspective. And Messinger, Fogel, and Dickson interpret smiling in infants from a dynamic systems perspective.

Part Four similarly examines specific topics but now from a broadly psychological and social perspective. Smith and Scott break emotion into specific psychological steps, which they call *components*, and discuss their separate links to facial behavior. Fernández-Dols and Ruiz-Belda focus on spontaneous facial behavior and the naturally occurring conditions under which it occurs. They illustrate how spontaneous behavior may be dramatically different from its posed and simulated counterpart and report evidence supportive of Fridlund's emphasis on the sociality of facial expression. Fernández-Dols and Carroll reexamine a traditional but lately dormant question of the relative roles of facial and situational information in the perception of emotion from facial expression. They challenge the traditional assumption that specific facial expressions have a specific meaning independent of the context in which they occur (that the frown is a "facial expression of anger" whatever the context). Russell similarly focuses exclusively on the observer in the process of facial communication. The final two chapters in this part illustrate a social communicative perspective on facial behavior. In the first, Chovil reviews research and writing emerging from this perspective. In the second, Bavelas and Chovil describe their own research on facial behavior during dialogue.

Finally, Part Five is an epilogue by Ginsburg summarizing and integrating themes that emerge from the previous chapters and offering his own reconceptualization. Readers who like to begin with a more detailed summary of each chapter might want to turn now to Ginsburg's chapter.

References

Allport, F. M. (1924). *Social psychology*. Boston: Houghton-Mifflin.

Andrew, R. J. (1963). Evolution of facial expression. *Science, 141,* 1034–1041.

Aristotle. (1913). Physiognominica. In W. D. Ross (Ed.) & T. Loveday & E. S. Forster (Trans.), *The works of Aristotle* (pp. 805–813). Oxford: Clarendon.

Averill, J. R. (1980). A constructivist view of emotions. In R. Plutchik & H. Kellerman (Eds.), *Emotion: Theory, research, and experience*. New York: Academic Press.

Behavioral Science Task Force of the National Advisory Mental Health Council (1995). Basic behavioral science research for mental health: A national investment: Motivation and emotion. *American Psychologist, 50,* 838–845.

Bell, C. (1806). *Essays on the anatomy of expression in painting*. London: Longman, Hurst, Rees, & Orme.

Birdwhistell, R. L. (1963). The kinesic level in the investigation of the emotions. In P. H. Knapp (Ed.), *Expression of the emotions in man* (p. 123–139). New York: International Universities Press.

Birdwhistell, R. L. (1970). *Kinesics and context*. Philadelphia, PA: University of Pennsylvania Press.

Brakel, J. van (1994). Emotions: A cross-cultural perspecitive on forms of life. In W. M. Wentworth & J. Ryan (Eds.), *Social perspectives on emotion* (Vol. 2). Greenwich: JAI Press.

Bruner, J. S., & Tagiuri, R. (1954). The perception of people. In G. Lindzey (Ed.), *Handbook of social psychology* (Vol. 2). Cambridge: Addison-Wesley.

Buzby, D. E. (1924). The interpretation of facial expressions. *American Journal of Psychology, 35,* 602–604.

Cacioppo, J. T., Berntson, G. G., & Klein, D. J. (1992). What is an emotion? The role of somatovisceral afference, with special emphasis on somatovisceral "illusions." *Review of Personality and Social Psychology, 14,* 63–98.

Camras, L. A., Malatesta, C., & Izard, C. E. (1991). The development of facial expression in infancy. In R. Feldman & B. Rime (Eds.), *Fundamentals of nonverbal behavior*. New York: Cambridge University Press.

Carlson, J. G., & Hatfield, E. (1992). *Psychology of emotion*. New York: Holt, Rinehart, & Winston.

Coleman, J. C. (1949). Facial expressions of emotion. *Psychological Monographs, 63* (1, Whole No. 296).

Cornelius, R. R. (1996). *The science of emotion.* Upper Saddle River, NJ: Prentice-Hall.

Damasio, A. R. (1994). *Descartes' error.* New York: G. P. Putnam's Sons.

Darwin, C. (1965). *The expression of the emotions in man and animals.* Chicago: University of Chicago Press. (Original work published 1872)

Duchenne de Boulogne, G. B. (1990). *The mechanism of human facial expression.* R. A. Cuthbertson (Ed. and Trans). Cambridge: Cambridge University Press. (Original work published 1862)

Duffy, E. (1957). The psychological significance of the concept of arousal on activation. *Psychological Review, 64,* 265–275.

Eibl-Eibesfeldt, I. (1972). Similarities and differences between cultures in expressive movements. In R. A. Hinde (Ed.), *Nonverbal communication.* Cambridge University Press.

Ekman, P. (1972). Universals and cultural differences in facial expressions of emotion. In J. Cole (Ed.), *Nebraska symposium on motivation, 1971* (pp. 207–283). Lincoln: University of Nebraska Press.

Ekman, P. (1973). *Darwin and facial expression: A century of research in review.* New York: Academic Press.

Ekman, P. (1980). *The face of man: Expressions of universal emotions in a New Guinea village.* New York: Garland STPM Press.

Ekman, P. (1992). Are there basic emotions? *Psychological Review, 99.* 550–553.

Ekman, P. (1994). Strong evidence for universals in facial expression: A reply to Russell's mistaken critique. *Psychological Bulletin, 115.* 268–287.

Ekman, P., & Friesen, W. V. (1975). *Unmasking the face.* Englewood Cliffs, NJ: Prentice-Hall.

Ekman, P., & Friesen, W. V. (1976). *Pictures of facial affect.* Palo Alto, CA: Consulting Psychologists Press.

Ekman, P., Friesen, W. V., & Ellsworth, P. (1972). *Emotion in the human face.* New York: Pergamon.

Ekman, P., & Rosenberg, E. (in press). *What the face reveals: Basic and applied studies of spontaneous expression using the Facial Action Coding System (FACS).* New York: Oxford University Press.

Fehr, B., & Russell, J. A. (1984). Concept of emotion viewed from a prototype perspective. *Journal of Experimental Psychology: General, 113.* 464–486.

Fernberger, S. W. (1928). False suggestion and the Piderit model. *American Journal of Psychology, 40.* 562–568.

Fridlund, A. J. (1992). Darwin's anti-Darwinism in *The expression of the emotions in man and animals.* In K. Strongman (Ed.), *International review of emotion* (Vol. 2, pp. 117–137). Chichester: Wiley.

Fridlund, A. J. (1994). *Human facial expression: An evolutionary view.* San Diego: Academic.

Frijda, N. H. (1953). The understanding of facial expression of emotion. *Acta Psychologica, 9,* 294–362.

Frijda, N. H. (1958). Facial expression and situational cues. *Journal of Abnormal and Social Psychology, 57,* 149–154.

Frijda, N. H. (1969). Recognition of emotion. In L. Berkowitz (Ed.), *Advances in experimental social psychology IV.* New York: Academic Press.

Harré, R. (Ed.). (1985). *The social construction of emotions.* Oxford: Blackwell.

Hinde, R. A. (1985a). Expression and negotiation. In G. Zivin (Ed.), *The development of expressive behavior* (pp. 103–116). Orlando, FL: Academic Press.

Hinde, R. A. (1985b). Was "The Expression of the Emotions" a misleading phrase? *Animal Behaviour, 33,* 985–992.

Hjortsjö, C. H. (1969). *Man's face and mimic language.* Lund, Sweden: Studentlit-teratur.

Hochschild, A. R. (1983). *The managed heart.* Berkeley: University of California Press.

Hooff, J. A. R. A. M. van (1976). The comparison of facial expression in man and higher primates. In M. von Cranach (Ed.), *Methods of inference from animal to human behavior* (pp. 165–196). Chicago: Aldine.

Ingram, J. (1994). *The burning house: Unlocking the mysteries of the brain.* London: Penguin.

Izard, C. E. (1971). *The face of emotion.* New York: Appleton Century Crofts.

Izard, C. E. (1977). *Human emotions.* New York: Plenum.

Izard, C. E. (1991). *The psychology of emotions.* New York: Plenum.

Izard, C. E. (1992). Basic emotions, relations among emotions, and emotion-cognition relations. *Psychological Review, 99.* 561–565.

Izard, C. (1994). Innate and universal facial expressions: Evidence from developmental cross-cultural research. *Psychological Bulletin, 115,* 288–299.

James, W. (1950) *The principles of psychology.* New York: Dover. (Original work published 1890)

Kagan, J. (1978). On emotion and its development: A working paper. In M. Lewis & L. A. Rosenblum (Eds.), *The development of affect.* New York: Plenum.

Klineberg, O. (1938). Emotional expression in Chinese literature. *Journal of Abnormal and Social Psychology, 33,* 517–520.

Klineberg, O. (1940). *Social psychology.* New York: Holt.

Kraut, R. E., & Johnston, R. E. (1979). Social and emotional messages of smiling: An ethological approach. *Journal of Personality and Social Psychology, 37,* 1539–1553.

LaBarre, W. (1947). The cultural basis of emotions and gestures. *Journal of Personality, 16,* 49–68.

Landis, C. (1924). Studies of emotional reactions: II. General behavior and facial expression. *Journal of Comparative Psychology, 4,* 447–509.

Landis, C. (1929). The interpretation of facial expression in emotion. *Journal of Genetic Psychology, 2,* 59–72.

Landis, C. (1934). Emotion: II. The expressions of emotion. In C. Murchinson (Ed.), *Handbook of general experimental psychology* (pp. 312–351). Worcester: Clark University Press.

Landis, C., & Hunt, W. A. (1939). *The startle pattern.* New York: Farrar, Straus, & Giroux.

Levenson, R. W. (1992). Autonomic nervous system differences among emotions. *Psychological Science, 3,* 23–27.

Lewin, K. (1927). Kindlicher ausdruck. *Zeitschrift fur Paedagogie und Psychologie, 28,* 510–526.

Lorenz, K. Z. (1970). *Studies on animal and human behavior* (Vols. 1 & 2). Cambridge, MA: Harvard University Press.

Lutz, C. (1982). The domain of emotion words in Ifaluk. *American Ethnologist, 9,* 113–128.

Mandler, G. (1975). *Mind and emotion.* New York: Wiley.

Matsumoto, D., & Ekman, P. (1988). *Japanese and Caucasian facial expressions of emotion (JACFEE).* Slide set and brochure available from first author, San Francisco State University.

Mehrabian, A. (1972). *Nonverbal communication.* Chicago: Aldine-Atherton.

Merleau-Ponty, M. (1964). *Sense and non-sense.* (H. L. Dreyfus & P. A. Dreyfus, trans.). Chicago: Northwestern University Press. (Original work published 1961)

Munn, N. L. (1940). The effect of knowledge of the situation upon judgment of emotion from facial expressions. *Journal of Abnormal and Social Psychology, 35*, 324–338.

Oatley, K. (1992). *Best laid schemes: The psychology of emotions.* Cambridge: Cambridge University Press.

Oatley, K., & Jenkins, J. M. (1996). *Understanding emotion.* Cambridge, MA: Blackwell.

Ortony, A., & Turner, T. J. (1990). What's basic about basic emotions? *Psychological Review, 97*, 315–331.

Osgood, C. E. (1955). Fidelity and reliability. In H. Quastler (Ed.), *Information theory in psychology* (pp. 374–384). Glencoe: Free Press.

Osgood, C. E. (1966). Dimensionality of the semantic space for communication via facial expressions. *Scandinavian Journal of Psychology, 7*, 1–30.

Parkinson, B. (1995). *Ideas and realities of emotion.* London: Routledge.

Plutchik, R. (1962). *The emotions: Facts, theories, and a new model.* New York: Random House.

Russell, J. A. (1994). Is there universal recognition of emotion from facial expression? *Psychological Bulletin, 115*, 102–141.

Russell, J. A. (1995). Facial expressions of emotion: What lies beyond minimal universality? *Psychological Bulletin, 118*, 379–391.

Schachter, S., & Singer, J. E. (1962). Cognitive, social, and physiological determinants of emotional state. *Psychological Review, 69*, 379–399.

Schlosberg, H. (1941). A scale for judgment of facial expressions. *Journal of Experimental Psychology, 29*, 497–510.

Schlosberg, H. (1952). The description of facial expressions in terms of two dimensions. *Journal of Experimental Psychology, 44*, 229–237.

Schlosberg, H. (1954). Three dimensions of emotion. *Psychological Review, 61*, 81–88.

Sherman, M. (1927). The differentiation of emotional responses in infants: II. The ability of observers to judge the emotional characteristics of the crying of infants and of the voice of an adult. *Journal of Comparative Psychology, 7*, 335–351.

Shweder, R. A. (1992). The cultural psychology of the emotions. In M. Lewis & J. Haviland (Eds.), *Handbook of emotions.* New York: Guilford.

Smith, W. J. (1977). *The behaviour of communicating.* Cambridge, MA: Harvard University Press

Smith, W. J. (1985). Consistency and change in communication. In G. Zivin (Ed.), *The development of expressive behavior* (pp. 51–75). Orlando, FL: Academic Press.

Sorenson, E. R. (1975). Culture and the expression of emotion. In T. R. Williams (Ed.), *Psychological anthropology* (pp. 361–372). Chicago: Aldine.

Sorenson, E. R. (1976). *The edge of the forest: Land, childhood and change in a New Guinea protoagricultural society.* Washington, DC: Smithsonian Institution Press.

Tagiuri, R. (1969). Person perception. In G. Lindzey & E. Aronson (Eds.), *Handbook of social psychology* (Vol. 3, pp. 395–449). Reading, MA: Addison-Wesley.

Tinbergen, N. (1939). On the analysis of social organization among vertebrates, with special reference to birds. *American Midland Naturalist, 21*, 210–234.

Tinbergen, N. (1952). "Derived" activities: Their causation, biological signifi-

cance, origin and emancipation during evolution. *Quarterly Review of Biology,*
27, 1–32.

Tomkins, S. S. (1962). *Affect, imagery, consciousness* (Vol. 1: The positive affects).
New York: Springer.

Triandis, H. C., & Lambert, W. W. (1958). A restatement and test of Schlosberg's
Theory of Emotion with two kinds of subjects from Greece. *Journal of Abnormal and Social Psychology, 56,* 321–328.

Turhan, M. (1960). Ueber die Deutung des Gesichtsausdrucks. *Psychologigische
Beitraege, 5,* 495–497.

Turner, T. J., & Ortony, A. (1992). Basic emotions: Can conflicting criteria converge? *Psychological Review, 99,* 566–571.

Vinacke, W. E. (1949). The judgment of facial expressions by three national-racial
groups in Hawaii: I. Caucasian faces. *Journal of Personality, 17,* 407–429.

Vinacke, W. E., & Fong, R. W. (1955). The judgment of facial expressions by three
national-racial groups in Hawaii: II. Oriental faces. *Journal of Social Psychology, 41,* 184–195.

Wierzbicka, A. (1992). *Semantics, culture, and cognition.* New York: Oxford.

Woodworth, R. S. (1938). *Experimental psychology.* New York: Holt.

Woodworth, R. S., & Schlosberg, H. (1954). *Experimental psychology.* New York:
Holt, Rinehart, & Winston.

Zajonc, R. B. (1994). Emotional expression and temperature modulation. In S. H.
M. van Goozen, N. E. van de Poll, & J. A. Sergeant (Eds.), *Emotions: Essays
on emotion theory.* Hillsdale, NJ: Erlbaum.

Zajonc, R. B., Murphy, S. T., & Inglehart, M. (1989). Feeling and facial efference:
Implications of the vascular theory of emotion. *Psychological Review, 96,* 396–
416.

2. Methods for the study of facial behavior

HUGH L. WAGNER

In the present chapter, I first survey the main methods that have been applied to the study of faces and indicate how different methods relate to different types of research questions. I make no claim that this survey is complete; space would not permit this. In particular, I do not consider ethological approaches (see Eibl-Eibesfeldt, 1989, especially chapters 2 and 6). Following this brief survey, I focus on judgment studies and examine the components of such studies in some detail, reexamining the assumptions underlying the usual practices in the application of judgment methods and their analysis. It will become apparent that these usual practices, while mostly appropriate for addressing certain questions about facial behavior, lack generalizability to many other important questions.

Ways of studying facial behavior

The range of questions that may be asked about facial behavior is apparent from the other chapters of this volume. A consideration of these questions suggests that they may be differentiated from one another on the basis of which of two general aims the study of the face has. An examination of the methods available indicates that they are not equally applicable to questions with different general aims. Many questions involve describing or measuring facial behavior. Such questions include: What can facial behavior tell us about the number and nature of distinct emotions? (That is, are there "basic," or "fundamental," emotions?) How is facial behavior involved in the experience of emotions? Does facial behavior directly reflect emotional experience? Are there individual differences (and gender differences) in facial behavior? Essentially, these questions do not involve any consideration of what is communicated by facial behavior or how it is interpreted by others. Ekman, Friesen, and

Ellsworth (1972/1982a) referred to studies of such questions as "component studies." Here, to emphasize the methodological distinction, we call them *measurement studies*. The investigation of questions like these requires methods that provide a description or measurement of actual changes in the face.

Other questions are about the information conveyed by facial behavior. For example: Can we judge a person's personality from his or her facial behavior? Can we tell what people are feeling from their facial behavior? Are there individual differences (and gender differences) in the ability to interpret facial behavior? How well can we establish deception or truth from facial behavior? Questions like these need to be investigated using methods that rely on observers responding to facial behavior; they do not involve asking what the nature of the facial behavior actually is. Almost always, in research on humans, this means conducting *judgment studies*. Other questions include both aspects; that is, they ask both what the facial behavior is and what it signifies to the observer. These include: How is facial behavior involved in communication? How is facial behavior involved in person perception? How is facial behavior related to interpersonal skills? Is expressive behavior related to health and illness? These require a combination of methods. Of course, the groups are not independent of one another; some questions in the last group may be subdivided into measurement and judgment issues, and questions in the first two groups might have important corollaries that demand a different approach. For example, once the conditions under which truth and deception may be distinguished have been established using judgment methods, investigators might be interested in describing the facial behavior that accompanies truth and deception, using measurement methods.

In this section, I look briefly at the three most widely used general approaches to the study of facial behavior. Two are measurement methods, and one is judgment methodology.

Electromyography

Electromyography (EMG) provides the most objective way we have of measuring facial behavior. A full treatment of EMG methodology, including its application to facial behavior, was given by Cacioppo, Tassinary, and Fridlund (1990). A less technical account is available in Fridlund and Izard (1983). Briefly, as usually applied, facial EMG recording involves the placement of small surface electrodes over the muscles (or muscle groups) involved in changing the facial appearance. The electrodes detect aggregated muscle action potentials from underlying muscle fibers, and the signal, suitably filtered, amplified, and smoothed, is taken to be approximately proportional to the strength of contraction of the underlying muscles. One of the earliest applications of this technique to the study of emotion (Schwartz, Fair, Salt, Mandel, & Klerman, 1976) demonstrated that recording from over the corrugator (brow), frontalis (forehead), depressor (below mouth corners), and masseter (jaw) muscles permitted the discrimination of conditions in which subjects imagined scenes evoking for them happiness, sadness, anger, and "a typical day." These states were discriminable even in the absence of visible changes of expression. This, and other early studies, have been criticized for their use of univariate statistical procedures – for example, by Fridlund and Izard (1983), who advocated a multivariate, pattern-classification approach. Nevertheless, the techniques have since been fruitfully applied in a number of areas of research, addressing questions of our first type. It is also, of course, extremely useful in situations where we want to assess covert (that is, not observable) facial behavior, for which the remaining two types of method are totally unsuited.

Disadvantages of the use of EMG are that it is intrusive: Sticking electrodes onto a person's face might directly change his or her facial movements. It is also obtrusive: It draws the subject's attention to the face, which is also likely to modify behavior. Like other psychophysiological methods, it is relatively expensive, may be relatively unreliable, and may result in a relatively high rate of subject attrition owing, for example, to mechanical or electrical faults in the recording system.

"Objective" coding systems

These are based on the identification and measurement of visible units of facial behavior. They are distinguished from judgment methods because (although they clearly involve judgments being made by observers) the judgments are intended to be purely descriptive, not interpretive. The aim is for the observer to act as a neutral system of measurement rather than as a reactive recipient of communication. Three of these methods were based on theoretical considerations: the identification of the patterns of facial movement known or believed to be associated with particular emotions, believed to be "universal" emotions. Ekman, Friesen, and Tomkins (1971) devised the *Facial Affect Scoring Technique* (FAST), which consisted of 77 descriptions of six such emotions. Izard

(1979) and Izard and Dougherty (1980) similarly produced the *Maximally Descriptive Facial Movement Coding System* (MAX) and the *System for Identifying Affect Expression by Holistic Judgment* (AFFEX), respectively. All three systems were based on early studies of the universality of the recognition of certain configurations of facial actions as particular facial expressions. These systems have a variety of limitations. None, for example, permits the measurement of intensity of behavior, nor the measurement of actions other than those theoretically judged to be important at the time of constructing the systems. MAX and AFFEX were developed for use with infants and omit many configurations that might be relevant for those studying older children and adults.

The alternative to a theoretically based approach is one based on the anatomy of the facial musculature. Although Landis (1924) made an early attempt to describe facial muscle actions, as well as using judgment methods, the first systematic treatment of the precise actions of all the facial muscles was provided by Hjortsjö (1969). Through a process of learning to fire his own facial muscles voluntarily, he developed a precise description of the changes in facial appearance resulting from the action of each facial muscle. His book provided a coding system, based on numbers assigned to each muscle action, which could be used by observers, as well as a classification of the expressions produced by these muscles and their combination. This was partially validated by the application of the coding system to photographs of persons posing these expressions. (See Eibl-Eibesfeldt, 1989, chapter 6, for examples of Hjortsjö's illustrations of single muscle actions and their combination into facial expressions.)

Ekman and Friesen (1978) followed Hjortsjö's method, using Hjortsjö's results to confirm their own. They formalized the descriptions as the FACS, which was intended to provide "a comprehensive system that would distinguish all possible visually distinguishable facial movements." Not all different muscles produce different facial appearances, and so each individually producible facial movement was denoted an *action unit*, and these AUs, of which there are 44, form the basis of the coding and measurement system. Each AU may be scored on a five-point intensity scale. Eibl-Eibesfeldt (1989, Table 6.1) shows how closely the FACS action units correspond to the earlier muscle unit descriptions of Hjortsjö. Hjortsjö's coding system for facial behavior has been eclipsed by its development by Ekman and Friesen into FACS and seems not to have been used in much research. The application of FACS to dynamic facial behavior is very time-consuming, needing slow-motion replay of videotape excerpts. Further, for many purposes, a full description of the facial movements is not necessary; all that might be required is a description of the actions assumed to be involved in emotional behavior. For these reasons, Ekman and Friesen have derived a version called EM-FACS, which scores "only the AUs and AU combinations that are best supported by empirical findings or theory as emotion signals" (Ekman & O'Sullivan, 1991, p. 171).

These systems have been widely used in researching many different questions. They are appropriate, of course, where the questions involve the description or measurement of facial behavior rather than the assessment of the information conveyed by facial behavior. In this regard, it is curious to note that one hotly debated question – that concerning the existence and nature of universal emotions with universal expressions, which is manifestly a question about facial behavior rather than about information transmission – has rarely been investigated by the use of these measurement techniques (or EMG). Instead, the evidence for universality is almost entirely based on judgment studies. That is, the question investigated is actually a corollary of, or as Russell (1994) has put it, one of four aspects of, the basic question: Namely, is the facial behavior produced by human beings labeled similarly by people in different cultures? Izard (1994) recently recognized this: "I think that methods dependent on language and semantic attribution are not the best way to establish the [innateness-universality hypothesis]" (p. 291).

Judgment studies

Judgment methodology is the most widely used in investigations of facial behavior. We look at the methodology in some detail in the remainder of this chapter. Here I draw attention to the major varieties of these techniques. Judgment studies are necessary to address those questions concerned with the information conveyed by facial expression – questions about the use people make of facial behavior to infer the states or characteristics of others, or of the verbal messages they are conveying. Ekman et al. (1972/1982a) examined the obverse question – of when it is possible to reach conclusions about components of facial behavior from judgment studies. They stressed that answers to measurement questions may be inferred only when the judgment study produces results showing accuracy. Even so, there are still problems with using judgment studies for this purpose. First, agreement amongst, or accuracy of, observers might fail not because of the absence of particular behaviors but because they are unnoticed or misinterpreted. Second, agreement may be reached, or accuracy attained, by the use of cues other than facial behavior (e.g., lip bites, hesitations, sighs, etc.). In view of these difficulties, it is clear that measurement questions are best addressed with direct measurement methods, as described in the preceding sections.

Judgment studies are of two main types. The first involves *category judgments* and may usefully be subdivided depending on how the judgment categories originate. Most commonly, judges are given a short list of response categories, which may be based on theoretical considerations (e.g., Ekman, 1972; Izard, 1971) or derived from the terms commonly used by members of the subject pool (e.g., Wagner, 1990). This approach is known as the *forced-choice method*. The judge is shown a series of stimuli, usually one at a time, and has to try to assign each stimulus to (usually) a single response category (that is, to choose one response label) from those provided. A neutral or "don't know" category is sometimes permitted. Less frequently used has been the *free-response method*, in which judges are allowed to choose freely what label to apply, although that freedom is likely to be constrained by telling the subject what type of label (e.g., emotional) is required (e.g., Izard, 1971; Russell, 1991a). The second general approach, the *rating method*, allows judges to rate the extent to which each of a number of properties is shown in the stimulus faces (e.g., Schlosberg, 1954). Once again, the properties rated are usually provided by the investigator on the basis of theoretical notions.

For Ekman, Friesen, and Ellsworth (1972/1982b), the choice between category and rating methods is determined by which of two distinct theoretical perspectives is taken on the information available in the face. Category judgments, it was argued, are used by those who postulate a set of distinct primary affects, often in attempts to identify the unique (and universal) facial actions associated with each affect (e.g., Izard, 1971; Woodworth, 1938). Rating methods (which they called "dimensional" methods), on the other hand, were used by theorists who postulate that emotion categories (and facial behavior) may be accounted for by variations in a small number of independent dimensions (e.g., Osgood, 1966; Schlosberg, 1954). However, this simple relation between theory and method fits neither the uses to which these methods have been put nor the methods used by particular theorists. First, the dimensional theorist Osgood (1966), as Ekman et al. (1972/1982a) recognized, actually used a category judgment method, in which labels for 40 emotional states drawn from earlier studies were available to judges, who had to select one for each posed stimulus. The three-dimensional semantic space accounting for the judgments was derived by factor analytic methods. Second, the theoretical positions are not mutually exclusive. It is possible for one theorist to hold both that a set of basic or fundamental emotions exists and that it may be described by a smaller number of dimensions. Frijda (1969), for example, used data from both category and dimension methods to examine a theoretical position that permits both types of description. Third, the dimensional method has also been used with judges rating not supposed underlying dimensions but the emotions themselves (e.g., Wagner, Buck, & Winterbotham, 1993). One reason for this is the existence of blends of emotion and facial behavior, as pointed out, for example, by Plutchik (1962). Nummenmaa (1992), it may additionally be noted, has for some years used a combination of category judgment and dimension judgment methods to investigate the ways in which the facial behavior associated with basic emotions may be blended. Nummenmaa's basic category judgment method is unusual in that it is *exhaustive*, by which I mean that there are equal numbers of stimuli and response categories, and all are presented to a judge simultaneously, so that the task is to sort the k stimuli individually into k categories.

The methodology of judgment studies

Ekman et al.'s (1972/1982a) chapter on methodological decisions in research on emotion in the human face may be taken as the basic guide for such research. It proposes a set of "standards" to be achieved in both measurement and judgment studies, standards that have been widely followed. This source has been enormously useful in guiding research design in judgment studies, providing a wealth of advice and information. However, as it is nearly 25 years since it first appeared, it is time to reappraise its prescriptions. Later methodological accounts have been provided by Rosenthal (1982, 1987), paying particular attention to statistical issues. Many of Ekman et al.'s standards are common sense, or general experimental standards, but where they become more specific, they are applicable only to a subset of questions about facial behavior. In particular, the proposed standards seem to have been derived from a concentration on the use of judgment studies to address questions essentially of our first type. Furthermore, they are not all directly relevant to questions concerning *naturally occurring* facial behavior. This is not to say that the standards are wrong; these authors performed a major service for the field in producing them. My aim here is to examine the standards and to see how they may be made more generally applicable. A consequence of this reappraisal is that the prescriptions will be found to be too narrow and will have to be replaced by more flexible guidance. This is inevitable if judgment methods are to be applied to a wide range of research questions. I use the framework provided by Ekman et al. to reexamine the methodology of judgment studies, and I use the subheadings of that chapter as a guide.

Choosing the eliciting circumstance

Ekman et al.'s requirements here were threefold: "(1) There must be some basis for claiming the circumstance has relevance to emotion. (2) There must be some way to determine when emotion is aroused or stimulated and, if possible, which emotion is aroused or stimulated when, so as to provide an accuracy criterion for use in either component or judgment studies. (3) A clear record must be obtained if the crucial components are to be either measurable or evident to observers" (p. 25). The first two requirements are unexceptionable, as far as they go. If we are to examine judgments of facial behavior related to emotions, we must clearly be able to determine that they *are* related to emotions. However, what is not remarked here is that we need to be able, also, to exclude determinants of facial behavior *other than* emotion; otherwise, we cannot conclude that the information conveyed by facial behavior is caused by, or otherwise inextricably linked to, emotion rather than, say, intentions to act in a particular way.

The third requirement requires closer scrutiny. On the surface, it is again unexceptionable, since nobody would seriously argue against the need to obtain a clear record. However, from their subsequent discussion, it seems that what Ekman et al. are concerned with is not the recording process as such but rather the production of clear (that is, obvious or noticeable) examples of the behavior in question. This may be justifiable if the judgment method is to be used in a measurement study, but it would seriously compromise the ecological validity of many more appropriate uses of judgment methods. If, for example, we are investigating the question *Can a person tell from observing another's facial behavior what emotion the other reports experiencing?*, we cannot permit ourselves to exclude subjects, or portions of the record, that do not satisfy some criteria that we ourselves impose regarding how measurable or visible the facial actions are. That is, the sample of behavior shown to judges must be representative of (or randomly sampled from) the behavior of the subject in the situation under investigation. However, the selection might need to be guided by the need to exclude portions of the record in which we have reason to believe something other than the particular emotion (or other condition) under investigation might have occurred. For example, if we are making a continuous videotape record of facial behavior while people are describing some unpleasant event that had occurred to them, we would probably want to exclude that portion of the record made after a subject has run out of things to say, since they are no longer in the condition we are investigating. Of course, for other purposes – for example, if our interest is in the reactions of people who dry up in this way – the later sections of the record would be of crucial importance.

Ekman et al.'s recommended "standards" for choice of eliciting circumstances are (1) that experiments should include more than one eliciting circumstance; (2) that an assessment should be attempted of whether or not the circumstance leads to a particular emotion for subjects in general, as well as the particular subject; and (3) that if "artificial" induction (including posing) is used, an attempt should be made to estimate the generalizability to naturally occurring emotions. Each of these standards, like the third requirement, seems to reflect the standards' origins in the use of judgment methodology to address measurement questions. However, each is inapplicable to a wide range of questions about facial behavior. If, for example, we are interested in people's behavior in the presence of an opposite sex stranger in a neutral waiting-room setting, it would not help us to combine these observations with records made when solving a puzzle, with a friend viewing a movie, or posing to a camera (although, of course, we might wish to compare or contrast behavior produced in other situations). The second standard is also clearly restrictive. Since we are often interested in the responses of individuals, it might even be preferable to adopt the reverse strategy, that is, to tailor the eliciting circumstances to the individual subject.

Sampling persons

The standard proposed for this by Ekman et al. is a widely adopted one in human experimental psychology – namely, "Studies employing many subjects are more trustworthy than those using only a few" (p. 29). Ekman et al. caution, further, that the subjects employed are those showing "the intended response." However, we must be careful, in the general context of judgment studies, that this does not involve exclusion of subjects who fail to produce the facial behavior expected by the investigator, unless the judgment is to be of particular components or patterns of such behavior. Once again, this restrictive caution would limit the ecological validity of many types of study.

Rosenthal (1982) provided a thorough analysis of matters to do with the sampling of both senders and judges. In particular, his chapter should be consulted for detailed discussion of assessing and improving the reliability of judges, and for the solution of problems to do with treating either senders or judges as the unit of analysis in ANOVA of judgment studies. Briefly, if we have a sample of senders and a sample of judges, we may focus on whichever is the more important for our particular investigation. For example, if we are addressing a research question about gender differences in ability to interpret facial behavior, we would treat judge gender as a between-subjects factor, making sender gender a within-subjects factor. A straightforward two-way ANOVA of this design will overestimate the effect of sender gender compared to an alternative analysis with senders as the focus (and sender gender as a between-subjects factor), and judge gender as the within-subjects factor. The reason for this is that within-subjects error terms are smaller than those between subjects. It is clear that the appropriate analysis is one in which the variable of main interest is the between-subjects factor, since it is only when a factor is thus treated as a random variable that its effects may be generalized to other subjects. One simple approach that would avoid this confusion would be simply to average across senders, or judges, whichever is not the focus of the study. However, if it is the aim of the study to look at both sender and judge performance, then care must be taken to select appropriate error terms that will allow generalization of both (ignoring temptations to use a within-subject analysis to get a significant result, which would tell us about nobody but the particular subjects in the study). Rosenthal describes how this may be carried out.

Sampling behavior from a record

Under this heading, Ekman et al. recognized some of the issues of generalizability already mentioned. Their standard for this is that the investigator should specify how the sampling was done, so that generality of the result may be determined. They argued that the need to sample behavior may be reduced by careful selection of eliciting circumstances, instructions, and subjects, all of which, however, might in some cases reduce the generalizability of the results and their relevance to the questions under investigation. Sampling from the behavior record should be based not on subjective decisions of the investigator but on criteria such as the points in a record when posers report that they were producing a good pose, or when during a review of the recording, subjects indicated when they felt the emotion most strongly, or when a psychophysiological marker indicates that some event has taken place. Once again, however, for application to the widest range of investigations, sampling of this sort should be done circumspectly.

Sampling emotions

Here Ekman et al. touched on, but did not develop, one of the more serious problems surrounding the performance of judgment studies. As they put it, "Over- or underrepresentation of some emotions within a sample of facial behavior may seriously bias the outcome of both judgment or component studies" (p. 31). The problem, thus stated, is that presenting to judges unequal numbers of stimuli of different types produces a stimulus bias, meaning that accuracy for those stimuli might be overestimated if accuracy rates are not corrected. I examine this issue in the section on assessing accuracy. However, it is not clear that this is the particular problem addressed here by Ekman et al., since they illustrate the problem by contrasting the ease with which expressions of happiness are recognized and distinguished from other emotions, compared with the difficulty of discriminating some other emotions, such as fear and surprise. Such emotions, they say, "are probably more similar to each other in both facial components and semantic connotations than either is to disgust" (p. 31). Thus, the issue addressed seems to do with similarity of facial behaviors rather than statistical bias due to unequal numbers of each stimulus class.

The recommended standard for dealing with this problem involves providing a full description of what emotions have been sampled and of results broken down by each category. Beyond this, we are advised that "The more emotions sampled, the greater the generality" (p. 32), a suggestion that, once again, is not compatible with many research questions.

Sampling emotion words, categories, or dimensions

This is a key issue in the application of judgment studies. Ekman et al.'s recommended standards are that we should pay attention to the representative sampling of emotion terms to be used as response categories, including more rather than fewer, and at some points in the research program to use free responses (as opposed to forced choice). We should also make allowance for the existence of emotion blends in the face by letting judges note the occurrence of more than one emotion. Where the research involves questions about the emotion vocabulary, or about "the basic or primary emotion categories," these considerations are particularly important, since the use of a limited number of forced-choice categories may determine the conclusions drawn. The use of a preselected emotion vocabulary in the judgment task may, however, be justified as an economical procedure where the experiment involves, for example, the comparison of accuracy judgments based on observation of different parts of the face. However, even then, the investigator must be able to demonstrate that the judgment categories are sufficiently comprehensive.

This is perfectly proper advice, which has not always been followed. In particular, as pointed out earlier, the evidence for universals in facial expression has been based almost entirely on judgment studies, and these judgment studies have almost all used forced-choice methods, sometimes with as few as two or three response choices available to the subjects at any time (Ekman & Friesen, 1971). The evidence for the universality of certain facial behaviors is frequently cited as indicating the basic or primary emotion categories. Thus, studies of universality are exactly the type of study that should avoid the limited forced-choice methodology.

A number of problems relating to the sampling of response categories may be identified, particularly in studies of universality. (See Russell, 1994, for a critical review of the use of forced-choice methodology in this context.) First, as I have already remarked, the selection of categories will alert judges to the type of response that is required. In the present context, since the question under investigation has been the universality of facial expressions *of emotions*, the choices available to subjects were emotion labels. The fact that other categories of label have not been used in this type of study means that certain alternative interpretations of the results cannot be excluded – for example, there is universality of the facial behavior associated with particular *intentions* to act in particular ways, or with particular *patterns of appraisal* of stimulus situations. In some studies of isolated cultures, a modified forced-choice judgment paradigm introduced by Dashiell (1927) was used. In this, essentially a reversal of the standard format, the judge is told a very brief story, such as "someone has just met a friend and is happy," and is given the task of selecting from a limited number of photographs of facial behavior the one that is appropriate for the story. Apart from other problems that this method introduces (including, here, a very limited number of response options), the story quite clearly confounds the emotion label and the other aspects of the story, so that the results are equally open to other, not necessarily emotional, interpretations.

The second problem relating to the selection of response categories is, of course, that they limit the judges' range of choices even *within* the designated category. Thus, for example, Ekman's earlier list of emotions that show high levels of agreement (for example, Ekman, 1972) did not include contempt, although Izard's (1977) list did. There has been some debate about whether or not Izard's evidence actually established contempt as a *separate* universally recognized category. Ekman and Friesen (1986) stated that nobody had explored this issue and claimed the first discovery of a universally recognizable contempt display. In response, Izard and Haynes (1988) cited earlier data supporting the existence of a pan-cultural contempt expression. However, Ekman and Friesen (1988) subsequently pointed out that these apparently successful earlier studies did not use "contempt" as a separate response category but rather always combined it with other labels such as "scorn," "sneering," and "haughty." The important point for our purposes is that unless a response category is provided for judges in a forced-choice paradigm, they cannot use it, and hence the paradigm cannot have anything to say about what is represented by that label. Although this is an apparently obvious and even trivial point, it is essential to keep it in mind when interpreting the results of judgment studies, just as it is essential to notice that studies have often included more than one term in a particular response category, without demonstrating that they are exact synonyms.

The third problem involves the *balance* of response categories provided to judges. The particular problem here is that judges will probably not find all discriminations equally easy or difficult to make. In part, this was addressed by Ekman et al., in their consideration of sampling emotions, when they pointed out that some emotions are more similar in facial components and semantic connotations than are others (see earlier discussion). From the point of view of judgment studies, however, the problem is that the apparent ease with which a particular label may be accurately applied will depend on the *other* labels from which it has to be distinguished. Wagner (1990) pointed out that sets of response categories are not balanced, in particular, in relation to the number of "pleasant" and "unpleasant" categories provided. Thus, the apparent relative accuracy with which the label "happiness" can be applied, even to non-posed expressions (Wagner, MacDonald, & Manstead, 1986), could result from the use of sets of categories in which pleasant terms are in the minority. In the (not atypical) case of Wagner et al., only two pleasant categories ("happiness" and "surprise"; stimuli in the latter class showed people in situations described as producing pleasant surprise) were included, with four unpleasant categories ("anger," "sadness," "disgust," and "fear"), and "neutral." Wagner suggested that a judge who is able to discriminate pleasant from unpleasant facial behavior has a simpler choice if the face appears pleasant (with the chance of guessing the correct pleasant face of 50%) than if it appears unpleasant (with a probability of being correct by chance of 25%). Using a set of response categories with arguably equal numbers of pleasant and unpleasant categories, derived from the free responses to the eliciting stimuli of members of the subject pool, Wagner (1990) showed that "happy" was not applied with accuracy significantly better than chance (although "amused," "peaceful," and the possibly unpleasant "puzzled" were).

In attempts to avoid these and other problems associated with the use of forced-choice paradigms, free-response methods have sometimes been used. However, such methods have often suffered from some of the same problems as forced-choice studies and hence introduce new difficulties. As an example of shared problems, it may be noted that free choices are usually not entirely free but are constrained in some way. The way that they are constrained is, typically, to specify that the labels or descriptions required are of *emotions* (e.g., Izard, 1971). The reason for so constraining judges is, presumably, that they would otherwise not generate emotion labels. This is what Frijda (1953) reported; most of his subjects, asked simply to comment freely on a series of photographs of people, described situations in which the photographs might have been taken rather than emotions that subjects might have been experiencing. Thus, we have the same interpretive problem as noted earlier: Studies that have specified that emotion descriptions should be produced by judges have obscured the possibility that other descriptions might be equally valid. Indeed, in this case, we have evidence from Frijda's study that other types of description are *more* readily applied than are emotion terms to pictures of facial behavior.

The additional difficulty that arises with free-choice paradigms is common to any research method that permits unconstrained, open-ended responding: *How do we summarize the data?* In the context of studies, such as those on universality, intended to assess recognition of facial behavior, the question becomes: *How do we decide which freely chosen responses are correct?* Indeed, it is usually to avoid this problem that forced-choice methods are most frequently used. As Russell (1994) has pointed out, reports of studies based on free-labeling methods usually do not give a full account of how it was decided which responses were equivalent to one another, let alone a full list of judges' responses. Where examples are given, it is easy to take issue with the way that words have been combined into the same response category. Thus, for example, Russell argued that some words accepted as correct by Izard (1971) are not even emotions (e.g., "deliberating," "observation," and "clowning"), while sets of words accepted by Izard as correct responses for the same facial behavior are not all synonyms (e.g., "distress," "loneliness," "pain," "pity," and "worry" were accepted as correct for expressions intended to be sad). This difficulty will clearly be even greater when groups of judges who do not share a common language are compared, as is the case with cross-cultural studies of universality. Russell (1991b) reviewed evidence that different language groups might categorize emotions in somewhat different ways. Most extremely, terms describing emotions that are widely believed to be "basic" or "fundamental" by English-speaking theorists do not have direct translations in some other languages.

Choosing a method of recording

The basic issue here is whether to use still or moving records of facial behavior. The issue is largely decided by the type of investigation. "Stills may be appropriate when the information obtainable from the muscle actions at the apex of facial movement is of interest" (Ekman et al., 1972/ 1982a, p. 34). On the other hand, if our research questions require ecological validity, then stills may not be appropriate. As Ekman et al. put it, "In spontaneous eliciting circumstances . . . still photographs may mutilate the natural flow of behavior into meaningless units" (p. 35).

Occasionally, particularly in earlier research, artists' representations of facial behavior were used. Although such stimuli may allow control over factors other than facial behavior (including physiognomy, demographic characteristics, and lighting), we cannot be sure that other aspects of the behavior have not been altered or omitted, and so such stimuli are not considered to be very useful for investigating most types of questions about facial behavior. Ekman et al. suggest that this view might change once a systematic means of scoring facial behaviors is widely accepted. Even though this has been the case for some years now, particularly the

FACS, there would seem to be little advantage in using such stimuli rather than photographic or video records.

Presentation of stimuli

Russell (1994) has drawn attention to issues having to do with the way in which stimuli are presented (beyond choice of static versus dynamic), which were not addressed by Ekman et al. The underlying principle here is that *all judgments are relative*. Almost all judgment studies of facial behavior have used within-subject designs, so that the stimuli presented are presented within the context of all the other stimuli in the set, and the responses made are made within the context of the responses already given. Russell cited a number of studies that have demonstrated such context effects within judgment studies of facial behavior. It is even possible, by selection of particular stimulus sets, to cause "basic" expressions such as anger to be judged as "contempt," "disgust," or "frustration" (Russell, 1993). He argued that the practices of previewing – that is, showing the subject the full set of stimuli before any overt judgments are made – and of giving subjects a number of trials at the whole stimulus set (sometimes using only data obtained on the last trials) similarly serve to emphasize similarities and differences within the set.

To avoid these problems, we would ideally use between-subject designs, although this would clearly be a very inefficient approach. It has been found that recognition accuracy is lower for between-subject than for within-subject designs, confirming the importance of considering context effects (Russell, 1991a). The problems may be reduced in within-subject designs by attention to balancing of the order of presentation, so that at least the *immediate* context of each judgment is different for different subjects.

Assessing accuracy

This is another issue not addressed by Ekman et al. Category judgment studies are normally conducted to address either or both of two types of question about performance: (1) *how accurate is the observer overall*, and (2) *how accurate is the observer at identifying each one of the categories of stimulus*? In each case, we want both to provide a measure of accuracy and to assess accuracy in relation to levels of recognition to be expected by chance. The results of a category judgment study may be represented as a confusion matrix, showing how the observer's responses map onto

Table 2.1. *Confusion matrix resulting when a judge assigns responses "X,"
"Y," and "Z" to a number of stimuli of type X, Y, and Z*

Stimulus	Response			
	"X"	"Y"	"Z"	Total
X	a	b	c	$a+b+c$
Y	d	e	f	$d+e+f$
Z	g	h	i	$g+h+i$
Total	$a+d+g$	$b+e+h$	$c+f+i$	n

Note: Entries are frequencies with which each response is assigned to each stimulus type.

the stimulus categories (see Table 2.1). Three common types of error have been noted in the description and analysis of the data arising from such studies (Wagner, 1993). In the next section, I focus on two types of error that have received little previous attention. The third frequent error made is the common one of failure to ensure that only independent observations are entered into analyses using chi-squared or binomial distributions. For a detailed account of the three types of error, the reader is referred to Wagner (1993).

Assessing accuracy in judgment studies

Measuring accuracy

Wagner (1993) examined eighty-six published papers addressing the differential accuracy question. The vast majority of the reported studies measured accuracy by the use of a simple hit rate, H (the proportion of target stimuli correctly identified). It has long been recognized in other areas of research that H (or the false alarm rate, F; the proportion of nontarget stimuli wrongly identified as targets) is not an adequate measure of performance. As Macmillan and Creelman (1991) put it, "A subject for whom $H = .80$ and $F = .40$ is much more sensitive than someone for whom $H = .80$ and $F = .80$, an agnosiac who cannot distinguish [two types of stimulus] at all" (p. 12). To take an extreme case, suppose the judge in our example replied "X" to each and every one of the stimuli. All stimuli of type X would be correctly labeled, but none of type Y or Z would be. It would clearly be meaningless to use H as a measure of accuracy here, implicitly asserting that type X stimuli are perfectly recognized, simply because the strategy of responding "X" to every stimulus has meant that every pleasant stimulus receives the appropriate response.

Evaluating accuracy

The approach adopted by almost all researchers wishing to test the statistical significance of observed accuracy is to use the binomial distribution to compare the number correct with the number expected by chance, using the a priori probability (the proportion of stimuli of each type actually presented) as the chance probability. In Table 2.1, the a priori probability that, for example, a stimulus of type X will be correctly recognized is $(a + b + c)/n$. (If equal numbers of stimuli of each type are presented, this would be 0.33.) However, in adopting the a priori probability, we implicitly assume that the judge guessed randomly, which should result in equal numbers of guesses of the three categories. This is usually not the case in such studies. The true probability of any guess being correct by chance is properly estimated by the proportion of guesses that are of each category. The number expected to be correct by chance is this true probability multiplied by the number of stimuli presented of that type. Thus, for category X, the actual probability of a guess being correct is $(a + d + g)/n$, and the number expected by chance is this multiplied by $(a + b + c)$. There is nothing peculiar about this calculation; it is exactly the same as that used to compute expected values for chi-squared tests. Evaluating performance using a priori probabilities overestimates accuracy for categories receiving more than the a priori proportion of judgments. This problem is equivalent to using H as a measure of accuracy; both stem from failing to take account of observer bias.

It is important to note that it is not only tests on the accuracy of separate categories that may be affected by response bias. In situations where there is also stimulus bias (unequal numbers of stimuli in different categories), the overall hit rate is an adequate measure of accuracy, since it averages over unequal sizes of stimulus category (contrary to the assertion by Rosenthal, 1982, p. 332). However, testing the significance of overall accuracy should not use the average a priori probability to calculate the number expected by chance. Instead, the number expected by chance should be the sum of the number expected for each category, based on the true chance level for each category.

These arguments should *not* be interpreted as recommending that response bias should be treated *only* as a source of variation from a priori chance probabilities, to be controlled for in analysis. Indeed, as Rosenthal (1982) has pointed out, not only response bias but the full confusion matrix is likely to be of great importance in addressing some research questions, and it also should be examined "in a spirit of exploratory data analysis" (Rosenthal, 1982, p. 332). The former could lead us to examine the characteristics of the individual judge (or group of judges) that have resulted in the bias. The latter can provide important information about which stimuli (or responses) are more or less difficult to distinguish. The common principle here is that response biases are common in judgment studies. On the one hand, this makes it necessary to correct measures of accuracy, to remove the confound between accuracy and response bias, and to compute actual chance levels, to avoid errors in analysis. On the other hand, response biases are themselves data, which need to be examined and explained.

Correcting for response bias in judgment studies

Since the hit rate is clearly often not suitable for the description and analysis of the results of category judgment studies, we need an alternative measure that, to be of the widest utility in research on nonverbal behavior, should have the following properties:

1. It should be insensitive to response bias.
2. It should be insensitive to stimulus bias.
3. It should allow separate analyses of accuracy for each stimulus type (including cases with only two stimulus types and two response classes).
4. It should allow comparison of performance between studies with different numbers of response classes.

We have already seen the importance of the first two requirements. Essentially, they suggest that a measure should correct a raw hit frequency for both the proportion of responses of the target class and the proportion of stimuli of the target class. The other two properties have been included to improve generalizability across studies. Several researchers have used measures that attempt to avoid the problems of the use of the hit rate. Wagner (1993) examined these measures, and all failed for one or more reasons to meet the requirements. The interested reader is referred to that paper for more detail.

A recommended measure of accuracy

In view of the absence of a fully acceptable measure of accuracy, Wagner (1993) suggested a solution that is simple to compute and relatively easy to interpret. The proposed measure (the *unbiased hit rate*, or H_U) takes account of possible stimulus bias and response bias, combining the conditional probability that a stimulus will be recognized (given that it is presented) and the conditional probability that a response will be correct (given that it is used) into an estimate of the joint probability of both outcomes. This is done by multiplying together the two conditional probabilities, each of which is the cell entry in a frequency matrix divided by the appropriate marginal total. For example, in Table 2.1, for category X, H_U is $a/(a + b + c) \times a/(a + d + g)$.

This measure has all the properties that we require of a measure of accuracy. Since it expresses accuracy as proportions of both response frequency and stimulus frequency, it is insensitive to response bias, to proportions of stimuli of different types, and to the number of categories. It also allows separate measurement of individual categories even when there are only two categories. When no stimuli of a particular type are correctly identified, H_U has the value zero. When a stimulus type is always correctly identified and the corresponding response category is always correctly applied, H_U has the value $+ 1$. Variations in either or both of these components of accuracy result in values between 0 and 1. If either the frequency of presentation of a stimulus or the frequency of use of a response category is 0, then the conditional probability, and hence H_U, are both indeterminate. The former case presents no problem, since it cannot arise in practice; a stimulus category that is never presented is simply not included in the confusion matrix. The latter case could occur, however, but since the cell entry would be 0, we need not proceed to calculate the indeterminate H_U and may simply define it as 0.

The index H_U may be applied in the analysis of experimental data by using it (after arcsine transformation) as the dependent variable in inferential statistical procedures such as the analysis of variance. For this purpose, it has to be applied to the individual judges (if we are interested in judge performance), to the individual stimulus persons (if they are the units of analysis), or to individual sender–judge pairs (if we are interested in both levels of analysis). To clarify the computation, let us turn our general confusion matrix into a numerical one. Table 2.2 presents data extracted from an unpublished study from my laboratory (Wagner,

Table 2.2. *Confusion matrix showing the number of judges (out of 58) responding with the labels "anger," "contempt," and "disgust" to one stimulus intended to portray each emotion*

	Response			
Stimulus	"Anger"	"Contempt"	"Disgust"	Total
Anger	35	2	21	58
Contempt	1	40	17	58
Disgust	3	2	53	58
Total	39	44	91	174

1995) in which 58 judges viewed a number of facial stimuli, including three photographs claimed to represent: (1) an unilateral contempt expression (Ekman & Friesen, 1986, Fig. 1), (2) anger (Ekman & Friesen, 1975, Fig. 37, lower-left panel), and (3) disgust (Ekman & Friesen, 1975. Fig. 27A). Judges chose one of the terms "anger," "contempt," or "disgust" that they thought best described the expression on each face. The question we wish to ask of these data is: How accurate are the judges at identifying the intended emotion in each photograph? Raw hit rates show that $35/58 = 60\%$ of anger expressions, $40/58 = 69\%$ of contempt expressions, and $53/58 = 91\%$ of disgust expressions are correctly identified, making accuracy for disgust appear considerably better than accuracy for anger or contempt. But notice that the response categories are not used equally often; "disgust" is used more often than the other two together. Therefore, the relative sizes of these hit rates are misleading, being confounded with response bias. Computing H_U for each of these gives a better indication of the relative accuracy of recognition. Thus, for anger, $H_U = 35/39 \times 35/58 = .54$; for contempt, $H_U = 40/44 \times 40/58 = .63$; and for disgust, $H_U = 53/91 \times 53/58 = .53$. It is clear that correcting the hit rates for the response bias shows that disgust is actually correctly identified about as well as anger.

If we wish to compare performance with that to be expected by chance, we may estimate the joint probability of the co-occurrence by chance of the stimulus and response of a particular class by multiplying together the independent probabilities of each of these. For example, the joint probability for category X in Table 2.1 is $(a + b + c)/n \times (a + d + g)/n$. In the numerical example of Table 2.2, chance for anger is $58/174 \times 39/174 = .082$; for contempt, it is $58/174 \times 44/174 = .084$; and for disgust, it is $58/174 \times 91/174 = .174$. These figures may be used to compare the performance of a group of subjects with chance, by entering them along with corresponding values of H_U into a repeated measures t-test. We may also calculate the number expected by chance (just as in the application of chi-squared), by multiplying each probability by the total number of judgments (174), which gives for anger 13, for contempt 14.7, and for disgust 30.3. Notice also that we may similarly compute numbers expected by chance in the incorrect cells. Thus, for example, we can observe that the 21 misclassifications of the anger face as "disgust" are actually fewer than we would expect by chance, which is also 30.33 (.174 × 174; since there are equal numbers of each of the three stimulus types in this example, the chance probability is the same for all three stimulus types within each response category).

Summary and conclusions

The most important conclusion from this examination of methods of research into facial behavior is that the method selected should be appropriate to the research question. That is, if in a particular study we are examining a question that concerns the *structure* of facial behavior per se, then we should use a method that provides the most direct and objective measure possible of facial behavior. Whereas it is possible to use judgment methods to address these questions, the difficulties I have outlined here, together with considerations of reliability and validity, make it quite clear that they should be avoided. Instead, we must use either electromyography or objective scoring methods, the choice being determined largely by considerations of time, expense, obtrusiveness, and availability of equipment and expertise. On the other hand, if the study concerns a question about the *information* available to others in facial behavior, then we have to use a judgment method. Many studies, of course, will be concerned with both types of question, and in these we have to be particularly careful not to use the judgment methodology, which is essential for addressing the information questions, to address also the structural questions. Research of this type must adopt a mixture of methods.

Given that we have to use judgment methodology to address questions concerned with the information available in facial behavior, we must clearly take care to consider the issues discussed in this chapter. However, the general message that I want to put across here is that earlier lists of "standards" or requirements for such research are too restrictive.

They were formulated to deal with questions that did not necessarily require a high level of ecological validity, and, as we have seen, will be misleading if applied to many questions that concern researchers today.

References

Cacioppo, J. T., Tassinary, L. G., & Fridlund, A. J. (1990). The skeletomotor system. In J. T. Cacioppo & L. G. Tassinary (Eds.), *Principles of psychophysiology: Physical, social, and inferential elements* (pp. 325–384). Cambridge/New York: Cambridge University Press.

Dashiell, J. F. (1927). A new method of measuring reactions to facial expression of emotion. *Psychological Bulletin, 24,* 174–175.

Eibl-Eibesfeldt, I. (1989). *Human ethology.* New York: Aldine de Gruyter.

Ekman, P. (1972). Universals and cultural differences in facial expressions of emotion. In J. K. Cole (Ed.), *Nebraska symposium on motivation, 1971* (pp. 207–283). Lincoln, NE: University of Nebraska Press.

Ekman, P., & Friesen, W. V. (1971). Constants across cultures in the face and emotion. *Journal of Personality and Social Psychology, 17,* 124–129.

Ekman, P., & Friesen, W. V. (1975). *Unmasking the face: A guide to recognizing emotions from facial clues.* Englewood Cliffs, NJ: Prentice-Hall.

Ekman, P., & Friesen, W. V. (1978). *The facial action coding system.* Palo Alto, CA: Consulting Psychologists Press.

Ekman, P., & Friesen, W. V. (1986). A new pan-cultural facial expression of emotion. *Motivation and Emotion, 10,* 159–168.

Ekman, P., & Friesen, W. V. (1988). Who knows what about contempt: A reply to Izard and Haynes. *Motivation and Emotion, 12,* 17–22.

Ekman, P., Friesen, W. V., & Ellsworth, P. (1972/1982a). Methodological decisions. In P. Ekman (Ed.), *Emotion in the human face* (pp. 22–38). Cambridge/New York: Cambridge University Press.

Ekman, P., Friesen, W. V., & Ellsworth, P. (1972/1982b). What emotion categories or dimensions can observers judge from facial behavior? In P. Ekman (Ed.), *Emotion in the human face* (pp. 39–55). New York: Cambridge University Press.

Ekman, P., V. Friesen, W., & Tomkins, S. S. (1971). Facial Affect Scoring Technique: A first validity study. *Semiotica, 3,* 37–38.

Ekman, P., & O'Sullivan, M. (1991). Facial expression: Methods, means, and moues. In R. S. Feldman & B. Rimé (Eds.), *Fundamentals of nonverbal behavior* (pp. 163–199). Cambridge/New York: Cambridge University Press.

Fridlund, A. J., & Izard, C. E. (1983). Electromyographic studies of facial expressions of emotions and patterns of emotions. In J. T. Cacioppo & R. E. Petty (Eds.), *Social psychophysiology: A sourcebook* (pp. 243–286). New York: Guilford Press.

Frijda, N. H. (1953). The understanding of facial expression of emotion. *Acta Psychologica, 9,* 294–362.

Frijda, N. H. (1969). Recognition of emotions. *Advances in Experimental Social Psychology, 4,* 167–223.

Hjortsjö, C. H. (1969). *Man's face and mimic language.* Lund, Sweden: Studentlitteratur.

Izard, C. E. (1971). *The face of emotion.* New York: Appleton Century Crofts.

Izard, C. E. (1977). Human emotions. New York: Plenum.

Izard, C. E. (1979). The maximally discriminative facial movement coding system (MAX). Newark, DE: University of Delaware Office of Instructional Technology.

Izard, C. E. (1994). Innate and universal facial expressions: Evidence from developmental and cross-cultural research. Psychological Bulletin, 115, 288–299.

Izard, C. E., & Dougherty, L. M. (1980). A system for identifying affect expressions by wholistic judgments. Newark, DE: Instructional Resources Center.

Izard, C. E., & Haynes, O. M. (1988). On the form and universality of the contempt expression: A challenge to Ekman and Friesen's claim of discovery. Motivation and Emotion, 12, 1–16.

Landis, C. (1924). Studies of emotional reactions. II. General behavior and facial expression. Journal of Comparative Psychology, 4, 447–509.

Macmillan, N. A., & Creelman, C. D. (1991). Detection theory: A user's guide. Cambridge : Cambridge University Press.

Nummenmaa, T. (1992). Pure and blended emotion in the human face: Psychometric experiments. Helsinki: Suomalainen Tiedeakatemia.

Osgood, C. E. (1966). Dimensionality of the semantic space for communication via facial expressions. Scandinavian Journal of Psychology, 7, 1–30.

Plutchik, R. (1962). The emotions: Facts, theories, and a new model. New York: Random House.

Rosenthal, R. (1982). Conducting judgment studies. In K. R. Scherer & P. Ekman (Eds.), Handbook of methods in nonverbal behavior research (pp. 287–361). Cambridge/New York: Cambridge University Press.

Rosenthal, R. (1987). Judgment studies: Design, analysis, and meta-analysis. New York: Cambridge University Press.

Russell, J. A. (1991a). The contempt expression and the relativity thesis. Motivation and Emotion, 15, 149–168.

Russell, J. A. (1991b). Culture and the categorization of emotions. Psychological Bulletin, 110, 426–450.

Russell, J. A. (1993). Forced-choice response format in the study of facial expression. Motivation and Emotion, 17, 41–51.

Russell, J. A. (1994). Is there universal recognition of emotion from facial expression? A review of the cross-cultural studies. Psychological Bulletin, 115, 102–141.

Schlosberg, H. (1954). Three dimensions of emotion. Psychological Review, 61, 81–88.

Schwartz, G. E., Fair, P. L., Salt, P., Mandel, M. R., & Klerman, G. L. (1976). Facial muscle patterning to affective imagery in depressed and nondepressed subjects. Science, 192, 489–491.

Wagner, H. L. (1990). The spontaneous facial expression of differential positive and negative emotions. Motivation and Emotion, 14, 27–43.

Wagner, H. L. (1993). On measuring performance in category judgment studies of nonverbal behavior. Journal of Nonverbal Behavior, 17, 3–28.

Wagner, H. L. (1995). On differentiating anger, contempt, and disgust. Unpublished manuscript, University of Manchester.

Wagner, H. L., Buck, R., & Winterbotham, M. (1993). Communication of specific emotions: Gender differences in sending accuracy and communication measures. Journal of Nonverbal Behavior, 17, 29–53.

Wagner, H. L., MacDonald, C. J., & Manstead, A. S. R. (1986). Communication of individual emotions by spontaneous facial expressions. Journal of Personality and Social Psychology, 50, 737–743.

Woodworth, R. S. (1938). Experimental psychology. New York: Henry Holt.

PART II

Three broad theoretical frameworks

3. Emotions and facial expressions: A perspective from Differential Emotions Theory

CARROLL E. IZARD

In my first major effort at elaborating Differential Emotions Theory (DET), I proposed that personality was a supersystem consisting of five separate though highly interacting subsystems (Izard, 1971). The emotions were conceived as one of the subsystems of personality, and, following Tomkins (1962), the emotions were viewed as the primary motivational system for human behavior. Furthermore, each discrete emotion was interpreted as a system with distinct though interacting components. Although DET has changed to accommodate new thought and data, the essence of the systems approach has remained integral (cf. Izard et al., 1995). The systems concept is important in presenting a perspective on facial expressions, because the perspective I present hinges on the concepts of systems and separate, dissociable components.

Facial expression (as well as vocal, postural, gestural expression) is conceived as an evolved, genetically influenced but highly modifiable and dissociable component of emotion. However, as stated on previous occasions (e.g., Izard, 1977), *observable expression is not viewed as a necessary component of emotion.* One goal of this chapter is to summarize the argument for this position and to place it in perspective by addressing two kinds of counterarguments, argument against the evolutionary–genetic origin of facial expressions and argument against their links to emotion (feeling/motivational) states. Another goal is to reaffirm the theoretical significance of the concept of patterns. In DET, the term *pattern* refers to one of two phenomena: A set of movements that index a discrete emotion or a set or cluster of discrete emotions that interact to produce complex affective phenomena such as anxiety and depression (Izard & Youngstrom, 1996).

On the innateness and universality of facial expressions

Understanding DET's emphasis on an interactive systems approach is key to understanding the theory's perspective on facial expressions. The first substantial body of evidence offered in support of DET was based on recognition of facial expression of emotion (Ekman, Sorenson, & Friesen, 1969; Izard, 1971; Tomkins & McCarter, 1964). Actually, those data on facial expression, obtained from widely different literate and preliterate cultures, inspired work on two theories: the development of Ekman's (1971) neurocultural theory and elaboration of my own DET. Ekman's theory focused on an explanation of universal and cultural differences in facial expression of emotion. In contrast, even rudimentary versions of DET (Izard, Wehmer, Livsey, & Jennings, 1965) focused on the functions of emotions and their role as components of the principal motivational system for human behavior.

The cross-cultural data inspired further attempts to explicate the functions of the various discrete emotions that were recognized or labeled ("validated") cross-culturally. Both Ekman and I interpreted the cross-cultural data as evidence of the universality of a limited set of emotion expressions. Although this interpretation has been widely accepted for a couple of decades, it has also been the subject of a recent debate (Ekman, 1994; Fridlund, 1994; Izard, 1994; Russell, 1993, 1994). This debate was extensive, and the existing literature relating to it is the best source of information on the details of the disagreement. Some central issues in the debate were terminology for emotion categories, categories versus dimensions or continua for describing facial expressions, methodology for obtaining subjects' responses to expression stimuli, and interpretations of data. I give here only a brief synopsis of my view of the issue.

The universality debate

The debate was not really about the innateness and universality hypothesis (IUH) of facial expressions. It was about the universality of semantic attributions, because most of the data that inspired the debate were indeed based on semantic attributions. Despite the importance of this distinction, no one had ever explicitly stated a semantic attribution hypothesis or considered the implications of basing claims of innateness and universality of expressive behavior solely (or mainly) on language-based data. Although the debate (and other literature) has shown that semantic attributions are influenced by culture, methodology, and a host of other factors, both sides of the debate agreed that the cross-cultural data based on them provide support for the universality of at least a few expressions.

I am comfortable with the notion that the language-based data provide some support for the universality part of the IUH. They are consistent with, but not directly related to, the innateness part.

The innateness issue

Other types of data that could address the IUH as it relates to human facial expressions are quite scarce. Perhaps the most significant data will come from objective, nonattributional coding in cross-cultural, longitudinal studies of the ontogeny of facial behavior. This poses an extremely formidable task in terms of time and money, and it may never be accomplished by human observers (coders). It took several years of facial coding by numerous people to show for a single middle-class American sample that certain facial expressions hypothesized to signal emotions were present by 3 months and morphologically stable through 9 months of age (Izard et al., 1995). The prospects of automated coding of facial movements keeps hope alive for further research in this domain.

Despite the paucity of supporting data, I followed Darwin's lead (1872/1965), took encouragement from the cross-cultural data and ethological research on nonhuman facial displays (e.g., van Hooff, 1967; Tinbergen, 1973), continued to assume that the facial expressions of some basic emotions were innate, and presented evidence of discrete emotion expressions in young infants (e.g., Izard, Hembree, Dougherty, & Spizzirri, 1983; Izard, Huebner, Risser, McGinnes, & Dougherty, 1980). So did a number of other investigators (e.g., Haviland & Lelwica, 1987; Malatesta, Culver, Tesman, & Shepard, 1989; Weinberg & Tronick, 1994). The argument for innateness, like that for universality, was widely accepted for more than a decade; then the supporting evidence for the hypothesis became the subject of debate (Izard et al., 1995; Oster, Hegley, & Nagel, 1992). In this debate, the issue was not so much the innateness of discrete expressions as the time of their emergence in ontogeny, the question of developmental changes, and the methods of measurement.

At present, there is no generally accepted resolution of the developmental issues. There is robust evidence for the early emergence and morphological stability of certain facial patterns in infants (Izard et al., 1995). These data suggest that some of the infant patterns are morphologically identical to the corresponding patterns in adults, and research reviewed by Ekman and Oster (1979) shows that newborn infants are capable of making the movements of emotion. Nevertheless, there is still disagreement regarding the interpretation of these patterns.

"Prototypical" full-face expressions and component signals

Different views as to what constitutes a facial expression of emotion continue to cloud the issue. The false notion that there is *one* full-face "prototypical" expression for each of several basic emotions has undoubtedly created much misunderstanding. DET has hypothesized a set of elements for several full-face emotion-specific configurations, but the theory does not propose a single configuration (or single component) as the sole means of signaling any given emotion. The false idea that DET proposes a single prototypical infant expression as the sole means of signaling a particular emotion has been another distractor from the central tenets of the theory. The facial behavior coding system most frequently used by proponents of DET (MAX: Izard, 1979b) has always defined rules whereby a movement in a single region of the face can signal a hypothesized emotion; so can different combinations of regional movements. For example, MAX hypothesizes that oblique brows (inner corners raised) on an otherwise neutral face are a signal of sadness. This position is similar to the componential approach described by Smith (1989) and Smith and Scott (chapter 10, this volume).

On the number of emotion feelings and facial expressions

DET has also proposed that the number of basic emotions and emotion feelings are not limited to the number of basic or universal facial signals. Shame, shyness, and guilt are considered basic emotions, but they are not consistently associated with a particular facial pattern. Gaze behavior, posture, head and body movement, and psychophysiological indexes have proved useful in the coding of some of these emotions (see Izard, 1991, for a review).

From the perspective of DET, the failure to distinguish emotion and cognition has led to misunderstanding about the number of emotions. Some investigators (e.g., Kagan, 1994) repeatedly reaffirm the Jamesian notion that there is an infinite variety of emotions: feelings and expressions. I have argued that there are two factors that account for this view. One is that emotion feelings vary on a dimension of intensity, and subtle shades of feeling can rapidly alternate in focal awareness. Furthermore, each subtle feeling of joy or sadness can become associated with different thoughts. This might make a few basic emotions seem like a limitless number. Second, a core feeling, say sadness, can be associated with a very large number of distinctly different images and thoughts. Thoughts of an absent loved one or home may create nostalgia. Thoughts of the death of a loved one or a home destroyed by fire may create the deep and profound feelings of grief. In both cases, the core feeling is sadness; it is the associated cognition that is different. In DET then, there is indeed an infinite variety of affective–cognitive structures, schemas, and thought–feeling streams. This infinite variety of emotion–cognition phenomena can be built with a limited set of basic emotion feeling states, each of which varies along a very wide dimension of intensity (cf. Gelernter, 1994) and becomes associated with a limitless number of images and thoughts (cf., Izard, 1992). Both the behavioral indicators of discrete emotions and their associated cognitive representations can be used to discriminate among affective–cognitive structures and schemas.

The idea that the variety of emotional experiences is due largely to the multiplicity of links between emotion feeling states and cognitive representations contrasts sharply with the notion that basic emotions *mix* to form new secondary emotions. One theorist maintains that the mixing of primary emotions to make new emotions is like primary colors mixing to form pastels (cf. Plutchik, 1962). He proposes, for example, that the basic emotions of anger and joy actually mix in some way to form the secondary emotion of pride. In this scheme, it is not clear what happens at the neural level or what happens to the distinct motivational properties and other inherent functions of the constituent basic emotions. DET proposes that a given emotion feeling, depending on its level of intensity and other factors, becomes associated with different thoughts and images. Pride is explained as joy associated with thoughts of mastery or achievement. And whereas Kagan (1994) might see different achievements (developing a new idea, scaling El Capitan) as producing different types of pride, DET views such differences in terms of the content of the associated cognition.

On the role of context in emotion communication

The question of context as a factor in signal detection or emotion-expression recognition is in one sense a pseudoissue or nonissue. I can hardly imagine any serious student of emotion or social communication thinking that any form of perception or cognition is uninfluenced by context. Even children as young as 2.5 or 3 years have some appreciation of situational effects on emotion (e.g., Izard, 1971; Stein & Jewett, 1984). Hence, context would be expected to affect their judgment of emotion expressions. Despite the seemingly obvious role of context and the need to minimize (or otherwise control for) contextual cues to determine the independent signal value of facial expressions, some have criticized the early cross-cultural research on expression identification because subjects were shown slides of faces out of context. The critics raise the question of the ecological validity of relatively context-free expression recognition.

This may be unwarranted criticism of the early cross-cultural research on expression recognition. The investigators who did the early cross-cultural studies on emotion-expression recognition and labeling attempted to eliminate or minimize contextual cues because they wanted to examine the independent signal value of the facial signals. They assumed that appropriate context would inflate "accuracy" of signal (emotion) recognition.

Nevertheless, the criticism regarding the question of ecological validity is not without merit. There are still many questions relating to the relative power of facial and contextual features in determining judgments of the significance of patterns of facial movement. When judging facial expression within an environmental context or scene, there might be two types of information – emotion-relevant cues and emotion-irrelevant cues – or cues that vary on a dimension of affectivity. There could well be cultural as well as individual differences that help to determine the significance of the different types of information. The ecological validity issue points to the need for research on the signal value of facial patterns in naturally occurring and controlled situations. As Ekman (1994) observed, little is known about the information that people typically infer from facial expressions. The cross-cultural research of decontextualized faces only showed what facial patterns *can* signal, not what they always or necessarily signal in interpersonal interactions.

Developmental issues are the source of some of the most intriguing questions concerning the relative importance of facial versus contextual cues in emotion recognition. For example, are facial cues relatively more important in early infancy? There are reasons to think this might be the case. Although the evidence is incomplete, a number of emotion researchers have proposed that infants have an innate capacity for face recognition and the extraction of emotion information from facial and vocal patterns (Izard, 1971; Neisser, 1976; cf. Morton & Johnson, 1991). Some developmentalists have argued that the infant is primarily an affective being (Spitz, 1965) and particularly dependent on and sensitive to emotion information (Bowlby, 1973). Furthermore, contextual information varies along a dimension of complexity, and the greater the complexity, the greater the demands on cognitive capacity. It follows that the relative influence of facial and contextual cues in decoding facial expressions is, at least in part, a function of cognitive development.

The ontogeny of facial expressions

During the early years of the contemporary period of scientific interest in emotions, many investigators apparently interpreted DET as another theory of facial *expressions* rather than as a broad theory of emotions, personality, and social behavior. Partly because of the success of the early research on facial expressions and partly because of the labor-intensive and time-consuming nature of constructing and applying a microanalytic facial behavior coding system, even the proponents of DET seemed more preoccupied with expressions than anything else. This was true despite the theory's emphasis on the functions of emotions and their role in the development of personality and social relationships in the original statements of the theory. Numerous theory pieces explicating the proposition that emotions motivate and organize perception, cognition, and action (e.g., Barrett & Campos, 1987; Emde, 1980; Izard, 1979a; Malatesta ct al., 1989) failed to shift attention away from facial expressions. This was probably true because the evidence marshalled in favor of the theoretical propositions often came from studies of facial expressions. In any case, in the eyes of many researchers, DET tended to become identified with facial expression and the innateness-universality hypothesis.

Actually, proponents of DET (e.g., Izard et al., 1983; Malatesta et al., 1989) were regularly interpreting the data on facial expressions in young infants as evidence of discrete emotions and their role in the development of personality and social relationships. Others' interpretations and criticisms of this research tended to focus on the validity and measurement of infant facial expressions (e.g., Oster et al., 1992) rather than on the functions of emotions as complex systems involving neural, neuromuscular, and experiential components.

Preoccupation with facial expression detracted so much from the central theme of DET – the functions of emotions in motivating and organizing perception, cognition, and action – that DET was used as a foil in presenting a new emphasis on functionalism in emotion theory (Campos, 1994).

The key to the argument for facial expression as a component of emotion, albeit a dissociable component, is found in the aforementioned central assumption of DET. Emotions are inherently motivational. Emotions organize and motivate all forms of behavior, including social behavior. Emotions are central in developing and maintaining social relationships. The role of emotions and their motivational properties in interpersonal affairs is mediated by emotion signals, chiefly facial expressions.

Emotion expressions and emotion feeling motivational states

There are several aspects to the issue of linkage between facial behavior and internal (subjective) states. One question concerns the nature of the information contained in various configurations of facial activity, everyone apparently having agreed that each pattern has some kind of signal value or provides a basis for inferences that are similar across individuals and cultures. A second aspect concerns the ontogeny of the link between a particular expression and a congruent mental state. DET has proposed that the emergence of congruent emotion feeling co-occurs with the emergence of a stable expressive pattern that can be reliably encoded over a long enough period of time to enable the coupling of neural substrates of expression and feeling. DET acknowledges that the fleeting expressions of neonates can lack a congruent feeling or a stable expression-feeling connection because of the immaturity of neural substrates of emotion feelings (cf. Kalin, 1993). A third aspect of the issue of expressions and internal states relates to the possible role of voluntary and involuntary facial activity in the generation of internal states (mental and physiological). Darwin (1872/1965) clearly believed that expressions were related to "states of mind." He is repetitiously explicit on this point. He is not as clear as to what he meant by "state of mind," and his language in various sections of his volume on expressions makes it possible to interpret this phrase as referring to emotion feeling states or behavioral intentions or both.

A number of emotion theorists (e.g., Ekman, 1971; Izard, 1971; Malatesta, 1982; Tomkins, 1962) have argued that, under certain conditions, a particular facial expression signals a corresponding emotion feeling state. Others (e.g., Fridlund, 1994) have maintained that facial behavior is better conceived as displays (not "expressions") that signal behavioral intentions or social motives. In this latter view, facial displays (or "expressions") have no necessary relation to emotions. Because both feeling and intentions are unobservable mental states with a variable relation to actions, Fridlund's (1994) criticisms of an expression-feeling connection seem to apply equally well to a display-intention connection. Nevertheless, a connection between facial signal and future behavior is thought necessary for the evolution of such signals (Andrew, 1963).

The facial (somatosensory) feedback hypothesis of emotion activation

Since Darwin (1872/1965) and James (1884), psychologists have discussed the possible connection between facial expression and emotion experience. It was not until about 20 years ago that this issue became the focus of psychological experiments (Laird, 1974), and the results of these experiments generated yet another controversy relating to the functions of facial expression (for reviews and critiques, see Fridlund, 1994; Izard, 1990; Laird, 1974; Matsumoto, 1987; Winton, 1986; Zajonc, Murphy, & Inglehart, 1989). The weight of the published evidence suggests that expression does, in some instances and under some conditions, play a direct (Matsumoto, 1987) or indirect (Zajonc et al., 1989) role in the generation of emotion experience or feeling states. However, the point here is not to try to resolve this controversy, an accomplishment that will require both psychology and behavioral neuroscience, but to note its impact on the study of facial expression and on the emotion theories that considered them. Of particular interest to me was the extent to which this controversy detracted from DET's early focus on the role of expressive behavior in emotion *regulation* and the DET ideas that emotions constitute a system within the personality supersystem, that most emotions operate in sets or patterns, and that each discrete emotion is a system that contains expressive behavior as a dissociable component.

From the early days of DET (Izard, 1971, 1977), it was argued that emotion could be generated without facial expression. Indeed, the theory presented several caveats in interpreting expression as a sign of emotion or its activator. First, the neuromuscular ("expressive") component of emotion need not result in observable muscle movement or facial expression. Second, whatever role facial movement plays in emotion activation could be accomplished through the subtle movement of muscles involved in only one regional component of a full- or whole-face facial expression. Third, the "expressive" factor in emotion activation might not be expression or display at all. It might consist only of efferent activity in a reafferent loop and not affect muscles or expression in any way. DET went on to propose that the sensorimotor system (expressive behavior, efferent activity) was only *one* of four types of emotion-activating systems (Izard, 1993).

Facial expressions in social relationships

An essential argument for a link between facial expression and emotion feeling or motivational state is that intrapsychic states must be communicated in order to sustain a social relationship. A social relationship is based on shared thoughts and feelings. Both feeling and thought are communicated verbally, but DET holds that neither is communicated effectively or fully in a social relationship without emotion signals (cf. Zajonc, 1980). And emotion signals are most efficiently and parsimoniously communicated by facial expression.

A number of empirical studies have shown that predictable facial expressions occur in emotion-eliciting interpersonal situations. The spontaneous expressions of young infants vary in predictable fashion in different types of mother–infant interactions (Haviland & Lelwica, 1987; Izard et al., 1995). Infants of 2 to 9 months smile to mother's nodding face (Izard et al., 1995), whereas 13-month-old infants display anger and sadness when mother leaves them in a strange situation (Izard, Haynes, Chisholm, & Baak, 1991). These observations are consistent with the expression-feeling congruence hypothesis and the stability of a core feeling state for each discrete emotion over the lifespan (Barrett & Campos, 1987; Izard & Malatesta, 1987), but confirming this hypothesis requires more evidence on expression-behavior relations.

Facial expression and self-report of emotion feelings

A study assessing congruence of expression and feeling found evidence for a relation between spontaneous emotion expression and self-report of emotion feeling (Rosenberg & Ekman, 1994). Subjects were shown brief films that elicited expressions of disgust and fear while their faces were being videorecorded without their knowledge. On a subject-controlled replay of the emotion-eliciting film, the subjects stopped the film at each point where they remembered experiencing emotion, and they identified the specific feeling. The proportion of observed matches between emotion expressions and congruent feeling states exceeded the proportion expected by chance. Thus, the investigators found evidence of correspondence between film-induced expressive behavior and temporally synchronous reports of feelings (cf. Fernández-Dols & Ruiz-Belda, chapter 11, this volume).

Theoretical grounds for an expression-feeling link

Two characteristics of emotions, as described in DET but often ignored or denied in other theories, make the foregoing propositions regarding the link between feeling/motivational states and facial expression more believable. First, any emotion feeling can and does vary widely on a dimension of intensity. This proposition is such a significant part of DET that, as in Tomkins' theory (1962), formal rubrics for emotions consist of two terms: one more descriptive of lower intensities and the other of high intensities. Thus, we have double category labels such as interest-excitement, enjoyment-joy, anger-rage, fear-terror.

One argument against an expression-feeling connection is the notion that there is an infinite variety of emotion feeling states. I think that one reason that theorists from James (1890/1990) to Kagan (1994) conceptualize an infinite variety of qualitatively different emotions is their failure to accept fully the intensity principle as it applies to each discrete emotion. James thought somatosensory processes (such as those stemming from expressive behavior) were essential to emotion, and thus he struggled for an explanation of the "subtle" emotions. Contemporary theorists can elect a position that stems from the work of Cannon (1927) and attribute the subtle (and other) emotion states solely to central processes, but some neuroscientists continue to emphasize input from somatosensory processes in the activation of emotion feeling states (Damasio, 1994). On the output side, quantitative differences in feeling/motivational states can have very different effects on brain and body, but with respect to emotion category, these differences are quantitative, not qualitative.

The second DET principle that lays the groundwork for espousing an expression-feeling connection is the idea that a given emotion typically operates as part of a pattern or cluster of emotions. Patterns of emotions such as those found in depression (Blumberg & Izard, 1986) operate as subsystems of the emotions system. A corollary of this principle is that, with the partial exception of the emotion of interest, discrete emotions typically do not operate singly for very long periods of time. The activation of a new emotion is usually followed within a period ranging from a few milliseconds to 4 or 5 seconds by another emotion, the latter often being elicited by new information interacting with the first emotion and its consequences.

The idea of discrete emotions functioning in sets or subsystems may appear to create more problems for the expression-feeling connection hypothesis than it solves. One thing that offsets the seeming confusion that might be thought to stem from the patterning idea is the proposition that, even though discrete emotions often operate in patterns or subsystems of emotions, no emotion ever loses its distinct motivational properties. Thus, the behavioral consequents of, for example, a sadness-anger-shame pattern (one of the depression patterns) must be examined closely for thoughts and actions that stem from the motivational properties of all three of these emotions and their interactions. Among other things, this means that the causal processes for human behavior are highly complex and nonlinear (Izard, 1995; Lewis, 1995). Tracing expression-feeling connections is also very complex. Several factors contribute to this complexity. First, facial expressions normally continue for less than 5 seconds, and they are often observable for less than one second. Facial expressions that last only a second or so may often be shorter in duration than their corresponding experiential counterparts. Facial expressions may be visible only during the very brief time required for emotion activation. As a result, direct correspondence between facial expression and feeling may not be the rule but the exception, congruence often being confined to the brief period of the emotion activation process. Second, a fleeting veridical expression (linked to a congruent feeling state) may be quickly replaced by a more enduring nonveridical expression motivated by the desire to hide or to regulate one's feelings. Third, expressions, like feelings, vary in intensity, and low-intensity expressions that are also micromomentary may frequently escape conscious recognition. Fourth, expressions may be complex in that they contain signals of two or more emotions, and this may make the decoding process more difficult.

In DET, complex expressions are not *blends* of basic emotions, in the sense that primary emotions mix or blend to form new emotions. The term *blend* is a misleading misnomer insofar as it invites the inappropriate analogy of mixing primary colors to form pastels. DET has always argued that a given discrete emotion state, though often occurring within a *pattern* of other discrete emotion states, retains its unique motivational properties. Although each emotion experience motivates a particular (usually adaptive) type of cognition and action, the impact of a particular emotion state on behavior is modulated by other emotion states within the pattern. The diversity in affective symptomatology in the variety of anxiety and depressive disorders is best explained by the pattern of interacting emotion states that characterizes each of them (Blumberg & Izard, 1986).

Facial expressions of emotions or displays of social motives?

Arguments regarding the meaning of patterned facial muscle movements are probably about as old as humankind and language. References to the face as the window to emotion states can be found in Homer, the Bible, and other ancient documents. Some of these same documents also contain questions about the veridicality or reliability of the information in facial actions. Nevertheless, neither ancient nor contemporary writers, nor any observer of animal faces, human or nonhuman, doubt that facial patterns have signal value or provide information.

Decoding the information in the face does not seem to be a significant problem for ordinary people. The information in verbal and nonverbal (facial) signs and symbols appears to be a natural part of social interactions and relationships. Parallel processing and integration of verbal and nonverbal information usually proceed without a hitch, or, at least, without relationship-destroying miscommunications. It is not common for individuals to make facial or nonverbal information of any kind a part of the agenda in an interpersonal transaction, though this undoubtedly varies with age, sex, and culture.

In contrast to the usual ease with which ordinary people deal with facial expressions, the scientists who have concerned themselves with the face as a social stimulus seem always to have had some disagreements about the interpretation of facial information. The heart of the issue is the question of the existence and nature of an internal referent for facial expressions in phylogenetic and ontogenetic perspective. A second issue is the question of whether the referent is best described as a behavioral intention, social motive, or emotion feeling state. The assumption that patterns of facial movement have some kind of internal referent gives rise to several other questions. Is the referent congruent with the pattern? Does a given pattern of movements convey information about the underlying referent with a significant degree of reliability? Is social communication the sole function of facial patterns? Do they have a role in regulating emotion feeling states?

Discussion of these questions should be facilitated by a note on terminology. DET and several other emotion theories typically have described certain configurations of facial behavior as emotion "expressions." They might be called "facial expressions" if conditions (data) do not warrant the inference of underlying emotion feeling/motivational states. Ethologists and behavioral ecologists prefer the term *facial display*. DET has also used the term *pattern* to describe an interacting and co-occurring set of emotion feeling/motivational states (e.g., Izard & Youngstrom, 1996). It has also used the term to describe a set of coordinated facial muscle actions. All three terms (*expression, display, pattern*) will be used in this discussion, but the term *pattern* is seen as the most objective or neutral of the three in that it does not call for the attribution of any particular correlate. As applied to facial behavior, it merely indicates the occurrence of a set of coordinated muscle actions. Whereas *expression* and *display* tend to imply an act of communication in a social context, the term *pattern* has no such implication. A facial movement *pattern*, like an *expression* or *display*, can occur in a single area of the face or in multiple areas to form a whole face configuration.

Did patterns of human facial movements evolve because they conveyed socially useful information? The answer here is an unequivocal *yes*. "Before selection can begin to shape a response into a component of a display, the response must, on occasion, convey information to the animal's fellows about the future behavior of the animal that makes it" (Andrew, 1963, p. 142). Does communication remain a contemporary function of human facial expressions or displays? Again, the answer is *yes*. Although there is disagreement about the nature, significance, and correlates of facial patterns, no one doubts that they convey information.

Although proponents of quite different views regarding the referents for facial patterns agree that they have an evolutionary origin and that some of them probably evolved from movement patterns that originally served functions different from the ones they serve today, there is some disagreement about the underlying evolutionary mechanisms. Some theorists argue that facial displays have their origins in adaptations that evolved as a result of natural selection (e.g., Andrew, 1963, 1965; Fridlund, 1994). It seems likely, however, that some human facial displays may have evolutionary origins that cannot be attributed to natural selection. They may represent what Gould (1991) calls "exaptations," structures *not* built as an adaptation but "later coopted for utilities just as vital". Despite several efforts to do so, no one has presented a convincing case for the origin of the zygomatic major and its contraction (the human smile) as the result of natural selection and adaptation. The same is true for the concurrent medial frontalis and corrugator muscle actions that form the oblique brows that according to Darwin and many other emotion theorists signal sadness and, according to the behavioral ecology view, signal a request for succorance (Fridlund, 1994). Gould (1991) argued that exaptations account for all forms of "mental expression not in the initial repertoire of large brained populations" (p. 59), and I suggest that some of the facial expressions associated with emotions meet this criterion.

In any case, there is agreement across differing theories that at least some facial patterns evolved, whether as adaptations or exaptations, *to communicate information*. There remains some disagreement regarding their clarity, specificity, extent of their innateness and universality, and whether they relate to emotions, social motives, behavioral intentions, or to all three. There are readily available and extensive reviews of various aspects of these controversial issues (e.g., Ekman, 1994; Fridlund, 1994; Izard, 1994; Russell, 1994). I make only a few comments here about the DET position regarding an emotion-expression – emotion-feeling link, and Fridlund's (1994) behavioral ecology view (BEV) of a facial-display – social-motive connection. I hasten to add that I believe that DET is consistent with the notion that human facial patterns may convey emotion feeling/motivational states, or social motives, or behavioral intentions, or merely facilitate greetings, approvals, disapprovals, and other aspects of social communication. Nevertheless, DET does hold that a limited set of facial patterns are linked phylogenetically and ontogenetically to emotion feeling/motivational states. This does not mean that the expression-feeling link is immutable. DET theory has also emphasized that an expression can be dissociated from its corresponding emotion feeling and associated with other mental states.

Both DET and BEV lean on the literature on human evolution for support of the different positions. Darwin (1872/1965) entitled his famous treatise on communicative behavior "The Expression of the Emotions in Man and Animals," and it is abundantly clear that he believed that human facial expressions were associated with emotions. His account of the origins of the expressions is unsatisfactory in some respects (e.g., its dated neurophysiology and Lamarckianism), but he is unswerving in his effort to link expressions and "states of mind" (pp. 13ff). In beginning his work on emotions, he resolved, "in the first place, to observe infants; for they exhibit many emotions" (pp. 13ff). He even identified the expression (blushing) that he thought was associated with the most distinctly human emotion (shame).

The view of some contemporary evolutionists is apparently not so clear. BEV frequently cites R. J. Andrew as favoring the view that human facial patterns are not expressions at all but rather signals of behavioral intentions (e.g., Fridlund, 1994, p. 130). I acknowledge that Andrew's position is subject to different interpretations. I chose the following quote to represent the thrust of his argument:

> The expressions were perpetuated by natural selection and evolved into exaggerated displays because they had communicative value. In the course of evolution the expressions, particularly in man, came to represent not only intentions but also emotional states (although a given expression may indicate different emotions in different contexts). (Andrew, 1965, p. 90)

Furthermore, I take his parenthetical statement to be consistent with the DET notion of the dissociability of expression and emotion feeling state.

A specific example should help to clarify the difference between the DET and BEV positions on the matter of what is communicated by facial patterns. What DET would call an expression associated (under certain circumstances) with anger feeling is interpreted in BEV as "readiness to attack" (Fridlund, 1994, p. 129). Although an anger expression *might* convey a readiness to attack, and such readiness could well be facilitated by the organizing and motivating properties of anger feeling, I propose that more often than not, one feels angry without the slightest intention of attacking anyone (cf. Averill, 1983).

DET has argued that communication of emotion feeling states is essential to the forming and maintaining of social relationships (Izard & Malatesta, 1987; cf. Hobson, 1993). The very first significant social relationship, infant–mother (caregiver) attachment has been described by virtually all students of this phenomenon as an affective or emotional bond (Bowlby, 1973; Cicchetti, 1990; Sroufe, 1988). These theorists also point to emotion communication and maternal sensitivity and responsiveness to the infant's affective signals as the chief determinant of the quality of the attachment relationship. Infant facial patterns classified as negative emotion expressions are predictive of insecure attachments (Izard et al., 1991). Several studies have shown that infants as young as 2 or 3 months respond differentially to maternal facial patterns classified as emotion expressions (Haviland & Lelwica, 1987; Izard et al., 1995; Weinberg & Tronick, 1994).

The idea that the signaling of emotion states through facial patterns contributes to infant–mother attachment and the development and maintenance of other social bonds is consistent with my reading of ethologists' work on the origin and functions of displays and the evolution of human facial expressions. For example, van Hooff (1962) observed that in some higher (nonhuman) primates, the silent bared teeth display, a progenitor of the human smile, functions as an affiliative behavior, a "reassuring signal or even a sign of attachment" (p. 215). Some ethologists seem comfortable with the notion that displays represent emotion states.

Of course, neither ethologists nor human emotion theorists propose a lifetime lock step relation between a specific facial pattern and corresponding emotion state. The chroniclers of human history, as well as DET and other contemporary emotion theories, recognize the human ability to use expressions as a social tool and as a means of regulating feelings and to dissociate expression and feeling completely. Yet the role of facial patterns in primate social life seems to demand that at least on some occasions, there must be a reasonably good fit between the observable pattern and the underlying motivational state of the sender of the signal. DET defines emotion experience as a feeling/motivational state. It proposes that in some cases, the feeling state may correspond to, or be associated with, social motives or intentions and that in other cases, the sender may have one kind of feeling, another kind of facial pattern, and still another kind of intention. Such may be the case when the feeling is fear, the expression is a smile, and the intention is to escape as soon as it is physically and psychologically safe to do so. Regardless of differences in interpretations of the meaning of facial signals, BEV and DET are in agreement regarding the co-evolution of the capacity for their encoding and their decoding. I believe this to be Darwin's position as well.

In answer to Fridlund's query (chapter 5, this volume) about DET, it has from its inception (Izard, 1971, 1979a; cf. Tomkins, 1962) defined the subjective experience or feeling state of a discrete emotion as an affectively unique type of *motivation*. Because many emotion experiences are social in nature, what Fridlund calls "social motive" can be an aspect of the "motivational feeling state" of DET. Furthermore, DET (following Darwin) has always explicitly included "social motivation" in describing the functions of facial expressions (e.g., Izard, 1971, 1979a). This does indeed make it difficult to draw a distinction between the constructs that Fridlund and I have designated as referents for facial expressions or displays. Both referents (what is signaled by an expression or display) are facets of inner experience, require the same sort of criteria for specifying their occurrence and linkage to expression, and should be equally inferable from observed behavior and other convergent data.

One distinction between Fridlund's "social motive" and the DET construct of emotion experience/feeling state is that the latter is broader and has several aspects (Izard, 1993). In some instances (e.g., acrophobia, object-elicited disgust or anger), emotions are not social, and their expressions and feeling states necessarily have aspects other than "social motivation." Another distinction, in the case of some emotions, is that the "emotion feeling state" of DET includes an action tendency or action readiness and in this regard is similar to Frijda and Tcherkassof's concept of emotion experience.

The approach of Frijda and Tcherkassoff (chapter 4, this volume) and DET have significant common ground. We agree that facial expressions are related to emotion experiences and that the latter significantly influence cognition and action. In focusing on emotion as action readiness and relational activity, Frijda and Tcherkassof have contributed an excellent detailed analysis of emotion experience and the way it relates to behavior.

Concluding remarks

From the perspective of DET, new approaches to the study of facial patterns should verify the conditions under which particular patterns do and do not correspond to feeling/motivational states, or social motives, or action intentions. I think it is of great importance to stay focused on the *functions* of facial patterns in the larger context of personality development and the development and maintenance of social relations. It is equally important to move away from simplistic linear models of cause–effect relations and to consider the nonlinear causal processes that characterize all complex organic systems (Izard, 1995; Lewis, 1995). In this framework, one might study the reciprocal causal influences among facial patterns, feeling/motivational states, social motives, intentions, perception, appraisal processes, and actions.

Acknowledgments

This work was supported by NSF Grant No. SBR-9108925.
Special thanks to Erika Rosenberg for her helpful comments on an earlier draft of this manuscript.

References

Andrew, R. J. (1963). Evolution of facial expression. *Science, 142*, 1034–1041.
Andrew, R. J. (1965). The origins of facial expressions. *Scientific American, 213*, 88–94.
Averill, J. R. (1983). Studies on anger and aggression: Implications for theories of emotion. *American Psychologist, 38*, 1145–1162.

Barrett, K. C., & Campos, J. J. (1987). Perspectives on emotional development II: A functionalist approach to emotions. In J. D. Osofsky (Ed.), *Handbook of infant development* (2nd ed., pp. 555–578). New York: Wiley.

Blumberg, S. H., & Izard, C. E. (1986). Discriminating patterns of emotions in 10- and 11-year-old children's anxiety and depression. *Journal of Personality and Social Psychology, 51,* 852–857.

Bowlby, J. (1973). *Attachment and loss* (Vol. 2: Separation). London: Pelican.

Campos, J. J. (1994, Spring). The new functionalism in emotion. *SRCD Newsletter,* pp. 1, 7, 9–11, 14.

Cannon, W. B. (1927). *Bodily changes in pain, hunger, fear and rage: An account of recent researches into the function of emotional excitement.* New York: Appleton-Century-Crofts.

Cicchetti, D. (1990). Perspectives on the interface between normal and atypical development. In D. Cicchetti (Ed.), *Development and psychopathology* (Vol. 2, pp. 329–333). New York: Cambridge University Press.

Damasio, A. R. (1994). *Descartes' error: Emotion, reason, and the human brain.* New York: Putnam.

Darwin, C. R. (1965). *The expression of the emotions in man and animals.* Chicago: University of Chicago. (Original work published 1872).

Ekman, P. (1971). Universality and cultural differences in facial expressions. In J. K. Cole (Ed.), *Nebraska Symposium on Motivation* (Vol. 19, pp. 207–283). Lincoln: University of Nebraska Press.

Ekman, P. (1994). Strong evidence for universals in facial expressions: A reply to Russell's mistaken critique. *Psychological Bulletin, 115,* 268–287.

Ekman, P., & Oster, H. (1979). Facial expressions of emotion. *Annual Review of Psychology, 30,* 527–554.

Ekman, P., Sorenson, E. R., & Friesen, W. V. (1969). Pan-cultural elements in facial displays of emotions. *Science, 164,* 86–88.

Emde, R. N. (1980). Levels of meaning for infant emotions: A biosocial view. In W. A. Collins (Ed.), *Development of cognition, affect and social relations: Minnesota Symposia on Child Psychology* (Vol. 13, pp. 1–38). Hillsdale, NJ: Erlbaum.

Fridlund, A. J. (1994). *Human facial expression: An evolutionary view.* San Diego: Academic Press.

Gelernter, D. H. (1994). *The muse in the machine.* New York: Free Press.

Gould, S. J. (1991). Exaptation: A crucial tool for an evolutionary psychology. *Journal of Social Issues, 47*(3), 43–65.

Haviland, J. J., & Lelwica, M. (1987). The induced affect response: 10-week-old infants' responses to three emotion expressions. *Developmental Psychology, 23,* 97–104.

Hobson, P. (1993). The emotional origins of social understanding. *Philosophical Psychology, 6,* 227–249.

Hooff, J. A. R. A. M. van (1962). Facial expressions in higher primates. *Symposia of the Zoological Society of London, 8,* 97–125.

Hooff, J. A. R. A. M. van (1967). Facial displays of catarrhine monkeys and apes. In D. Morris (Ed.), *Primate ethology* (pp. 7–68). London: Weidenfield & Nicholson.

Izard, C. E. (1971). *The face of emotion.* New York: Appleton-Century-Crofts.

Izard, C. E. (1977). *Human emotions.* New York: Plenum.

Izard, C. E. (1979a). Emotions as motivations: An evolutionary-developmental perspective. In R. A. Dienstbier (Ed.), *Nebraska Symposium on Motivation: Vol. 26. Perspectives on human emotions* (pp. 163–200). Lincoln: University of Nebraska Press.

Izard, C. E. (1979b). *The maximally discriminative facial movement coding system (MAX)*. Newark, DE: University of Delaware, Computer and Network Services, University Media Services.

Izard, C. E. (1990). Facial expressions and the regulation of emotions. *Journal of Personality and Social Psychology, 58*, 487–498.

Izard, C. E. (1991). *The psychology of emotions*. New York: Plenum.

Izard, C. E. (1992). Basic emotions, relations among emotions, and emotion–cognition relations. *Psychological Review, 99*, 561–565.

Izard, C. E. (1993). Four systems for emotion activation: Cognitive and noncognitive processes. *Psychological Review, 100*, 68–90.

Izard, C. E. (1994). Innate and universal facial expressions: Evidence from developmental and cross-cultural research. *Psychological Bulletin, 115*, 288–299.

Izard, C. E. (1995). Cognition-emotion feedback and the self-organization of developmental paths – Commentary. *Human Development, 38*, 103–112.

Izard, C. E., Fantauzzo, C. A., Castle, J. M., Haynes, O. M., Rayias, M. F., & Putnam, P. H. (1995). The ontogeny and significance of infants' facial expressions in the first nine months of life. *Developmental Psychology, 31*, 997–1013.

Izard, C. E., Haynes, O. M., Chisholm, G., & Baak, K. (1991). Emotional determinants of infant–mother attachment. *Child Development, 62*, 906–917.

Izard, C. E., Hembree, E., Dougherty, L. M., & Spizzirri, C. C. (1983). Changes in facial expressions of 2- to 19-month-old infants following acute pain. *Developmental Psychology, 19*, 418–426.

Izard, C. E., Huebner, R. R., Risser, D., McGinnes, G., & Dougherty, L. (1980). The young infant's ability to produce discrete emotion expressions. *Developmental Psychology, 16*, 132–140.

Izard, C. E., & Malatesta, C. Z. (1987). Perspectives on emotional development I: Differential emotions theory of early emotional development. In J. D. Osofsky (Ed.), *Handbook of infant development* (2nd ed., pp. 494–554). New York: Wiley.

Izard, C. E., Wehmer, G. M., Livsey, W., & Jennings, J. R. (1965). Affect, awareness, and performance. In S. S. Tomkins & C. E. Izard (Eds.), *Affect, cognition, and personality* (pp. 2–41). New York: Springer.

Izard, C. E., & Youngstrom, E. A. (1996). The activation and regulation of fear and anxiety. In D. A. Hope (Ed.), *Nebraska Symposium on Motivation: Vol. 43. Perspectives on anxiety, panic, and fear*. Lincoln: University of Nebraska Press.

James, W. (1884). What is emotion? *Mind, 4*, 188–204.

James, W. (1990). *The principles of psychology*. Chicago: Encyclopedia Brittanica. (Original work published 1890)

Kagan, J. (1994). *Galen's prophecy: Temperament in human nature*. New York: Basic Books.

Kalin, N. H. (1993, May). The neurobiology of fear. *Scientific American*, 94–101.

Laird, J. D. (1974). Self-attribution of emotion: The effects of expressive behavior on the quality of emotion experience. *Journal of Personality and Social Psychology, 29*, 475–486.

Lewis, M. D. (1995). Cognition–emotion feedback and the self-organization of developmental paths. *Human Development, 38*, 72–102.

Malatesta, C. Z. (1982). The expression and regulation of emotion: A lifespan perspective. In T. Field & A. Fogel (Eds.), *Emotion and early interaction* (pp. 1–24). Hillsdale, NJ: Erlbaum.

Malatesta, C. Z., Culver, C., Tesman, J. C., & Shepard, B. (1989). The development of emotion expression during the first two years of life: Normative trends and patterns of individual differences. *Monographs of the Society for Research in Child Development, 54* (1–2, Serial No. 219).

Matsumoto, D. (1987). The role of facial response in the experience of emotion: More methodological problems and a meta-analysis. *Journal of Personality and Social Psychology, 52,* 769–774.

Morton, J., & Johnson, M. H. (1991). CONSPEC and CONLERN: A two-process theory of infant recognition. *Psychological Review, 98,* 164–181.

Neisser, U. (1976). *Cognition and reality.* New York: Freeman.

Oster, H., Hegley, D., & Nagel, L. (1992). Adult judgments and fine-grained analysis of infant facial expressions: Testing the validity of a priori coding formulas. *Developmental Psychology, 28,* 1115–1131.

Plutchik, R. (1962). *The emotions: Facts, theories, and a new model.* New York: Random House.

Rosenberg, E. L., & Ekman, P. (1994). Coherence between expressive and experiential systems in emotion. *Cognition and Emotion, 8,* 201–229.

Russell, J. A. (1993). Forced-choice format in the study of facial expression. *Motivation and Emotion, 17,* 41–51.

Russell, J. A. (1994). Is there universal recognition of emotion from facial expression? A review of the cross-cultural studies. *Psychological Bulletin, 115,* 102–141.

Smith, C. A. (1989). Dimensions of appraisal and physiological response in emotion. *Journal of Personality and Social Psychology, 57,* 329–353.

Spitz, R. A. (1965). *The first year of life.* New York: International Universities.

Sroufe, L. A. (1988). The role of infant–caregiver attachment in development. In J. Belsky & T. Nezworski (Eds.), *Clinical implications of attachment* (pp. 18–30). Hillsdale, NJ: Erlbaum.

Stein, N. L., & Jewett, J. L. (1984). A conceptual analysis of the meaning of negative emotions: Implications for a theory of development. In C. E. Izard & P. B. Read (Eds.), *Measuring emotions in infants and children* (Vol. 2, pp. 238–267). New York: Cambridge University Press.

Tinbergen, N. (1973). *The animal in its world: Explorations of an ethologist 1932–1972: Vol. 2. Laboratory experiments and general papers.* London: George Allen & Unwin.

Tomkins, S. S. (1962). *Affect, imagery, consciousness: Vol. 1. The positive affects.* New York: Springer.

Tomkins, S. S., & McCarter, R. (1964). What and where are the primary affects? Some evidence for a theory. *Perceptual and Motor Skills, 18,* 119–158.

Weinberg, M. K., & Tronick, E. Z. (1994). Beyond the face: An empirical study of infant affective configurations of facial, vocal, gestural, and regulatory behaviors. *Child Development, 65,* 1503–1515.

Winton, W. M. (1986). The role of facial response in self-reports of emotion: A critique of Laird. *Journal of Personality and Social Psychology, 50,* 808–812.

Zajonc, R. B. (1980). Feeling and thinking: Preferences need no inferences. *American Psychologist, 35,* 151–175.

Zajonc, R. B., Murphy, S. T., & Inglehart, M. (1989). Feeling and facial efference: Implications of the vascular theory of emotion. *Psychological Review, 96,* 395–416.

4. Facial expressions as modes of action readiness

NICO H. FRIJDA AND ANNA TCHERKASSOF

Many questions one could ask about facial expressions seem to be fixed by the use of the very word *expression*. *Facial expression*, first, refers to facial behavior that suggests emotional meaning to an outside observer. Second, the term carries the implication that that facial behavior has the function or purpose of conveying such meaning. Third, it suggests that there exists something (say, an inner feeling) independently of that behavior to which the behavior called *expression* is added as an extra.

These aspects are not necessarily all true of the same behaviors. Facial behaviors may suggest emotional meanings to observers, but that may not be their function or purpose. Receiving the epithet "expressive" in fact says nothing about the nature of the behavior concerned. "Hasty" or "greedy" behaviors, for instance, are made to arrive as fast as one can at the object of desire, and not to inform others about one's state of mind. Also, nonbehavior may on occasion be highly expressive, such as underacting in the theater and Jesus's remaining silent under accusation. And there are phenomena that are expressive by suggesting emotional meanings in which no inner feelings of whatever produced the phenomena are involved, such as joyful bird songs, angry bursts of wind, sad music, nervous lines, and solemn penguins.

Most past and current theorizing on facial expression starts from the assumption that it expresses emotional feelings and exists for the sake of doing so. The study of expression pretty much originated in the philosophical problem of the knowledge of other minds. It sought to solve the riddle of how it is possible to obtain knowledge of others' unspoken inner feelings (e.g., Bain, 1859; Berkeley, 1709; Lipps, 1905). That expressions manifest inner feelings probably is dogma to many researchers; at least it was when the first author started his work. Advance has been possible only by abandoning this dogma, recognizing that perception of emotional meaning does not necessarily imply attribution of inner feeling. The advance was due to phenomenology (Buytendijk & Plessner, 1925; Sartre, 1939; Gestalt psychology) and Wittgenstein.

We think, therefore, that the category of facial *expression* (and other bodily expressions) should be defined as a category of *impression*. Facial expression is facial behavior that suggests emotional meaning. This leaves the relations to whatever is expressed and what "expressing" means, a matter of empirical and theoretical analysis. For simplicity, we continue to use the term *expression* to refer to the facial behavior concerned.

Questions for research on facial expression

Analysis of facial expression has to address the following major questions:

1. *What* does facial expression "express"? That is, what information do observers perceive or infer from facial expressions (the receiver question), and what psychological states or processes produce them (the sender question)? What does a smile convey to an observer, and what state or process actually underlies that smile?
2. *Why* do certain psychological states or processes lead to particular expressions? That is, what is the functional explanation of facial expression? Why do we smile when happy (*if* we smile when happy and if we smile when *happy*)?
3. Why is that content *so* expressed? Why do facial expressions look the way they do and have the temporal properties that they have? Why do we *smile* when happy (if indeed happiness is what makes us smile)? Why its temporal and topographic variations?
4. *When* is that content expressed? When do expressions occur? Do facial expressions appear whenever the expressed state occurs, or, if not, what are the conditions?

Traditional theory has simple answers to all four questions:

1. Facial expressions express emotional states, particularly feelings. Different emotions or feelings correspond to different facial expressions (at some level of categorization of "different emotions").
2. Facial expressions exist for the sake of communicating emotions to others.
3. Presumably, Darwin's (1872) three principles provide a satisfactory

account of the nature and origin of expressions. However, most contemporary theorists are silent on why expressions are as they are. Other explanatory principles (notably, those from Bühler, 1934; Dumas, 1933a, 1947; Piderit, 1867) are largely ignored, except in some ethological work.

4. Expression occurs whenever the corresponding emotional state occurs, except insofar as it is suppressed by control processes.

The basic facts of facial expression

This chapter is concerned mainly with the first question: What does facial expression express? Our answer follows from what we consider to be the basic data on facial expressions.

1. There is a clear and distinct affinity between particular facial expressions and particular categories of emotion. This affinity exists crossculturally and probably universally.
2. Emotion categories and facial expressions do not possess more than an affinity, however. A given kind of emotion may give rise to different facial expressions or to no facial expression at all.
3. A given facial expression may be common to different kinds of emotion as well as to psychological processes that are not distinctly emotional.

"Affinity" between expressions and emotions, the first basic fact, means first of all that certain expressions form the preferred or paradigmatic representations of certain emotions, such as crying being typically linked to sadness or grief, laughter to joy, and wide open eyes, lifted brows, and dropped jaw to amazement or surprise (Ekman & Friesen, 1975). This affinity forms the substance of traditional analyses of facial expression, throughout history and across cultures. These analyses are surprisingly consistent, from at least Lebrun (1667), Engel (1785), and Camper (1792) onward.[1] They also tend to be consistent with the 2,000-year-old mudras, coded facial expressions from the Indian baratha natyam dance repertoire (see, for instance, Gopal, 1951), and their equivalents in kathakali dancing. They are said to follow the rules of "rasabhinava," which means "communication of emotional states by expressions of the face" (Bonneau-Le Breton, 1994, p. 175). Analysis by FACS (Facial Action Coding System) could and should be made to verify the similarities.

"Affinity" also refers to the fact that these same expressions are consistently assigned to six or so major emotion categories when judges are forced to choose from among those six or so (Ekman, 1982; Izard, 1977). Such assignments are not usually made with 100% consistency, and major confusions occur repeatedly (Russell, 1994); still, agreement generally is way above chance and tends to occur across cultures (Ekman, 1982; Russell, 1994). The affinity also appears from indications that the paradigmatic expressions actually tend to occur under the expected emotional conditions, and again cross-culturally so. For laughter, smiling, and crying, there need hardly be discussion on this point. Subtler indications came, for instance, from Darwin's (1872) observations and from the questionnaires he sent to about threescore missionaries. For instance, the facial expression of surprise, as described earlier, was made by the inhabitants of Tierra del Fuego "when the Beagle fired some rockets" (Darwin, 1872).

Each of these three sources of evidence is open to valid criticisms (Fridlund, 1994; Russell, 1994). However, together they constitute a solid body of indications, sufficient to establish an emotion-expression affinity as a basic fact that expression theory has to explain.

Yet there is no more than an affinity. The second basic fact of facial expression is that the expressions actually shown in emotional conditions often differ drastically from the paradigmatic ones. Crying in happiness and nervous giggling provide obvious examples. It is true that such crying or giggling is usually taken as evidence that the system is upset, but deviations from what theory expects are also common under normal conditions. For instance, in a study of the ecology of facial expression (Frijda, 1953), a large number of emotional and other reactions were provoked in two women in a conversational setting. Their facial expressions were filmed, their introspections were obtained after each segment, and detailed recordings made of each eliciting event. Very many expressions differed from those one would theoretically expect, given the eliciting event. For instance, a self-reported incident of deep happiness was accompanied only by concentrated staring into space, and one of anger led only to looking away. Wagner, MacDonald, and Manstead (1986), too, found a high proportion of nonparadigmatic expressions under natural conditions. Fernández-Dols and Ruiz-Belda (chapter 11, this volume) present observations along the same line.

Emotions may be accompanied by no facial expression at all, or not by characteristic ones (Fridlund, 1994; Frijda, 1986; Izard, 1977). This applies even to very strong emotions, and not only because of self-control. The expression researcher Dumas (1933a) reproduced photographs of victims of the Chinese torture called "fragmentation into a thousand fragments." Victims' faces were bland, or showed merely gasping. And ever since antiquity, philosophers have discussed the story of the Egyptian king Psammenitus, related by Herodotus (*Histories*, III, 14). When taken prisoner by Cambyses of Persia, Psammenitus was forced to watch his daughter passing by dressed as a slave, and his son on his way to execution. The king was observed to keep a bland, unmoved face. However, he burst out weeping when noticing a friend reduced to a beggar. When questioned by Cambyses, Psammenitus answered that some griefs are too great for tears, an interpretation accepted by Cambyses and by later philosophers.

The third basic fact is that expressions tend to be common to several states, emotional as well as nonemotional. This fact is suggested by the range of emotion interpretations given to almost every expression in recognition experiments, and by the range of conditions under which any given expression actually occurs.

It is rare to find an expression in a recognition experiment that is interpreted by the subjects in one sole way (Russell, 1994). For instance, the expressions described by Ekman and Friesen (1975) as expressions of surprise were considered to be fear expressions by a nonnegligible proportion of the subjects in several studies. Also, providing the subjects with more labels to choose from than the seven emotion names increases the range of interpretations (Russell, 1994). Yet the choices do not become random. These data have led to the conclusion that facial expressions do not correspond to particular emotions, but to regions in a two- or three-dimensional emotion plot (Russell, 1980; Woodworth & Schlosberg, 1954) or to relatively broad emotion classes (Ekman, 1993; Russell & Bullock, 1986; Woodworth, 1938). In experiments that leave the subject entirely free in what interpretations to make, ranges are still larger. In one such experiment (Frijda, 1953), most interpretations of a given expression could indeed be viewed as falling within an emotion region or class that also contained the emotion label considered "correct" (that is, the one given by the filmed subject or the filming experimenter). However, a sizable number of the interpretations could not easily be seen as belonging to such a region or class. They did not refer to emotions but to cognitive or instrumental responses, such as "deep thought" for a startle response, and "water is splashed in her face" for the reaction to a gruesome story. The reverse also occurred: Expressions of physical effort or concentration were often interpreted as expressions of emotion (e.g., pulling a rope as aversion and deep thought as distress).

Interestingly, the "errors" in interpretation usually appear quite reasonable. Although some of them appeared to be due to neglect of some subtle feature of the stimulus pattern, in most cases the expressions might very well have come from the states to which the subjects attributed them. Startle, distress, and deep thought may well on occasion present the same frown, bent head, and forcefully closed eyes. We can conclude that the same or similar facial expressions can occur with different states, emotional as well as nonemotional.

Certain facial expressions occur under conversational rather than emotional conditions. They are the more voluntarily produced conversational signals called *emblems* by Ekman and Friesen (1969) and *mimiques* by Dumas (1933b, 1947). Distinctions between voluntary and less voluntarily produced expressions are perhaps hard to make on a neurological basis (Fridlund, 1994); in actual practice, they seem to be made smoothly. We leave emblems or *mimiques* out of our discussion.

What is inferred from facial expressions?

The three basic facts discussed lead us to a paradox. On the one hand, there are reasons to doubt a strict correlation between particular emotions and particular expressions. On the other hand, there is a general tendency to attribute emotions to other people on the basis of their facial expressions.

But is that tendency indeed so general? Do people indeed attribute emotions to other people whenever such others show facial expressions? Is "attribution of emotion" the best way to characterize what people do under such circumstances? Data on the process whereby people assess the meaning of expressions suggest otherwise.

Not many studies have looked at process. Standard expression recognition experiments do not allow us to do so because they force the subjects to select an emotion label; subjects cannot respond in other ways. Some information does come from experiments that allow subjects to respond freely, as in the experiment by Frijda (1953). In that experiment, subjects were presented with the film segments of spontaneous expressions described earlier, and with slides taken from those films. They were asked to describe "what might be going on in the person shown or what might have happened to her." Responses were recorded verbatim, or nearly so. Various conclusions could be drawn.

First, quite often the subjects mentioned no emotion label. Fitting an emotion label to a perceived expression is clearly not an ubiquitous element when interpreting expressions. When an emotion label was mentioned, it often was not the first and most direct step in the response process. It usually followed and was an inference from other kinds of response.

Second, the most direct response was often to imagine and describe an emotionally charged situation that appeared to fit the perceived expression. For instance, one film clip showed the target person waiting for an electric shock with manifest tenseness, anxious attention, and trying to brace herself. One subject described it as follows: "As if she is looking at something with fixed attention, a game or something tense, two cars which almost get into collision, but nothing happens" (Frijda, 1953, p. 314). One of the slides showed the target person dreamily thinking of her work (painting). It was given the interpretation: "She looks the way you look at a small child playing." A film clip of the target's head when pulling a rope: "Just like she sees something very nasty." Sometimes an emotion label was added that was felt to fit the target's response to the imagined situation. "Something of contempt in it, a bit tense" was the label given for the response to the almost-collision situation (Frijda, 1953, p. 312).

Third, the expressions were perceived as parts of the target person's interaction with her environment. The slides and films showed only the target person's head and shoulders; yet she was perceived in a situation. She was perceived not as "displaying a facial expression" that signaled some emotional state "within" her but as a person actively responding to an event in her environment or her thoughts, attending to something or as explicitly *not* attending to something. She was seen as shielding herself from something, withdrawing from something, accepting or not accepting something, opening up to it or closing off from it, or some combination of these. In brief, the target persons were seen as interacting with their environment, and the facial expressions were seen as behaviors that were part of the interaction. The behavioral and interactive nature of the expressions was particularly evident in the film clips, where it contributed to the accuracy of interpretations (accuracy scores for the films were 50% higher than for the slides; Frijda, 1953, p. 306).

Fourth, it should be strongly emphasized that what the expressions convey is essentially emotional, even if the information grasped from them is not best represented by emotion labels. The situations were imagined for their emotional significance: as suspenseful, frightening, nasty, or endearing situations, to fit the expressions. An expression evidently suggests a situation with a particular emotional content. It would be erroneous to regard the free descriptions as the results of recalling situations that had been linked to the expressions in the past, as Fridlund (1994, pp. 276–277) seems to suggest. The facial expressions did not remind the subjects of situations in which they had seen them before. They invented or imagined the situations, as several subjects made clear (see also Ruckmick, 1921, for similar observations). They creatively imagined situations that fit the expressions' apparent emotional implications.

Recognizing expressive information

The fact that subjects imagined situations that they felt fit the expressions has an important implication. It means that the expressions contain information. Terms like *attribution* or *inference* obscure the fact that expressions possess a meaning that the subject perceives or deciphers *in* them rather than adds *to* them. Indeed, that meanings are inherent in expressive phenomena has been the accepted view in earlier discussions of perceiving such phenomena; Gestalt psychologists coined the term *physiognomic perception* (Koffka, 1935; Köhler, 1929; Werner, 1926/1948).

Expressions dictate a Gibsonian view. There is information contained in them that can be picked up by an observer *before* interpretations or attributions are made. This raises the question of what that information is. The preceding has shown that it is not "emotions." Attributing emotions goes beyond the information that the expressions contain because emotion labels may vary with one particular expression. We think that the information contained in expression can be identified by examining what in fact is conveyed by them in daily interactions.

In such a context, it rarely is some verbal or abstract categorization, as in expression recognition experiments. People do not usually mutter something like "Lo, anger!" to themselves. Under many conditions categorization would not even be possible – for instance, when confronted with the dynamic expressions found in ballet, mime, or music. But in daily interactions, people give evidence that another person's expression is recognized or understood, be it correctly or incorrectly, in at least three nonverbal, nonabstract ways. All three can be traced in the protocols from the Frijda (1953) experiment.

> *Environmental expectation.* Another person's facial expression may direct one's attention to a particular object and evoke an expectation about that object that fits the expression. Recognizing a fearful expression may just mean looking around for a threat or perceiving

a given object as a threat. Understanding the meaning of someone's crying may just mean that one wonders what loss occurred.

Affective response and behavioral expectation. Another person's facial expression may modify one's affective state and evoke expectations about how the other person will respond in further interactions that fit the expression. Understanding someone's angry expression often just means becoming frightened and expecting further hostile behavior. "Understanding" of this nature has been observed even in babies under 6 months (Schwartz, Izard, & Ansul, 1985).

Empathic identification response. Another person's facial expression may engender an empathic response: imitatory movement, or just the sense that one can identify the perceived expression in terms of one's own expressive repertoire. Expression empathy is best considered a nonverbal categorization or identification act. Recognizing an angry face sometimes just means sensing the contraction and nasty, pushing forward movement implied, or even involuntarily producing them by motor mimicry (see Frijda, 1953, 1956, for observations and discussion).

None of these three kinds of recognition response implies attribution of a feeling state to the perceived person nor any form of explicit categorization. Attribution and categorization, by contrast, would seem to depend upon prior nonverbal recognition of expressive meaning and to involve going beyond that meaning.

What does facial expression express? The notions of relational activity and action readiness

Identifying the information contained in expressions is of double interest. It clarifies the process of understanding expressions by an observer and of his or her making emotion attributions on that basis. And it identifies what in fact is expressed in expression – that is, what the states or processes are in a sender that most directly cause the expressions.

How do we characterize that which is expressed? The information contained in facial expressions is, we think, that which is common in raising appraisal expectations, evoking affect and behavior expectations in interactions, and empathic responses. It is, in addition, what is common to the various conditions under which a given expression arises and to the various emotional and nonemotional states that may elicit a given expression.

The data discussed lead to the hypothesis that expressions correspond to something more general than "emotions," or at a different plane of analysis – namely, the subject's "positionality" (Frijda, 1953) or "relational activity" (Frijda, 1986). Facial expressions represent the manner in which the individual at that particular moment relates (or does not relate) to the environment. They represent the position taken: accepting or refusing, moving toward (in the sense of proximity seeking), moving away, or moving against. They represent the activity or lack of activity in taking position: highly or weakly active, or inactive as in apathy or rest. They also represent the manner of that activity: whether it is being deployed freely or under restraint, inhibited as in anxiety paralysis, or lacking in direction as in nervousness.

Because of their temporal dynamics, among other things, facial expressions usually point to the motivational states that engender the relational activity. We call them *states of action readiness*. Facial expressions express states of action readiness, which we specify as states of readiness to establish, maintain, or change a particular kind of relationship with some object in the environment or in thought, or with the environment as a whole (Frijda, 1986, chapter 2). States of action readiness vary according to their aim (obtaining proximity, avoiding contact, neutralizing obstruction, etc.) and their degree and manner of activation (hyperactivation, hypoactivation, tenseness). Major modes of action readiness correspond with major modes of subject–environment interaction or major interactional goals (cf. Roseman, Wiest, & Swartz, 1994). Theoretically, only a limited number of modes of subject–environment interaction can be distinguished, and these can meaningfully be called *basic*, as all states of action readiness represent one or more of these modes.

State of action readiness implies a tendency to control behavior. That is, states of action readiness have the property of "control precedence" (Frijda, 1986). They are likely to lead to action and to interfere with ongoing actions. They are involuntary and "impulsive" or unplanned in nature. Because they are motivational states or goals, each state of action readiness may get expressed through a variety of behaviors, including mere mental actions (wishes, plans, fantasies). Therefore, although facial expressions point to states of action readiness, the reverse is not always true. They may or they may not appear in expression or in other behavior. States of action readiness can remain impulses or states of readiness and nothing more.

Different modes of action readiness correspond to the 6 to 10 dimensions derived from theory (Frijda, 1986) and from questionnaire research

(Davitz, 1969; Frijda, Kuipers, & Terschure, 1989). The notion of states of action readiness thus allows for more differentiation than the two or three dimensions of expression posited by Schlosberg (1954) and Russell (1980). This is as it should be. The information contained in facial expressions is richer than variation along two or three dimensions. This appears from several studies. In one study, ratings were made on 22 bipolar scales of 30 posed facial expressions. Factor analysis of the ratings yielded four orthogonal factors when average ratings per photograph were used (Frijda & Philipszoon, 1963), and six when the individual ratings were used: pleasantness, activation, attentional activity, spontaneity–reactivity, surprise, and simple–complex (Frijda, 1969). Almost the same factors appeared in a second study with posed photographs of a different target person (Frijda, 1969). In a third study, subjects were asked to check which of 110 emotion adjectives applied to each of 62 posed expressions of an actress and 68 posed expressions of an actor. Factor analysis of the frequencies of co-occurrence of the adjectives yielded 17 or 18 unipolar factors with over 1% contribution to variance; the factors from both sets were rather similar. Other subjects rated the same photographs on 40 bipolar 7-point scales, which resulted in seven bipolar factors. Cluster analyses yielded similar differentiation (Frijda, 1970, 1973).

Most of these factors, if not all, do not just represent the semantics of emotion words. In Frijda (1969), significant correlations were obtained between the factor scores and ratings of various simple and complex facial feature measures (e.g., smiling, frowning, approach–avoidance score, tenseness) for both target persons.

Expressions and action readiness: Empirical support

If facial expressions correspond to states of action readiness, subjects should have little trouble associating particular states of action readiness with particular facial expressions. Support for this prediction was obtained in a preliminary experiment (Tcherkassof, in preparation). Subjects were presented with 28 facial expression slides from Matsumoto and Ekman's (1989) series, four for each of the seven emotion categories. They rated each expression on 34 action readiness items. The items came from the questionnaire used by Frijda et al. (1989), with slight adaptations, and were presented as 3-point scales (*not applicable, somewhat applicable,* and *very much applicable*). Items for *crying* and *laughing* were included. In a second round, subjects rated each slide on seven 3-point

Table 4.1. *Action readiness ratings: Percentages of "somewhat applicable" and "very much applicable" ratings (entries of 60% or over)*

Action readiness mode	Facial expression group						
	Anger	Sadness	Disgust	Fear	Contempt	Surprise	Joy
Approach							81
Being with							76
Protect oneself			74	77			
Avoid			75	81			
Attending	81	69	72	90	77	95	76
Keep distance	70		83	81			
Reject			95	92		81	
Boil inwardly	89						
Agonistic	92		90.5	71.5			
Reactant	88						
Interrupt				71.5		90.5	
In command					72.5		82
Submitting		69					
Helplessness		92		93		84.5	
Tensely contracted[a]	93	83	94	100			
Open					65.5	64	96
Crying		80					
Laughing							92

[a]The phrase "tensely contracted" translates the French "crispation." The latter has a defensive, inhibitory overtone that the English designation does not have.

emotion items representing the Matsumoto and Ekman (1989) emotion labels.

Table 4.1 gives the percentages of subjects who checked the action readiness items for each group of slides meant to represent a given emotion category. (Scores for the four slides in a group are combined, as are ratings of "somewhat applicable" and "very much applicable"; the "very much" scores alone give almost the same picture. To save space, only the items showing variation over the seven groups are included in the table.)

The subjects clearly found the task meaningful. A large majority agreed upon at least one of the action readiness items for each slide group; for all but the *contempt* slides, at least one item was checked by over 90% of the subjects for the four slides in the group together. The subjects showed unanimity on at least one item for 21 of the 28 individual slides. All but two of the slides (both from the *contempt* group) showed at least one action readiness item with 90% agreement or over.

One would predict that those action readiness items in particular will be checked that figure prominently in the semantics of the emotion label of the slide group concerned. Specific predictions were derived from questionnaire data on action readiness ratings for emotion incidents (Frijda et al., 1989). For *contempt*, no predictions could be derived. The predicted entries have been underlined in Table 4.1. All of them were checked by 77% of the subjects or more. A number of nonpredicted high scores also emerged, however.

We hypothesized that emotion attributions are inferences from assessments of states of action readiness. This implies that expressions labeled differently probably differ in terms of action readiness. The present experiment gives clear cues that this might indeed be the case. Discriminant analysis (using all 34 items), with the emotion group labels as the criterion, yields 74.8% correct assignments. Our hypothesis further implies that agreement on action readiness assignments to expressions should be at least as high as on emotion attributions (Table 4.2), provided that all expressions given the same emotion label contain the same mode of action readiness. This latter condition was not fulfilled, however. For instance, two of the *sadness* photographs were rated as distinctly agonistic, while the other two were not. The prediction could also not be rigorously tested because the number of action readiness items was about five times that of emotion items. Yet it is interesting to compare the two types of ratings. Two results are worthy of note. First, the highest percentages in comparable columns of Tables 4.1 and 4.2 do not differ much, and as already mentioned, almost all individual slides showed such a high percentage on at least one action readiness item. Second, similar confusion patterns occur for both rating types. Expressions meant to depict *contempt* do less well than those from other groups in both rating types, while the similarity in action readiness patterns of the *sadness, fear*, and *disgust* groups in Table 4.1 (and as evident in the discriminant analysis) is reflected in the off-diagonal elements in Table 4.2.

The behavioral context

To view expressions as forms of relational activity is strengthened by examining the behavioral context in which facial expressions usually appear. Facial expression literature curiously neglects that context. The expressions are generally treated as if they stand on their own. This neglect most probably is a mistake. Facial expressions tend to appear in a context of head and body orientations, gross body movements, posture changes,

Table 4.2. *Emotion ratings: percentages of "somewhat applicable" and "very much applicable" ratings (entries of 60% or over)*

Checked emotion	Facial expression group						
	Anger	Sadness	Disgust	Fear	Contempt	Surprise	Joy
Anger	87						
Sadness		97		62			
Disgust		62	98.5	60			
Fear		(57)		97			
Contempt			84		68		
Surprise				92		98.5	
Joy							93.5

and other object-related actions with a similar relational sense. One would expect a frightened face made when confronting a material event to be at least accompanied by withdrawal movements of head and shoulders, if it is not accompanied by crouching or flight. During anger, the facial expression is often accompanied by general muscular tensing, fist clenching, and forward bending or stiffly erect posture. A relaxed smile tends to be accompanied by a slowing down of respiration (Dumas, 1948). In fact, respiration changes accompany facial expressions that are adopted voluntarily, and they are probably responsible for the autonomic changes observed by Ekman, Levenson, and Friesen (1983)(Boiten, 1996).

Although little or no research exists on this issue, there are scattered descriptions, mostly of emotional expressions of mentally ill people (e.g., Darwin, 1872; Dumas, 1933a) and of children (Bonneau-Le Breton, 1994), that support the suppositions of behavioral context with a similar sense, and so does available work on posture (e.g., De Meijer, 1991). Recognition studies show that the information conveyed by posture and gross body movement primarily concerns action readiness in the most literal sense, approach-address versus withdrawal-avoidance and dominance–submission, and activation control (tenseness) (Riskind, 1984; see De Meijer, 1991, for review and empirical data).

What kinds of behavior are facial expressions?

"Expressive behavior" is not a substantive category but an impression notion, as we said earlier. One cannot, therefore, expect facial expressions to be all of a kind. States of relational action readiness are indeed reflected by different kinds of behavior. Even instrumental behavior like eating is expressive (of greed, for instance) when its dynamic properties show the intensity of readiness to get to the goal.

Facial behavior that carries expressive information can be subsumed under four headings (1) relational activity proper; (2) social signals; (3) activation and deactivation manifestations; and (4) inhibition manifestations.

1. *Relational activity proper* is behavior that directly modifies the individual's relationship to its environment. It is the kind of behavior from which Darwin derived his first principle, but that was discussed more elaborately by Engel (1785), Piderit (1867), and Wundt (1902). Some facial expressions are actions to decrease or increase sensory intake (e.g., opening or closing the eyes or nostrils, head aversion, mouth movements in response to aversive tasting substances; Chiva, 1985). Other expression features are parts of approach and withdrawal movements, such as wincing, and probably raising the eyebrows in surprise (Fridlund, 1994; Frijda, 1986). The surprise expression as a whole is an orienting reaction. Frowning is a curious case of relational behavior. It is relational in that it corresponds with the effort of maintaining focus upon one's goal under difficulty (Schänzle, 1939; Smith, 1989); it seems to be effective in that function (Frijda, 1986, p. 21), although it is obscure how.

Many expressive movements are intention movements, the initial stages of relational actions proper (*Handlungsinitien*, action onsets, Bühler, 1934). Readying one's jaw or fist for aggressive approach in anger is an example. Intention movements are evident states of readiness.

2. Certain facial expressions are *social signals* meant to influence the behavior of others. They are nonverbal requests or commands (Frijda, 1982, 1986), and are extensively discussed by Fridlund (1994, and chapter 5, this volume). A threat display discourages approach or persistence in whatever elicits it. Certain smiles signal willingness to establish contact without aggressive intent. Crying tends to induce succorance and probably is meant to serve that purpose.

Relational activity proper and social signals are functionally not so different. Relational activity proper serves the prevailing state of action readiness directly: It directly helps to maintain, achieve, or modify a given type of relationship. Facial social signals likewise serve that prevailing state, but they do so indirectly by invoking the activity of an interactant. The aim of aggression is to end an obstruction by neutralizing the obstructor; the aim of threat is to obtain the same end by way of intimidating the obstructor, who has to "cooperate" by understanding the threat and responding to it (Fridlund, 1994; Frijda, 1982, 1986).

3. *Activation and deactivation manifestations.* Activation is defined as "tonic readiness to act" (Pribram & McGuiness, 1975). Activation and activation loss are equivalent to Darwin's third principle of "direct action of the nervous system" as sources of expressive movement. Activation variation was considered the major explanatory principle for expression by both Spencer and Dumas (1933a). There are different modes of activation: that involved in relational or instrumental actions, that coming from physical effort such as the face made when cracking a nut, "superfluous" activation such as characterizes much joyful behavior, and restrained activation that goes by the name of "tenseness." Deactivation is illustrated by the drooping features of relaxation, fatigue, and sadness.

4. *Inhibition* involves response blocking under activating conditions. Freezing in rodents is usually quoted as exemplifying inhibitory process, and so is generalized response blocking in anxiety (Gray, 1982); both can be understood as cautionary responses to unpredictable or aversive conditions. Facial expression features that are best explained as inhibitory features are the sagging jaw in amazement, and the rigid, drooping and bland features in anxiety and certain anger reactions (Darwin, 1872; Dumas, 1933a).

Facial expression is here given a functional analysis. Expressions are the way they are because the relational activity, social influencing, and activation implement the aims of the state of action readiness at hand. Facial expression at any given instant of time can be understood from the functions of the composing elements in protection, orientation of attention, motor realization of activation, signaling affiliative intent, and the like. This analysis clearly leads to a componential view of facial expressions, such as proposed by Scherer (1992) and Smith (1989, and chapter 10, with Scott, this volume). Individual components of expression each have their functions, either as independent bits of relational activity or as modifiers or intensifiers of other components. Scherer (1992) and Smith and Scott (chapter 10, this volume) primarily link the components to their appraisal antecedents. We link them to their action readiness sources and relational functions.

Components belonging to different modes of relational activity may coexist. For instance, protective eye closure coexists with keeping the eyes open to maintain visual contact in some fearful expressions. Each facial expression can be read in terms of composing modes of action readiness, as in this example. Traces of relational activity can be subtle. A tinge of reserve may occur in an expression that is otherwise open and receptive; that is, some slight narrowing of the eyes, or the head being held somewhat stiffly, may occur with directed attention and forward stretching of the head. Systematic variation on facial components allows analysis of how the information content of expressions varies correspondingly. A nice example is found in a study by Garotti, Caterina, Brighetti, Giberti, & Ricci-Bitti, (1993). They systematically varied specific features in schematic drawings of smiles (e.g., eye narrowing, opening the mouth) and, submitting the drawings to subjects in a recognition experiment, obtained clearly different emotion attribution patterns for each variation.

The process of expression understanding

How is it possible to understand facial expressions, the old philosophical question with which expression study began? Understanding facial expressions becomes rather transparent from the present perspective, which may be taken as an argument in its favor (Frijda, 1956).

Usually, one of the three traditional explanations – associative learning (Berkeley, 1709), "reasoning by analogy" (Bain, 1859), and "empathy" (Lipps, 1907) – is taken for granted. None provides a satisfactory explanation. Associative learning does not because it renders novel expressions (like those in ballet dancing) unintelligible. Reasoning by analogy does not because it appears too sophisticated for, for instance, animal recognition of expressions. Empathy does not because it itself is largely an interpretative response (Frijda, 1956).

An ability to grasp the sense of relational activity and activation, however, is not a great mystery. It merely requires that movements be viewed as behavior – that is, as purposive, as movements related to the organism's environment and as guided by aims in relation to that environment. It requires, in short, that movements are perceived from an intentional stance (Dennett, 1978), which presumably implies a process of the same elementary nature as perceiving causality (Michotte, 1950).

Recognizing action readiness in behavior requires no great step either. It just amounts to picking up the cues that tell that things may come from the things that are. From here, the three recognition modes of daily life are not so difficult to understand. Once relational activity is grasped as involving relational action readiness, the material is there from which to generate expectations about environmental events and about possibly forthcoming behavior by the observed person, and to identify the perceived readiness in terms of one's own felt readiness repertoire. Knowledge and imagination then help out, given the time and the inclination, to construct hypothetical representations of the viewed person's emotion or other state, and to find a fitting label for it.

Facial expressions and emotions

We claim, then, that facial expressions are relational activities, social signals, activation manifestations, and inhibitions, all of which flow from a state of readiness to maintain or change the relationship with the environment. Does this mean that facial expressions have nothing to do with emotions? Not at all. On the contrary. Emotions and facial expressions are intrinsically related for the simple reason that emotions are states of action readiness. More precisely, emotions are best viewed as action dispositions (Lang, 1995) or states of action readiness elicited by antecedent events as appraised and manifesting some degree of control precedence (see Arnold, 1960; Frijda, 1986; Lang, 1995; Scherer, 1984, for convergent views). Also, a change in state of action readiness is perhaps the major aspect of behavior or experience that leads to use of the word "emotion," both to denote one's own state and that observed in others. The word *emotion* is rarely used for mere feelings that do not involve some claim on change in action readiness.

The emotion-expression relationship is greatly clarified by the componential approach to emotions (e.g., Frijda, 1986; Lang, 1995; Lazarus, 1991; Mandler, 1984; Scherer, 1984). According to that approach, emotions are structures of moderately correlated components. Affect, appraisal, action disposition, and physiological response are the major components. Emotional feelings are considered as one's awareness of one or more of these components. Different emotions can be viewed as structures that differ in one or more of these components. Emotion words specify such structures at a given level of specification, though not necessarily with regard to all components together.

Many emotion words specify a particular state of action readiness. In several languages there exist close links between major emotion categories and modes of action readiness (Davitz, 1969; Frijda et al., 1989; Frijda, Markam, Sato, & Wiers, 1995; Roseman et al., 1994). The links between major emotion categories and modes of action readiness parallel those between major emotion categories and facial expressions. For instance, hostile or threatening impulse is one of the major semantic components of "anger" and its nearest equivalents in many other languages, and a prototypical angry expression translates a hostile or threatening action readiness. This explains Ekman's (1982, 1993; Ekman & Friesen, 1975) findings. It accounts for the affinity between particular emotions and particular expressions, the first basic fact mentioned.

Yet those links between emotions and expressions are neither necessary nor exclusive, as follows from multicomponential emotion theory. First, emotion words are generally used in fuzzy, nondeterministic fashion, to denote now this, then that of the moderately correlated components (Fehr & Russell, 1984; Russell, 1991; Shaver, Schwartz, Kirson, & O'Connor, 1987). They may primarily indicate particular appraisals rather than modes of action readiness. "Anger" is often used to denote the response to an event appraised as blameworthy, regardless of the nature of the resulting state of action readiness. That may be an impulse to break off contact rather than hostile impulse, or drastic loss of action readiness, as when paralyzed and almost fainting from anger. Other emotion words do not specify the state of action readiness at all. "Being upset" suggests that action readiness is somehow interfered with – action is interrupted – but no more. The links between emotion categories and modes of action readiness, while sometimes clear and intrinsic, thus are in no way fixed or absolute.

Second, not all states of action readiness (and thus, not all emotions) give rise to facial expression or to a very specific facial expression. The emotion of desire, understood as the impulse to get closer in order to possess, is an example. Facial expression, moreover, is only one among many kinds of action that a given state of action readiness may command. Each kind of action has its own determinants in addition to the state of action readiness. One additional determinant for facial expression is physical context: A fearfully contorted face is more likely in front of a threatening physical object than when facing failing an examination. Another determinant is prevailing activation mode. For instance, the nonsocial smile may represent "active rest" or "sense of mastery" rather than just generally pleasure or joy (Buytendijk, 1947; Frijda, 1986; Sroufe & Waters, 1976); and Ellgring (1989) notes that facial expressions in depressed patients depend more upon their initial behavioral level than upon the prevailing emotion or mood. Other determinants again are social influence and expected effectiveness, as extensively examined by Fridlund (1994). All this accounts for the second basic fact: the loose and variable relation between particular emotions and particular expressions.

Third, there is no simple relationship between action readiness and overt behavior, including facial expression. As we mentioned, states of action readiness are not always expressed in overt behavior, and they may lead to widely divergent overt behaviors. In addition, control processes, including social display rules, obviously work to widen the split.

Moreover, there is no simple relation between the impact of an emotional event and action readiness. The event aspect that controls action readiness, or which mode of action readiness controls behavior, is not always the central aspect of the event's impact. We earlier gave the example of a target person in the Frijda (1953) experiment who was thinking with feelings of deep happiness about some work she had been doing. Her face mostly showed her concentrated attention, and not so much the happiness. Similar observations are made by Kraut (1982) and Fernández-Dols and Ruiz-Belda (chapter 11, this volume). They found that events causing important satisfaction or happiness frequently do not lead to happy expressions; the subjects smile only when facing the public. Part of the explanation may be that concentration and exhaustion after effortful feats overlay or delay actual feelings of joy or triumph.

Then both action readiness and facial expression may vanish when action appears meaningless. Brehm (1994) advances the hypothesis that the relationship between event intensity and emotional response has the shape of a sawtooth rather than being monotonic. In maximally intense emotions, response magnitude drops steeply. The hypothesis is corroborated by the Chinese torture report and the story of Psammenitus. These considerations, too, account for aspects of the second basic fact.

Fourth, relational actions, social signals, and activation manifestations need not originate in a state of action readiness. They may come just from physical exercise or represent hypotonic boredom reactions that look like dumb amazement. They may also come from voluntary intent to signal a particular event appraisal to others ("how awful is what you tell me") or to suggest a state of action readiness that is not really there. These are the conditions for *mimiques* or emblems (Dumas, 1933b; Ekman & Friesen, 1969).

Attributing emotions necessarily involves going beyond the information given by expression. One has to add that the relational action, social signal, or activation state was elicited by an appraised event, and that these actions involve a state of action readiness with control precedence. One frequently has to add hypotheses on the nature of the eliciting event and appraisal – hence, the confusions in recognition experiments. This accounts for the third basic fact, the looseness of the emotion-expression relationship.

As indicated before, the major forms of action readiness can be considered basic forms of subject–environment interaction. They form discrete categories, very much as the basic emotions in Izard's (1977) theory. Since certain emotions paradigmatically embody these forms of action readiness, and the corresponding states may paradigmatically be manifest in certain facial expressions, it makes sense to consider these emotions as basic emotions, and certain facial expressions to represent them. However, recognizing basic emotions in this sense in no way implies the lore around that notion: unitary biological predispositions, felt *qualia*, solid links between the various components, a stiff emotions hierarchy. That lore, in fact, we firmly reject.

Conclusions

Facial expressions, we propose, "express" the individual's state of relational action readiness or unreadiness. State of action readiness is the proper content of facial expressions, and that which observers infer from them in the first place. Expressions "express" it, in the sense that an action expresses its underlying intention. They implement or effectuate action readiness. That is, they do so unless they come from a different source, such as social habit, deceit, or voluntary intent.

Because the core of what one calls "emotions" consists, by and large, of variations in the individual's state of action readiness, facial expressions can be said to "express" emotions. Facial expressions, *when* they are contingent upon states of action readiness, are intimately bound to emotions. Emotions are expressed in facial expressions and lead to such expressions *when* additional conditions are appropriate for state of action readiness to do so. Facial expressions thereby are often fairly diagnostic for the prevailing states of action readiness and, with sufficient cues (behavior context, time course, information that there is some eliciting event) for emotion.

At the same time, from the point of view of the observer, the issue is not simple. Facial expressions represent relational activities, activation modes, social signals, and inhibitory states. Correctly recognizing emotion needs those additional "sufficient cues" just mentioned, which allow going from relational activity to action readiness to correctly assessing whether the action readiness is the response to an appraised event.

The relationship between facial expressions and emotions, as felt or as defined by eliciting event, type of appraisal, or action readiness, is variable. Manifest state of action readiness may be peripheral to what is central to experience. Occurrence of facial expression depends upon other factors, in addition to feeling, event appraisal, and action readiness. These factors dilute the link between emotions and expressions. They do, however, in no way sever it. Although the link is neither exclusive nor necessary, it is an intrinsic one.

Acknowledgment

This manuscript was prepared with the assistance of the members of the CERE group, and the support of the Maison des Sciences de l'Homme, Paris, and the Université de Paris-X Nanterre.

Note

1 Lebrun was a painter, Engel a theorist of the stage, and Camper a Dutch anatomist (in fact, the founder of comparative anatomy).

References

Arnold, M. B. (1960). *Emotion and personality* (Vols. 1 and 2). New York: Columbia University Press.
Bain, A. (1859). *Emotions and the will*. London: Longmans and Green.
Berkeley, G. (1709). *An essay towards a new theory of vision*. London.
Boiten, F. A. (1996). Autonomic response patterns during voluntary facial action. *Psychophysiology, 33*, 123–131.
Bonneau-Le Breton, C. (1994). *Expression faciale des émotions: comparaison des mimiques évoquées et provoquées, dans une perspective developpementale*. Ph.D. thesis, Université de Paris-X Nanterre.
Brehm, J. (1994). *The intensity of emotions*. Unpublished manuscript.
Bühler, K. (1934). *Ausdruckstheorie*. Jena, Germany: Fisher.
Buytendijk, F. J. J. (1947). *De eerste glimlach van het kind* [The infant's first smile]. Nijmegen: Dekker en van der Vegt.
Buytendijk, F. J. J., & Plessner, H. (1925). Die Deutung des mimischen Ausdrucks. *Philosophische Anzeiger, 1*, 26–48.
Camper, P. (1792). *Redencoeringen over de Wyze om de onerscheiden Hartstochten op onze Wezens te Verbeelden* [Discourses on the manner to depict the various passions on our creatures]. Utrecht.
Chiva, M. (1985). *Le doux et l'amer* [The sweet and the bitter]. Paris: Presses Universitaires de France.
Darwin, C. (1872). *The expression of emotions in man and animals*. London: John Murray.
Davitz, J. R. (1969). *The language of emotion*. New York: Academic Press.
De Meijer, M. (1991). *Emotional meaning in large body movements*. Tilburg, Netherlands: Tilburg University Press.
Dennett, D. C. (1978). *Brainstorms: Philosophical essays on mind and psychology*. Montgomery: Bradford Books.
Dumas, G. (1933a). L'expression des émotions. In G. Dumas (Ed.), *Nouveau traité de psychologie. Tome 3* (pp. 39–292). Paris: Alcan.
Dumas, G. (1933b). Les mimiques. In G. Dumas (Ed.), *Nouveau traité de psychologie. Tome 3* (pp. 293–360). Paris: Alcan.
Dumas, G. (1947). *La vie affective*. Paris: Presses Universitaires de France.

Ekman, P. (1993). Facial expression and emotion. *American Psychologist, 48,* 384–392.

Ekman, P. (Ed). (1982). *Emotion in the human face* (2nd ed.). New York: Cambridge University Press.

Ekman, P., & Friesen, W. V. (1969). The repertoire of nonverbal behavior: Categories, origins, usage and coding. *Semiotica, 1,* 49–98.

Ekman, P., & Friesen, W. V. (1975). *Unmasking the face.* Englewood Cliffs, NJ: Prentice-Hall.

Ekman, P., Levenson, R. W., & Friesen, W. V. (1983). Autonomic nervous system activity distinguishing among emotions. *Science, 221,* 1208–1210.

Ellgring, H. (1989). *Nonverbal communication in depression.* Cambridge: Cambridge University Press.

Engel, J. J. (1785). *Ideen zu einer Mimik.* Berlin: Mylin.

Fehr, B., & Russell, J. A. (1984). Concept of emotion viewed from a prototype perspective. *Journal of Experimental Psychology: General 113,* 464–486.

Fridlund, A. J. (1994). *Human facial expression: An evolutionary view.* New York: Academic Press.

Frijda, N. H. (1953). The understanding of facial expression of emotion. *Acta Psychologica, 9,* 294–362.

Frijda, N. H. (1956). *De betekenis van gelaatsexpressies* [The meaning of facial expressions of emotion]. Amsterdam: Van Oorschot.

Frijda, N. H. (1969). Recognition of emotion. In L. Berkowitz (Ed.), *Advances in experimental social psychology* (Vol. 4, pp. 167–223). New York: Academic Press.

Frijda, N. H. (1970). Emotion and recognition of emotion. In M. B. Arnold (Ed.), *Feelings and emotions: The Loyola symposium* (pp. 241–250). New York: Academic Press.

Frijda, N. H. (1973). The relation between emotion and expression. In M. von Cranach & I. Vine (Eds.), *Social communication and movement* (pp. 325–340). New York: Academic Press.

Frijda, N. H. (1982). The meanings of facial expression. In M. Ritchie-Kye (Ed.), *Nonverbal communication today: Current research* (pp. 103–120). The Hague: Mouton.

Frijda, N. H. (1986). *The emotions.* Cambridge, England: Cambridge University Press.

Frijda, N. H., Kuipers, P., & Terschure, E. (1989). Relations between emotion, appraisal, and emotional action readiness. *Journal of Personality and Social Psychology, 57,* 212–228.

Frijda, N. H., Markam, S., Sato, K., & Wiers, R. (1995). Emotion and emotion words. In J. A. Russell, J-M. Fernández-Dols, A. S. R. Manstead, & J. Wellenkamp (Eds.), *Everyday conceptions of emotion* (pp. 121–144). Dordrecht: Kluwer.

Frijda, N. H., & Philipszoon, E. (1963). Dimensions of recognition of emotion. *Journal of Abnormal and Social Psychology, 66,* 45–51.

Garotti, P. L., Caterina, R., Brighetti, G., Giberti, E., & Ricci-Bitti, P. E. (1993). Il ruolo del sorriso come indicatore di stati emotivi differenziati [The role of the smile as indicating differentiated emotional states]. *Rassegna di Psicologia, 10,* 29–53.

Gopal, R. (1951). *Indian dancing.* London: Phoenix House.

Gray, J. A. (1982). *The neuropsychology of anxiety: An enquiry into the functions of the septo-hippocampal system.* Oxford: Oxford University Press.

Izard, C. E. (1977). *Human emotions.* New York: Plenum.

Koffka, K. (1935). *Principles of Gestalt psychology.* New York: Harcourt Brace.

Köhler, W. (1929). *Gestalt psychology.* New York: Liveright.

Kraut, R. E. (1982). Social presence, social feedback, and emotion. *Journal of Personality and Social Psychology, 42,* 853–863.

Lang, P. J. (1995). The emotion probe. *American Psychologist, 50,* 372–385.

Lazarus, R. S. (1991). *Emotion and adaptation.* New York: Oxford University Press.

Lebrun, C. (1677). *Conférences sur l'expression des différents charactères des passions* [Lectures on the expression of the different passions]. Paris.

Lipps, T. (1905). Die Erkenntnis from fremden Ichen [The knowledge of other minds]. *Psychologische Untersuchungen, 1,* 1–53.

Lipps, T. (1907). Zur Einfühlung [On empathy]. *Psychologische Untersuchungen II,* 73–102.

Mandler, G. (1984). *Mind and body: The psychology of emotion and stress.* New York: Norton.

Matsumoto, D., & Ekman, P. (1989). American-Japanese cultural differences in intensity ratings of facial expressions of emotion. *Motivation and Emotion, 13,* 143–157.

Michotte, A. E. (1950). The emotions as functional connections. In M. Reymert (Ed.), *Feelings and emotions* (pp. 114–126). New York: McGraw-Hill.

Piderit, T. (1867). *Mimik und Physiognomik.* Detmoldt: Meyer.

Pribram, K. H., & McGuiness, D. (1975). Arousal, activation, and effort in the control of attention. *Psychological Review, 82,* 116–149.

Riskind, J. H. (1984). They stoop to conquer: Guiding and self-regulatory functions of physical posture after success and failure. *Journal of Personality and Social Psychology, 47,* 479–493.

Roseman, I. J., Wiest, C., & Swartz, T. S. (1994). Phenomenology, behaviors, and goals differentiate discrete emotions. *Journal of Personality and Social Psychology, 67,* 206–221.

Ruckmick, C. A. (1921). A preliminary study of the emotions. *Psychological Monographs, 30.*

Russell, J. A. (1980). A circumplex model of affect. *Journal of Personality and Social Psychology, 39,* 1161–1178.

Russell, J. A. (1991). In defense of a prototype approach to emotion concepts. *Journal of Personality and Social Psychology, 60,* 425–438.

Russell, J. A. (1994). Is there universal recognition of emotion from facial expression? A review of the cross-cultural studies. *Psychological Bulletin, 115,* 102–141.

Russell, J. A., & Bullock, M. (1986). Fuzzy concepts and the perception of emotions in facial expression. *Social Cognition, 4,* 309–341.

Sartre, J. P. (1939). *Esquisse d'une theorie phenomenologique des emotions.* Paris: Hermann (The Emotions, New York, Philosophical Library, 1948).

Schänzle, J. (1939). *Der mimische Ausdruck des Denkens* [The facial expression of thinking]. Berlin: Grafe.

Scherer, K. R. (1984). On the nature and function of emotion: A component process approach. In K. R. Scherer & P. Ekman (Eds.), *Approaches to emotion* (pp. 293–317). Hillsdale, NJ: Erlbaum.

Scherer, K. R. (1992). What does facial expression express? In K. T. Strongman (Ed.), *International review of studies of emotion* (Vol. 2, pp. 139–165). New York: Wiley.

Schlosberg, H. (1954). Three dimensions of emotion. *Psychological Review, 61,* 81–88.

Schwartz, G. M., Izard, C. E., & Ansul, S. E. (1985). The 5-month-old's ability to discriminate facial expressions of emotion. *Infant Behavior and Development, 8,* 65–77.

Shaver, P., Schwartz, J., Kirson, D., & O'Connor, C. (1987). Emotion knowledge: Further exploration of a prototype approach. *Journal of Personality and Social Behavior, 52,* 1061–1086.

Smith, C. A. (1989). Dimensions of appraisal and physiological response to emotion. *Journal of Personality and Social Psychology, 56,* 339–353.

Sroufe, L. A., & Waters, E. (1976). The ontogenesis of smiling and laughter: A perspective on the organization of development in infancy. *Psychological Review, 83,* 173–189.

Tcherkassof, A. (in preparation). *La perception des expressions émotionelles faciales.* Unpublished doctoral dissertation, Université de Paris-X Nanterre.

Wagner, H. L., MacDonald, C. J., & Manstead, A. S. R. (1986). Communication of individual emotions by spontaneous facial expression. *Journal of Personality and Social Psychology, 50,* 737–743.

Werner, H. (1948). *Comparative psychology of mental development.* New York: Science Editions. (Original work published 1926)

Woodworth, R. S. (1938). *Experimental psychology.* New York: Holt.

Woodworth, R. S., & Schlosberg, H. (1954). *Experimental psychology* (rev. ed.). New York: Holt.

Wundt, W. (1902). *Grundzüge der pysiologischen Psychologie* (Vol. 3). Leipzig: Engelmann, 5th. Ausgabe.

5. The new ethology of human facial expressions

ALAN J. FRIDLUND

Historically, researchers on facial expressions have tried to forge links between movements of the face and those ineffable states called "emotions" (e.g., Mandler, 1984). The advocates of this "Emotions View" are not homogeneous in all their axioms and precepts, but they share the belief in the centrality of emotion in explaining facial movements. I myself worked within this tradition for many years (e.g., Ekman & Fridlund, 1987; Fridlund, Ekman, & Oster, 1987; Fridlund & Izard, 1983; Fridlund, Schwartz, & Fowler, 1984; Matsumoto, Ekman, & Fridlund, 1990) but began to be troubled by certain insurmountable problems with the approach. My apostasy led to a search for a better way to understand our facial expressions.

I have proposed an alternative (e.g., Fridlund, 1991a, 1994), termed the *Behavioral Ecology View*, because it derives from modern accounts of the evolution – both genetic and cultural – of signaling behavior.[1] This account, based on work by biologists like Maynard Smith, Hinde, Smith, Krebs, Davies, and Marler, contrasts with the Emotions View of faces (see Izard; Frijda & Tcherkassof; Smith & Scott; chapters 3, 4, and 10, respectively, this volume) in its view of how facial expressions evolved, what they signify, and how they function in our everyday lives. This chapter presents the fundamentals of the Behavioral Ecology View, followed by the reasons why it may afford the better understanding of human facial expressions.

The Behavioral Ecology View of faces

Most theorists within the Emotions View essentially espouse a two-factor model, depicted in Figure 5.1, that posits two basic kinds of faces. First are the innate reflex-like faces that read out ongoing emotion; these are "facial expressions of emotion." Second are learned, instrumental faces

103

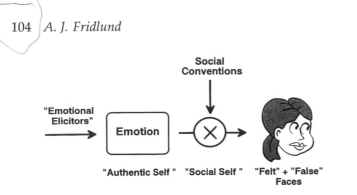

Figure 5.1. The Emotions View of facial expression.

that connote emotion that is not occurring; these reflect everyday social dissimulation such as the smile of phony politeness.

The two-factor Emotions View is also permeated by an implicit but familiar Western romanticist portrait of human nature, which draws heavily from Rousseau – which most psychologists know via Sigmund Freud's *id* and *ego*, and which I believe explains both its appeal and its persistence. I schematize this romanticist view in Table 5.1.

The Behavioral Ecology View of facial displays does not treat them as "expressions" of discrete emotional states, or the outputs of modular affect programs, or as a compromise between the opposing forces of a Janusian self. For the contemporary ethologist or the behavioral ecologist, facial displays are simply messages, which influence others' behavior because vigilance for and comprehension of signals co-evolved with the signals themselves. Early on (Fridlund, 1986), I provided this scenario:

> Millions of years ago, if you crossed my turf, I might bite your head off [at some risk to me, if you decided to retaliate]. If you had advance warning, you might escape death through retreat or protective defense, and we'd both survive.
>
> But you'd need cues to retreat or protect. I'd have to give them, and you'd have to notice them. Here's the scenario: because of a lucky gene, I adventitiously bared one tooth for ½ second before I pounced. Your lucky gene made you look at my head. I bared my tooth, and you looked in the right place, not because I wanted to display my feelings, or because you wanted to see how I felt. We both acted out of pure dumb genetic luck. That we survived our skirmish increases the chances that our lucky genes will proliferate, and that my odd tooth-baring and your odd vigilance for it will both disseminate in our progeny.

The vignette is simplistic, and the evolution it describes is genetic (cultural evolution operates similarly, but ontogenetic learning replaces phylogenetic predisposition). Nonetheless, its message is that displays

Table 5.1. *Romanticist* leitmotif *underlying "two-factor" theories of facial expression*

Aspect of expression	"Emotional" expressions	"Social" expressions
Creature domain	Animal (savage)	Human (noble)
Context of occurrence	Natural (private)	Civil (public)
Type of issuance	Released	Rule-governed
Quality of expression	Reflexive	Instrumental
Veridicality	Authentic	Deceptive
Governing mechanism	Endogenous "facial affect programs"	Exogenous "cultural display rules"
Neurological bases	Subcortical ("passion")	Neocortical ("will", "reason")

co-evolve with vigilance for them. This prediction from modern evolutionary theory carries several implications. In the first place, *the co-evolution of facial displays and vigilance for them could occur only if displays provided reliable, graded, mutually beneficial signals of contingent future action.* These signals would allow interactants to proceed with reciprocation or counteraction that promoted mutual survival (Alcock, 1984; Hinde, 1985a; Smith, 1977, 1986).

Second, *the dictates of economy and privacy would select against any involuntary displays of internal state that might betray information detrimental to the displayer.* Evolution should suppress any movements – such as the "emotional expressions" of Emotions theorists – that ostensibly erupt despite one's efforts to hide them (cf. Krebs & Dawkins, 1984). In order to flourish, one must issue faces that primarily serve social motives, not any quasi-reflexive emotion (Andrew, 1963a, b, 1964, 1972; Hinde, 1985b). Indeed, instead of there being six or seven expressions of "fundamental emotions" (for example, anger), there may be any number (whether 1 or 100) "about to aggress" displays appropriate to the identities and relationship of the interactants and to the context in which the interaction occurs.[2] All of these factors, in turn, determine one's aims within the interaction. The topography of any "about to aggress" display would likely depend upon contextual features such as whether the interactant is dominant or nondominant, conspecific or extraspecific, and whether one is defending territory or young, contesting for access to a female, or retrieving stolen food or property. And as noted by Marler and Evans (chapter 6, this volume) and Ginsburg and Harrington (1993), the context of any interaction includes the history of previous interaction.

Third, *survivors of conflicts would not only include those who produced more schematized facial behavior (technically, "ritualized" if the evolution is genetic and "conventionalized" if it is cultural) but also those with a heightened sensitivity to faces* (see Nelson & de Haan, chapter 8, this volume) and who exhibited more "social cognition" (see Brothers, 1992). This "ecology" of signaling and vigilance, countersignaling and countervigilance, is analogous to the balance of resources and consumers, and predator and prey, that characterizes all natural ecosystems.

Fourth, *the costs and benefits of signaling, and of emitting a particular kind of signal, would vary with the momentary social context and the animal's intentions within it.* This sociality of animal signals is well documented in a number of animals and a variety of social settings (see Fridlund, 1994; and Marler & Evans, chapter 6, this volume). Human signals, like the signals of other animals, should be no less dependent upon motive and context. How, then, does the Behavioral Ecology View interpret everyday human facial expressions?

Table 5.2 compares typical facial displays as interpreted by the Emotions View and the Behavioral Ecology View. In each case, an "emotional expression" is replaced by the signification of a social motive. This isn't just a replacement of terms, for two reasons. First, "emotions" are ineffable entities about which there is no consensual definition – as the relevant chapters in this volume attest (more on this later). "Motives," on the other hand, can be deduced from behavioral observation. Second, the Behavioral Ecology interpretation disposes of the romanticized split between the "authentic" self that embodies the impulse to make a face and the social self that wants to withhold it or modify it. Thus, in contexts in which one would try to appease another, any smile one issued would tend to be labeled a "false smile" in the Emotions View, which would connote a smile that masks some other emotion with its associated facial expression. For the behavioral ecologist, the same smile would likely be labeled an "about to appease" display, and it would deliver the same message as the words, "I give in" or "Whatever you say."

Note from Table 5.2 that I have not depicted prototype faces for each category. This is because, *contra* the Emotions View, the Behavioral Ecology View does not require them. Rather, because displays exert their influence in the particular context of their issuance, they may only be interpretable within that context. By analogy with language, I may use the word *pen* to denote a writing implement in one context and a holding area in another, and there is no requirement that the writing *pen* be pronounced any differently than the cattle *pen* – the context determines

Table 5.2. *Emotions and Behavioral Ecology interpretations of common human facial displays*

Emotions view ["facial expressions of emotion"]	Behavioral Ecology view [signification of intent]
"Felt" ("Duchenne") smile (Expression of happiness)	Readiness to play or affiliate ("Let's play [keep playing]," or "Let's be friends")
"False" smile (Feigned happiness)	Readiness to appease ("Whatever you say," or "I give in")
"Sad" face	Recruitment of succor ("Take care of me," or "Hold me")
"Anger" face	Readiness to attack ("Back off or I'll attack")
"Leaked" anger (Inhibited anger)	Conflict about attacking ("I want to attack and I don't want to attack")
"Fear" face	Readiness to submit or escape ("Don't hurt me!")
"Contentment" face	Readiness to continue current interaction ("Everything [you're doing] is just fine")
"Contempt" face	Declaration of superiority ("I can't even bother with you")
"Poker" face (Suppressed emotion)	Declaration of neutrality ("I'm taking no position [on what you're doing or saying]")

the word's signification. Similarly, I may smile both when I am giving a gift and when I am exacting revenge. The context determines whether the smiles signify "I like you" or "Gotcha!," and the faces needn't be different. The evidence supports this: For example, a face interpreted as "contemptuous" in one context may be interpreted as "exasperated" or even "constipated" in another (Russell, chapter 13, this volume, and 1994). And needless to say, because displays are specific to intent and context, the practice within the Emotions View of simultaneously proposing a small set of fundamental affects, and then invoking "blends" of them to explain the range of everyday displays, is considered procrustean, tautological, and self-confirming (see Ortony & Turner, 1990, for a lexical critique of theories of "basic emotions").

Fifth, *because facial displays are the results of a formalized co-evolution with vigilance for them, they are not readouts but "social tools" (Smith, 1977) that aid the negotiation of social encounters.* Displays are declarations that signify

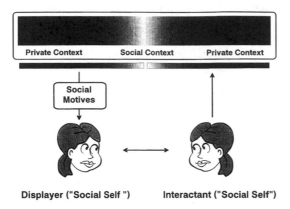

Figure 5.2. The Behavioral Ecology View of facial displays.

our trajectory in a given social interaction (i.e., what we will do in the current context, or what we would like the other to do). And this "context" depends considerably not only on the structural features of the situation but on the succession of interactants' displays and their responses to them.

I have depicted my conception of the Behavioral Ecology View in Figure 5.2. In Figure 5.2, the "facial expressions of emotion" of the Emotions View (cf. Figure 5.1) actually serve the social motives of the displayer. No distinction is made between "felt" and "false" displays issued by "authentic" and "social" selves; instead, *all* displays are considered to arise out of social interaction, thus there is *only* a social self. Finally, displays are deployed and interpreted within the context of the interaction ("social context" in the figure). This context is formed from both its structural features (e.g., the setting as well as the relations of the interactants) and, as the Ginsburg and Harrington quote suggests, the accreted "common ground" that arises from any previous interactions. Finally, the "private context" of the participants consists of that set of expectations, needs, and so on, that each brings to the interaction, and these in turn result in great part from one's prior interactions. For this reason, the figure depicts the interactants' private contexts as melding with their shared social context.

Shortcomings of the Emotions View

The previous summary focused on how the behavioral ecologist understands human facial expressions. As I mentioned earlier, I came to adopt this view not only because of its solid biological grounding but because of insurmountable problems I encountered in trying to make an Emotions View of facial expression "work." I now discuss some of the difficulties I encountered, and I indicate the resolutions suggested by the Behavioral Ecology View.

The Emotions View neglects the costs of automatic expression.

Signals do not evolve to provide information detrimental to the signaler. Displayers must not signal automatically but only when it is beneficial to do so (i.e., when such signaling serves its aims within an interaction). Automatic readouts or spillovers of drive or emotion states (for example, "facial expressions of emotion") would thus be extinguished early in phylogeny in the service of deception, economy, and privacy. What about those cases in which people can be seen trying to "hide their emotions"? For the behavioral ecologist, these cases represent not incomplete suppression of automatic, emotional expression ("leakage") but simple conflict behavior. For example, an individual who momentarily shows a pursed lip on an otherwise impassive face is not showing leakage of anger but conflicting intentions (cf. Tinbergen, 1953) (e.g., probably to show stolidity *and* to threaten).

The Emotions View omits the recipient's co-evolutionary role in the origin and persistence of display.

The recipient is indispensable in the process of formalization. Signals that are not received and then acted upon cannot be selected. Recipients of displays should only attend to cues that provide predictions about the future *behavior* of the displayer, regardless of how the displayer "feels." This does not imply that recipients can *only* use formalized cues; everyday behavior in a given context also allows prediction of the others' next moves (Argyle, 1972; Kendon, 1981). Nonetheless, only those cues to which recipients reliably attend *can* evolve (whether genetically or culturally). Behavioral intentions must therefore drive displays.

The Emotions View erroneously presumes that infant faces are "authentic" and that maturation breeds dissimulative faces.

The most reflex-like human faces are seen in infants, and in the Emotions View they are held to reflect an "innate expression-feeling concordance" (cf. Izard & Malatesta, 1987). In the Behavioral Ecology View, the seeming reflexiveness of infant displays just reflects the selection pressures on the infant. The late-maturing human infant's social milieu is relatively simple; the infant merely needs to garner caretaker attention, and the caretakers discern the required response. Thus, the primary selection pressures on children are to capture and hold the attention of caretakers, especially if competition originally occurred among infants of multiple caretakers. Indeed, it would be well to conceive of the infant not as an innocent but as a servomechanism cleverly shaped by natural selection to emit the displays that will optimally promote and maintain parental care (i.e., they should be intense attention grabbers).

What displays should evolution "choose" to grab adult attention? Conceivably, infants may have evolved merely to be good emulators of the requisite adult displays. Those infants who are good emulators can better exploit the extant adult signal system. Thus, by virtue of the fact that adults succor other adults who are crying, those infants who produce loud cries will receive more reliable care. Because adults are engaged when other adults smile, then babies who produce "flashbulb" social smiles will more readily engage caretakers and obtain similar advantage. Because infants who did not emit pronounced cries or smiles would have been comparatively neglected and less viable, natural selection should directly shape the production of exaggerated, plangent, canonical infant displays. (The emulation may be due to natural selection, with the infant a hard-wired emulator, and/or it may occur via early imitation of the caricatured faces that caretakers make toward neonates [Meltzoff & Moore, 1977].)

When should infants display? In the case of crying, infants should of course cry when hungry, tired, in pain or need of diapering, and so forth. The so-called distress cries of the newborn, in this account, are protolinguistic protests that mean, "Make it better!" or "Get me outta here!" These displays are "honest" (i.e., occurring when the infant needs a caretaker's direct intervention). The infant, however, cleverly shaped by natural selection, should issue additional cries, or convincingly urgent ones, periodically and unpredictably. These "deceptive" cries should be issued often enough to insure steady caretaker attention, but not so often or so needlessly that the attention extinguishes. Caretaker attention is a risky commodity, as suggested by the high rates of child abuse and infanticide worldwide, and most likely it is infants' ingratiation strategies (i.e., looking cute and issuing endearing smiles) that explain why so many thrive.

Is the displaying infant "emotional"? Prerequisite to any answer is a consensual definition of emotion, which proponents of the Emotions View have failed to supply.[3] For the behavioral ecologist, individuals of any age who show the right displays at the right time will survive, even if they are anhedonic (arguably, the psychopath fits this criterion). Displays function as manipulations, and infant cries and smiles are manipulations that merely serve to garner caretaker attention and intervention. No emotion is implied or required; whether infants are emotional when they issue displays is a separate problem whose resolution requires evidence independent of the displays.

Compared to infants, older children start showing more subtle and variegated displays. In the Emotions View, this change from plangency to subtlety reflects learned dissimulation (i.e., "socialization of emotion" [cf. Lewis & Michalson, 1982, 1985] or the internalization of "display rules" [Saarni, 1978], the effect of which is the uncoupling of the innate expression-feeling concordance [Izard & Malatesta, 1987]). In the Behavioral Ecology View, the increased subtlety of more mature displays may be due to either maturation or socialization.

Conceivably, increased variation in facial display with maturation would simply reflect normal developmental differentiation of both morphology and behavior (Baer, 1828). More likely, the increased subtlety of display *is* social, but it is not dissimulative. Rather, the apperception of more complex social relations leads directly to more complex social motives. Thus, the infant merely has to cry or smile to garner the attention of a caretaker who discerns how to respond. In contrast, the normal adult rarely has such an attentive, discerning caretaker. Satisfying needs requires sophisticated signals to negotiate a complex social terrain that includes one's relatedness to those present, as well as a context of interaction that may involve varying social roles, past interactions, modes of reciprocation, and moral notions of entitlement.

The Emotions View fails to account for the poor relationship between emotions and facial displays.

Adults may have "emotions" (as commonly defined), but the relation of adult display to emotion is adventitious. Displays serve social motives, which themselves may depend little upon whether, for example, people say that they are emotional. Everyday smiling is illustrative. We may be courteous, loving, amusing, or reassuring, and smile accordingly, if we are so moved – regardless of whether we feel happy, sad, angry, or fearful. I know of no evidence that we smile more when we are happy, but if we do, it is likely so for two reasons. We may simply prefer (and report being "happier" in) situations that engender such motives. More likely, social motives served by smiles (e.g., humor, play, affiliation) may arise more frequently during those periods when we say that we're happy, and at these times, our impulse is to tell someone. This impulse may reflect personal disposition or cultural tradition about whether one "shares one's happiness" with another or simply thanks God quietly for one's blessings.

Clearly, people often do *not* show facial behavior when the Emotions theorist would predict it. When people feel immensely wounded by another, or praised overwhelmingly by an audience, their faces will remain motionless – except, perhaps, for moist eyes. In fact, it is altogether common to say that a person is especially "moved" when her face isn't! (See Fernández-Dols & Ruiz-Belda, chapter 11, this volume, for especially persuasive data.)

The multiple determinants of other prototype "emotional expressions" also vitiate the Emotions View. In emotion theories, the display characterized by wincing, down-turned mouth, and frequent tears (i.e., the "cry" face) is thought to express sadness. Nonetheless, we also cry when we would say that we are happy, angry, frightened, or relieved. From the Behavioral Ecology View, the function of the cry-face display in all cases is to signal readiness to receive attention or succor, regardless of one's emotional status. Similarly, the display comprised of a knit brow, pursed lips or retracted lip corners with bared teeth, and fixated gaze (i.e., the "about to attack" face) is held in the Emotions View to express anger. For the behavioral ecologist, making an "about to strike" face serves to repel an interactant, and acting this way can occur for many reasons and amid circumstances that could connote many emotions. Indeed, we make this face not only when we are angry, but when we are helpless, frightened ("defensive"), frustrated, exasperated, bored, or engaging in a fit of bravado.

The social-motive analysis of threat displays follows that for smiles. I know of no evidence that we make threatening "attack" faces more when we are angry. If we do, it may be because when we are angry we often seek out another to provoke. We make threat faces in the process, but the faces serve the provocation rather than the anger occasioning it (again, anger is just *one* emotion that can lead us to provoke another). Moreover, our attacking another in anger may occur only if we believe that events that anger us mandate confrontation and retaliation; alternatively, our anger should occasion smiling if we believe that anger mandates supplication or even a sly con. These beliefs may be individual or cultural.

Displays should generally be issued when they are likeliest to benefit the displayer. In no case would they be readouts of varying states like "emotion." When is a display maximally beneficial? (Predicting such optimality mathematically is the focus of the "game-theoretic" analysis of displays in modern ethology [Caryl, 1979; Maynard Smith, 1982].) A loud bellow when conditions are *not* threatening – or, for that matter, every fifteen minutes around the clock – may alert others of one's RHP (Resource Holding Potential) and forestall predation far better than one issued contingent upon another's attack. To continue the logic: (1) one should not cry whenever one is saddest, but when succor is needed and most readily available; (2) one should not produce a "fright" display when afraid unless submission is advantageous or rescue is desired, and these conditions may hold even when one happens not to be afraid. The form and intensity of a display, and the alignment of the display with personal resources or intentions, would depend on contextual factors such as common interests, availability of resources, and presence of kin, intruders, or predators (Ricklefs, 1979).

The Emotions View takes a crypto-moralistic view of deception.

Within the Emotions View, what is "hidden" in deception is ostensibly detectable through "leakage" from unmanaged behavior (Ekman, 1981; Ekman & Friesen, 1969). The Emotions View thus makes deception something that requires some cognitive sophistication – since infants are not supposed to be able to do it, and since people must *learn* to do it by counteracting the expression of their "authentic" selves. The facts belie this.

Deception is *not* restricted to socialized humans, nor does it require learning or cognitive sophistication. Far from it. It spans the animal and botanical kingdoms. Morphological deceptions (mimicries) are common in plants and insects. Behavioral deceptions are widely reported in insects, crustaceans, fish, birds, and marsupials (see Fridlund, 1994, for review). Deception appears commonplace among mammals generally, including monkeys (Cheney & Seyfarth, 1990) and the great apes (e.g., de Waal, 1982, 1989). Given these nonhuman deceptions, it is difficult to argue that our progenitors were naive, authentic expressors of felt emotion who were forced inexorably to dissimulate as human culture developed. Nonhuman signals do not resemble the "emotional expressions" of two-factor theories. Rather, nonhuman displays seem as thoroughly embedded in social relations as the faces we make ourselves (see review by Fridlund, 1994).

Various studies have claimed to show leakage of emotion in deceit (DePaulo, 1992), but these studies have found only signs of agitation or "displacement behaviors" like lip biting. True demonstrations of "leakage" require not only that the "leaked" emotion be detectable but that it be *decodable* (i.e., what one "leaks" must predict the emotion that one is attempting to hide). These demonstrations have not been forthcoming.

For the behavioral ecologist, the leakage conception is a Freudian atavism, and again, "leakage" reflects conflict among intentions (i.e., "I want to indicate X and I *don't* want to indicate X."). That many researchers have retained the view that deception *qua* deception produces leakage results from the studies they have designed, which typically required that subjects deceive by stating counterfactuals or taking morally objectionable positions. Consequently, for most subjects, *deception was confounded with conflict about deceiving*. This conflict can be moral (wanting to comply by lying versus believing that one shouldn't lie anyway) or pragmatic (wanting to comply by lying versus expecting nonetheless that there will be hell to pay). I know of only one study that included the obvious controls to rule out conflict as the source of "leakage" – the inclusion of situations contrived such that subjects both deceive *and* endorse their deception. Bavelas and colleagues devised such a situation and thereby established the importance of the conflict view (Bavelas, Black, Chovil, & Mullett, 1990). Subjects had to lie in order to keep secret a friend's surprise birthday party. They lied perfectly and showed no "leakage."

The Emotions View holds erroneously that the existence of "facial expressions of emotion" is demonstrated by the dual neurological control of facial expressions.

Within the Emotions View, one ground for claiming the existence of hard-wired, prototypical "facial expressions of emotion" depends upon neurology. The logic goes as follows: There is neurological "dual control" of the face shown in studies of neurological lesions. Damage to neocortical areas results in the loss of voluntary facial expressions but the sparing of "emotional" expressions, which are controlled by the primitive subcortex. Conversely, damage to subcortical areas results in the loss of "emotional expressions" but the sparing of voluntary ones.

This constitutes validation for the "two-factor" Emotions View of facial expression as representing a blend of "emotional" and "social" faces. In actuality, there is nothing unique about the neurology of facial expressions, because the same kinds of phenomena occur outside of the face.

There do appear to be two sets of neural controls of facial expression. The evidence comes from two phenomena in clinical neurology. The first is that of *central facial paralysis* (also, *corticobulbar palsy*), which occurs with a stroke or other brain lesion that damages the upper motor neurons emanating from the precentral motor strip. Individuals with this syndrome have intact facial reflexes and can produce normal symmetrical smiles when told jokes or tickled. When they are asked to move their lower facial muscles, however, their movements are dramatically weakened. (They are weaker on the side of the face contralateral to the lesion; symmetrical movement is retained in the upper face. The reasons are arcane and are found in the details of facial embryology [see Fridlund, 1994].)

The second syndrome is termed *reverse facial paralysis* (and, oftentimes, *mimetic palsy* or *amimia*). As expected, those afflicted with this syndrome can make facial movements to command, but their faces are largely immobile and almost masklike, missing the apparently spontaneous faces that occur in greeting, joking, and everyday conversation. Reverse facial paralysis occurs with an intact motor strip and upper motor neurons, and thus another brain area or areas must be damaged to account for the deficient facial behavior. What exactly is the brain locus? One of the clues derives from brain autopsies from individuals who suffered reverse facial paralysis. Another derives from the disorder of Parkinson's disease, which produces the same masklike amimia, along with the preservation of movements to command. Both seem to involve the destruction of structures such as the basal ganglia (which includes structures like the caudate nucleus, putamen, globus pallidus, and the claustrum), substantia nigra, red nucleus, thalamus, the pontine reticular formation, and an assortment of other subcortical areas that, collectively, are known as the *extrapyramidal motor system*. Wilson (1924) first proposed that the faces preserved in central facial paralysis were controlled by this system.

It is clear, then, that central and reverse paralysis form a classic two-by-two double dissociation between lesion and behavior (Teuber, 1955) – following lesions in one region but not another, certain faces are spared but others are impaired. But what do we call the faces that are spared and those that are impaired? As I mentioned, the faces spared and impaired in central versus reverse facial paralysis have often been distinguished as "nonemotional" and "emotional" and used to buttress a two-factor Emotions View. But evidence from two other neurological disorders argues that this interpretation is too parochial.

The first is a type of aphasia (speech disorder) known as *apraxia of speech*. Individuals with this syndrome cannot "propositionize" (to use J. Hughlings Jackson's term), or construct a speech utterance from their verbal lexicons (Head, 1926). Depending upon the severity of the syndrome, sufferers of apraxia of speech can with some effort push out words when coaxed, but most often they communicate by resorting to pantomime and other gesticulation. Curiously, some speech remains even in the most severe cases; it is usually termed *automatic speech*. What remains are utterances that require no construction; these are overlearned phrases like rhymes and songs, exclamations, prayers, the alphabet, counting, and the days of the week or months of the year. Once cued, those with apraxia of speech can usually sound off the sequence with reasonable fluency. When asked what they just uttered, they cannot verbalize their response (Martin, 1988).

The second disorder is termed *ideomotor apraxia*, and it affects nonspeech limb and finger movements (e.g., Brown, 1972). As in apraxia of speech, musculoskeletal function is uncompromised, but sufferers are unable to execute even simple movements to command. For example, patients with ideomotor apraxia may be unresponsive when asked to lick their lips, purse their lips and blow, or extend one hand and turn it. And like apraxia of speech, certain movements remain. If asked to drink, they show normal lip licking after swallowing. If a lit match is held to the mouth, they will likely blow it out. If a key is pressed into the one hand and a locked padlock is presented, they can place the key in the lock and turn it.

Both apraxia of speech and ideomotor apraxia are manifest by impairments in constructing movements but the retention of overlearned, habitual speech or movements. It is reasonable, then, to wonder whether central facial paralysis should be considered a type of apraxia. The same kinds of commands that fail to produce faces in central facial paralysis fail to elicit speech-related movements in apraxia of speech and instrumental movements in ideomotor apraxia. The same kinds of routinized cues that produce automatic speech in apraxia of speech ("Recite the Lord's Prayer") and instrumental acts in ideomotor apraxia (e.g., holding a match to the lips) are duplicated in tasks designed to elicit "emotional" faces (e.g., joke telling). It thus seems unnecessary to use the "emotional" versus "nonemotional" dichotomy for faces when the results of neurological lesions can be cast in the "constructed" versus "habitual" terms of generic dual motor control.

The Emotions View neglects the sociality that is implicit even when displayers are alone.

Solitary faces do of course occur, and this fact is often touted as definitive evidence for some faces being by nature readouts or expressions of emotion rather than social, communicative displays (see Buck, 1984, 1985; Cacioppo & Tassinary, 1987). As Buck (1984) put it,

> When a sender is alone . . . he or she should feel little pressure to present a proper image to others, and any emotion expression under such circumstances should be more likely to reflect an actual motivational/emotional state. (p. 20)

Ekman took the same tack when he described a study of differences in facial displays among Japanese and Americans. Ekman stated,

> In private, when no display rules to mask expression were operative, we saw the biologically based, evolved, universal facial expressions of emotion. (Ekman, 1984)

The most pointed declaration of the reliance of the emotions view upon the supposed emotional nature of solitary faces was provided by Ekman, Davidson, and Friesen (1990), who stated,

> Facial expressions do occur when people are alone . . . and contradict the theoretical proposals of those who view expressions solely as social signals. (p. 351)

The belief that faces observed in solitude constitute the definitive evidence for "facial expressions of emotion" is instantiated in the experiments typically conducted by proponents of the Emotions View. Experimental subjects are usually isolated in a laboratory room and presented various kinds of "emotional" elicitors. Many of these are depicted in the panels of Figure 5.3. These include panels: (A) face-to-face contact; (B) contact through a partition or laboratory wall; (C) watching television; (D) imagery tasks; and (E) viewing slides. Because subjects are physically alone in panels (B) though (E), any facial displays elicited in subjects are considered "expressions of emotion." The exception is panel (A), face-to-face contact, which is considered "social" and therefore produces a combination of both emotional and conventional faces.

Contrary to this categorization, I contend that a binary view of what

Figure 5.3. Disguised sociality in common methods of eliciting "emotional" facial expressions.

is "social" and what is "nonsocial" is too absolutist. It is much more reasonable to suggest instead that the manipulations in Figure 5.3 vary in their sociality. Everyone considers face-to-face contact (A) quite social, but does speaking through a glass or partition (B) make it nonsocial? I think not, but then what if the glass is a TV screen (C)? Asserting that watching a televised image is not social would be news to soap-opera lovers who consider the characters to be intimate acquaintances, and to sports fans who throw things at the screen. And what if the image is not on the TV but in my mind's eye (D)? Finally, what if I freeze a frame of an image and show a photo (E)? Would this make viewing a face nonsocial? Not necessarily, as sales of baby and family albums would attest; the photos in them are not mere spots of chromatic dye – they are cues to the reconstruction of interactions (i.e., panel D). In this sense, a still image of a face is a projective stimulus. When a patient examines a TAT (Thematic Apperception Test) card and begins to shake, blanch, and then burst into tears, it's not the ink on the card. Ditto for still images, but their use has nevertheless been canonized as the "slide-viewing technique" (Buck, 1979), and pictorial depictions were used in nearly all studies of "facial expressions of emotion" among different populations (see Russell, 1994).

Sociality does not conform to the all-or-none law. Instead, the varying types of "emotional elicitors" in Figure 5.3 represent simply different kinds of sociality. Even when an interactant has been physically removed from the room, he or she may still be present psychologically. This implicit sociality view is far from novel. Even though Darwin (1872, pp. 6–8) dismissed it given his overriding interest in building a Lamarckian, reflexive model of faces as vestiges of once-serviceable habits (Fridlund, 1992, 1994; Montgomery, 1985), Wundt (1896), Piderit (1858, 1886), Gratiolet (1865), and Ribot (1897) all proposed "imaginary object" accounts of solitary faces made toward absent others.

It seems obvious to me that the physical presence of others is one of the *least* important ways of assessing the sociality of facial displays. There are several ways in which people can be structurally alone, with their facial behavior implicitly social.

First, *when we are alone we often treat ourselves as interactants*. We talk to ourselves; reward or punish ourselves; hit, touch, and stroke ourselves; and deploy facial displays in the course of these acts. Can it be said that talking to ourselves is not communicative but a "readout"? If so, what is being read out? In this sense, the faces made to oneself are as communicative as our "self-talk." That we are social interactants with ourselves at first seems absurdly solipsistic, but it is entirely consistent with views that emphasize the "private, authentic self" as a social construction (Mead, 1934) and the dialogical nature of thought as internalized speech (Bakhtin, 1981; Vygotsky, 1962; Wertsch, 1985).

Second, *we often act as if others are present when they are not*. We curse them, or utter words of love to them, or rehearse what we will say to them when we see them. In many of these acts, we deploy facial displays. Our acting as if others are there when they are not is usually done with prior knowledge of their absence (e.g., practicing for a play, talk, or interview). Occasionally, it is done without prior knowledge of others' absence, as when we speak to and make faces to a person we believe is in the next room – when the other has in fact departed and can no longer hear us. With or without prior knowledge, these faces, too, are communicative, although they are emitted when we are alone.

Third, *we often imagine that others are present when they are not*. In our imagination we engage in interactions with others who are not there (i.e., we "simulate" interaction with them). We imagine talking to them, arguing with them, making love with them, and we often deploy facial displays. As in the previous example, we usually have prior knowledge that the others are absent. However, we sometimes become lost in reverie, and we momentarily forget that the imaginary others are actually absent. The facial displays made in reverie are also communicative, both when we are lost in reverie and *believe* they are there, and when we know that they are not. When we imagine a lover, and then smile and become sexually aroused, if we say that the smile was nonsocial, would we say that the arousal was nonsexual?

That implicit audiences mediate solitary faces has been documented in several experiments. Fridlund et al. (1990) established the role of imaginary audiences in mediating private faces. Subjects provided, and were then asked to imagine, situations that they enjoyed either alone (low-social) or with other people (high-social). We measured smiling during the imagery using facial electromyography (EMG) overlying the *zygomatic major* muscles, and we asked subjects to rate how happy they felt during the imagery. These happiness ratings were then controlled statistically. Subjects showed more EMG activity in their *zygomatic major* sites in high-social than low-social imagery, even when their happiness ratings were equalized. For Fridlund et al., this increase implied that subjects were displaying to the "people in their heads." Fridlund, Kenworthy, and Jaffey (1992) later extended these findings to dysphoric imagery using a standard imagery protocol.

Fridlund (1991b) attempted to circumvent the slipperiness of imagery manipulations by directly manipulating implicit audiences. Subjects watched an amusing videotape in one of four viewing conditions: (1) alone; (2) alone, but with the belief that a friend nearby was performing an irrelevant task; (3) alone, but with the belief that a friend nearby was viewing the same videotape in another room; and (4) when a friend was physically present. Viewers' smiles were measured using facial electromyography (EMG) over the *zygomatic major* muscles responsible for smiling. Smiling (measured using EMG) among solitary viewers who believed a friend was viewing nearby equaled that shown in the actual presence of the friend but was greater than that shown by subjects who simply viewed alone. Reported happiness did not differ among the viewing conditions, and within conditions it correlated negligibly with smiling.

Similar findings emerged from another study involving gradations in sociality, where Chovil (1991) visually coded the types of gestures made in different social contexts. Her subjects (here, all females) heard stories about close calls in one of four conditions: (1) alone, from an audio tape recording; (2) alone, over the telephone; (3) from another subject across a partition; and (4) talking to another subject face-to-face. When these conditions were ordered according to their "psychological presence," as determined by separate raters, Chovil's subjects exhibited facial displays – largely wincing and grimacing – that increased monotonically with sociality, a finding that mapped nearly identically onto that provided by Fridlund (1991b).

In these sociality studies, face-to-face interaction resulted in maximal facial behavior. This should not always be the case, however, because in many contexts we do *not* issue communications to others. Friends sharing a humorous experience face-to-face should exhibit greater facial behavior than if they are separated by a partition; friends asked to play poker should make less. One important determinant of our facial behavior is our social role with respect to our potential interactants. Commuters on a subway may be within inches of each other yet pretend not to notice; if they are friends, however, their talk and facial behavior may be incessant. (There are exceptions, as when we "spill our guts" to a total stranger on a plane, and here, our faces pour out with our words.) Just this kind of finding was reported by Wagner and Smith (1991), who videotaped pairs of subjects while they "rated their emotions" to slides. The facial behavior of the subjects was more discernible if the two were friends than if they were strangers. In the Behavioral Ecology View, the subjects' faces were no more than a running commentary on the series of slides. Had they been permitted, the friends would have chatted while they made faces; and the strangers would have done neither. And it is hard to strip an experiment of the influence of such social roles. To the solitary subject, the experiment is a judge, and the subject is in temporary solitary confinement awaiting parole for "good behavior." Two male or two female subjects in the same room may make a contest out of the experiment, whereas an experiment with a (heterosexual) male–female pair may become a "blind date."

Fourth, *we often forecast interaction and deploy displays appropriately*, consciously or not, even though no interactant is immediately present. These displays function in the service of seeking or shunning interaction. Most species have displays that function to deter potential interactants. In both gorillas and humans, a tongue-showing display deters others (Smith, Chase, & Lieblich, 1974; Dolgin & Sabini, 1982). If we are in a bad mood, we scowl upon entering the office in the morning; the scowl discourages potential greeting. On the other hand, solicitation of interaction is omnipresent (cf. the "readiness to interact" displays described by Smith, 1977). We deploy a smile seconds before greeting a neighbor at the front door. As T. S. Eliot stated, "I must prepare a face to meet the faces that I meet." Indeed, Kraut and Johnston (1979) found that bowlers were very unlikely to smile when they had just made a spare or strike but were very likely to do so when they turned around to meet the gaze of those in their bowling party. And like the bird who calls continuously in case a suitable mate should fly past (Smith, 1977), the human infant solving a problem deploys a "cognitive mastery" smile (Sroufe & Waters, 1976). The smile usually seduces any potential pedagogues who may encounter the infant.

This was confirmed by Sue Jones and colleagues, who developed an infant analog to Kraut and Johnston's (1979) bowling study. Infants were positioned such that they could either look at toys or at their mothers, and Jones et al. observed their facial behavior toward each. As early as 10 months of age, infant smiling was almost entirely dependent upon visual contact with the caregiver (Jones & Raag, 1989; Jones, Collins, & Hong, 1991).

Fifth, *we often treat nonhumans, and animate and inanimate objects, as interactants.* That we often treat nonhuman animals as humans is self-evident to any pet owner. We talk to them, confide in them, praise and curse them, and make faces and gesture to them. Most people have no difficulty according pets agency and treating them as autonomous interactants. What is more reluctantly acknowledged is the extent to which we accord agency to inanimate objects and regard *them* as interactants. Devotees of indoor gardening talk, gesture, and make faces to their houseplants. Children do the same to their stuffed animals, dolls, or toy soldiers. In outbursts of animism, most of us have pummeled intransigent soda machines that "stole our money" or television sets that "lost our station," or gesticulated wildly at willful, errant bowling balls, and in so doing we scolded them, called them names and, in the act, we made faces and gestures.

Is this implicit sociality account viable? In the implicit sociality view, implicit or imaginary interactants can never be excluded. Even recruiting subjects alone and leading them to believe that they are "unobserved" (e.g., using a hidden camera) do not eliminate the implicit social context. At the limit, the *experimenters* still constitute an implicit audience; with the wall of the laboratory – with the experimenters behind it – constituting a de facto partition condition just as in Figure 5.3 (B). The power of such an arrangement is commonly acknowledged as "experimental demand," "experimenter effects," or "evaluation apprehension" (Latané, 1981).

Subjects' thoughts will *always* be populated, I believe, by thoughts or images either of the experimenter, or the others in their lives, or even themselves; moreover, we convert inanimate objects into interactants. I call this process *restitutional interaction* (after Bleuler). Achieving pure "aloneness" is a *reductio ad absurdum* that would require narcotization so complete that daydreaming stops, and this would terminate most overt subject behavior, not just facial movement. This fact undercuts any presumption that isolating subjects or minimizing their physical contact with others actually "purifies" their facial productions in any way. Our solitary faces may thus be just as conventional as our "social" ones. When subjects are alone versus in the presence of others, what differs is not the "amount" of sociality but its directness, or the degree to which one's social engagement is entrained to *specifiable* others (i.e., those planted in the room by the experimenter).

It might be objected that the implicit sociality view is nondisconfirmable. In fact, it probably is unfalsifiable *in extremis*, but this is no impediment to its viability as a scientific concept. This feature is shared with many useful and established theories whose limiting cases are unattainable. One clear example is superconductivity theory: Even though the temperature of absolute zero seems unattainable, potent and useful superconductivity effects can be observed as one approaches it. Likewise, implicit sociality can be studied quite easily within experimentally manipulable ranges.

The strict falsifiability objection is also instructive in that it reveals the extent to which we view most animals (especially humans) atomistically instead of as components of, and agents within, an encompassing web of social relations – even when alone (see Mead, 1934). Indeed, "solitude" – not implicit sociality – may be the odder concept.

Summary

In the Behavioral Ecology View, facial expressions are not readouts of "emotional state," nor are they the compromise formations of an "authentic" self inhibited by a "social" one. Displays evolve, phylogenetically or culturally, in particulate fashion in response to specific selection pressures, and they necessarily co-evolve with others' responsivity to them. Displays have meanings specifiable only in their context of occurrence, and they are issued to serve one's social motives in that context. These motives bear no necessary relation to *emotion* as the term is commonly used, and indeed, a range of "emotions" can co-occur with any social motive. As manipulations serving intent, displays are issued when they will optimally enhance cultural or genetic inclusive fitness. The faces made in solitude are no more or less "social" than those observed in public, because people are always implicitly social even when schematically alone. Experimental methods that isolate subjects in order to observe "emotional expressions" merely disguise the sociality that governs them.

Is the Behavioral Ecology View antagonistic to *emotion*? Not in the slightest. It simply regards the term as unnecessary to understand how our facial expressions both evolved and operate in modern life. Perhaps what I stated in *Human Facial Expression* (Fridlund, 1994) offers the best coda:

> I suggest that facial displays can be understood without recourse to emotions or emotion terms, and I show that certain tenets of the Emotions View are improbable or unworkable. What cannot be done is to show that emotions have no role in facial displays, because excluding emotion would require a definition that allowed it. At present, arguing against "emotion" in any form is shadow-boxing.
>
> In the end, emotion may be to the face as Ryle's "ghost" (Ryle, 1949) was to the machine. "Emotions" and homuncular "ghosts" may both be constructions borne of a transcendentalist wish for something more than function or mechanism. If psychology's "Cognitive Revolution" dispatched the need for a managerial homunculus in the nervous system, so then we must finally dispatch the notion that the face mirrors the passions of the soul. But this conclusion may be premature. For the time being, the only rejoinder to those who question whether any facial display might be related to emotion is, "What do you mean by emotion"? (p. 186)

Acknowledgment

Portions of this chapter are from Fridlund (1994), reprinted with permission.

Notes

1 "Behavioral ecology" is, technically, the branch of zoology in which behavior is examined for the ways that it contributes to reproductive success (see Krebs & Davies, 1987). Behavioral ecologists thus study how behavior emerges within an animal's "ecology" – that is, within its social organization and its environmental niche. Because it conceives of expressive movements and receptivity for them as highly interdependent, the terms *interactional* or *communicative* could easily be substituted. (See Chovil, chapter 14, this volume, for a linguistically based and compatible communicative account.)

2 There are constraints on the number of displays within any species or for any motive. For example, the added specificity of separate displays for, say, exasperation versus constipation (Russell, 1994) would create an extra perceptual burden for recipients. Moreover, little such evolution would occur if the displays were needlessly specific because the context carried the necessary information (e.g., the contexts for exasperation and constipation are wholly different). Tallying the numbers of displays is complicated in any case, since display taxonomies can be structural or functional, and the functional taxonomies must also tabulate the contexts in which displays are deployed.

3 Throughout this chapter, I use the word *emotion* only as a prop, because the

proponents of the Emotions View all use the term but mean different things by it. This is evident in the contributions to this volume by Izard and by Frijda and Tcherkassof. Despite their excellent defenses of two variations on the Emotions View, both illustrate the difficulties inherent in trying to retain "emotion" as an explanation for human facial expression. The pivotal question to ask of each is, "When should facial expressions occur and when should they not?"

For Izard (see chapter 3, this volume), "facial expression . . . is conceived as an evolved, genetically influenced but highly modifiable and dissociable component of emotion," but he then states that "observable expression is not viewed as a necessary component of emotion." Thus, emotion can include facial expression, but it can occur without an expression, and furthermore, expression can occur without emotion. What are the conditions of linkage and dissociation that would produce each? Izard is unclear. He appends the term *motivational* to *emotional* to describe states that might elicit facial expressions, while also suggesting that emotion can occur without occasioning motives, after having stated earlier that "emotions motivate and organize perception, cognition, and action." When, then, should a facial expression occur: When emotion motivates, when it does not, or doesn't it matter? This I cannot glean from Izard's chapter.

The chapter by Frijda and Tcherkassof contains a corresponding set of semantic tangles. After a quite literate introduction to the problems faced by a traditional Emotions View of facial expression, the authors conclude that facial expressions are not adequately described in terms of "emotion." Instead, facial expressions usually point to a motivational state . . . which we call the individual's *states of action readiness*. Facial expressions express states of action readiness. After these declarations, do the authors forsake emotion? Far from it, because emotions are states of action readiness. In fact, they constitute the "core" of emotions. Here this theory parallels Izard's on emotion and motivation. Emotion can engender action readiness, but action readiness is only one of the moderately correlated components of emotion, and can occur without emotion. On the question of when a facial expression occurs, Frijda and Tcherkassof logically concluded, where Izard demurred, that facial expressions of emotion occur if and only if the emotion is accompanied by a state of action readiness. In taking this step, the authors remove emotion from the direct causal chain, since action readiness is only one moderately correlated component of emotion, and since many factors other than emotion can occasion action readiness.

What is also notable from the two chapters – and is frankly pandemic among expositors of the Emotions View – is that the differences in how they use the term *emotion* indicate that they are talking about two different constructs. Neither offers a proper technical definition of emotion, one which would stipulate criteria – independent of facial expression – for when emotion is occurring (an inclusion criterion) and when it is not (an exclusion criterion). How can we entertain a theory whose critical term cannot be defined concretely and consensually?

References

Alcock, J. (1984). *Animal behavior: An evolutionary approach* (3rd ed.). Sunderland, MA: Sinauer.

Andrew, R. J. (1963a). Evolution of facial expression. *Science, 141,* 1034–1041.

Andrew, R. J. (1963b). The origin and evolution of the calls and facial expressions of the primates. *Behavior, 20,* 1–109.

Andrew, R. J. (1964). The displays of the primates. In J. Buettner-Janusch (Ed.), *Evolutionary and genetic biology of primates* (Vol. 2, pp. 227–309). New York: Academic Press.

Andrew, R. J. (1972). The information potentially available in displays. In R. A. Hinde (Ed.), *Nonverbal communication.* New York: Cambridge University Press.

Argyle, M. (1972). Non-verbal communication in human social interaction (pp. 243–269). In R. A. Hinde (Ed.), *Nonverbal communication.* New York: Cambridge University Press.

Baer, K. E. von (1828). *Entwicklungsgeschichte der Thiere: Beobachtung und Reflexion.* Königsberg, Germany: Bornträger.

Bakhtin, M. M. (1981). *The dialogical imagination* (M. Holquist, Ed.). Austin, TX: University of Texas Press.

Bavelas, J. B., Black, A., Chovil, N., & Mullett, J. (1990). Truths, lies, and equivocations: The effects of conflicting goals on discourse. *Journal of Language and Social Psychology, 9,* 135–161.

Brothers, L. (1992). Perception of social acts in primates: Cognition and neurobiology. *Seminars in the Neurosciences, 4,* 409–414.

Brown, J. D. (1972). *Aphasia, apraxia, and agnosia.* Springfield, IL: Charles Thomas.

Buck, R. (1979). Measuring individual differences in the nonverbal communication of affect: The slide-viewing paradigm. *Human Communication Research, 6,* 47–57.

Buck, R. (1984). *The communication of emotion.* New York: Guilford.

Buck, R. (1985). Prime theory: An integrated view of motivation and emotion. *Psychological Review, 92,* 389–413.

Cacioppo, J. T., & Tassinary, L. G. (1987). The relationship between EMG response and overt facial actions. *Face Value, 1,* 2–3.

Caryl, P. G. (1979). Communication by agonistic displays: What can games theory contribute to ethology? *Behaviour, 68,* 136–169.

Cheney, D. L., & Seyfarth, R. M. (1990). *How monkeys see the world.* Chicago: University of Chicago Press.

Chovil, N. (1991). Social determinants of facial displays. *Journal of Nonverbal Behavior, 15,* 141–154.

Darwin, C. R. (1872). *The expression of the emotions in man and animals.* London: Albemarle.

DePaulo, B. M. (1992). Nonverbal behavior and self-presentation. *Psychological Bulletin, 111,* 203–243.

de Waal, F. (1982). *Chimpanzee politics.* New York: Harper & Row.

de Waal, F. (1989). *Peacemaking among primates.* Cambridge, MA: Harvard University Press.

Dolgin, K., & Sabini, J. (1982). Experimental manipulation of a human non-verbal display: The tongue show affects an observer's willingness to interact. *Animal Behaviour, 30,* 935–936.

Ekman, P. (1981). Mistakes when deceiving. *Annals of the New York Academy of Sciences, 364,* 269–278.

Ekman, P., Davidson, R. J., & Friesen, W. V. (1990). The Duchenne smile: Emotional expression and brain psysiology II. *Journal of Personality and Social Psychology, 58,* 342–353.

Ekman, P., & Fridlund, A. J. (1987). Assessment of facial behavior in affective disorders. In J. D. Maser (Ed.), *Depression and expressive behavior.* Hillsdale, NJ: Erlbaum.

Ekman, P., & Friesen, W. V. (1969). Nonverbal leakage and clues to deception. *Psychiatry, 1,* 88–105.

Fridlund, A. J. (1986, October). *Emotion – How we have strayed from Darwin and lost our way.* Paper presented at the Historical Symposium on Emotion, 26th Annual Meeting of the Society for Psychophysiological Research, Montreal.

Fridlund, A. J. (1991a). Evolution and facial action in reflex, social motive, and paralanguage. *Biological Psychology, 32,* 3–100.

Fridlund, A. J. (1991b). Sociality of solitary smiling: Potentiation by an implicit audience. *Journal of Personality and Social Psychology, 60,* 229–240.

Fridlund, A. J. (1992). Darwin's anti-Darwinism in *The expression of the emotions in man and animals.* In K. Strongman (Ed.), *International review of emotion* (Vol. 2, pp. 117–137). Chichester: Wiley.

Fridlund, A. J. (1994). *Human facial expression: An evolutionary view.* San Diego, CA: Academic Press.

Fridlund, A. J., Ekman, P., & Oster, H. (1987). Facial expressions of emotion. In A. Siegman & S. Feldstein (Eds.), *Nonverbal behavior and communication* (2nd ed., pp. 143–224). Hillsdale, NJ: Erlbaum.

Fridlund, A. J., & Izard, C. E. (1983). Electromyographic studies of facial expressions of emotions and patterns of emotions. In J. T. Cacioppo & R. E. Petty (Eds.), *Social psychophysiology: A sourcebook* (pp. 243–286). New York: Guilford Press.

Fridlund, A. J., Kenworthy, K. G., & Jaffey, A. K. (1992). Audience effects in affective imagery: Replication and extension to affective imagery. *Journal of Nonverbal Behavior, 16,* 191–212.

Fridlund, A. J., Sabini, J. P., Hedlund, L. E., Schaut, J. A., Shenker, J. I., & Knauer, M. J. (1990). Social determinants of facial expressions during affective imagery: Displaying to the people in your head. *Journal of Nonverbal Behavior, 14,* 113–137.

Fridlund, A. J., Schwartz, G. E., & Fowler, S. C. (1984). Pattern-recognition of self-reported emotional state from multiple-site facial EMG activity during affective imagery. *Psychophysiology, 21,* 622–637.

Ginsburg, G. P., & Harrington, M. (1993, May). *Emotions as features of situated lines of action.* Paper presented at the Nag's Head Conference on The Experience and Expression of Emotion, Boca Raton, Florida.

Gratiolet, P. (1865). *De la physionomie et des mouvements d'expression.* Paris: J. Hetzel.

Head, H. (1926). *Aphasia and kindred disorders of speech.* Cambridge: Cambridge University Press.

Hinde, R. A. (1985a). Expression and negotiation. In G. Zivin (Ed.), *The development of expressive behavior* (pp. 103–116). Orlando, FL: Academic Press.

Hinde, R. A. (1985b). Was "The expression of the emotions" a misleading phrase? *Animal Behaviour, 33,* 985–992.

Izard, C. E., & Malatesta, C. Z. (1987). Perspectives on emotional development I: Differential emotions theory of early emotional development. In J. Osofsky (Ed.), *Handbook of infant development* (rev. ed.). New York: Wiley-Interscience.

Jones, S. S., Collins, K., & Hong, H.- W. (1991). An audience effect on smile production in 10-month-old infants. *Psychological Science, 2,* 45–49.

Jones, S. S., & Raag, T. (1989). Smile production in older infants: The importance of a social recipient for the facial signal. *Child Development, 60,* 811–818.

Kendon, A. (1981). Introduction: Current issues in the study of "nonverbal communication." In A. Kendon (Ed.), *Nonverbal communication, interaction, and gesture* (pp. 1–53). Paris: Mouton.

Kraut, R. E., & Johnston, R. E. (1979). Social and emotional messages of smiling: An ethological approach. *Journal of Personality and Social Psychology, 37*, 1539–1553.

Krebs, J. R., & Davies, N. B. (1987). *An introduction to behavioral ecology* (2nd ed.). Sunderland, MA: Sinauer.

Krebs, J. R., & Dawkins, R. (1984). Animal signals: Mind-reading and manipulation. In J. R. Krebs & N. B. Davies (Eds.), *Behavioural ecology* (2nd ed., pp. 380–402). Oxford: Blackwell.

Latané, B. (1981). The psychology of social impact. *American Psychologist, 36*, 343–356.

Lewis, M., & Michalson, L. (1982). The socialization of emotions. In T. Field & A. Fogel (Eds.), *Emotion and early interaction*. Hillsdale, NJ: Erlbaum.

Lewis, M., & Michalson, L. (1985). Faces as signs and symbols. In G. Zivin (Ed.), *The development of expressive behavior* (pp. 183–219). Orlando, FL: Academic Press.

Mandler, G. (1984). *Mind and body*. New York: Norton.

Martin, A. D. (1988). The assessment of verbal expression. In F. C. Rose, R. Whurr, & M. A. Wyke (Eds.), *Aphasia*. London: Whurr.

Matsumoto, D., Ekman, P., & Fridlund, A. J. (1990). Analyzing nonverbal behavior. In P. Dowrick (Ed.), *A practical guide to using video in the behavioral sciences*. New York: Wiley.

Maynard Smith, J. (1982). *Evolution and the theory of games*. Cambridge: Cambridge University Press.

Mead, G. H. (1934). *Mind, self, and society from the standpoint of a social behaviorist*. Chicago: University of Chicago Press.

Meltzoff, A. N., & Moore, M. K. (1977). Imitation of facial and manual gestures by neonates. *Science, 198*, 75–78.

Montgomery, W. (1985). Charles Darwin's thought on expressive mechanisms in evolution. In G. Zivin (Ed.), *The development of expressive behavior* (pp. 27–50). Orlando, FL: Academic Press.

Ortony, A., & Turner, T. J. (1990). What's basic about basic emotions? *Psychological Review, 97*, 315–331.

Piderit, T. (1858). *Grundzüge der Mimik und physiognomik*. Brunswick, Germany: F. Vieweg und Sohn.

Piderit, T. (1886). *Mimik und physiognomik*. Detmold, Germany: Meyer.

Ribot, T. (1897). *The psychology of the emotions*. London: Walter Scott.

Ricklefs, R. E. (1979). *Ecology* (2nd ed.). New York: Chiron Press.

Russell, J. A. (1994). Is there universal recognition of emotion from facial expression? *Psychological Bulletin, 115*, 102–141.

Ryle, G. (1949). *The concept of mind*. London: Hutchinson.

Saarni, C. (1978). Cognitive and communicative features of emotional experience, or do you show what you think you feel? In M. Lewis & L. Rosenblum (Eds.), *The development of affect*. New York: Plenum.

Smith, W. J. (1977). *The behavior of communicating*. Cambridge, MA: Harvard University Press.

Smith, W. J. (1986). An "informational" perspective on manipulation. In R. W. Mitchell & N. S. Thompson (Eds.), *Perspectives on human and nonhuman deceit* (pp. 71–87). Albany, NY: State University of New York Press.

Smith, W. J., Chase, J., & Lieblich, A. K. (1974). Tongue showing: A facial display of humans and other primate species. *Semiotica, 11*, 201–246.

Sroufe, L. A., & Waters, E. (1976). The ontogenesis of smiling and laughter: A perspective on the organization of development in infancy. *Psychological Review, 83,* 173–189.

Teuber, H. L. (1955). Physiological psychology. *Annual Review of Psychology, 6,* 267–294.

Tinbergen, N. (1953). *Social behaviour in animals.* London: Chapman and Hall.

Vygotsky, L. S. (1962). *Thought and language.* Cambridge, MA: MIT Press.

Wagner, H. L., & Smith, J. (1991). Facial expression in the presence of friends and strangers. *Journal of Nonverbal Behavior, 15,* 201–214.

Wertsch, J. V. (1985). *Vygotsky and the social formation of mind.* Cambridge, MA: Harvard University Press.

Wilson, S. A. K. (1924). Some problems in neurology. II. Pathological laughing and crying. *Journal of Neurology and Psychopathology, 16,* 299–333.

Wundt, W. (1896). *Outline of psychology* (C. H. Judd, Trans.). New York: Stechert.

PART III

With a biological and developmental focus

6. Animal sounds and human faces: Do they have anything in common?

PETER MARLER AND CHRISTOPHER EVANS

A survey of the literature reveals that many who have commented on the signaling of animals ascribe to the view that all of their communicative signals are manifestations of emotion or affect. If this view were correct, then animal signals would have much in common with certain human facial expressions, widely regarded by some, if not by all, as uniquely revealing signs of emotion. The prevalence of this interpretation of animal signals is evident in the comments displayed in Table 6.1 on the vocalizations of monkeys and apes, drawn from a wide range of disciplines. Either explicitly or implicitly, each of them assumes parallels with human expressions of emotion. One aim of a program of research extending over a period of 15 years has been to subject the interpretation of animal signals as emotion-based to a critical appraisal. This chapter reviews some of the evidence that has been forthcoming and the possibility that it bears on our understanding of human emotional expressions.

As a point of departure, we began our studies by consulting dictionary definitions of *emotion*, of which we take the following, from the Random House Dictionary of the English Language (1981, p. 467), to be representative. "Emotion: an affective state of consciousness in which joy, sorrow, fear, hate, or the like, is expressed, as distinguished from cognitive and volitional states of consciousness" – "usually accompanied by certain physiological changes, as increased heartbeat, respiration or the like, and often overt manifestation, as crying, shaking, etc." We thought it likely that commentators on animal signaling probably subscribed to something equivalent to this folk psychology view of emotion, especially since they felt no need to present a more formal definition of what they implied by the term *emotion*. In seeking experimental approaches to the question of emotion, we focused especially on the issues of volition and cognition.

133

Table 6.1. *Interpretations of monkey signals as manifestations of affect, emotion, or motivation*

1. "The noises made by monkeys express their mood, and are effective in communicating it to others." (Rowell & Hinde, 1962, zoologists)
2. "Nonhuman primates can send complex messages about their motivational states; they communicate almost nothing about the state of their physical environments." (Lancaster, 1965, anthropologist)
3. "... all signals appear to be clearly related to the immediate emotional states of the signaling individuals and their levels of arousal." (Bastian, 1965, linguist)
4. "The use of both the face and the voice by rhesus monkeys in their natural habitat seems to be restricted to circumstances that connote emotion." (Myers, 1976, neurobiologist)
5. "... the nonhuman primate does not use the auditory medium to communicate whatever conceptual knowledge it possesses. The vocal repertoire appears to relate to affective rather than cognitive dimensions, the nature of the signal reflecting the emotional disposition of the caller." (Marin, Schwarz, & Saffran, 1979, psychiatrists)
6. "... the signal emitted by an animal is an expression of its affective condition, and the reception of the signal indicates the infection of others by the same condition – nothing more." (Luria, 1982, psychologist)

One reason for the assumption that animal signals are not under volitional control is their presumed automaticity. Do animals have elective control of signal production, or is animal signaling a completely impulsive behavior? Do animal signals share with human emotional expression the attribute of "unbidden occurrence," to borrow Ekman's (1992) felicitous phrase? Another quotation, from Derek Bickerton's thought-provoking book *Language and Species* (Bickerton, 1990) again illustrates the widely held view that volitional control of animal signaling is lacking. In discussing the probable vocal behavior of the ancestral primate, *Australopithecus afarensis*, he states that "If the performance of modern apes is anything to go by, it (*A. afarensis*) descended from a line in which certain vocalizations (alarm calls on the appearance of predators, food barks on the discovery of food) are quite automatic and impossible to suppress" (p. 142). If these constraints apply to creatures as closely related to humans as apes and protohumans, presumably they are even more relevant to the behavior of other animals.

Our approach to the issue of impulsiveness was based on the presumption that, if animals possess any ability to control signal production, this might be revealed by varying the signaler's social circumstances. Do they call if no one is there to hear them? By studying what we came to refer to as "audience effects," we sought to determine whether presence or absence of a companion as a potential signal receiver would have any effect on whether or not signals are in fact given. If their production is completely impulsive, a companion should not make any difference.

In addition to the presumed impulsiveness of animal signals, we thought it likely that another factor favoring an emotional view was the widespread impression that the external situations eliciting animal vocalizations are typically generalized and relatively unspecific. By analogy, the antecedent external conditions for the production of human facial expressions are also global and unspecific. Greater involvement of cognition in the process of signal production would presumably open up the potential for more specific relationships between eliciting circumstances and signal production, as when linguistic labels are applied to particular objects and events in the environment. It was our impression that a presumed lack of what we call *input specificity* gives further encouragement to the view that animal signals and human facial expressions of emotion have attributes in common. We use this term to refer to the range of external stimuli with which a given signal is associated. Thus, a low degree of input specificity implies a wide range of eliciting external circumstances, thereby circumscribing the kind of information that may be conveyed to others. Insofar as the range of eliciting stimuli is one major determinant of what signals mean, the issue of input specificity is germane to understanding how signals function in social communication (Marler, 1978).

We take it that these two issues – of impulsiveness and input specificity – are also relevant to our understanding of human facial expressions of emotion and the ways in which they can influence patterns of social interaction. The results of our studies suggest that there are indeed some parallels with the signaling of animals, which may be helpful in framing new questions about human facial expressions.

Note that the issues of impulsiveness and input specificity are not necessarily interrelated. A signaling system that is automatic and involuntary could have a high degree of input specificity. Similarly, a signal accessible to a wide range of external inputs could be under voluntary control. It would nevertheless be of special interest if we should find cases of animal signaling behavior that are under volitional control and also display high input specificity, since this combination is a necessary antecedent for the evolution of human linguistic behavior.

Over the past several years, we have endeavored to address the issues of impulsiveness and input specificity in animals, most recently using bird displays as subjects (reviews in Evans & Marler, 1995; Marler, Evans, & Hauser 1992; Marler, Karakashian, & Gyger, 1990). The results of our studies raise questions about the role of cognition in animal communication and indicate the inadequacy of the folk psychology view of emotion as a complete explanation for the production of animal signals.

Is there evidence for volitional control of animal signals?

First we focus on the question posed by Bickerton. If an animal is faced with a situation designed to elicit an emotion such as fear, as when it is confronted with a predator, must it inevitably and uncontrollably emit alarm calls regardless of all other considerations? We have addressed this issue using Golden Sebright chickens (*Gallus gallus*) as subjects. This is a strain not far removed from the ancestral junglefowl stock. As with all gallinaceous birds, chickens have a large vocal repertoire, including some of especial interest for this study. They have an interesting array of alarm calls and a call associated with the discovery of food (Collias, 1987). Alarm and food calls lend themselves to our purpose because we have some prospect of specifying the stimuli that elicit them.

We began with observational studies of the behavior of birds confined in large outdoor aviaries and exposed to an array of potential predators and food items (Gyger & Marler, 1988; Gyger, Marler, & Pickert, 1987). This work confirmed that in addition to a food call, there are two classes of alarm call, with qualitatively distinct, virtually antithetical acoustic structure. One call type is associated with distant aerial predators, such as a hawk overhead; the other is elicited by ground predators, such as a raccoon or a weasel (Gyger et al., 1987).

The alarm calls of birds

We found it difficult to address Bickerton's question under field conditions, both because such studies are dependent upon the chance appearance of potential predators, and because there is inadequate control over the social circumstances of the focal animal. We therefore developed a laboratory approach that permitted systematic experimental manipulation of factors such as predator type and social context. The first step was to find reliable means of eliciting alarm calls, established initially by using hawk-shaped models (Evans & Marler, 1991) as in the classic studies by Lorenz and Tinbergen (e.g., Tinbergen, 1948). In later experiments, we substituted video recordings or computer-generated images of predators, finding them to be as effective as models, with the advantage that, once digitized, it is easy to vary the properties of video images systematically (Evans, Evans, & Marler, 1993; Evans, Macedonia, & Marler, 1993; Evans & Marler, 1992).

In the spirit of Fridlund's (1994, and chapter 5, this volume) Behavioral Ecology View of human facial expressions, we reasoned that there must be both costs and benefits to alarm calling of animals, with a balance that would be strongly affected by whether or not the caller, as a potential target of predation, is alone or in a group. The question was posed experimentally as follows: Confronted with a situation that is known to elicit antipredator behavior (a predator video image), does a male chicken behave differently when alone or when in the presence of a companion? We placed a second cage next to that in which the subject male was confined and introduced a range of companions, including other males, familiar and unfamiliar adult females, chicks, and also a female of a closely related galliform species, the bobwhite quail *Colinus virginianus*. In control trials, the cage was empty. We then presented hawk stimuli in each of these social conditions.

Audience effects on alarm calling

The results of this "audience effect" experiment were striking. There was a significantly greater production of aerial alarm calls in the presence of conspecific companions, whether male or female, than when the male was either alone or adjacent to a female of another species (Gyger, Karakashian, & Marler, 1986; Karakashian, Gyger, & Marler, 1988).

As we studied videotapes of this behavior, we made a most interesting observation. A solitary male that failed to vocalize was not indifferent to the simulated hawk. On the contrary, the full suite of escape behaviors was evoked, including upward scanning, scuttling behavior, feather sleeking, crouching, and freezing. We could detect no difference in the male's behavior when alone and with a companion other than the change in the frequency of alarm calling. This finding presented an immediate challenge to Bickerton's assumption that animals are incapable of withholding vocal signals. It also led us to infer that the alarm calls are not inextricably associated with what we take to be a manifestation of the emotion of fear in these birds. Fearful behavior as such was not subject to audience effects, as far as we could see. Audience effects imply an unexpected lack of automaticity in the vocal behavior of birds.

The degree of behavioral flexibility would nevertheless be limited if the only relevant rule were that birds call when companions are present but remain silent when they are not. But, of course, this is an over-simplification. In some situations, solitary birds vocalize a great deal. In fact, we have found several further complications to the "audience effect."

Are audience effects on calling behavior universal?

In addition to aerial predator calls, we can also reliably elicit in the laboratory the other major class of chicken alarm calls – the ground predator alarm call – in this case, with videotapes of a mammalian predator, such as a raccoon (Evans, Evans, & Marler, 1993). Here the call type is quite different. Whereas aerial alarm calls consist of a single, long, low-amplitude note, occasionally repeated, ground alarm calls are pulsatile, highly repetitive, and much louder and far-carrying. The accompanying behavior is conspicuous, in complete contrast to the cryptic behavior associated with aerial alarm calling (Evans et al., 1993), which shares with passerine alarms some characteristics that likely make it more difficult to locate (Brown, 1982; Marler, 1957).

What is the effect of providing or removing a companion for a male engaged in responding to a ground predator? The answer is that there is no change. In this same study, we were able to replicate the audience effect on aerial alarm calling, but we found no evidence of an audience effect on production of the ground predator call (Evans & Marler, un-published data).

Behavior that accompanies the ground predator alarm call, as given to a fox or a raccoon, is the opposite of cryptic. As has been demonstrated for some other cases of antipredator behavior, such as the stotting of gazelles in response to a cheetah (Caro, 1986), the ground predator call seems likely to have multiple addressees, including not only companions but also the predator itself. In these circumstances, a strong audience effect would be functionally inappropriate.

Further complications: For different calls, different audience specifications

What constitutes an optimal audience? In one of our studies, we showed that male chickens court females of their own strain more intensely than females of other strains and that the level of sexual display is proportional to morphological similarity (Evans & Marler, 1992). Courting males are also sensitive to familiarity, with unfamiliar females of any type evoking more courtship than familiar females of the same kind. One might expect to find parallels with audience effects, and perhaps even sensitivity to kin relationships (cf. Sherman, 1977). To our surprise, we found that several chicken strains were equally potent in potentiating aerial alarm calling (Evans & Marler, 1992). Nor does familiarity affect the number of calls produced, and we have found no evidence that kinship plays any role. Thus, the visual criteria for an adequate audience for aerial alarm calling seem to be relatively general. There are also auditory contributions to audience effects (Evans & Marler, 1991), and here the optional requirements might be more specific. This modality may be less preoccupied with the predator than the visual system.

The gender of the audience is also unimportant with aerial predator calls; a male is just as effective an audience as a female. But now if we look at audience effects in another context – namely, food calling – we find a different set of rules. When males discover a favored food, they give a distinctive call that is a strong attractant for females (Hughes, Hughes, & Covalt-Dunning, 1982; Marler, Dufty, & Pickert, 1986a, b; Gyger & Marler, 1988). A female approaches a food-calling male at a run. The male then drops the food item before her, picks it up and drops it, still calling, and allows her to eat it without competition. Broody hens have a similar call and associated behavior used to attract their chicks to share food (Sherry, 1977). The food call is another case of signal production influenced by the presence of an audience, but the rules are different from those for alarm calling. Whereas a female audience potentiates male calling when food is discovered, the presence of a male audience actively inhibits food calling.

This contrast in male and female audience effects on food calling in chickens is functionally appropriate. Food calling in the presence of a female is commonly a prelude to courtship. The proffering of valued foods by a male, even when he himself is hungry, is a clear case of a sexual investment. Such behavior would be functionally inappropriate if the recipient were a potential sexual competitor such as another male.

What about the issue of audience familiarity? In the case of food calling, the signaler is sensitive not only to the sex of an audience but also to prior acquaintanceship. A male food calls significantly more to a strange hen than to a familiar one. With alarm calls, there is no such distinction between familiar and strange audiences. There is also the question of audience species-specificity. This has not yet been fully defined but seems to vary between call systems. The degree of species-specificity for an optimal audience effect is high with food calling, but it is much lower with the aerial alarm call, at least in the visual domain, and even a member of another species may exert some audience effect (Evans & Marler, 1991).

It becomes clear that the rules for audience effects vary from one functional system to another, in ways that make functional sense.

Could audience effects result from social facilitation?

Unlikely as it may seem, given the variation in audience effect rules from one call system to another, it is still conceivable that the audience effect on calling is not a result of the specific potentiation or inhibition of vocalization but rather a case of social facilitation (Zajonc, 1965). Changes in call production could simply be an artifact associated with a lowering of the threshold for behavior in general, such as might be associated with changes in levels of arousal (Dewsbury, 1992). By requiring cockerels to key peck to obtain food, and showing that a female audience enhances food calling but does not change the rate of key pecking, we have effectively ruled out this interpretation (Evans & Marler, 1994).

So we have another line of evidence indicating a degree of dissociation of signal production from other associated behaviors within what might be viewed as a single "emotional" complex. Neither food calls nor aerial alarm calls are integral and inseparable parts of their associated physiological states, presumed to be emotional in the latter (i.e., fear), and motivational (hunger) in the former. Rather, the calls may be viewed as commentaries on those states that can be given or withheld according to the caller's social circumstances.

On the other hand, except in cases of possible deception, we are convinced that these bird signals are not independent of their associated physiological states. As far as we can tell, a bird giving an alarm call in response to a hawk overhead shows all the signs of autonomic arousal that we would expect to accompany a state of fearfulness. We presume that the emotion of fear is a typical concomitant of alarm-calling behavior and is perhaps a close correlate, and perhaps even a determinant, of the general *intensity* of antipredator behavior. The specification of response *quality*, however, appears to involve some kind of mechanism other than emotion.

What are the implications for volition and cognition?

We have shown that there are many nuances to the control of vocalization by a companion, providing considerable communicative flexibility, the extent and nature of which varies from one signal system to another. Do these complexities require us to conclude that the production of bird vocalizations is in the strictest sense voluntary, and perhaps even under cognitive control? Here we are faced with a much more complex issue. How should we seek to establish the existence of volition in a bird? As with much current experimentation on animal cognition, and perhaps with some child studies as well, it is sometimes hard to resist the temptation when confronted with complex behavior to indulge in overrich interpretations of the underlying mechanisms. There is a danger that such interpretations may extend beyond what the facts require us to infer. On the other hand, perhaps cognitive interpretations are indeed appropriate. Do birds really have an "intent to communicate"? Perhaps they have more cognitive resources than we give them credit for in seeking to control the behavior of others by communicative means? The occurrence of deception in food calling would certainly hint at some interesting possibilities.

It is possible, however, that we are too parsimonious in the degree of complexity that we are prepared to admit for reflexive mechanisms. If we are ready to accept that the initial responsiveness to the predator may be reflexive, why not add an additional reflexive "circuit" for audience stimuli, such that calling only occurs if this is also activated? It is true that our results require us to allow for further complications, with the nature of the circuitry varying from one call system to another. Nonetheless, the degree of complexity required is no greater than that which we know from physiological studies to be involved in the reflexive control of, for example, the locomotor behavior of invertebrates. We may therefore need to reflect more carefully about exactly what we would find acceptable as evidence for the existence of volition and cognition in the vocal behavior of animals, before rejecting the spirit of Bickerton's position.

The issue of input specificity

In addition to the issue of impulsiveness, there is also a widespread impression that animal signals display a lack of input specificity, adding to the conviction held by many that they are completely emotion-based. By input specificity, we refer to the assumption that a wide range of diverse stimuli converge on the same expressive output, appropriate to the emotion that is aroused. We also take this to be an underlying assumption of emotion-based interpretations of human facial expressions. This is another view of animal signals that is based on a misconception. In fact, many animal vocalizations have a high degree of input specificity, and this is especially the case with some alarm calls associated with a state of fearfulness.

Vocalizations given in response to specific stimuli

One of the first demonstrations of high input specificity in the natural vocal behavior of an animal was provided by nonhuman primates, from work in Africa on the alarm call system of the vervet monkey (*Cercopithecus aethiops*). Vervets have a large repertoire of calls (Struhsaker, 1967), including distinct alarm calls for each of their principal classes of predators: eagles, leopards, and snakes (Seyfarth, Cheney, & Marler, 1980). In adults, the associations between call type and predator type are quite specific. Playbacks of tape-recorded calls in the absence of predators elicit the same distinctive responses that are evoked directly by each of these three classes of predators (Cheney & Seyfarth, 1990). Analogous findings have been obtained in studies of captive ring-tailed lemurs (*Lemur catta*) (Macedonia, 1990).

We have found similarly specific relationships in chickens between predator type and the class of vocalizations elicited. Our experimental analyses have concentrated especially on the aerial alarm call of adults. Using digitized video images of a hawk flying overhead presented to male chickens in the laboratory, we have been able to define several of the necessary attributes of a stimulus for this class of calls (Evans et al., 1993). Those that are relevant include image size and speed, a birdlike shape, and a certain position in space. So there is no question that some bird signals have a high degree of input specificity. Furthermore, playback studies reveal that, as in vervet monkeys, companions understand what alarm calls mean.

Birds can decode the meanings of different calls

The meaning of alarm calls has been explored by presenting tape-recorded calls to female chickens in a sound-attenuated chamber, in the absence of any predators (Evans et al., 1993). Several alarm calls were selected for playback in order to sample the full range of variation in call structure. In all, we presented 12 alarm calls, arranged in six matched pairs so that total duration was identical. Calls were also matched for sound intensity. Hens were placed in a test cage, with a simulated bush in one corner to provide cover. They then heard in a random order playbacks of one of the pairs of alarm calls.

The responses evoked by playback of the two call types were reliably different, and similar to those elicited by the original video sequences of aerial and ground predators. The frequency with which hens ran into cover was high in response to the aerial predator call but low in response to the ground predator call and to a control sound. We also conducted frame-by-frame analyses of test session videotapes so that we could track changes in gaze direction. We found that horizontal scanning increased in response to both types of alarm call, and there was no significant difference between them. In contrast, there were striking differences in the frequency of upward scanning, which is conspicuous in these birds because they have a limited binocular vision and fixate objects by rolling the head abruptly to one side. Upward scanning was elicited much more often by aerial predator calls. We conclude that there must be a sense in which the aerial predator call represents danger overhead, and the ground predator call represents danger at eye level, a surprising parallel with the vervet monkey findings (Cheney & Seyfarth, 1990).

Similarly with food calls, it appears that hens understand their meaning when a cock gives them and the fact that a bout of rapid calling is likely to refer to a choice tidbit and a few calls to something more commonplace (Marler et al., 1986a; Evans & Marler, 1994). Another point of interest is that food calling sometimes appears to be given deceptively, by a male with something inedible in his bill, especially if the hen is too far way to see what he is presenting to her (Gyger & Marler, 1988). We should note that there is still uncertainty about the *kind* of information that the hen extracts from such a call – whether it should be thought of as a designative label for food, or as a prescription for a particular response, such as come and eat – a distinction that is inherently difficult to make with animal signals (Marler, 1961, 1992). Nevertheless, it is clear that in some sense birds do understand that food calls mean one thing, alarm calls another, and that different alarm calls have different meanings. Just as the degree of input specificity can be quite high, so meanings can be quite specific.

As we begin to accumulate comparative data, it becomes clear that, in birds and other animals, the degree of input specificity varies from species to species and from one vocalization to another. In some cases, the widely held view that input specificity is low is probably valid. The range of input stimuli for signals associated with alertness and vigilance is likely to be wide and generalized. In other cases, it begins to approach the high degree of specificity that we typically associate with linguistic labels (or commands). Certainly, the alarm calls of some animals serve at least one equivalent function of language: They convey to other individuals sufficient information about certain critically important external situations for them to be able to select an appropriate adaptive response without necessarily having access to the eliciting external situation themselves.

The concept of functional reference

The responses elicited by the signals we have studied are those appropriate to food or to particular subclasses of predators, a property for which we have coined the term *functional reference* (Evans et al., 1993; Macedonia & Evans, 1993; Marler et al., 1992). For example, chickens responded quite differently to playback of the two alarm call types, in ways that match those apparent when the predators themselves are present. One response class is designed to evade detection and capture by a distant but very fast-moving aerial predator, and the other to capture the attention and track the movements of a more deliberate slow-moving ground predator, nearer at hand. This response dichotomy is just what would be predicted if the calls function as noniconic symbols, with different predator types as the signal referents.

We view functional reference as we have defined it as one step, albeit a small one, in the direction of language, sometimes with a degree of input specificity exceeding that commonly associated with emotion-based signals (see Fridlund, 1994, p. 152). It is important to note, however, that even the most extreme interpretation of signaling behavior as a manifestation of emotion does not exclude the likelihood of some degree of referentiality. However broad the range of evoking stimuli may be, when an emotion is indeed externally elicited, each emotion will be called forth by a distinctive array of stimuli, as Ekman (1992) has pointed out. As a consequence, any environmentally triggered act that is expressive of a given emotion necessarily encodes information about the class of evoking stimuli, with the potential in social situations for others to decode that information and act upon it – the essence of functional reference. Thus, "when you see a person with a disgust expression, you know that the person is responding to something offensive to taste or smell" (Ekman, 1992, p. 177). The transmission of such knowledge is surely one of the functions that human facial expressions serve, and the same must also be true not only of those animal signals with highly specified referents but also of those that, as we presume to be the case with human facial expressions, have a relatively unspecific set of referents. In the vervet monkey, for example, in addition to those predator-specific alarm calls that have been most intensively studied, there are others of a more general nature. These have a lower degree of input specificity, being elicited by a wide range of stimuli for which an increase in vigilance is an appropriate response (Struhsaker, 1967). The sudden adoption of an alert, anxious posture by a vigilant animal must in turn serve itself as a potential signal conveying general information of this kind to others.

Of course, in both animals and humans, each signal operates in concert with a range of others. If a signal that itself has low input specificity is accompanied by another signal with different properties, the combination can result in communication with a greater degree of specificity. A monkey giving a generalized alarm call connoting mild anxiety achieves a more specific message by staring fixedly at the object of concern. The same would apply to a human fear face, or an expression of disgust, associated with a fixed gaze. And, of course, a speech accompaniment provides endless possibilities for further specification.

Premack (1975) has pointed out another way by which input specificity can be increased – namely, by individual idiosyncrasy. In a social group whose members are familiar with each other, one individual may be especially fearful of foxes and ready to alarm call to them freely, but may be relatively unconcerned about raccoons. Another may have a ferret phobia, and so on. The same call type might be used in all cases but with an overlay of individualistic vocal markers, such as occur frequently in animal sounds. Such an overlay might be viewed either as a separate signal or as part of the context in which a signal is presented (Leger, 1993). An educated listener, knowing the special quirks of his companions, could make a fair guess at the actual predator, despite the low input specificity of the call class itself. There is great potential for diversifying the properties of a system of functional reference by the exploitation of special responsive idiosyncrasies of the two sexes, contrasting vulnerabilities, and thus sensitivities of different age classes, and even of different species. A similar argument may also have some validity as applied to the communicative potential of human facial expressions, provided that the sender's biases are known to the receiver, whether peculiar to the individual or shared with other members of a class of which the sender is a member. And even when considered in isolation from other signals, it is surely the case that some human facial expressions display functional reference, whether cognition-based or not, in the same sense that this is true of animal vocalizations.

Social factors, birdcalls, and faces

It is clear that the social circumstances of an animal can have a profound effect on those behaviors, expressive in nature, that serve as vehicles for communication. There is a remarkable convergence here with recent findings on human facial expressions (Chovil, chapter 14, this volume, and 1992; Fridlund, 1992, 1994). The act of smiling, for example, proves to be a rather loose correlate of pleasurable emotional experiences, although not completely independent of them. A classical study by Kraut and Johnston (1979) found that people in a pleasurable situation often delayed smiling until they were face-to-face with a companion but smiled much more rarely when alone. As Chovil (chapter 14, this volume) expresses it, "Kraut and Johnston's study was a landmark in establishing that adult facial displays were sensitive to an available receiver." Infant smiling also proves to be potentiated by the presence of an appropriate receiver, such as the mother, with attentiveness to the infant and even eye contact as a significant factor (Jones, Collins, & Hong, 1991; Jones & Raag, 1989; reviewed by Chovil).

A baseline level of smiling is often reported that is not dependent on an overt audience effect. This suggests that if there is dissociation of the facial expression from the associated emotional state, the separation is only partial. Similarly, facial expressions of rage in infants were more intense when directed toward the mother than toward a stranger, suggesting a degree of selectivity in the audience effect (Stenberg, Campos, & Emde, 1983), again imposed on a significant baseline rate. It may be necessary to determine in this case, however, that the mother is indeed an audience and not a referent (more on this later). Similarly, a solitary cockerel is likely to give *some* food calls when he finds a succulent insect, even though he would give more with an appropriate, female audience. The same is true of the aerial alarm call, sometimes given by a solitary bird, although it is given more frequently when a companion is present.

In the typical case, audience effects appear to facilitate or inhibit production of a call, the basic causal determinants for which are already in place.

Some feel that audience effects on human facial expressions are so compelling that they throw doubt on the very presumption that the face reflects endogenous emotional states. Fridlund (1992, 1994, and chapter 5, this volume) has developed this viewpoint extensively in his "behavioral ecology" model of human facial expressions, bringing social considerations into a primary position in his analysis, and deemphasizing the role of endogenous emotional factors. In response to the presumption that performance in solitude implies endogenous wellsprings for facial expressive behavior, a counterargument is presented: Even when an individual knows that it is isolated, the possibility of an imagined audience can never be excluded (Fridlund, 1994). Fridlund's experiments demonstrate that an implicit audience can indeed affect the incidence of smiling significantly, as when a subject viewing an amusing videotape smiles more, knowing that an invisible companion is viewing the same tape in an adjacent room (Fridlund, 1991). Unfortunately, the notion of an imagined audience can never be disproved either. Applying this interpretation to the alarm or food calling of an isolated chicken seems even less plausible. In any case, in both humans and animals, the evidence suggests that any postulated imagined audience is less potent than the real thing.

On the basis of present evidence, the most appropriate way to view audience effects on the signaling behavior of animals seems to be as modulatory in nature rather than as primary motivators of expressive behavior. From this viewpoint, a neurocultural model of expressive behavior such as that of Ekman (1972) seems more appropriate than the Behavioral Ecology View of Fridlund (1994). The "neurocultural" viewpoint postulates innate endogenous motivational and emotional programs that can nevertheless be modulated by social factors, operating according to whatever social conventions have prevailed in the individual's developmental history. As applied to human facial expressions (see Ekman, 1972, 1977), this line of theorizing is designed to accommodate the fact that learning may play a significant role in the degree to which the expressive output from endogenous programs is masked or exaggerated, or even used deceptively. In the latter case, the expression can presumably be completely dissociated from its original endogenous motivation, although there is some evidence of feedback, such that going through the motions of an emotional expression engenders some aspects of the corresponding physiological state (Levenson, Ekman, & Friesen, 1990).

The animal data seem to fit well with a model of this type, even embracing the possibility of deception as we have indicated. A cockerel may give food calls, even when he has a food item in his beak that is actually unpalatable, especially when he is in the presence of a strange hen, who is far enough away that she cannot see whether he has food or not, than when he is alone (Gyger & Marler, 1988). In this case, the dependence of the behavior on social stimulation, rather than on the endogenous physiological processes that are triggered by the discovery of a preferred food, is maximal. We may note that this potential case of deception appears to conform more closely to Fridlund's Behavioral Ecology View than when the food calling is performed in an honest fashion.

There may be another message latent in the animal studies for students of audience effects on human facial expressions. The animal data indicate that audience effect rules can vary widely from one communicative subsystem to another in functionally significant ways, present in some cases and lacking in others. The emphasis on audience familiarity, gender, and even species can vary from one signal to another.

Could it be that some human facial expressions are more susceptible to audience effects than others? Most human studies have focused on smiling, where the effects of an audience are strong. Would the same be true, for example, of the facial expression of disgust, regarded by some as an emotional display (Ekman & Friesen, 1975; Izard, 1971). Perhaps not? One could imagine that, in a state of unhappiness, a sad face might be less subject to audience effects than crying. The precise effects of an audience may vary with the nature of the emotion, facilitating in some cases, inhibiting in others. Either effects might be global, or they could be more focused, changing the incidence of some components of facial expression while leaving others unchanged. The precise analytical techniques of Ekman and Friesen (1978), revealing that the motor patterns of smiling differ when subjects are truthful or deceptive about feeling pleasant (Ekman, Friesen, & O'Sullivan, 1988), would also be ideal for comparing the details of smiling in isolation and in the presence of different audiences, to determine whether or not subtly distinct expressions may be involved. Studies are needed both of audience effects on other facial expressions, in addition to those of pleasure and anger, and of the effects of different *types* of audience, before we can generalize with any confidence about social effects on emotional display.

Social intentions and audience effects

The concept of audience effects deals with only one limited aspect of the larger and much more complex issue of intentionality. As we have defined them, audience effects deal with the special case of a companion that is not, itself, a referent for the signal in question. This is the reason we have concentrated on alarm and food calls rather than, for example, calls associated with aggression. Aggressive calls are clearly given with social intent, and displays of anger are surely susceptible to audience effects. But unless great care is taken in the design of experiments, the roles of a companion as audience and a companion as referent may become indistinguishable. The territorial intruder that elicits an aggressive signal is itself the signal addressee. In a reductionistic spirit, we have chosen to restrict the concept of an audience effect to cases where there is no doubt that the role of a companion is as a witness to a signaling event of which it is not itself the primary instigator. Some studies of audience effects on human facial expressions such as smiling satisfy this criterion of nonreferentiality, whereas this is not obviously the case with other displays, such as expressions of rage (Stenberg et al., 1983). The value of the concept of an audience effect will be reduced if we allow it to become so broad as to encompass other aspects of social intent. On the other hand, we pay a price for this reductionistic stance by excluding more complex communicative interactions in which questions of intentionality in the deeper philosophical sense inevitably arise.

Functional reference and cognition

In developing the concept of functional reference, we intended it to be noncommittal about the nature of the underlying brain mechanisms (Marler et al., 1992), which could run the gamut from innate reflexive circuitry to cognitive mechanisms, sustained by neural systems that are shaped by individual experience. The breadth of the concept is such that it surely encompasses both birdcalls and human faces. In fact, human facial expressions are viewed by some as functioning symbolically. They sometimes appear to engage cognition in somewhat the same sense that this is true of language, as when they are being used as "emblems" (Ekman, 1982) although it is not always clear when this interpretation is being applied to emotional displays and when to other facial signals (see Chovil, chapter 14, this volume). However, it is more common for facial expressions to be used in a paralinguistic fashion to modulate the meaning of spoken words, to add emphasis, or initiate turn taking in a conversation (Chovil, 1991). The level of operation is obviously much simpler than that of speech, but the face must surely on occasion operate in a symbolic mode, presumably as a reflection of underlying cognitive processing. Would a similar inference be appropriate in animals, as when they respond appropriately to a predator-specific alarm call?

It may be that cognitive mechanisms are involved, and that when a chicken or a vervet monkey hears an alarm call, an internal representation of the appropriate predator class is elicited. We could imagine this representation being manifest as an internalized experience or as an expectation of a certain pattern of external stimulation, along with preparations for certain patterns of response.

Alternatively, perhaps hard-wired reflexive circuitry could provide a sufficient basis for these cases of functional reference? Without the benefit of introspection, it will be difficult for experiments conducted with adult nonhuman organisms to distinguish between the alternatives in a rigorous way. On the basis of the evidence presented so far, hard-wired interpretations would seem to be as acceptable as a cognitive view, especially if the behavior proves to be highly stereotyped and refractory to the effects of individual experience during ontogeny. If, on the other hand, the behavior proves to be developmentally plastic, and experience turns out to be important in the development of audience effects and input specificity, we might be more inclined to entertain cognitive interpretations. One obvious source of insight into this problem is an understanding of the ways in which such behavior develops, as Fridlund (1994) has argued eloquently and persuasively in the case of human facial expressions.

Preliminary evidence of experience dependence

The results of a first effort to explore the development of antipredator behavior in chickens already hint at the inappropriateness of reflexive interpretations. Rearing conditions appear to have a strong influence on alarm calling in chickens, reinforcing the inclination to take a cognitive approach seriously. Palleroni and Marler (in preparation) raised four broods of a total of 40 chicks with or without parents, and with or without access to predators. Predator experience was supplemented up to the age of 16 weeks by exposure twice a week to a live ferret and to a live peregrine falcon. Between 20 and 27 weeks of age, the young birds were studied for responsiveness to video recordings of a hawk and a hunting ferret moving toward the camera. We already knew that birds raised normally in outdoor enclosures with access to both parents and predators respond quite differently to these test stimuli, in ways that are functionally appropriate for evading the very different hunting techniques of these two predators.

We found that birds raised with parents and with predator experience behaved normally, but all others displayed varying degrees of abnormal behavior. Specific relationships between alarm-call type and predator type were almost absent, although not entirely so. The behavior of chicks raised without either parents or predator experience was the most aberrant of all. It seems clear that the development of normal antipredator behavior is influenced both by experience of predators and by the presence of parents, although the precise mechanisms involved still have to be elucidated. At this stage, it seems conceivable that a cognitive interpretation may be appropriate after all.

In a further check that these experimental deprivations might simply have delayed normal development, and that typical antipredator behavior might emerge if we waited long enough, we retested the birds a year later, after they had lived outdoors, exposed to local predators, with adults present (Palleroni & Marler, in preparation). There was almost no change, suggesting that the impairments imposed by parental and predator deprivations are permanent. Although the acoustic morphology of the calls of the deprived birds appeared normal, they were not used in appropriate circumstances. Normal development seems to have been quite precluded by these rather drastic ontogenetic manipulations. More refined experimentation will be required to determine which specific aspects of experience are relevant and whether deprived subjects are deficient in predator recognition, escape behavior in general, or in audience responsiveness. Meanwhile, it seems appropriate to keep an open mind about whether or not cognition is involved in the antipredator behavior of chickens.

Conclusions

If we are correct in invoking both volition (i.e., controlled impulsiveness) and cognition (i.e., developmentally flexible functional reference) to explain some aspects of the vocal behavior of birds, what becomes of the "emotional" hypothesis? It seems clear that the folk psychology version of Emotions Theory, as we have framed it, is inadequate to explain both the complex audience effects on call production and the degree of experience-dependent input specificity that we have described. On the other hand, we have no intention of demoting the crucial role of emotional factors in avian vocal behavior, which undoubtedly play a major, if not a universal, role not only in the production of animal calls but also in the control of other kinds of behavior. This becomes especially clear if we extend the term *emotional* to encompass both the traditional categories, such as fear and anger, and also other types of endogenously driven behavior, such as feeding or migratory activity. We have made the tentative suggestion elsewhere (Marler et al., 1992) that the term *motivational* might prove in the long run to be more apposite than *emotional* in conceptualizing the alternatives to cognitive and volitional control of vocal behavior. Indeed, it may be that the very notion of cognition-free emotion, invoked previously by many to explain animal vocalization (see Table 6.1), is itself an anachronism. That it is something of an anomaly is certainly the position held by many authorities on emotional theory (e.g., Ekman & Davidson, 1994; Plutchik, 1970; Russell & Fernández-Dols, chapter 1, this volume). There is general agreement, however, that the basic brain mechanisms underlying cognition and emotion are distinct (LeDoux, 1995), and psychological distinctions can often be made between cognitive and emotional activation, even though cognitive contributions are sometimes thought to be minimal and perhaps even nonexistent (Izard, 1994; Zajonc, 1994).

With regard to animals, we think it likely that both kinds of process, emotional and cognitive, make some contribution to virtually every utterance they produce. We visualize a continuum, with the balance favoring cognitive control in some cases and emotional factors in others, varying according to functional requirements. But even when there is a strong cognitive component, we doubt that emotional factors can ever be ignored.

The parallels between animal vocal behavior and human facial expressions are thought provoking. In both cases, there are indications of elementary, language-like properties, albeit quite primitive, but in both cases it is obvious that there is no real confusion with linguistic behavior. Social communication with vehicles of this type is necessarily limited by comparison with the extraordinary sophistication of language. However, there can be no question of the importance of this kind of "affective" signaling in social discourse, as much so in humans as in animals. It may be that we should begin thinking of more human and animal communicative signals as compounds, blending different kinds of information, some of which may be more effectively displayed by facial expressions, or by some of the nonlinguistic components of speech, rather than by language itself.

It is of some theoretical importance to determine whether, in animals, variation in emotional state is encoded in different signal properties, or in components of compound signals that are distinct from those properties that convey referential information (Partan & Marler, in preparation), as appears to be the case in our own speech (Scherer, 1979, 1985). Computer-generated emotion-free speech is a sadly impoverished vehicle for appraisive judgments. Evaluative assessments may be less readily made on the basis of the particular category of signal being used than by reference to such nonlinguistic, across-category attributes such as pitch and intonation, perhaps controlled more by emotion than cognition (cf. Scherer, 1994). Marler (1992) has indicated some of the acoustic features that are candidates for encoding appraisive information in primate calls and birdcalls. It may prove to be a widespread attribute of animal signals that emotion plays a special role in generating certain restricted features of vocal and visual displays, working in concert with those that have a cognitive basis to achieve maximal communicative efficiency.

A model of signaling behavior that combines both affective and symbolic components into signal compounds may prove to have heuristic value in understanding the many complexities of human facial expressive behaviors, especially if we take account of their frequent use in concert with other signals, with different properties. Signals used together with emotional expressions may emanate from the face or from other body parts, in order to contribute to compound visual signals, and may also engage other sensory modalities, of which audition is likely to be preeminent. Along with others (cf. Andrew, 1963), we often find ourselves wondering about the evolutionary implications of the extraordinarily close relationship in primates between the face and the voice. Perhaps avian evolution might have proceeded very differently if birds had been endowed not with elegant plumage but with an expressive face?

Acknowledgments

This paper would not have been written without the encouragement of Alan Fridlund, whose comments, sometimes acerbic, always thoughtful and constructive, have been a constant source of intellectual stimulation. We also acknowledge the value over the years of discussions with two of the pioneers in the study of human emotion, Paul Ekman and Klaus Scherer. We appreciate comments on the manuscript by Nicole Chovil, Gerald Ginsburg, Sarah Partan, and James Russell. Research described in the paper was supported by NSF grant BNS 8616925 to P.M. and by an NIMH Postdoctoral fellowship (MH09683) to C.E.

References

Andrew, R. J. (1963). The origin & evolution of the calls and facial expressions of the primates. *Behaviour, 20,* 1–109.

Bastian, J. (1965). Primate signalling systems and human languages. In I. DeVore (Ed.), *Primate behavior: field studies of monkeys and apes.* Holt, Rinehart and Winston: New York.

Bickerton, D. (1990). *Language and species.* Chicago: University of Chicago Press.

Brown, C. H. (1982). Ventriloquial and locatable vocalizations in birds. *Zeitschrift für Tierpsychologie, 59,* 338–350.

Caro, T. M. (1986). The functions of stotting in Thompson's gazelles: Some tests of the predictions. *Animal Behavior, 34,* 663–684.

Cheney, D. L., & Seyfarth, R. M. (1990). *How monkeys see the world.* Chicago: University of Chicago Press.

Chovil, N. (1991). Communicative functions of facial displays. *Journal of Nonverbal Behavior, 15,* 141–154.

Chovil, N. (1992). Discourse-oriented facial displays in conversation. *Research on Language and Social Interaction, 25,* 163–164.

Collias, N. E. (1987). The vocal repertoire of the red junglefowl: A spectrographic classification and the code of communication. *Condor, 89,* 510–524.

Dewsbury, D. A. (1992). Surplusage, audience effects and George John Romanes. *Behavior and Brain Sciences, 15,* 152.

Ekman, P. (1972). Universals and cultural differences in facial expressions of emotion. In J. Cole (Ed.), *Nebraska Symposium on Motivation (1971), 19,* 207–283.

Ekman, P. (1977). Biological and cultural contributions to body and facial movement. In J. Blacking (Ed.), *The anthropology of the body.* London: Academic Press.

Ekman, P. (Ed.). (1982). *Emotion in the human face* (2nd ed.). New York: Cambridge University Press.

Ekman, P. (1992). Are there basic emotions? *Psychological Review, 99,* 550–553.

Ekman, P., & Davidson, R. J. (1994). *The nature of emotion: Fundamental questions.* Oxford: Oxford University Press.

Ekman, P., & Friesen, W. V. (1975). *Unmasking the face.* Englewood Cliffs, NJ: Prentice-Hall.

Ekman, P., & Friesen, W. V. (1978). *The facial action coding system.* Palo Alto, CA: Consulting Psychologists Press.

Ekman, P., Friesen, W. V., & O'Sullivan, M. (1988). Smiles when lying. *Journal of Personality and Social Psychology, 54,* 414–420.

Evans, C. S., Evans, L., & Marler, P. (1993). On the meaning of alarm calls: Functional reference in an avian vocal system. *Animal Behavior, 46,* 23–38.

Evans, C. S., Macedonia, J. M., & Marler, P. (1993). Effects of apparent size and speed on the response of chickens (*Gallus gallus*) to computer-generated simulations of aerial predators. *Animal Behavior, 46,* 1–11.

Evans, C. S., & Marler, P. (1991). On the use of video images as social stimuli in birds: Audience effects on alarm calling. *Animal Behavior, 41,* 17–26.

Evans, C. S., & Marler, P. (1992). Female appearance as a factor in the responsiveness of male chickens during anti-predator behavior and courtship. *Animal Behavior, 43,* 137–145.

Evans, C. S., & Marler, P. (1994). Food-calling and audience effects in male chickens, *Gallus gallus*: Their relationships to food availability, courtship and social facilitation. *Animal Behavior, 47,* 1159–1170.

Evans, C. S., & Marler, P. (1995). Language and animal communication: Parallels and contrasts. In H. Roitblat & J. Arcady-Meyer (Eds.), *Comparative approaches to cognitive science.* Cambridge, MA: MIT Press.

Fridlund, A. J. (1991). Sociality of solitary smiling: Potentiation by an implicit audience. *Journal of Personality and Social Psychology, 60,* 229–240.

Fridlund, A. J. (1992). The behavioral ecology and sociality of human faces. In M. S. Clark (Ed.), *Review of personality and social psychology* (Vol. 13, pp. 90–121). Newbury Park, CA: Sage.

Fridlund, A. J. (1994). *Human facial expression.* New York: Academic Press.

Gyger, M., Karakashian, S., & Marler, P. (1986). Avian alarm calling: Is there an audience effect? *Animal Behavior, 34,* 1570–1572.

Gyger, M., & Marler, P. (1988). Food calling in the domestic fowl (*Gallus gallus*): The role of external referents and deception. *Animal Behavior, 36,* 358–365.

Gyger, M., Marler, P., & Pickert, R. (1987). Semantics of an avian alarm call system: The male domestic fowl, *Gallus domesticus. Behaviour, 102,* 15–40.

Hughes, M. K., Hughes, A. L., & Covalt-Dunning, D. (1982). Stimuli eliciting food calling in the domestic chicken. *Applied Animal Ethology, 8,* 543–550.

Izard, C. E. (1971). *The face of emotion.* New York: Appleton-Century-Crofts.

Izard, C. E. (1994). Cognition is one of four types of emotion-activating systems. In P. Ekman & R. J. Davidson (Eds.), *The nature of emotion: Fundamental questions.* Oxford: Oxford University Press.

Jones, S. S., Collins, K., & Hong, H.-W. (1991). An audience effect on smile production in 10-month-old infants. *Psychological Science, 2,* 45–49.

Jones, S. S., & Raag, T. (1989). Smile production in older infants: The importance of a social recipient for the facial signal. *Child Development, 60,* 811–818.

Karakashian, S. J., Gyger, M., & Marler, P. (1988). Audience effects on alarm calling in chickens (*Gallus gallus*). *Journal of Comparative Psychology, 102,* 129–135.

Kraut, R. E., & Johnston, R. E. (1979). Social and emotional messages of smiling: An ethological approach. *Journal of Personality and Social Psychology, 37,* 1539–1553.

Lancaster, J. (1965). *Primate behavior and the emergence of human culture.* New York: Holt, Rinehart and Winston.

LeDoux, J. E. (1995). In search of an emotional system in the brain: Leaping from fear to emotion and consciousness. In M. S. Gazzaniga (Ed.), *The cognitive neurosciences* (pp. 1049–1061). Cambridge: MIT Press.

Leger, D. W. (1993). Contextual sources of information and responses to animal communication signals. *Psychological Bulletin, 113,* 295–304.

Levenson, R. W., Ekman, P., & Friesen, W. V. (1990). Voluntary facial action generates emotion-specific autonomic nervous system activity. *Psychophysiology, 27,* 363–384.

Luria, A. (1982). *Language and cognition.* Cambridge: MIT Press.

Macedonia, J. M. (1990). What is communicated in the antipredator calls of lemurs: Evidence from antipredator call playbacks to ringtailed and ruffed lemurs. *Ethology, 86,* 177–190.

Macedonia, J. M., & Evans, C. S. (1993). Variation among mammalian alarm call systems and the problem of meaning in animal signals. *Ethology, 93,* 177–197.

Marin, O., Schwarz, M. F., & Saffran, E. M. (1979). Origins and distribution of language. In M. S. Gazzaniga (Ed.), *Handbook of behavioral biology II: Neuropsychology.* New York: Plenum.

Marler, P. (1957). Specific distinctiveness in the communication signals of birds. *Behaviour, 11,* 13–39.

Marler, P. (1961). The logical analysis of animal communication. *Journal of Theoretical Biology, 1,* 295–317.

Marler, P. (1978). Affective and symbolic meaning: Some zoosemiotic speculations. In T. A. Sebeok (Ed.), *Sight, sound, and sense* (pp. 112–123). Bloomington: Indiana University Press.

Marler, P. (1992). Functions of arousal and emotion in primate communication: A semiotic approach. In T. Nishida, W. C. McGrew, P. Marler, M. Pickford, & F. B. M. de Waal (Eds.), *Topics in primatology: Vol. 1. Human origins* (pp. 225–233). Japan: University of Tokyo Press.

Marler, P., Dufty, A., & Pickert, R. (1986a). Vocal communication in the domestic chicken I: Does a sender communicate information about the quality of a food referent to a receiver? *Animal Behavior, 34,* 188–193.

Marler, P., Dufty, A., & Pickert, R. (1986b). Vocal communication in the domestic chicken II: Is a sender sensitive to the presence and nature of a receiver? *Animal Behavior, 34,* 194–198.

Marler, P., Evans, C. S., & Hauser, M. D. (1992). Animal signals: Motivational, referential, or both? In H. Papousek, U. Jorgens, & M. Papousek (Eds.), *Nonverbal vocal communication: Comparative and developmental approaches* (pp. 66–86). Cambridge: Cambridge University Press.

Marler, P., Karakashian, S., & Gyger, M. (1990). Do animals have the option of withholding signals when communication is inappropriate? The audience effect. In C. Ristau & P. Marler (Eds.), *Cognitive ethology: The minds of other animals* (pp. 187–208). Hillsdale, NJ: Erlbaum.

Myers, R. E. (1976). Comparative neurology of vocalization and speech: Proof of a dichotomy. In S. Harnad, H. D. Steklis, & L. Lancaster (Eds.), *Origins and evolution of language and speech.* New York: Academy of Sciences.

Palleroni, A., & Marler, P. (in prep.). Development of anti-predator behavior in a galliform bird is experience dependent.

Partan, S., & Marler, P. (in prep.). Multimodal communication.

Plutchik, R. (1970). Emotions, evolution, and adaptive processes. In M. B. Arnold (Ed.), *Feelings and emotions.* New York: Academic Press.

Premack, D. (1975). On the origins of language. In M. S. Gazzaniga & C. B. Blakemore (Eds.), *Handbook of psychobiology.* New York: Academic Press.

Rowell, T. E., & Hinde, R. A. (1962). Vocal communication in rhesus monkey (*Macaca mulatta*). *Proceedings of the Zoological Society of London, 138,* 279–294.

Scherer, K. R. (1979). Nonlinguistic vocal indicators of emotion and psychopathology. In C. E. Izard (Ed.), *Emotions in personality and psychopathology* (pp. 493–529). New York: Plenum.

Scherer, K. R. (1985). Vocal affect signaling: A comparative approach. *Advances in the Study of Behavior, 15,* 189–244.

Scherer, K. R. (1994). An emotion's occurrence depends on the relevance of an event to the organism's goal-need hierarchy. In P. Ekman & R. J. Davidson (Eds.), *The nature of emotion: Fundamental questions.* Oxford: Oxford University Press.

Seyfarth, R. M., Cheney, D. L., & Marler, P. (1980). Monkey responses to three different alarm calls: Evidence of predator classification and semantic communication. *Science, 210,* 801–803.

Sherman, P. W. (1977). Nepotism and the evolution of alarm calls. *Science, 197,* 1246–1253.

Sherry, D. F. (1977). Parental food-calling and the role of the young in the Burmese red junglefowl (*Gallus gallus spadiceus*). *Animal Behavior, 25,* 594–601.

Stenberg, C., Campos, J. J., & Emde, R. N. (1983). The facial expression of anger in seven-month-old infants. *Child Development, 54,* 178–184.

Struhsaker, T. T. (1967). Auditory communication among vervet monkeys (*Cercopithecus aetheiops*). In S. A. Altman (Ed.), *Social communication among primates* (pp. 281–324). Chicago: University of Chicago Press.

Tinbergen, N. (1948). Social releasers and the experimental method required for their study. *Wilson Bulletin, 60,* 6–51.

Zajonc, R. B. (1965). Social facilitation. *Science, 149,* 269–274.

Zajonc, R. B. (1994). Evidence for non-conscious emotions. In P. Ekman & R. J. Davidson (Eds.), *The nature of emotion: Fundamental questions.* Oxford: Oxford University Press.

7. Yawns, laughs, smiles, tickles, and talking: Naturalistic and laboratory studies of facial action and social communication

ROBERT R. PROVINE

Inquiry about the experience, expression, physiological correlates, and neurological mechanisms of emotion is often shaped by semantics and embedded in elaborate theoretical frameworks. What, for example, are the criteria for emotions and facial expressions? What is the function of a smile? The present exploration of yawning, laughing, smiling, tickling, and talking avoids these issues, at least at the outset. This research observes spontaneous social behavior of people or animals in natural settings, sometimes recruiting subjects to keep logs of their ongoing behavior or retreating to the laboratory to test hypotheses. *Social behavior* is defined here as acts that are either evoked by or performed primarily in the presence of other individuals. This behaviorally oriented description of the who, where, when, what, and how of ongoing, overt behavior is an underused approach in human social science that produces data that can outlive the propositions that inspire it. Data from this basically atheoretical, descriptive research provide insights into topics ranging from the social role of facial actions (yawning and smiling), vocalizations (laughing and talking), and touch (tickling) to the neurological mechanisms of laughter and speech. Such descriptions of motor acts are the starting point for ontogenetic and phylogenetic analyses, and they provide a bridge between the study of human and animal social behavior (Provine, 1996a, c). Although the movements of organisms (including vocalizations) differ in their complexity, choreography, and motor control, at their root all are muscle contractions triggered by motor neurons. What sets the present set of behaviors apart from walking or breathing is that all are motor acts that in different ways, and to varying degrees, evolved to change the behavior of others.

The present research is unusual in that three of the five target behaviors – yawning, laughing, and tickling – although undeniably social in character, are not traditionally studied in the context of facial action and

158

emotion. (Smiling and talking have attracted considerable research.) No one seems to know quite what to do with laughter (Provine, 1996a), a social vocalization somehow related to positive affect and humor, or tickling, a footnote in the study of laughter and tactile sensation, or yawning, a facial social signal that has been ignored altogether. Yawning is not even considered to be a "facial expression." But why is yawning not a facial expression? Perhaps it is associated with the "emotions" of boredom or sleepiness (Provine & Fischer, 1989; Provine & Hamernik, 1986), two behavioral states that fail to make the list of approved emotions, possible victims of science by committee. The present treatment avoids these problems of definition. It describes yawning, laughing, smiling, tickling, and talking, as well as their social contexts. Special attention is directed to contagious yawning and laughter, bizarre and compelling behaviors that offer unique insights into a variety of issues in the neural, behavioral, and social sciences.

Laughing, smiling, and talking: Relation to social context

Laughing, smiling, and talking are among the most common and prominent human social signals. Although these activities differ at the level of motor act, sensory channel, message, and richness of information content, all are important in social discourse. Laughing and talking are principally auditory signals, functioning in light or darkness and around obstructions. Smiling, in contrast, is a visual signal that requires line-of-sight visual contact from the recipient to the illuminated face of the sender. Talking was selected for study because its role in communication is unquestioned and because it is seldom considered in concert with laughing and smiling.

The present analysis studies laughing, smiling, and talking using parallel procedures that facilitate direct comparisons between behavior and species (Provine & Fischer, 1989). It strips laughing, smiling, and talking of their richness and subtlety and treats them as motor acts distributed in time. This austere approach reveals overlooked and neglected phenomena and suggests ancient, common roots of vocal and gestural behavior.

A self-report, log-keeping procedure was used to collect 1-week-long samples of behavior from 72 subjects. Each subject recorded bedtimes and waking times and episodes of laughing, smiling, or talking (not each laugh, smile, or word) and the social context in which they occurred during hourly segments of the day. Also, subjects recorded the social context of the behavior by checking one of these categories: *alone with no social stimuli or media* (i.e., spontaneous laughter), *alone with media stimuli* (i.e., watching television alone, reading a book), *social with no media* (i.e., joking with friends), and *social with media* (i.e., watching television with friends). The effects of media, a form of vicarious social stimulation, were not evaluated. Results are reported as the probability of occurrence of at least one act in a given social condition during a given hour. The probability, not the frequency, of behavior is reported to reduce individual differences in subjects' record keeping.

The mean probabilities of laughing, smiling, and talking in various social and media contexts show that all are predominantly social acts. These activities are performed infrequently by solitary subjects without media stimulation. The social context effect was particularly strong in the case of laughing (no media), which was over 30 times as likely to be performed by subjects in social than in solitary settings. Smiling (no media) was over 6 times and talking was over 4 times as likely to occur in social than in solitary situations.[1] Solitary behavior did occur, however. Solitary talking in the form of rehearsing upcoming conversations, studying, cursing, singing, and "thinking out loud" were reported, occurring most often during the postwaking hour. Smiling, but not laughing, was a common element of these morning soliloquies. The social nature of the studied behaviors may actually be stronger than reported because some solitary acts may involve subjects displaying either to their image in a mirror or to social imagery, "the people in your head" (Fridlund et al., 1990). The self-report procedure was especially useful for collecting data on these potentially embarrassing solitary activities, which may be inhibited by the presence of observers. The social sanctions against private "conversations" and emotional expressions are well known.

Although a happy person probably laughs or smiles more than a sad one, these behavior patterns are performed primarily in response to face-to-face encounters with others, not as ongoing expressions of emotional tone. Thus, a happy person may show a relatively neutral facial expression and laugh or smile only when greeting or interacting with someone. We seldom laugh, smile, or talk in response to inanimate objects. By extension, if expressions of positive affect such as laughing or smiling are desired, perhaps for therapeutic reasons, it is important to seek the appropriate social context. Chovil (chapter 14, this volume) presents numerous additional examples of the social, phasic character of smiling. Lockard, Fahrenbruch, Smith, and Morgan (1977) provide further evidence of the social context of smiling and laughing, and they note differences between the frequency and intensity of these acts when performed in different social situations. Anger offers an interesting parallel to laughing and smiling; it too is a social response to the acts of people, not to the acts of nature or objects (Averill, 1983). Identical blows to the head by a stick generate very different emotional responses when provided by a human adversary than by the chance falling of a branch from a tree.

Talking may be more akin to laughing, smiling, and other nonverbal social signals than is often appreciated. For example, "small talk" may have evolved to facilitate or maintain social bonds among our tribal ancestors, a role independent of linguistic or information content and similar to that served by mutual grooming among members of contemporary primate troops (Provine & Fischer, 1989). This social bonding function is characteristic of the "phatic" speech of Malinowski (cited in Farb, 1974) "in which ties of union are created by a mere exchange of words" (p. 23). In this context, the act of speaking is often more important than what is said. The whispering found uniquely among affiliates or conspirators offers interesting parallels (see Fridlund, chapter 5, this volume).

Contagious yawning and laughter: Insights into the propagation of behavior

The contagiousness of yawning and laughter receives special attention here because it is both intriguing and useful.[2] Unlike many target behaviors in social psychology, contagious yawning and laughter are social acts that have strong biological determinants and provide the opportunity to explore mechanisms from the social to the neurological level of analysis. When you yawn in response to witnessing a yawn, or laugh in response to a laugh, you are not making a conscious effort to imitate someone. More likely, you are experiencing the triggering of a neurological "stimulus feature detector" (ethological "innate releasing mechanism," or IRM) that activates the species-typical, stereotyped ("fixed") action pattern of the yawn in the visual domain or laughter in the auditory domain (Alcock, 1989; Provine, 1986, 1989b, 1992, 1996a, c). Such sensory feature detectors are more likely to have evolved to select the simple, stereotyped, species-typical acts of yawning or laughter than more arbitrary and variable behavior learned during the lifetime of the individual. The study of contagious yawning offers advantages over competing approaches to the detection of faces or facial expressions (visual features) that rely on neuropsychological studies of rare clinical conditions (i.e., prosopagnosia) or the electrophysiological recording of face-specific brain neurons in animal models. In the auditory domain, the search for a detector for structurally simple, stereotypic and species-typical laughter offers advantages over more complex and culturally varied speech (Provine, 1992, 1993, 1996a, b). (The simplicity, stereotypy, and species-typicality of yawning and laughter offer similar tactical advantages in the search for the neural pattern-generating circuits producing the behavior [Provine, 1986, 1996c; Provine & Yong, 1991].) In the cases of both yawning and laughter, the contagious response can be used to study the activity of the underlying pattern recognition process. Also, behavioral contagion may offer insights into the general topic of imitation, a controversial example of which has been suggested for human neonates (Meltzoff & Moore, 1977, 1983). Contagious yawning and laughter are a familiar but overlooked precedent for similar "imitation" that involves neither imitative intent nor a unique, early developing process (Provine, 1989a).

Contagious yawning

Most people have experienced the contagiousness of yawning. As you may have noticed, even reading or thinking about yawning evokes yawns (Carskadon, 1991, 1992; Provine, 1986). Of particular interest here is the determination of the features of the yawning face that trigger the contagious response, presumably by activating a hypothetical, yawn-specific, neurological detector. For example, does the gaping mouth, one of the most prominent features of the yawning face, mediate the contagion response?

Several studies tested the yawn-evoking potency of features of a yawning face (Provine, 1986, 1989b). The yawn-evoking capacity of variations in a 5-min series of 30 monochrome videotaped repetitions of a yawning face (one yawn every 10 sec) were compared with each other and with a control condition of a series of 30 videotaped smiles (Provine, 1989b). Single frames of the video stimuli in mid-yawn or mid-smile are shown in Figure 7.1. The 360 subjects, 30 per stimulus condition, were tested individually in a small isolation chamber. A given subject participated in only 1 of the 12 experimental conditions. Subjects were instructed via videotaped instructions to observe the video monitor and to record their yawns, if any should occur, by pressing a button.

The normal yawning face (Figure 7.1a) was an effective stimulus, caus-

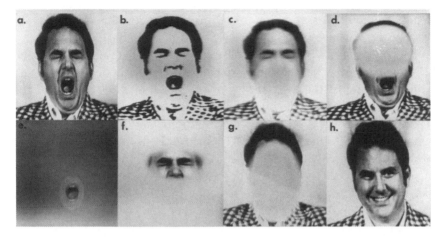

Figure 7.1. Single frames of video stimuli in mid-yawn or mid-smile. All stimuli were animate except for the single tonic (still) condition resembling (a). (a) Normal halftone yawn; (b) high-contrast yawn; (c) no-mouth yawn; (d) no-eyes yawn; (e) mouth-only yawn; (f) eyes-only yawn; (g) no-face yawn; (h) smile. From Provine (1989b).

ing 16 of 30 possible subjects to produce a total of 92 yawns, significantly more yawns than occurred in response to the smile (Figure 7.1h). (The potency of the contagion effect is greater if the response criterion is broadened to include those who "thought about yawning.") The yawn detection process was not axially specific; yawns in orientations of 90°, 180°, and 270° were as potent or nearly as potent as normal, upright, 0° yawns. The number of subjects who yawned in response to the high-contrast presentation of the yawn (Figure 7.1b) did not differ significantly from those who yawned in response to normal (halftone) yawns (Figure 7.1a) or smiles (Figure 7.1h). A tonic (still) yawn video frame of a yawner in mid-yawn (Figure 7.1a) produced a number of yawners midway between and not significantly different from that produced by normal, animate yawns or smiles.

The "no-mouth" yawn (Figure 7.1c) was the only stimulus with a deleted feature that produced as many yawning subjects as the complete face and significantly more yawners than the smile. (Thus, shielding one's mouth during a yawn may be polite, but it is ineffective in preventing contagious yawns.) This initially counterintuitive and disconcerting finding of potent "no-mouth" yawns was, however, consistent with the relative ineffectiveness of the "mouth-only" yawn (Figure 7.1e). The gaping mouth, one of the most obvious features of the yawning face, is not necessary to evoke contagious yawns. Outside of the facial context, the gaping mouth is an ambiguous stimulus that could be singing, yelling, or engaged in some other activity. The hypothetical yawn detector may be triggered not by a single feature but by the overall configuration of the yawning face, perhaps being driven by a constellation of cues such as the squinting of the eyes, tilting of the head, and movement of the jaw. The significance of the overall stimulus configuration and dynamic cues in the discrimination of facial expressions (smiles) is reinforced by Leonard, Voeller, and Kuldau (1991). In monkeys, a lack of axial and feature specificity in many face-specific brain neurons suggests a stimulus detection process of the sort described here for human yawns (Provine, 1989b). Monkeys even have neurons that fire only in response to yawning faces, but contagious yawning has not yet been detected in monkeys (Deputte, 1994). Although Ekman and Friesen (1982) comment on the onset, offset, and apex timing of human smiles ("felt smiles" last ⅔ to 4 sec), regrettably few studies have examined the important dynamic aspects of facial behavior.

The contagious yawn is not a reflex having a short and constant latency (Provine, 1986). Response latency was determined using a color version of the animate video stimulus of the normal yawning face in Figure 7.1a that recurred every 10 sec for 5 min. Yawns were triggered in 23 of the 42 subjects (55%) who yawned during a 5-min session in contrast to only 5 of 24 subjects (21%) who yawned while viewing a control series of animate smiles. The response latency was long and variable, and the proportion of subjects yawning while viewing yawns increased gradually during the 5-min session. These properties are consistent with the involvement of a complex, higher-order, polysynaptic, perceptual process, not a reflex.

Contagious laughter

Despite a wealth of research on laughter in the context of humor and its social dynamics, including the discovery that "canned" laughter increases audience laughter and the rated humorousness of comedy material, it went unnoticed that *laughter itself* can trigger laughter and mediate the phenomenon of contagion (Provine, 1992, 1996a). The hypothesis that laughter is a sufficient stimulus for laughter and/or smiles was investigated by observing the responses of subjects in three undergraduate psychology classes to a sample of laughter provided by a "laugh box" (a small, battery-operated record player obtained in a novelty store). The laugh stimulus lasted 18 sec and was repeated at the beginning of each of ten 1-min intervals.

A majority of subjects in two of the three classes laughed in response to the laugh stimulus on the first of the 10 trials. The laugh-evoking potency of the stimulus laughter declined over trials until only 3 of the 128 total subjects laughed on the last trial. On all trials, more subjects smiled than laughed in response to the laugh stimulus. (Smiles should not be viewed as low-amplitude laughs. However, in response to humorous material, or to signal positive affect, smiles are emitted more frequently and at lower thresholds than laughter.) Most subjects smiled in response to stimulus laughter on the first trial, but, as with laughter-evoked laughter, laughter-evoked smiling declined over trials, until few subjects smiled on trial 10. Although not studied systematically, contagious laughs and smiles have much shorter response latencies than contagious yawns.

The polarity of subjects' responses to the laugh stimulus shifted over trials. Although the question was not asked during earlier trials, after trial 10, most subjects answered "yes" when asked if they found the stimulus "obnoxious." As a veteran of many such experiments, I can attest to the aversiveness of repeated canned laughter. The dual (positive/negative) nature of laughter is consistent with everyday experience. To "laugh with" friends consolidates the social bonds between group members, but to "laugh at" someone is to mock them, to exclude them from the "in group." Jeering among adolescent gangs may even escalate into violence leading to injury or death. In this context, it is noteworthy that mobbing, a synchronized group response by some birds and mammals to drive often larger invaders from their territories, is functionally similar to human jeering, shows social facilitation, and involves a simple, staccato, repetitive cry similar to laughter (Eibl-Eibesfeldt, 1989, p. 315).

The power of contagious laughter as a social coupling process should not be underestimated. Consider a persistent epidemic of laughter that began among 12- to 18-year-old girls in a boarding school in Tanganyika and spread throughout a district, requiring the closing of schools (Rankin & Philip, 1963). The potency of the effect has long been recognized by the entertainment industry, which developed the technology of "canned" laughter for broadcast television comedy shows, "laugh boxes," and "laugh records" such as that produced by *Okeh*, one of the most popular novelty recordings of all time (Provine, 1992, 1996a).

In the present research, laughter itself was sufficient to evoke laughter in audiences. You can dispose of the joke and maintain much of the laughter. The characteristics of laughter described here are relevant to several central issues in speech science. Contagious laughter involves the replication in the perceiver of the motor pattern that originally generated the vocalization in the sender. This intimacy between laugh production and detection, characteristic of contagion, suggests a highly specialized functional correlation and/or co-evolution of vocalization and perception, a conclusion relevant to motor theories of speech perception and associated issues of modularization of function (Mattingly & Studdert-Kennedy, 1991).

Laughter in the speech stream

Laughter is an ancient vocalization in the universal human vocabulary that coexists with modern speech. The antiquity of laughter is suggested by its presence (but in somewhat different form) in other great apes (Marler & Tenaza, 1977; Provine, 1996a; Provine & Bard, 1994, 1995). Although laughter is sprinkled through speech, we do not "speak" laughter. Laughter is under weak voluntary control. Ask someone to laugh for you, and you will probably be informed that they cannot laugh on command, or you will be provided forced, artificial-sounding laughter.[3] Normal laughter is emitted during certain social encounters, perhaps reflecting the mechanism and circumstance of many animal vocalizations. (See Marler & Evans, chapter 6, this volume, for a discussion of animal communication.) Given the prominence of laughter in speech, it is curious that texts concerning speaking and listening ignore the subject.

To examine the placement of laughter in speech, 1,200 cases of naturally occurring laughter were observed in anonymous adults, mostly college students, in public places (Provine, 1993). Observers sought groups of laughing people and recorded who laughed (speaker or audience), gender of speaker and audience, and what was said immediately before laughter occurred. This straightforward descriptive study reveals new, sometimes counterintuitive, information about the relation between speech and language, laughter and humor, and gender differences in laugh patterns.

During conversation, laughter by either speaker or audience seldom interrupted the phrase structure of speech (8 in 1,200 cases by speaker, 0 by audience [Provine, 1993]). A speaker may say, "You are going where?! Ha-ha." but rarely "You are going – ha-ha – where?!" The reliability of this phenomenon is noteworthy, given the relatively unstructured nature of most conversational dialogue. Because laughter by speaker or audience occurred immediately after complete phrases, laughter can be said to "punctuate" speech. This punctuation effect is so strong that it may be confirmed by cursory observations of everyday social conversations.

The finding that laughter seldom interrupts speech indicates that there is a lawful and probably neurologically programmed process responsible for this temporal organization (Provine, 1993). The near absence of speech interruptions by laughter indicates further that speech has priority over laughter in gaining access to the single vocalization channel. Laughter's subservience to speech is similar to the situation with breathing and coughing, other airway maneuvers that occur almost exclusively during speech pauses. The placement of signed laughter in the stream of signed speech of congenitally deaf signers would be of considerable interest because their speech is not constrained by respiratory patterns or a common organ of vocalization (Provine, 1993). The degree of sparing of the pattern of laughter of speakers and audiences having various aphasias would provide information about the segregation of neural mechanisms of speech and laughter.

Contrary to folk wisdom, most laughter is not a consequence of structured attempts at humor such as joke or story telling (Provine, 1993). Only 10% to 20% of pre-laugh comments are even mildly humorous. Although opinions vary about what is funny, few would consider "I wouldn't say so" or "Here comes Andre" promising comedy material. Yet such is the stuff of most pre-laugh comments.

Another unexpected finding was that speakers, especially females, laugh more than their audience (Provine, 1993). Overall, speakers laughed 46% more than their audience. The difference was especially great when female speakers were conversing with a male audience, a condition producing 127% more speaker than audience laughter. Neither males nor females laughed as much to female as to male speakers.

Our observations of naturally occurring laughter reveal previously unappreciated facts about laughter, several of which require consideration in future studies (Provine, 1993, 1996a).

1. Laughter is a social vocalization that almost disappears in people placed in solitary situations (Provine & Fischer, 1989). Attempts to study individual subjects in a laboratory setting are unlikely to produce much laughter and may not be ecologically valid. Even comedy videos, a form of vicarious social stimulation, will seem funnier and evoke more laughs if they are observed in a group setting.

2. Most laughter is not a response to jokes or other formal attempts at humor (Provine, 1993). Research based on an audience's response to jokes or cartoons, although valid in its own domain, is of limited relevance to most everyday laughter. Most laughter is sprinkled through a rich stream of speech, facial expressions, gestures, and postural changes. The exclusive focus on humor deflects consideration of broader and deeper roots of laughter in human vocal communication and social interaction. Given these data, it is not surprising that over two thousand years of speculating on why jokes are funny (i.e., evoke laughter) has contributed little to our understanding of laughter.

3. Speaker and audience laughter must be differentiated. The finding that speakers laugh more than their audience indicates the limits of research that reports only audience behavior, the typical approach of humor research. The speaker and audience are engaged in a social relationship, and the contribution of both must be considered (Provine, 1993).

4. The pattern of speaker and audience laughter depends on gender. For example, neither males nor females laugh as much to female as to male speakers, and female speakers are especially likely to laugh when conversing with a male audience (Provine, 1993). These laugh patterns may be species-wide. Males in a variety of cultures engage in more laugh-evoking activity than females, and gender differences emerge as early as 6 years of age, when joking first appears (Castell & Goldstein, 1977; Chapman & Foot, 1976; Chapman, Smith, & Foot, 1980; McGhee, 1979).

Yawning as a motor act

There is a tendency in the behavioral and social sciences to describe the frequency of an act, or how it correlates with or predicts other behavior, and never to get around to describing the behavior. Yet such descriptions are necessary for future developmental, comparative, and neurophysiological analyses. So as not to repeat this error, I now provide brief descriptions and general information about two of the less well-known target behaviors, yawning and laughter (next section).

Yawns are slow, involuntary gaping movements of the mouth that begin with a slow inspiration and end with a briefer inspiration. Yawning is highly stereotyped in form (Provine, 1986). For example, during yawns, inhalation through the mouth is obligatory, in contrast to normal breathing, which can be done with equal facility through either nose or mouth. The typical yawn lasts about 6 sec, but some yawns are longer or shorter in duration. Yawns are under little conscious control. Whether occurring spontaneously or as a contagious response, yawns go to completion. Everyone is aware of the difficulty in stifling a yawn. When performed in series, yawns recur at variable intervals of about a minute. Yawns feel good. On a 1 (bad) to 10 (good) scale, people rate yawns as about 8.5.

Yawning is widespread among vertebrate animals (Baenninger, 1987; Deputte, 1994; Heusner, 1946; Provine, 1986). Behavior resembling yawning is performed by diverse animals including crocodiles, snakes, fish, birds, and mammals, although contagious yawning may be exclusive to humans. Spontaneous yawning begins near the end of the first trimester and remains prominent throughout life. However, contagious yawning may not develop until the second year (Provine, 1989a).

There is much folklore about yawning and its causes, some of which stands the test of scientific scrutiny. Sleepy or bored people do yawn a lot. This is the basis for simulated yawns being a rude gesture expressing drowsiness or boredom. Most yawning occurs during the hours shortly before bedtime and after waking (slightly more after waking), when people are presumably sleepy (Provine, Hamernik, & Curchack, 1987). Furthermore, people yawn more in boring than interesting situations (Provine & Hamernik, 1986).

Stretching and yawning occur concurrently after waking but not before bedtime (Provine et al., 1987). The coupling between yawning and stretching suggests that yawns may have evolved as a type of stretch involving the head and face. Provocative evidence for a relationship between yawning and stretching is the involuntary ("associated") stretching movements of the paralyzed limbs that some hemiplegics perform during yawns.

It is not known whether yawning hastens or impedes sleep or has neither or both effects (Provine et al., 1987). Yawning may have several functions. Although sleepy people yawn, so do paratroopers before their first jump. Yawning may facilitate the transition between states or activities such as sleep and wakefulness.

Contrary to folk wisdom, yawning *is not* triggered by a buildup of CO_2 or a low level of O_2 in the blood (Provine, Tate, & Geldmacher, 1987). Increasing blood CO_2 by breathing 5% CO_2 (over 100 times the amount in air) does not increase yawning, and the complementary process of breathing 100% O_2 does not inhibit yawning. However, both interventions have other major respiratory effects.

Laughter as a motor act in humans and chimpanzees

The simple, highly stereotyped acoustic structure of human laughter is characterized by one or more forcibly voiced, acoustically symmetric, vowel-like notes (i.e., "ha," "ho," "he") having durations of around 75 msec (Provine & Yong, 1991) (Figure 7.2). These laugh notes recur at regular intervals of around 210 msec and proceed with a decrescendo. Notes late in a sequence have progressively lower amplitudes. Laugh notes have strong harmonic structure, with females having higher-pitched average fundamental frequencies (H_o = 502 Hz) than males (H_o = 276 Hz). Variations of the characteristic theme usually involve the first or last note of a laugh episode (i.e., "haaa-ha-ha," "ha-ha-haaa," "cha-ha-ha") and are constrained within a narrow range by the vocalization apparatus. It is informative to experience the difficulty of laughing with notes or internote intervals that are shorter or longer than usual. The aspirant-like sounds occurring in the spaces between the laugh notes bear little information; laughter with these sounds edited out still sounds normal. Conversely, if the laugh notes are edited out and the spaces closed up, all that remains is a long breathy sigh that is very unlaughlike.

The notes of human laughter parse and are performed exclusively during expiration. Although we do not "speak" laughter (as noted previously, laughter is under weak conscious control), the notes of human laughter are formed in a manner similar to speaking "ha-ha-ha." Speech involves a modulation of expiratory airflow. In contrast to the human pattern, chimpanzee (*Pan troglodytes*) laughter resembles panting or grunting, with a single breathy vocalization being produced during each expiration and inspiration (Provine, 1996a; Provine & Bard, 1994, 1995). The chimpanzee vocalization is tied more closely to the respiratory cycle. If this coupling of vocalization to breathing is a general property of vocal control, it suggests an important and unappreciated constraint on the evolution of vocal speech in chimpanzees and probably other great apes (Provine, 1996a; Provine & Bard, 1994, 1995).

Tickling as communication: An enigma resolved

Most people are aware that you cannot tickle yourself. However, the significance of this fact for understanding tickle has not been fully appreciated. You cannot tickle yourself because tickle is a context-

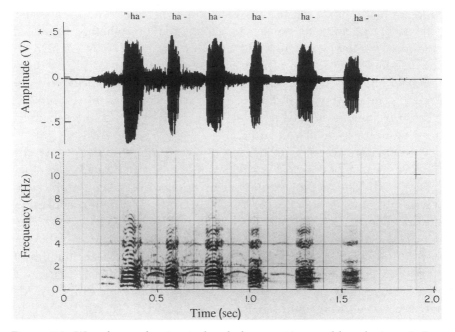

Figure 7.2. Waveform of a 6-note laugh from a 46-year-old male (*upper*). Frequency spectrum of the same laugh (*lower*). In the frequency spectrum, the stacks of evenly spaced horizontal bands of the voiced laughter are harmonics of the notes' fundamental frequency. Both the waveform and the frequency spectrum show the unvoiced aspiration that precedes and follows each voiced laugh note. Although the explosively voiced notes may have frequencies above 16kHz, most power is in frequencies below 8 kHz. From Provine & Yong (1991).

dependent social process that involves both the ticklee and the tickler (Provine, 1996b). As noted earlier with laughter, if a person is removed from the necessary social setting, the response almost disappears. Given the social nature of tickle, it is hardly surprising that the behavior has been grudging in divulging its secrets to anatomists and physiologists.

The proposal of tickle as social behavior is consistent with the sparse research data. In a study of tickling oneself, Weiskrantz, Elliott, and Darlington (1971) showed that the intensity of the tickle sensation varied inversely with the subject's control over and predictability of a tactile stimulus. They explained this result in terms of proprioceptive feedback (efference) that cancels self-produced stimulation. Without such efference, we would be constantly tickling ourselves by accident.

By inference, progressively less predictable (thus, increasingly nonself) stimuli are increasingly effective in evoking the sensation of tickle. The efference that inhibits self-tickling enhances the signal-to-noise ratio and detectability of animate, nonself tactile stimulation, whether produced by a mother's loving touch, a playmate, or a parasite. It is adaptive to defend against the source of nonself tactile stimulation of such vulnerable (and highly ticklish) body parts as the neck, back of knees, crook of elbows, genitals, thorax, and all body orifices. Consider, for example, a cat's ear flicking away a fly, or your strong defensive reaction to an insect crawling up the side of your neck.

The defensive response to nonself motile, tactile stimulation may be the circumstance of the most ancient form of tickle. In humans and other great apes, tickle has evolved into an act of tactile social communication between the tickler and ticklee in which tactile stimulation evokes an attenuated form of the defense reaction of the ticklee in addition to something new, laughter, a vocalization reinforcing the behavior of the tickler. In this new social context, we observe several paradoxical qualities of tickle: Even invited and presumably pleasant tickle is often accompanied by a fending away of the hand of the tickler; initially pleasurable tickle may become aversive if intense or prolonged; and the social context contributes much to the nature of the response. Consider the difference in response to similar, potentially tickling stimuli when administered by a playful friend versus a stranger. Clearly, tickle is not a simple reflex evoked by a simple, physically definable stimulus.

At this point, the story of tickle merges into that of laughter. (For an exploration of the relation between tickling and humorous laughter in the context of the Darwin-Hecker hypothesis, see Fridlund & Loftis, 1990.) When tickled, chimpanzees and other great apes produce a vocalization that resembles but is not identical to human laughter in sound or social context (Provine, 1996a; Provine & Bard, 1994, 1995). Although humans laugh when tickled, most adult human laughter occurs during conversation in which individuals have little, if any, physical contact. Chimpanzees, in contrast, laugh almost exclusively during physical contact, or threat of such contact, and during chasing games (the individual being chased laughs the most), wrestling, or tickling. Tickle games and laughter among both chimpanzees and humans may establish in-group bonds; we only tickle and are tickled by those with whom we have close social relationships such as friends, relatives, and lovers.

Tickle and laughter have another very important but unappreciated function, the establishment and maintenance of social interactions between the infant and its mother. Tickle and laughter responses develop early in chimpanzees and humans and involve a chain of mutually rewarding give-and-take stimulation and response between mother and infant that may encourage, sustain, and regulate the intensity of physical interaction (Plooij, 1979; Provine, 1996a; Provine & Bard, 1995). A baby's laughter is a positive reinforcer of maternal tickling. When the tickling becomes too intense, the baby's laughter turns to crying or fussing, a signal to the mother to stop or reduce the vigor of tactile stimulation. Nonspeaking primate babies possess powerful vocal reinforcers.

I close with a caveat and recommendation. In tickle and laughter, as in the earlier cases of yawning and smiling, we have ancient, stereotyped behaviors over which we exercise only modest conscious control. The traditional difficulty in discussing such behaviors is the likely consequence of attempting to reason about prelinguistic, largely unconscious processes of the affective domain. Language, a precision tool of the intellect, may not serve us as well in the realm of emotion, empathy, and intuition. It is useful to approach human behavior in an objective manner, as if we were studying another species, ethologists stalking not the rain forest but city sidewalks and shopping malls, with a fresh eye and naive curiosity that permits us to see the familiar in new ways.

Notes

1 These data, based on the *probability* (not frequency) of an event per hour, are effective in revealing circadian and social trends for a given act, but they are limited in their ability to provide direct comparisons between the relative frequency of behaviors, a purpose for which they were not intended (i.e., 1 or 10 performances of an act during a given hour would yield identical probabilities of 1.0.). Talking, for example, is much more than four times as frequent in social as in solitary situations.

2 Although any signal may synchronize the behavior or physiology of a group (i.e., an alarm cry triggers escape and/or fear), only a response in which the *identical* act is replicated in an observer is propagated as a behavioral chain reaction from individual to individual. If yawns evoked either a cardiovascular change or a knee jerk instead of yawns in others, there would be no contagion.

3 Although both laughter (primarily a vocal stimulus) and smiling (a visual stimulus) signal positive affect, we have much greater voluntary control over smiling than laughter. Differences between "false" and "felt" smiles aside (Ekman & Friesen, 1982), it is much easier to produce a smile than a laugh on command. Try it. Smiling is a better operant than laughter and is a much more flexible instrument of social discourse.

References

Alcock, J. (1989). *Animal behavior* (4th ed., pp. 26–27). Sutherland, MA: Sinauer Associates, Inc.

Averill, J. R. (1983). Studies on anger and aggression. *American Psychologist, 38,* 1145–1160.

Baenninger, R. (1987). Some comparative aspects of yawning in *Betta splendens, Homo sapiens, Panthera leo,* and *Papio sphinx. Journal of Comparative Psychology, 101,* 349–354.

Carskadon, M. A. (1991). Yawning elicited by reading: Is an open mouth a sufficient stimulus? *Sleep Research, 20,* 116.

Carskadon, M. A. (1992). Yawning elicited by reading: Effects of sleepiness. *Sleep Research, 21,* 101.

Castell, P. J., & Goldstein, J. H. (1977). Social occasions for joking: A cross cultural study. In A. J. Chapman & H. C. Foot (Eds.), *It's a funny thing, humour* (pp. 193–197). Oxford: Pergamon Press.

Chapman, A. J., & Foot, H. C. (Eds.). (1976). *Humor and laughter: Theory, research and applications.* New York: Wiley.

Chapman, A. J., Smith, J., & Foot, H. C. (1980). Humour, laughter and social interaction. In E. McGhee & A. J. Chapman (Eds.), *Children's humour.* New York: Wiley.

Deputte, B. L. (1994). Ethological study of yawning in primates. I. Qualitative analyses and study of causation in two species of old world monkeys (*Cercocebus albigena* and *Macaca fascicularis*). *Ethology, 98,* 221–245.

Eibl-Eibesfeldt, I. (1989). *Human ethology.* New York: Aldine de Gruyter.

Ekman, P., & Friesen, W. V. (1982). Felt, false, and miserable smiles. *Journal of Nonverbal Behavior, 6,* 238–252.

Farb, P. (1974). *Word play.* New York: Knopf.

Fridlund, A. J., & Loftis, J. M. (1990). Relations between tickling and humorous laughter: Preliminary support for the Darwin-Hecker hypothesis. *Biological Psychology, 30,* 141–150.

Fridlund, A. J., Sabini, J. P., Hedlund, L. E., Schaut, J. A., Shenker, J. I., & Knauer, M. J. (1990). Social determinants of facial expressions during affective imagery: Displaying to the people in your head. *Journal of Nonverbal Behavior, 14,* 113–137.

Heusner, A. P. (1946). Yawning and associated phenomena. *Physiological Review, 25,* 156–168.

Leonard, C. M., Voeller, K. K. S., & Kuldau, J. M. (1991). When's a smile a smile? Or how to detect a message by digitizing the signal. *Psychological Sciences, 2,* 166–172.

Lockard, J. S., Fahrenbruch, C. E., Smith, J. L., & Morgan, C. J. (1977). Smiling and laughter: Different phyletic origins. *Bulletin of the Psychonomic Society, 10,* 183–186.

Marler, P., & Tenaza, R. (1977). Signalling behavior of apes with special reference to vocalization. In T. A. Sebeok (Ed.), *How animals communicate* (pp. 965–1033). Bloomington: Indiana University Press.

Mattingly, I. G., & Studdert-Kennedy, M. (Eds.). (1991). *Modularity and the motor theory of speech perception.* Hillsdale, NJ: Erlbaum.

McGhee, P. E. (1979). *Humor: Its origins and development.* San Francisco: Freeman.

Meltzoff, A. N., & Moore, M. K. (1977). Imitation of facial and manual gestures by human neonates. *Science, 198,* 75–78.

Meltzoff, A. N., & Moore, M. K. (1983). Newborn infants imitate adult facial gestures. *Child Development, 54,* 702–709.

Plooij, F. (1979). How wild chimpanzee babies trigger the onset of mother–infant play – and what the mother makes of it. In M. Bullowa (Ed.), *Before speech:*

The beginning of interpersonal communication (pp. 223–243). Cambridge: Cambridge University Press.

Provine, R. R. (1986). Yawning as a stereotyped action pattern and releasing stimulus. *Ethology, 72,* 109–122.

Provine, R. R. (1989a). Contagious yawning and infant imitation. *Bulletin of the Psychonomic Society, 27*(2), 125–126.

Provine, R. R. (1989b). Faces as releasers of contagious yawning: An approach to face detection using normal human subjects. *Bulletin of the Psychonomic Society, 27,* 211–214.

Provine, R. (1992). Contagious laughter: Laughter is a sufficient stimulus for laughs and smiles. *Bulletin of the Psychonomic Society, 30,* 1–4.

Provine, R. R. (1993). Laughter punctuates speech: Linguistic, social and gender contexts of laughter. *Ethology, 95,* 291–298.

Provine, R. R. (1996a). Laughter. *American Scientist, 84,* 38–45.

Provine, R. R. (1996b). Ticklish talk: A letter to the editor and reply. *American Scientist, 84,* 100–101.

Provine, R. R. (1996c). Contagious yawning and laughter: Significance for sensory feature detection, motor pattern generation, imitation, and the evolution of social behavior. In C. M. Heyes & B. G. Galef (Eds.), *Social learning in animals: The roots of culture* (pp. 179–208). New York: Academic Press.

Provine, R. R., & Bard, K. A. (1994). Laughter in chimpanzees and humans: A comparison. *Society for Neuroscience Abstracts, 20,* part 1, p. 367.

Provine, R. R., & Bard, K. A. (1995). Why chimps can't talk: The laugh probe. *Society for Neuroscience Abstracts, 21,* part 1, p. 456.

Provine, R. R., & Fischer, K. R. (1989). Laughing, smiling, and talking: Relation to sleeping and social context in humans. *Ethology, 83,* 295–305.

Provine, R. R., & Hamernik, H. B. (1986). Yawning: Effects of stimulus interest. *Bulletin of the Psychonomic Society, 24,* 437–438.

Provine, R. R., Hamernik, H. B., & Curchack, B. C. (1987). Yawning: Relation to sleeping and stretching in humans. *Ethology, 76,* 152–160.

Provine, R. R., Tate, B. C., & Geldmacher, L. L. (1987). Yawning: No effect of 3–5% CO_2, 100% O_2, and exercise. *Behavioral and Neural Biology, 48,* 382–393.

Provine, R. R., & Yong, Y. L. (1991). Laughter: A stereotyped human vocalization. *Ethology, 89,* 115–124.

Rankin, A. M., & Philip, P. J. (1963). An epidemic of laughing in the Bukoba District of Tanganyika. *Central African Journal of Medicine, 9,* 167–170.

Weiskrantz, L, Elliott, J., & Darlington, C. (1971). Preliminary observations on tickling oneself. *Nature, 230,* 598–599.

8. A neurobehavioral approach to the recognition of facial expressions in infancy

CHARLES A. NELSON AND MICHELLE DE HAAN

To young infants who have not yet developed the capacity for language, the human face holds particular significance. After all, it is the face that conveys a range of nonverbal information, including identity, gender, age, affective state, and possibly intention (e.g., pursing of the lips suggestive of a forthcoming kiss). Although this visual information is also important to adults, they are less dependent on it since, unlike infants, they are able to take advantage of information conveyed through language.

Of the many types of information that the face transmits to the infant or young child, facial expressions may be the most important. Darwin (1896) first brought this to attention by suggesting that the display and recognition of facial expressions may represent an adaptation that serves the purpose of communication and survival. For example, an infant's recognition of an angry expression displayed by a stranger could facilitate a crying response, which will in turn bring the caregiver to protect the infant. Similarly, an infant's recognition of a happy expression displayed by the caregiver could facilitate the expression of happiness in the infant, which could contribute to the development of the attachment relationship (Bowlby, 1969).

How does the ability to recognize expressions develop?

Biological contributions

One factor that may contribute to the development of the ability to recognize expressions is development of the neural systems involved in recognition. In previous writings, one of us (Nelson, 1987, 1993) suggested that the ability to recognize facial expressions of emotion represents a selective adaptation resulting in the creation of specialized neural systems that subserve this ability. This argument is partly based on studies showing that infants just a few months old are able to discriminate among different "types" of expressions (e.g., happy, fear). This suggests some degree of "prewiring"; that is, the neural systems that mediate recognition of expressions may require little experience to develop.[1]

If recognizing expressions is adaptive for the infant, then these neural systems may emerge independent of any experience. For example, the development of these neural systems could be regulated by a genetic program that does not require experience and is common to all members of the species. This account remains unproven, however, for several reasons. First, simply because an ability emerges early in life does not mean that it is "innate" and uninfluenced by experience. It is entirely possible that the necessary experience occurs prenatally or shortly after birth. Moreover, experience with facial expressions themselves may not be necessary; for example, the necessary experience could be nonspecific (e.g., simply viewing faces or facelike stimuli is sufficient). Second, there have not been, nor will there likely be, studies in the human newborn showing that certain populations of neurons respond selectively to expressions; nor is there any evidence for genes that specifically regulate expression recognition. Moreover, although such data might be considered the strongest evidence of an adaptive ability that has been selected through evolution, resulting in dedicated neural hardware, they would still not prove that experience is unimportant for development. For example, experience could regulate the expression of genes related to expression recognition.

Experiential contributions

An alternative to this strongly maturational view is that the neural structures involved in recognition of expressions do require some type of experience in order to develop. Unfortunately, the nature of this experience has yet to be adequately catalogued. That is, we have little idea to what expressions the young infant is exposed; whether the infant actually attends to these expressions; and how much of this information actually "passes" through the visual system unimpeded (due to built-in constraints, such as an underdeveloped fovea, lateral geniculate nucleus, etc.; see Bronson, 1994; Nelson, 1987). Accordingly, we are unable to specify what role experience plays in the recognition of facial expressions until we document such experiences.

Even in cases where investigators have attempted to document infants' experience of expressions in the natural environment, it can be difficult to draw conclusions about how this experience affects development. For example, Kuchuk, Vibbert, and Bornstein (1986) found that infants who showed greater sensitivity to photographs of smiling faces had mothers who more frequently encouraged attention to themselves when they were smiling. One interpretation of these results is that encouraging infants to attend to certain expressions causes an increase in their sensitivity to those expressions. However, an alternative interpretation could be that infants who are "constitutionally" more sensitive to expressions elicit more expression-directed interactions from their caregivers.

How, then, does the ability to recognize facial expressions develop? The maturationist/evolutionary argument can account for the early emergence of the ability, but this argument is post hoc, and no data directly support it. On the other hand, little is known about the infant's early exposure to expressions (or other relevant stimuli), and it can be difficult to determine how this experience affects perception of expressions. One way to resolve this impasse may be to search for linkages between brain and behavior that collectively act in the service of expression recognition. For example, one can study the pattern of brain activation during the time a subject is recognizing the visual display of emotion. By adopting this approach, the intractable issue of proportioning variance to maturation (presumably under some form of genetic control) and to experience (presumably acquired through some learning mechanism) can be avoided, and instead we can simply focus on interpreting behavior in the context of its neurobiological underpinnings. We herein employ three strategies to facilitate this goal, with the hope of deriving a biologically plausible model for the processes underlying the recognition of facial expressions.

We begin our review by describing the behavioral literature on the development of the infant's ability to recognize facial expressions. From this review, we conclude that the components of this ability are present within the first few months of life but that the ability to recognize facial expressions is far from fully assembled even as "late" as the first year and beyond. Because these studies rely on observing the infant's overt behavior, the data reviewed in this section of the chapter do not permit us to address the issue of the neural mechanisms that mediate expression recognition. Accordingly, in the next two sections, we turn our attention to the neurophysiological literature on this subject. Here we focus first on the nonhuman primate and human adult, and second on the nonhuman primate and human infant. Although the types of studies done with these two populations differ considerably, a pattern emerges from this review that points to some common underlying mechanisms.

What are "facial expressions of emotion"?

Humans, and most likely other primates, display emotion through a number of sensory channels – for example, through the auditory system (vocalizations), the somatosensory system (sense of touch), possibly the olfactory system (e.g., odor emitted under conditions of fear), and certainly the visual system. With regard to vision, the various physical components of the face (e.g., mouth, eyes, brow, etc.) are capable of reliably arranging in certain ways that give rise to labelable or identifiable expressions (at least by adult human standards). These expressions, in turn, can, under certain circumstances, reflect an underlying affective state. Thus, as Ekman (e.g., 1972) and many others have demonstrated, there are characteristic movements of the face that adults readily identify as representing discrete emotions. *For the purposes of the present chapter, we are simply concerned with whether infants treat these expressions as discrete entities that are discriminable from one another.* That is, can infants discriminate one expression from another, and do they perceive different examples of the one type of emotion as belonging to the same category? Although a distal goal may well be to determine whether infants recognize these expressions as representing emotion per se, our proximal goal is simply to determine whether they discriminate these expressions in ways similar to that of adults. It is assumed that these two goals are intimately related in development, with the recognition process perhaps scaffolding onto the discrimination process.

One final point should be stressed when talking about the "recognition" of facial expressions. Unlike adults who can verbally label an expression (e.g., "that is happy, that is fear," and so on), infants must convey their recognition through nonverbal means. Developmental psychologists have devised a number of clever methods to evaluate recognition and discrimination, but we must concede at the outset that what the adult does and what the infant does may well reflect two different processes (e.g., the infant may respond to an expression as a collection of perceptual attributes that may or may not possess some signal strength such as "fearfulness," whereas the adult may respond to the same expression as a holistic pattern that represents a particular underlying affect). Although we suspect (and certainly hope) that this is not the case, we are unable to address this point because the types of studies done with infants have not been done with adults.

The perception of facial expressions as inferred from behavior

This literature has been reviewed in recent years by a number of authors (e.g., Nelson, 1985, 1987, 1993; Nelson & Ludemann, 1989; Oster, Daily, & Goldenthal, 1989; Walker-Andrews, 1988), and the reader is encouraged to consult these sources. For present purposes, we simply summarize this work, directing most of our attention to studies published since approximately 1990.

A number of investigators in the first half of this century examined the extent to which infants and young children could discriminate facial expressions as portrayed by live actors (e.g., Ahrens, 1954; Buhler & Hetzer, 1928; Spitz & Wolf, 1946). Although the findings from this work suggested that the ability to discriminate facial expressions appears relatively early in life (e.g., 5–6 months), methodological problems made interpretation of the findings difficult (e.g., observers were not blind to the facial actions of the model; often no control conditions were used; because live models were used, stimuli may not have been consistent across subjects). Although more recent attempts improved upon how live faces were used to examine infants' perception of expressions (e.g., independent observers verified that a particular expression was actually posed; Field, Woodson, Greenberg, & Cohen, 1982), other methodological concerns persisted (e.g., the person posing the expressions also held the infant, so body movements and not only expressions could have influenced infants' responses).

As the methods of experimental psychology improved, studies began to be undertaken in which testing conditions and stimuli were better controlled. The results of this work suggest that infants may be able to discriminate among expressions even earlier than was initially thought. For example, 3-month-olds can discriminate happy and sad faces from surprised faces (Younge-Browne, Rosenfeld, & Horowitz, 1977) and smiling faces from frowning faces (Barrera & Maurer, 1981). By 4 months, infants can discriminate joyful expressions from angry or neutral ones (LaBarbera, Izard, Vietze, & Parisi, 1976); by 5 months, they can discriminate among sad, fearful, and, under certain conditions, angry expressions (Schwartz, Izard, & Ansul, 1985); and between 5 and 7 months, they can discriminate among happy, surprised, and "woe" (presumably sadness) expressions (Spieker, 1985). During this age period, infants can also discriminate among different examples of the same type of expression. For example, 3-month-olds can discriminate among smiling faces that vary in intensity (e.g., very vs. mildly happy; Kuchuk et al., 1986), 4-month-olds can discriminate between mild and intense examples of happy faces (Nelson & Ludemann, 1986), and 7-month-olds can discriminate between mild and intense examples of happy and fearful faces (Ludemann & Nelson, 1988).

Studies such as these (and others; see reviews cited earlier) provide evidence that infants are capable of discriminating the features of the face that to an adult denote expression. However, because in these studies only a single model posed all of the expressions, it is not clear whether (1) infants' responses were specific to the particular model's face selected for study rather than responses to expressions in general, and (2) infants were simply discriminating local differences in pattern information (e.g., upturned vs. downturned mouth) or were responding to the configuration of features that make up an expression. One way to address these issues is to test whether infants are capable of generalized discrimination of expressions. That is, do they recognize that an expression is the same even when it is posed by several different models? If infants are able to do this, it suggests that their responses are not limited to a particular model's face and are unlikely to be based on local differences in pattern information. For example, Nelson, Morse, and Leavitt (1979) habituated 7-month-olds to different models posing a happy expression. Following habituation, the infants saw a new model posing a happy expression and a fearful expression. Nelson et al. found that infants looked longer at the fearful expression than at the happy expression. This suggests that the infants recognized the happy expression as familiar, despite the change in model, and were able to discriminate this expression from the fearful expression (i.e., the infants showed generalized discrimination or categorization of happy). In contrast to these results, infants at this age did *not* show generalized discrimination if they were first habituated to different models posing fearful expressions. Subsequent studies replicated and extended these findings. For example, 7-month-olds showed generalized discrimination of happy from fear following habituation to happy faces posed by (1) multiple male or female models (Nelson & Dolgin, 1985), and (2) female models that varied in how intensely the expression was depicted (e.g., slightly happy with no teeth showing and very happy with teeth showing [Ludemann & Nelson, 1988]). However, it was observed rather consistently that 6- to 7-month-olds showed no evidence of generalized discrimination when first habituated to faces showing a fear or surprise face and then tested with happy faces (Caron, Caron, & Myers, 1982; Ludemann & Nelson, 1988; Nelson & Dolgin, 1985).

It is not clear whether infants younger than 6 to 7 months are also capable of generalized discrimination of facial expressions. In one study (Caron et al., 1982), 30-, 24-, and 18-week-olds were habituated to four different models posing happy or surprise expressions and then tested with a new model posing both expressions. Thirty-week-olds showed generalized discrimination following habituation to either expression, 24-week-olds showed generalized discrimination only after habituation to happy, and 18-week-olds showed no evidence of generalized discrimination. These results suggest that categorization of expressions does not emerge until 6 to 7 months. However, this conclusion is drawn into question by the results of a more recent study (Serrano, Iglesias, & Loeches, 1992). In this study, a small ($n = 12$) group of 4- to 6-month-olds were habituated to several models depicting either anger, fear, or surprise. Following habituation, they were presented with new models depicting the familiar expression and one novel expression. When habituation trials were compared to test trials, infants showed reliable evidence of discrimination in all conditions, except when first habituated to surprise and then tested with surprise and fear. These results suggest that infants younger than 7 months categorize fear, anger, and possibly surprise expressions as representing discrete entities. However, an alternative interpretation is that infants did not categorize all the angry (or fearful, or happy, or surprise) faces as similar but instead failed to discriminate among the different examples of that expression. Recall that generalized discrimination of an expression involves perceiving the similarity of different examples within a category of expression despite discriminable differences between those examples. Because these authors did not test to see if infants could discriminate between the different models used, it is unclear whether the infants in their study were showing generalized discrimination or simply failing to notice that a new model was shown during the test.

Even by 7 months of age, infants' ability to categorize expressions may be limited. For example, they may have difficulty grouping expressions into broader categories, such as positive and negative expressions. This was demonstrated in a study in which 7- and 10-month-olds habituated either to a variety of models portraying various prototypical positive expressions (e.g., happy) or a variety of models portraying mixed or blended expressions collectively labeled by adults as representing "positive" affect (Ludemann, 1991). Following habituation, infants saw either novel models portraying a positive expression (to test for generalized discrimination) or novel models portraying negative expressions (anger and fear; to test for discrimination of negative from positive expressions). Ten-month-olds, but not 7-month-olds, could recognize the familiar expression and discriminate it from the novel expression following habituation to prototypical positive expressions. In contrast, neither age group showed evidence of generalized discrimination following habituation to blended positive expressions (i.e., infants neither recognized the new model as portraying the same affect as the habituation models nor did they discriminate the positive from negative affect). These results suggest that it is not until 10 months that infants are able to categorize expressions as positive or negative. Even by this age, infants' knowledge of facial expressions may be bound by prototypes, since infants did not recognize the expression when nonprototypical examples were used.

Summary

The data reviewed thus far suggest that even very young infants (e.g., within a few months of birth) are able to discriminate the features of the face that to an adult denote facial expressions. However, it may not be until after 6 to 7 months that infants begin to recognize that an expression remains the same despite discriminable differences in the intensity of the expression, identity, or gender of the model, and so on. Yet even at this age, infants' ability to categorize expressions is limited: They show evidence of categorization only after habituation to a particular expression (happy and sometimes surprise); they cannot categorize blends of expressions; and they cannot categorize different types of expressions into broader categories. What are the mechanisms underlying these changes in infants' responses to facial expressions? As discussed at the outset of this chapter, we do not know the extent to which experience with facial expressions contributes to the ability to subsequently perceive expressions. Nor do we know with any certainty with human infants (or children) what neural structures or systems subserve this ability. Recent experimental work with nonhuman primates and case studies with hu-

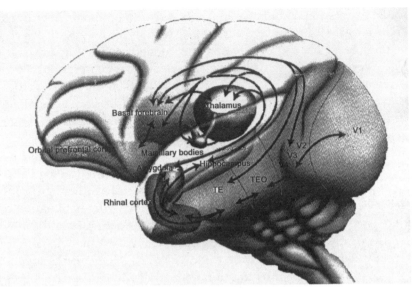

Figure 8.1. Some of the temporal lobe areas thought to be involved in monkeys' ability to recognize facial expressions. (From Bachevalier, Pascalis, & Overman, 1994, and reprinted with permission.)

man adults provide some suggestive evidence on the neural bases of expression recognition, and it is reviewed next. This is followed by a description of electrophysiological studies with human infants that builds on this nonhuman primate work.

Neural bases of expression recognition

Face-selective cells

Several investigators have reported the existence of neurons in the adult monkey brain that respond selectively to faces (reviewed in Desimone, 1991). These cells are found in several areas of the temporal cortex but are especially common in area TPO of the superior temporal polysensory area and areas TEa and TEm of the inferior temporal cortex, where they constitute between 10% and 20% of all visually responsive cells (see Figure 8.1; Baylis, Rolls, & Leonard, 1987; Rolls & Baylis, 1986; Yamane, Kaji, & Kawano, 1988). Face-selective cells are also found in other areas of the brain that receive projections from the temporal cortex, such as the amygdala (see Figure 8.1; Leonard, Rolls, Wilson, & Baylis, 1985;

Rolls, 1984) and the frontal cortex (Pigarev, Rizzolatti, & Scandolara, 1979).

To identify face-selective neurons, investigators usually begin by recording a cell's firing rate (i.e., number of action potentials over time) while showing the monkey a variety of face and nonface (e.g., sine waves, three-dimensional objects) stimuli. The activity of an individual cell can be measured by lowering small microelectrodes into the cortex and measuring the small voltage changes that occur at the tip of the electrode. These voltage changes emanate from the brain cell closest to the tip (Perrett & Mistlin, 1990). In general, if the magnitude of the cell's response to faces is at least two times greater than the magnitude of its largest response to any nonface object, then the cell is considered to be face-selective (e.g., Rolls & Baylis, 1986). Investigators report that 50% of cells identified in this way fire 5 to 10 times more in response to faces than to other objects (Hasselmo, Rolls, & Baylis, 1989; Rolls & Baylis, 1986).

Several investigators have attempted to determine whether cells identified in this way are truly selective for faces *qua* faces. For example, one possibility is that face-selective cells are actually responding to the visual complexity of a stimulus or to its meaningfulness. However, the results of several studies show that face-selective cells do *not* respond to other visually complex, meaningful stimuli such as food, a snake, and so forth (Baylis, Rolls, & Leonard, 1985; Bruce, Desimone, & Gross, 1981; Rolls & Baylis, 1986). Furthermore, the responses of face-selective cells are only minimally influenced by a variety of manipulations of properties such as size (Rolls & Baylis, 1986) or spatial frequency composition (Rolls, Baylis, & Leonard, 1985). The results of these studies suggest that the responses of face-selective cells cannot be accounted for by visual complexity, stimulus meaningfulness, or simple perceptual properties of faces.

Expression-selective cells

A few investigators have included faces with emotional expressions in the set of faces shown to monkeys during recording of single-cell activity in the superior temporal sulcus (see Figure 8.1; Perrett et al., 1984) and amygdala (see Figure 8.1; Leonard et al., 1985). In both studies, investigators reported the existence of a small number of cells that responded more to certain expressions (e.g., yawn, open-mouth threat) than to others. However, in neither study was it clear whether these cells were truly selective for expressions, since facial expression and facial identity were not systematically varied. In a more detailed study, Hasselmo and colleagues (1989) recorded from cells in the temporal cortex while monkeys watched pictures of three other monkeys, each showing either a calm expression, a slight threat, or a full open-mouth threat. Of the 45 face-selective neurons identified, 9 cells responded to expression regardless of identity, 15 responded to identity regardless of expression, and 3 responded to both expression and identity. The expression-selective cells tended to be found in the upper (part of area STP) and lower (part of area TE) banks of the superior temporal sulcus, while the identity-selective cells were found in the inferior temporal gyrus (part of area TE). These results suggest that information about facial expressions may be processed separately from information about facial identity.

Investigators have also reported the existence of cells responsive to facial gestures and direction of gaze. For example, Perrett et al. (1984) observed that some cells respond to the opening of a mouth, lowering of a head, or lowering of eyes. In the anterior portion of STP, many cells responded to combinations of these gestures (e.g., both lowering of the head and opening of the mouth). These cells may play a role in the recognition of emotional expressions since (1) facial expressions involve movement of the face, and (2) most expressions involve alterations in combinations of facial features (e.g., the threat expression involves opening the mouth, lowering the head, and raising the eyebrows).

Summary

Studies of individual neurons' responses to faces suggest that there are cells that are more responsive to faces than to other objects. Some of these cells may be more sensitive to differences in facial identity, whereas others may be more sensitive to differences in facial expression. However, these differences are *relative* differences, not absolute ones. Specifically, there are no cells that respond *only* to one expression and not to any others, nor are there any that respond *only* to faces and not at all to any other object.

Moreover, the existence of cells selective for faces is not necessarily evidence that faces or facial expressions are "special" patterns or that there is any innate "wiring" for recognizing faces. Other arbitrary objects can receive the same kind of processing (i.e., selective responses at the single-cell level) as faces (Perrett & Oram, 1993). For example, there are cells in the amygdala selective for particular foods (e.g., watermelon; Ono & Nishijo, 1992) or nonfood items (e.g., model of a spider). In the temporal cortex, investigators have found cells selective for hands (Gross, Rocha-Miranda, & Bender, 1972) and for movements of body parts other than faces (e.g., the whole body walking; Oram & Perrett, 1994). In fact, one can find cells selective even for arbitrary patterns of learned significance. For example, Miyashita (1988, 1990) found that after training on a delayed-match-to-sample task using colored patterns, some cells fired only during the delay following a particular stimulus. Like the responses of face selective cells, the responses of these cells to the preferred pattern generalized across changes in size, position, and color. This suggests that cells selective for faces could exist even if the ability to recognize faces is not specifically "prewired" but is completely learned from experience with faces in the visual environment.

Based on the work with single cells, most investigators have concluded that the representation of both faces and other objects probably involves the pattern of firing across a population of cells with varying selectivity to particular features or combinations of features of the object (Gross, Rodman, Gochin, & Colombo, 1993; Perrett & Oram, 1993). The neural representation of faces may differ from that for other objects only in that there may be (1) a larger population of cells that participate in encoding faces than for other types of objects, and (2) more specificity in the responses of the face-selective cells than in the responses of cells that participate in the encoding of other objects (Gross et al., 1993). These differences may arise because it is more critical for monkeys (and humans) to tell apart individual faces than to tell apart individual members of other categories (e.g., fruit; Gross et al., 1993), and because faces are more similar to one another than are most other stimuli among which the monkey (or human) must discriminate (Damasio, Tranel, & Damasio, 1990; Gross et al., 1993).

Imaging studies in humans

There is a limited amount of evidence to suggest that there are neural responses specific to faces in adult humans. In humans, one way to measure the neural activity that occurs during recognition of a face is with electrodes placed on the scalp or directly on the cortical surface (the latter typically applies only to patients who are candidates for neurosurgery). For example, Ojemann, Ojemann, and Lettich (1992) recorded the brain activity of epileptic patients undergoing neurosurgery while subjects participated in several tasks including one where they were required to label slides of facial expressions. The activity of 3/21 populations of neurons, all in the middle temporal gyrus, increased when subjects labeled emotional expressions. These results suggest that there may be neurons in the human middle temporal gyrus that are specifically involved in the recognition of facial expressions. However, the results of this study should be interpreted with caution because (1) only a small number of faces ($n = 8$) was used, and (2) other interpretations of the results are possible (e.g., that the response has something to do with generating a verbal label for objects in general rather than recognizing facial expressions per se).

Another method that has been used to study the neural activity that occurs during recognition of facial expressions is positron emission tomography (PET). During a PET scan, regional cerebral blood flow is measured by observing the patterns of accumulation of a radioactively labeled substance injected into the subject's bloodstream. The pattern of regional cerebral blood flow can then be used to infer the pattern of brain activity.

Regions with greater blood flow are assumed to be more active. In one study (George et al., 1993), this method was used to image brain activity while subjects saw two faces at the top of a screen and one face at the bottom. The subject's task was to press a button to indicate which of the two top photos matched the bottom one. In one condition, the subject had to match the expression of the faces (varying degrees of neutral, sad, or happy), and in the other, the identity of the faces. The brain activity occurring during the identity matching task was then subtracted from the brain activity occurring during the expression matching task. This was done so that the brain activity related to the motor, motivational, and object-recognition aspects of the task was eliminated, leaving just the activity specific to the task of recognizing facial expressions. George et al. found that compared to the identity matching task, during emotional expression matching, there was right anterior cingulate and bilateral prefrontal/frontal (left greater than right) activation.

Although these results suggest that there may be specific areas of the brain involved in recognizing expressions, they should be interpreted with caution for several reasons. First, subjects made significantly more errors on the emotion matching task than on the identity matching task. Thus, differences between the two conditions could reflect nonspecific effects of task difficulty rather than specific effects of emotion recognition. Second, the faces used in the identity matching task also differed in facial expression. As the authors acknowledge, it is possible that subjects processed this information about the faces even though the task did not require them to do so. If this is the case, then activation of some of the areas involved in recognition of emotional expressions might have been "subtracted out" when the identity matching and facial expression matching tasks were compared.

These concerns notwithstanding, George et al.'s (1993) results suggest that the anterior cingulate cortex and regions of the frontal cortex may be involved in recognizing facial expressions. These areas differ from the areas in which most face-selective cells are found in the monkey brain. In those studies, face-selective cells were found primarily in the inferior temporal cortex and amygdala. It is interesting that in the study by George et al. (1993), the anterior temporal lobe (possibly reflecting the activity of the amygdala) *was* activated. But it was activated in *both* the expression matching task and the identity matching task. Thus, this activation "disappeared" when the two conditions were subtracted. This suggests that the anterior temporal region may be involved in both identity and expression matching. One reason why this region was activated during both tasks may be, as already mentioned, that the faces in the identity matching task did have facial expressions. If the anterior temporal region is specifically involved in recognizing facial expressions, it may have been activated in both identity matching and expression matching tasks if subjects processed the facial expressions during both tasks.

Case studies in humans

A different approach to understanding the neural mechanisms underlying recognition of expressions is to study patients with brain damage. If patients with damage to a particular area show impairments in recognizing expressions, it would suggest that this area is normally involved in that ability. For example, Adolphs, Tranel, Damasio, and Damasio (1994) recently studied the recognition of expressions in a patient (S. M.) with bilateral destruction of the amygdala caused by Urbach-Weithe disease, a rare genetic disease in which the tissue of the amygdala is replaced by mineral deposits. S. M. appears to have no trouble recognizing facial identity, but she has difficulty recognizing facial expressions. For example, in one task, S. M. was shown a series of photographs of angry, surprised, fearful, happy, disgusted, and sad expressions and asked to rate for each face how much of a given emotion was present (on a scale of 1 to 5). S. M. consistently rated the angry, fearful, and sad faces as less intense than did healthy controls or controls with damage to brain areas other than the amygdala. In other tasks, S. M. showed impairments in recognizing blends of expressions and in perceiving the similarity between different types of expressions. These results suggest that the amygdala may be involved in recognizing emotional expressions. Unfortunately, this conclusion may be tempered somewhat by the authors' failure to include appropriate control conditions. For example, S. M. was not asked to label expressions, nor was it determined whether her impairment was due to errors in making prototypicality judgments or errors in making intensity judgments with other stimuli (e.g., sunsets, phases of the moon, etc.).

Summary

The results of human imaging and case studies suggest that there are areas of the brain that are specially involved in the recognition of faces and facial expressions. The results of Adolph et al.'s case study, together with the single-cell work in monkeys, suggests that the anterior temporal lobe and/or amygdala play a central role in the recognition of facial expressions.[2] These results are, however, somewhat discrepant from the results of George et al.'s (1993) PET study. One reason for this apparent discrepancy may be the lack of spatial resolution inherent in PET studies. Perhaps improvements in this procedure as well as others (e.g., functional Magnetic Resonance Imaging, or fMRI) will eventually bring the sets of findings reviewed herein closer in concert. Another possible reason for discrepancies between studies is that different studies used different tasks to assess recognition of expressions. For example, in the studies with monkeys, animals typically perform a simple discrimination task while viewing the faces in order to maintain their attention/motivation (e.g., the monkey must learn not to lick to avoid an aversive taste when a circle is shown but is rewarded with juice for licking if any other object/face is shown); in George et al.'s study, subjects were required to match faces to sample; in Adolph et al.'s study, S. M. was asked to rate whether certain verbal labels applied to faces. These differences in task requirements may influence how expressions are processed and thus what neural processes are activated during recognition of expressions.

Developmental literature

Because the studies described so far have been conducted with adults, they do not address the question of how responses to facial expressions develop. One approach to this question is to look at the development of those structures (e.g., TE, STP, amygdala) that have been implicated in mediating the recognition of facial expressions in the adult human and nonhuman primate.[3] In so doing, we may be able to develop a theoretical link between the behavioral literature on the recognition of facial expressions and the neurobiological literature. This, in turn, may allow us to advance a model that accounts for the ontogeny of the ability to recognize facial expressions of emotion.

This section begins with a brief overview of developmental neuroanatomy, targeting for discussion the development of those brain regions implicated in the recognition of facial expressions. We then review the few studies that have been done with human infants in a cognitive neuroscience context that attempt to link structure and function.

Developmental neuroanatomy

Area TE. Work by Bachevalier and colleagues suggests that in the monkey, area TE is still immature during the first half-year of life (1 month in the infant monkey's life is thought to equal about 4 months in the infant human's life). For example, the metabolic activity of TE as measured by 2-DG uptake is barely detectable at 3 months and is not adultlike until 6 months (Hagger et al., 1988), and certain types of visual learning that depend on TE are not evident until after 3 months (Bachevalier, Brickson, Hagger, & Mishkin, 1990). In addition, lesions of TE, which cause severe deficits in visual recognition in adults, have only a minimal effect on visual recognition in infants less than 12 months old (Bachevalier & Mishkin, 1994). The connections between TE and other areas of the brain are also somewhat different in infants than adults in that (1) some connections are more widespread in infants than in adults, and (2) some additional connections exist in infants that are not present in adults (Rodman & Consuelos, 1994; Webster, Ungerleider, & Bachevalier, 1991). Together, these results suggest that area TE is not fully mature during the first half-year of life in the monkey.

However, there is also some evidence that other aspects of TE functioning are adultlike. Work by Rodman and colleagues (Rodman, Skelly,

& Gross, 1991) has shown that the activity of single cells in IT (which is the same area as cytoarchitectonic area TE) is remarkably adultlike when measured in alert infant monkeys. The percentage of cells responsive to visual stimuli, the latency and robustness of responses, and the selectivity of responses were qualitatively similar to responses of adults in monkeys as young as 5 weeks. However, some differences were noted when monkeys were tested under anesthesia. Under these conditions, there were many fewer visually responsive cells in infants than in adult monkeys. In adults, about 80% of cells were responsive to visual stimuli, about 50% in 4-to 7-month-old monkeys, and about 10% in monkeys less than 4 months (and all but one of the responsive cells were found in monkeys older than 3 months). Infants' greater sensitivity to anesthesia suggests that the physiological properties of IT cells in infants are different from those in adults. The authors speculate that this difference may be related to developmental changes in cells' energy metabolism or synapse formation.

In studying these cells, Rodman and colleagues (1991) found a small number of cells that were responsive to faces. Thus, face-sensitive cells appear to be present early in life. Although some faces with expressions (e.g., threat, yawn) were shown to the monkeys, the authors do not report any cells that responded selectively to the expressions. In addition, it is not clear that the "face-selective" cells of infant monkeys show all of the same properties as the face-selective cells of adult monkeys (e.g., that they are not responding to stimulus visual complexity or meaningfulness, etc.; see earlier discussion), since these cells have not been studied as extensively in infants.

STP. Unfortunately, little is known about the development of STP. The results of one study of area STP and surrounding cortical areas showed that these cortical areas showed some plasticity at birth (i.e., under conditions of damage to other areas, they are capable of taking on the functions that the damaged areas would have subserved [Webster, Bachevalier, & Ungerleider, 1988]). These results suggest that STP and surrounding areas may not be fully mature at birth.

Amygdala. Relatively little is known about the development of the human amygdala, although, anatomically, the amygdala, like a functionally related area that sits in close proximity – the hippocampus – appears to develop early (for review of hippocampal development, see Nelson,

1995). Most of what is known about the functional development of the amygdala comes from studies of the effects of lesions of the monkey amygdala. For example, Bachevalier and Mishkin (1994) have shown that, in contrast to the effects of TE lesions already described, lesions of the amygdala (and hippocampus) disrupt memory in infants. This finding is consistent with the idea that the amygdala and hippocampus are more mature at birth, and thus may possess less plasticity, than cortical areas. Bachevalier (1991) has shown that amygdala (and hippocampal) lesions disrupt infant monkeys' social behavior. For example, at 6 months of age, these monkeys show blank and inexpressive faces, as well as poor eye contact and body expression.

Summary. In summary, the available evidence suggests that in the monkey, cortical area TE, and possibly area STP, is functionally not fully mature during the first half-year of life (approximately 2 years in the human), although cells responsive to faces are present in area TE by this time. In contrast, the amygdala may mature earlier than these cortical areas. This suggests that the amygdala may contribute more to the recognition of faces early in life, while the influence of areas TE and STP develops later or more slowly.

Human developmental cognitive neuroscience literature

In contrast to the rapid gains made in elucidating the relation between brain and cognitive and emotional function in adults, relatively little work has been done in the context of development. In this section, we describe two notable exceptions: the use of the eye-blink startle response and of event-related potentials (ERPs).

Eye-blink startle response. The eye-blink startle response is a reflex blink initiated involuntarily by sudden bursts of loud noise. In adults, these reflex blinks are augmented (i.e., made larger) by viewing slides of unpleasant scenes and pictures, and they are inhibited (i.e., made smaller) by viewing slides of pleasant or arousing scenes and pictures (see Lang, Bradley, & Cuthbert, 1990, 1992). Balaban (1995) used a procedure very similar to that used with adults to examine the psychophysiology of infants' responses to facial expressions. Five-month-old infants watched slides depicting eight different adults posing happy, neutral, and angry expressions. Each slide was presented for 6 sec, followed 3 sec later by an acoustic startle probe (a 95-dB, 75-msec burst of white noise). Consistent with the adult literature, infants' blinks were augmented when they viewed the angry expressions and were reduced when they viewed the happy expressions, relative to when they viewed neutral expressions.

This work is significant for understanding the underlying neurobiology of infants' recognition of facial expressions. It has been speculated by a number of authors (e.g., Davis, 1989) that at least in rats, fear-potentiated startle (increased blink responses to aversive stimuli) is mediated by the central nucleus of the amygdala, which in turn directly projects to brain-stem centers. If the central nucleus also mediates this response in humans, then Balaban's (1995) results suggest that by 5 months of age, at least portions of the amygdala circuitry underlying the response to facial expressions is "on-line" and functional. This interpretation of the results would also be consistent with the study by Adolphs et al. (1994; reviewed earlier), suggesting that the amygdala is involved in recognizing expressions.

Event-related potentials. The startle-blink reflex represents one approach to studying the neural mechanisms involved in recognizing facial expressions. Although this approach has the advantage of being noninvasive and easily used with both infants and adults, it has the disadvantage of being spatially remote from the brain itself – that is, it is a peripheral measure of brain activity. A different approach that gives a more central measure of brain activity and is also noninvasive is the recording of event-related potentials (ERPs). ERPs are recorded by electrodes placed on the surface of the scalp while the subject is engaged in some task. By time-locking the subject's brain response to the occurrence of discretely presented stimuli, it is possible to ascertain the timing of mental events with great precision (on the order of milliseconds). The spatial coordinates of the neural generators responsible for the observed brain responses can also be determined to some degree (although temporal resolution of this procedure is far superior to its spatial resolution).

We used ERPs to study infants' responses to facial expressions in two experiments designed to parallel previous behavioral studies (e.g., Nelson & Dolgin, 1985). We were specifically interested in examining the ERP equivalent of infants' visual preferences for facial expressions – that is, infants' reactions to expressions in a task where they were not required to remember or discriminate a particular expression. Thus, in both experiments, 7-month-olds were shown slides of two different expressions presented with equal probability. While infants watched the slides, ERPs were recorded from electrodes placed along the midline of the anterior–posterior axis of the head and along each side of the head.

In the first experiment (Nelson & de Haan, 1996), we chose to look at infants' brain-wave responses to happy and fearful expressions, since previous behavioral studies indicate that infants respond differently to these two expressions. For example, they look longer at a fearful face than at a happy face when the two are presented side by side (Nelson & Ludemann, 1986), and they take longer to habituate to a fearful face than to a happy face (Nelson et al., 1979). In the second experiment, we chose to look at infants brain-wave response to two negative expressions, anger and fear. Previous behavioral studies suggest that infants are able to discriminate these expression by 7 months of age (e.g., Schwartz et al., 1985). However, there are no studies comparing infants' preference between fearful and angry faces to show what their reactions to these expressions would be without prior habituation to one expression.

We observed that the ERPs invoked by happy differed from those invoked by fear (see Figure 8.2, *left*). However, no such differences were observed when fear and anger were used (see Figure 8.2, *right*) (for a discussion of the functional significance of these differences, see Nelson & de Haan, 1996). The results of the first experiment are consistent with the behavioral findings reviewed earlier, which suggest that infants of this age respond differently to fearful and happy expressions in behavioral tests of visual preference. The results of the second experiment are consistent with the explanation that infants simply could not discriminate between the two expressions. Since these experiments were designed to examine the electrophysiological equivalent of a visual "preference," rather than discrimination, these responses may reflect the brain's obligatory reaction to different expressions.

It is difficult to draw conclusions from scalp-recorded activity about the location of the neural generators underlying the observed ERP responses, particularly when only a small number of electrodes (in our case, six) are used. However, based on the animal studies, on the Adolphs et al. (1994) study, and on Balaban's (1995) findings, it is tempting to speculate that the ERPs observed to happy, fear, and anger reflect

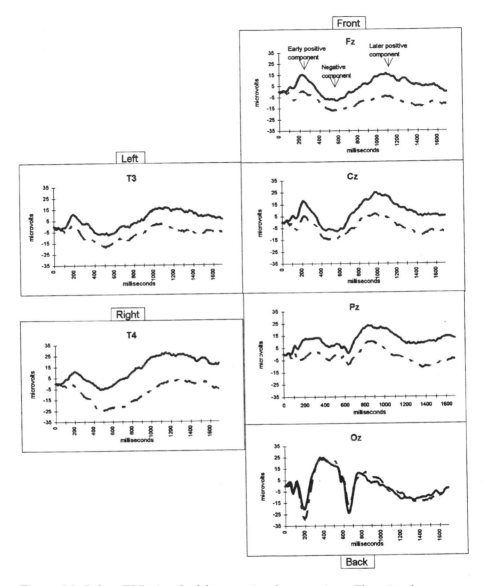

Figure 8.2. Infant ERPs invoked by emotional expressions. The stimulus was shown during 0–500 msec. Cz = midline, T3 = left anterior temporal, T4 = right anterior temporal. (From Nelson & de Haan, 1996, reproduced with permission.) *Left*: Solid line = Happy, dashed line = Fearful. *Right*: Solid line = Angry, dashed line = Fearful.

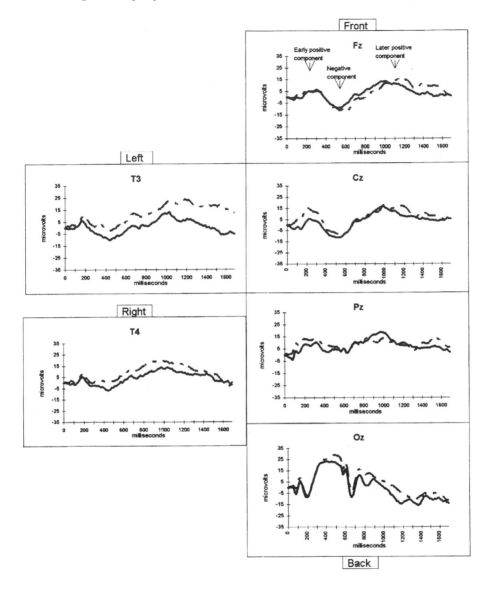

the activity of the anterior and medial temporal lobe (e.g., amygdala). We hope in the future to use more sophisticated methods of inferring neural generators from scalp-recorded ERPs (e.g., current source density analysis; brain electrical source analysis) to investigate this hypothesis in greater detail.

Conclusions

Our review of the behavioral literature on infants' perception of facial expressions suggests that infants just a few months old are capable of discriminating the features of the face that to an adult denote facial expressions. However, it may not be until after 6 to 7 months of age that infants begin to recognize that a facial expression is the same despite changes in intensity of the expression, identity of the model, and so forth. Even at this age, infants may be limited to categorizing particular, prototypical positive expressions.

Our review of the neurophysiology and neuropsychology of recognizing facial expressions suggests that anterior temporal and medial temporal lobe structures are disproportionately involved in recognizing facial expressions. There is, however, no evidence that there are cells in these regions of the brain that respond *exclusively* to facial expressions; rather, a more parsimonious interpretation is that certain cells in the amygdala and areas of the anterior temporal lobe (e.g., STP) are more responsive to facial expressions than to other patterned stimuli. Although it is possible to speculate that such specificity has come about through selection pressures, and that such specificity is adaptive for the organism (e.g., the expression anger or disgust signaling a flight response), the lack of data on the role of experience in recognizing facial expressions would make such speculation premature.

The few studies conducted with young monkeys suggest that the brain structures that in adults are necessary for recognizing facial expressions are functional early in life, although when they become fully mature is not known. The physiological and anatomical data suggest that the human amygdala is likely adultlike between 6 and 12 postnatal months, although temporal regions like area TE and STP probably have a much more protracted course of development. Interestingly, these data are consistent with the results of behavioral studies. Those studies indicate that although elements of the ability to recognize expressions are clearly in place within a few months of birth, infants are still far from expert at recognizing certain expressions (particularly negative expressions such as fear and anger) even as "late" as 12 to 18 months and beyond (Nelson, 1987).

Both the behavioral studies with humans and the anatomical studies with monkeys suggest that there are periods when the ability to recognize expression may change. For example, 6- to 7-month-olds can respond to expressions as categories, but younger infants may respond to expressions more on the basis of individual instances or isolated features. It might be worthwhile to look at the ERPs elicited by expressions over this time to see how these responses change as the ability to perceive expressions categorically emerges. In monkeys, there is some suggestion that the various neural structures thought to be involved in expression recognition mature at different rates. For example, the amygdala may contribute more to the recognition of faces early in life, whereas the influence of temporal cortical areas may emerge later or more slowly. If this is true, then early lesions of the amygdala, but not TE or STP, might impair expression recognition early in life, and lesions to either area might impair recognition later in life.

We have said little about the role of experience in the development of expression recognition, partly because relatively little work has been done in this area. In the future, it may be informative to document more carefully the types of expressions that occur in the infant's environment and relate this information to behavioral and psychophysiological measures of infants' perception of expressions. For example, Camras and colleagues have shown that on behavioral tests of recognition, children from abusive/neglectful families respond differently to emotional expressions than do children from nonabusive families. Moreover, the expressivity of the mothers also differed in the two types of family (Camras et al., 1990). It might be informative to look at brain-behavior relations to see if they are organized differently in children from abusive/neglectful families than in children from nonabusive families.

In summary, the ability to recognize facial expressions of emotion is reasonably sophisticated within the first year of life, although this ability continues to develop through childhood. At the neurobiological level, this observation can be accounted for by the relatively early maturation of structures such as the amygdala, and the relatively late development of cortical structures such as TE, STP, and so on. Although the behavioral manifestation of recognizing facial expressions is clearly due to changes in the underlying neural substrate, what remains to be determined is how this neural substrate is itself modified and sculpted by experience. The nature of experience with facial expressions, and how this experience in turn influences (or fails to influence) the ontogeny of the ability to recognize facial expressions, remains to be determined.

Notes

1 By 3 months of age, infants can also recognize and discriminate differing patterns of dots (Bomba & Siqueland, 1983). Thus, the observation that infants can discriminate expressions early in life is not necessarily proof of the existence of a prewired neural system that is specialized for facial expressions. Although this is plausible, an alternative possibility is that there is a more general system that emerges early in life and mediates discrimination of several different types of patterned information.
2 These findings are consistent with the single-cell work reviewed earlier, which showed that cells responsive to facial expressions are present in the amygdala. However, the observation that S. M. has no trouble recognizing facial identity is discrepant with the observation that cells responsive to facial identity are present in the amygdala.
3 One must be cautious, however, in making such inferences, since the structures that mediate a behavior in adults may not be the same structures that mediate that ability earlier in life (e.g., Bachevalier & Mishkin, 1994).

References

Adolphs, R., Tranel, D., Damasio, H., & Damasio, A. (1994). Impaired recognition of emotion in facial expressions following bilateral damage to the human amygdala. *Nature, 372,* 669–672.

Ahrens, R. (1954). Beitrag zur Entwicklund des Physiognomie und Mimikerkennes. *Zeitschrift fur Experimentelle und Angewandte Psychologie, 2,* 412–454.

Bachevalier, J. (1991). An animal model for child autism. In C. A. Tamminga & S. C. Schulz (eds.), *Advances in neuropsychiatry and psychopharmacology: Vol. 1. Schizophrenia research* (pp. 129–140). New York: Raven Press.

Bachevalier, J., Brickson, M., Hagger, C., & Mishkin, M. (1990). Age and sex differences in the effects of selective temporal lobe lesions on the formation of visual discrimination habits in rhesus monkeys. *Behavioral Neuroscience, 104,* 885–889.

Bachevalier, J., & Mishkin, M. (1994). Effects of selective neonatal temporal lobe lesions on visual recognition memory in rhesus monkeys. *The Journal of Neuroscience, 14,* 2128–2139.

Bachevalier, J., Pascalis, O., & Overman, W. (1994). *The development and neural basis of visual recognition memory in primates.* Unpublished manuscript.

Balaban, M. T. (1995). Affective influences on startle in five-month-old infants: Reactions to facial expressions of emotion. *Child Development, 66,* 28–36.

Barrera, M. E., & Maurer, D. (1981). The perception of facial expressions by the three-month-old infant. *Child Development, 52,* 203–206.

Baylis, G. C., Rolls, E. T., Leonard, C. M. (1985). Selectivity between faces in the responses of neurons in the cortex in the superior temporal sulcus of the monkey. *Brain Research, 342,* 91–102.

Baylis, G. C., Rolls, E. T., & Leonard, C. M. (1987). Functional subdivisions of the temporal lobe neocortex. *The Journal of Neuroscience, 7,* 330–342.

Bomba, P. C., & Siqueland, E. R. (1983). The nature and structure of infant form categories. *Journal of Experimental Child Psychology, 35,* 294–328.

Bowlby, J. (1969). *Attachment and loss: Vol. 1. Attachment.* New York: Basic Books.

Bronson, G. W. (1994). Infants' transitions toward adult-like scanning. *Child Development, 65,* 1243–1261.

Bruce, C., Desimone, R., & Gross, C. G. (1981). Visual properties of neurons in a polysensory area in superior temporal sulcus of the macaque. *Journal of Neurophysiology, 46,* 369–384.

Bühler, C., & Hetzer, H. (1928). Das erste Verstandis für Ausdruck im ersten Lebensjahr. *Zeitschrift für Psychologie, 107,* 50–61.

Camras, L. A., Ribordy, S., Hill, J., Martino, S., Sachs, V., Spaccarelli, S., & Stefani, R. (1990). Maternal facial behavior and the recognition and production of emotional expression by maltreated and nonmaltreated children. *Developmental Psychology, 26,* 304–312.

Caron, R. F., Caron, A. J., & Myers, R. S. (1982). Abstraction of invariant face expressions in infancy. *Child Development, 53,* 1008–1015.

Damasio, A., Tranel, D., & Damasio, H. (1990). Face agnosia and the neural substrates of memory. *Annual Review of Neuroscience, 13,* 89–109.

Darwin, C. (1896). *The expressions of the emotions in man and animals.* New York: Appleton.

Davis, M. (1989). The role of the amygdala and its efferent projections in fear and anxiety. In P. Tyrer (Ed.), *Psychopharmacology of anxiety.* Oxford: Oxford University Press.

Desimone, R. (1991). Face-selective cells in the temporal cortex of monkeys. *Journal of Cognitive Neuroscience, 3,* 1–8.

Ekman, P. (1972). Universal and cultural differences in facial expressions of emotion. In J. K. Cole (Ed.), *Nebraska Symposium on Motivation* (Vol. 19, pp. 207–283). Lincoln: University of Nebraska Press.

Field, T. M., Woodson, R. W., Greenberg, R., & Cohen, C. (1982). Discrimination and imitation of facial expressions by neonates. *Science, 218,* 179–181.

George, M. S., Ketter, T. A., Gill, D. S., Haxby, J. V., Ungerleider, L. G., Herscovitch, P., & Post, R. M. (1993). Brain regions involved in recognizing emotion or identity: An oxygen-15 PET study. *The Journal of Neuropsychiatry and Clinical Neurosciences, 5,* 384–394.

Gross, C. G., Rocha-Miranda, C. E., & Bender, D. B. (1972). Visual properties of neurons in inferotemporal cortex of the macaque. *Journal of Neurophysiology, 35,* 96–111.

Gross, C. G., Rodman, H. R., Gochin, P. M., & Colombo, M. W. (1993). Inferior temporal cortex as a pattern recognition device. In E. Baum (Ed.), *Computational learning and cognition: Proceedings of the 3rd NEC research symposium (Siam)* (pp. 44–72).

Hagger, C., Bachevalier, J., Macko, K. A., Kennedy, C., Sokoloff, L., & Mishkin, M. (1988). Functional maturation of inferior temporal cortex in infant rhesus monkeys. *Neuroscience Abstracts, 14,* 2.

Hasselmo, M. E., Rolls, E. T., & Baylis, G. C. (1989). The role of expression and identity in the face-selective responses of neurons in the temporal visual cortex of the monkey. *Behavioural Brain Research, 32,* 203–218.

Kuchuk, A., Vibbert, M., & Bornstein, M. H. (1986). The perception of smiling and its experiential correlates in 3-month-old infants. *Child Development, 57,* 1054–1061.

LaBarbera, J. D., Izard, C. E., Vietze, P., & Parisi, S. A. (1976). Four- and six-month-old infants' visual responses to joy, anger, and neutral expressions. *Child Development, 47,* 535–538.

Lang, P. J., Bradley, M. M., & Cuthbert, B. N. (1990). Emotion, attention, and the startle reflex. *Psychological Review, 97,* 377–395.

Lang, P. J., Bradley, M. M., & Cuthbert, B. N. (1992). A motivational analysis of emotion: Reflex-cortex connections. *Psychological Science, 3,* 44–49.

Leonard, C. M., Rolls, E. T., Wilson, F. A. W., & Baylis, G. C. (1985). Neurons in the amygdala of the monkey with responses selective for faces. *Behavioural Brain Research, 15,* 159–176.

Ludemann, P. M. (1991). Generalized discrimination of positive facial expressions by seven- and ten-month-old infants. *Child Development, 62,* 55–67.

Ludemann, P. M., & Nelson, C. A. (1988). Categorical representation of facial expressions by 7-month-old infants. *Developmental Psychology, 24,* 492–501.

Miyashita, Y. (1988). Neuronal correlate of visual associative long term memory in primate temporal cortex. *Nature, 335,* 817–820.

Miyashita, Y. (1990). Associative representation of visual long term memory in the neurons of the primate temporal cortex. In E. Ewai & M. Mishkin (Eds.), *Vision, memory and the temporal lobe* (pp. 75–87). New York: Elsevier.

Nelson, C. A. (1985). The perception and recognition of facial expressions in infancy. In T. M. Field & N. A. Fox (Eds.), *Social perception in infants* (pp. 101–125). Norwood, NJ: Ablex.

Nelson, C. A. (1987). The recognition of facial expressions in the first two years of life: Mechanisms of development. *Child Development, 58,* 889–909.

Nelson, C. A. (1993). The recognition of facial expressions in infancy: Behavioral and electrophysiological correlates. In B. de Boysson-Bardies, S. de Schonen, P. Jusczyk, P. MacNeilage, & J. Morton (Eds.), *Developmental neurocognition: Speech and face processing in the first year of life* (pp. 187–198). Dordrecht, The Netherlands: Kluwer Academic.

Nelson, C. A. (1995). The ontogeny of human memory: A cognitive neuroscience perspective. *Developmental Psychobiology, 31,* 723–738.

Nelson, C. A., & de Haan, M. (1996). Neural correlates of visual responsiveness to facial expressions of emotion. *Developmental Psychobiology, 29,* 1–18.

Nelson, C. A., & Dolgin, K. (1985). The generalized discrimination of facial expressions by 7-month-old infants. *Child Development, 56,* 58–61.

Nelson, C. A., & Ludemann, P. M. (1986, May). *The discrimination of intensity changes of emotion by 4- and 7-month-old infants.* Paper presented at the Midwest Psychological Association, Chicago, IL.

Nelson, C. A., & Ludemann, P. M. (1989). Past, current, and future trends in infant face perception research. *Canadian Journal of Psychology, 43,* 183–198.

Nelson, C. A., Morse, P. A., & Leavitt, L. A. (1979). Recognition of facial expressions by seven-month-old infants. *Child Development, 50,* 1239–1242.

Ojemann, J. G., Ojemann, G. A., & Lettich, E. (1992). Neuronal activity related to faces and matching in human right nondominant temporal cortex. *Brain, 115,* 1–13.

Ono, T., & Nishijo, H. (1992). Neurophysiological basis of the Kluver-Bucy syndrome: Responses of monkey amygdaloid neurons to biologically significant objects. In J. P. Aggleton (Ed.), *The amygdala* (pp. 167–190). New York: Wiley-Liss.

Oram, M. W., & Perrett, D. I. (1994). Responses of anterior superior temporal polysensory (STPa) neurons to "biological motion" stimuli. *Journal of Cognitive Neuroscience, 6,* 99–116.

Oster, H., Daily, L., & Goldenthal, P. (1989). Processing facial affect. In A. Young & H. Ellis (Eds.), *Handbook of research on face processing* (pp. 107–161). Amsterdam: North Holland Press.

Perrett, D. I., & Mistlin, A. J. (1990). Perception of facial characteristics by monkeys. In W. C. Stebbins & M. A. Berkley (Eds.), *Comparative perception: Vol. 2. Complex signals* (pp. 187–215). New York: Wiley.

Perrett, D. I., & Oram, M. W. (1993). The neurophysiology of shape processing. *Image and Vision Computing, 11,* 317–333.

Perrett, D. I., Smith, P. A. J., Potter, D. D., Mistlin, A. J., Head, A. S., Milner, A. D., & Jeeves, M. A. (1984). Neurons responsive to faces in the temporal cortex: Studies of functional organization, sensitivity to identity and relation to perception. *Human Neurobiology, 3,* 197–208.

Pigarev, I. N., Rizzolatti, G., & Scandolara, C. (1979). Neurons responding to visual stimuli in the frontal lobe of macaque monkeys. *Neuroscience Letters, 12,* 207–212.

Rodman, H. R., & Consuelos, M. J. (1994). Cortical projections to anterior inferior temporal cortex in infant macaque monkeys. *Visual Neuroscience, 11,* 119–133.

Rodman, H. R., Skelly, J. P., & Gross, C. G. (1991). Stimulus selectivity and state dependence of activity in inferior temporal cortex in infant monkeys. *Proceedings of the National Academy of Science USA, 88,* 7572–7575.

Rolls, E. T. (1984). Neurons in the cortex of the temporal lobe and in the amygdala of the monkey with responses selective for faces. *Human Neurobiology, 3,* 209–222.

Rolls, E. T., & Baylis, G. C. (1986). Size and contrast have only small effects on the responses to faces of neurons in the cortex of the superior temporal sulcus of the monkey. *Experimental Brain Research, 65,* 38–48.

Rolls, E. T., Baylis, G. C., & Leonard, C. M. (1985). Role of low and high spatial frequencies in the face-selective responses of neurons in the cortex in the superior temporal sulcus in the monkey. *Vision Research, 25,* 1021–1035.

Schwartz, G., Izard, C., & Ansul, S. (1985). The 5-month-old's ability to discriminate facial expressions of emotions. *Infant Behavior and Development, 8,* 65–77.

Serrano, J. M., Iglesias, J., & Loeches, A. (1992). Visual discrimination and recognition of facial expressions of anger, fear, and surprise in 4- to 6-month-old infants. *Developmental Psychobiology, 25,* 411–425.

Spieker, S. (1985, April). *Infant discrimination and generalized recognition of dynamic facial expressions.* Paper presented at the Biennial Meeting of the Society for Research in Child Development, Toronto, Ontario.

Spitz, R., & Wolf, K. M. (1946). The smiling response: A contribution to the ontogenesis of social relations. *Genetic Psychology Monographs, 34,* 57–125.

Walker-Andrews, A. (1988). Infants' perception of the affordances of expressive behaviors. In C. Rovee-Collier & L. P. Lipsitt (Eds.), *Advances in infancy research* (Vol. 5, pp. 173–221). Norwood, NJ: Ablex.

Webster, M. J., Bachevalier, J., & Ungerleider, L. G. (1988). Plasticity of memory circuits in developing monkeys. *Society for Neuroscience Abstracts, 14,* 4.

Webster, M. J., Ungerleider, L. G., & Bachevalier, J. (1991). Connections of inferior temporal areas TE and TEO with medial temporal-lobe structures in infant and adult monkeys. *Journal of Neuroscience, 11,* 1095–1116.

Yamane, S., Kaji, S., & Kawano, K. (1988). What facial features activate face neurons in the inferotemporal cortex of the monkey? *Experimental Brain Research, 73,* 209–214.

Younge-Browne, G., Rosenfeld, H. M., & Horowitz, F. D. (1977). Infant discrimination of facial expressions. *Child Development, 48,* 555–562.

9. A dynamic systems approach to infant facial action

DANIEL S. MESSINGER, ALAN FOGEL, AND
K. LAURIE DICKSON

What does it mean when a baby smiles? Is it an expression of enjoyment, a signal to a partner that rewards effective caretaking, or simply a muscular contraction? Do physically different types of smiles indicate different things? Should the social context in which an infant smiles inform our understanding of the smile? To address these questions, we apply insights and ideas from a dynamic systems perspective to anatomical, social interactive, and neurophysiological data on the development of infant facial action (Fogel, 1993; Fogel & Thelen, 1987; Thelen, 1995; Thelen & Smith, 1994).

Two methodological and theoretical approaches to the study of facial action and to our initial questions can be identified. The Differential Emotions approach postulates that certain facial displays are expressions of discrete emotions while others are not (Ekman, 1994). The approach has generated research investigating the production (Izard, Hembree, Dougherty, & Spizzirri, 1983b) and recognition (Ekman, Friesen, & Ellsworth, 1972) of a set of facial displays thought to be prototypical expressions of a limited set of discrete emotions. The research has productively explored the physiological (e.g., Levenson, Ekman, & Friesen, 1990), cerebral (e.g., Fox & Davidson, 1988), and situational (e.g., Izard et al., 1983b) correlates of these facial displays. Using this approach, however, the coordination inherent in complex facial displays is a reality to be accepted, not a puzzle to be explored.

Is there more to facial action than displays of discrete emotion? Camras (1992) argues that a key premise of the differential perspective is that discrete emotions are associated with distinct eliciting conditions. Certain situations, for example, should typically elicit sadness, while others should elicit anger. Among infants, however, anger displays response to all negative elicitors, and sad displays are not a predominant response to any elicitor (Camras, 1992). Michel, Camras, and Sullivan (1992) have also demonstrated that discrete displays may be part of larger action structures that may not be emotional. For example, brow raising is a component of what have been posited to be interest expressions (Izard, 1983). However, in an experimental paradigm, brow raising during such expressions was typically related to infants raising their heads and/or eyes to gaze at an object presented above their line of sight (Michel et al., 1992). Thus, questions have been raised about the accuracy of viewing prototypical displays as expressions of discrete emotions, and about nonemotional factors involved in the formation of these displays.

The Dynamic Systems Approach explored in this chapter emphasizes the description of co-occurring and sequential patterns of facial action in relatively spontaneous social interactions (see Fernández-Dols & Ruiz-Belda, chapter 11, this volume; Oster & Ekman, 1977; Oster, 1978). We explain these patterns in terms of the interplay of muscular, cerebral, neural, attentional, experiential, and interactive constituents of what can be broadly described as emotional phenomena. We see the effort to explain patterns of facial actions as part of a dialogue with functional (e.g., Barrett, 1993; Campos, Mumme, Kermoian, & Campos, 1994), ethological (e.g., Fridlund, 1991; Fridlund, chapter 5, this volume), and differential approaches (e.g., Ekman, 1994; Izard, chapter 3, this volume; Izard & Malatesta, 1987) to facial action and emotion.

From a Dynamic Systems perspective, the mutual influence of facial actions with neurophysiological and interpersonal factors constitutes a form of "bottom–up" self-organization. These mutual influences mean that facial actions index interrelationships between relevant constituents. In Dynamic System's terms, facial action is a collective variable. It is a key to ongoing changes in the system that it helps to constitute.

A dynamic systems approach to two types of smiles

The theme of this chapter is that organization emerges from the mutual influence of the constituents of a system. First we describe how our observations of infants led us to conceptualize different kinds of smiles as co-occurrences of independent facial actions. Next we discuss different types of mutual influence at work in the formation of these two types of smiling. We also review patterns of neural activity that interface with interactive patterns to support the development of these two types of smiling. We argue that top–down mechanisms alone are inadequate to coordinate these smiles. A more macroscopic perspective characterizes the final section that illustrates an application of a systems axiom: Complex configurations of facial action have properties different from the properties of their constituents. The conclusion explores the role of a Dynamic Systems perspective in integrating other approaches to facial action and emotion.

How did the Dynamic Systems Approach emerge in our own work? As students of infant emotional development, we were influenced by theoretical perspectives that argued for the importance of infant emotion as an organizer and motivator of infant behavior and development (Tomkins, 1962). As observers of social interaction, we watched many face-to-face interactions in which a parent (often the mother) played with a young infant (generally below 6 months of age). To our surprise, many of the infant facial actions that occurred during these sequences did not seem to be described – much less explained – by dominant theoretical perspectives. Infant facial expressions were often fleeting. They sometimes occurred on only one side of the infant's face or were stronger on one side than the other. Smiles sometimes seemed to emerge from and contain elements of grimaces that did not appear to be positive at all. Changes in infant facial action were fast-paced. Infant smiles and other actions would come during a sequence of parental entreaties and seem to change in response to equally swift reactions on mother's part. It was out of this fast-paced interactional matrix that more stable, recognizable expressions seemed to develop. How could we generate data that would reflect these observations?

The Facial Action Coding System (FACS) (Ekman & Friesen, 1978; Friesen & Ekman, 1992) provided an important strategy for understanding and then objectively measuring (via an application of FACS to infants) [Oster & Rosenstein, in press]) these observations (see Wagner, chapter 2, this volume). Other coding systems identify facial action as discrete emotions or blends of discrete emotions (e.g., AFFEX [Izard, Dougherty, & Hembree, 1983a]). That is, one codes "enjoyment" directly from an infant's facial action. FACS, on the other hand, identifies anatomically based action units that are the functional constituents of facial displays. One codes the action of the zygomatic major as it pulls the corners of the lips upward and to the side of the face to create a smile. Such a strategy allows one to analyze facial configurations or displays into their constituent actions.

We became interested in the different types of smiling created by the combination of lip corner raising with other facial actions. In the Duchenne smile (see Figure 9.1), the lip corners are raised; the contraction of the orbicularis oculi raises the cheeks and, in adults, typically crinkles

Figure 9.1. Lip corner raising due to zygomatic major contraction co-occurs with orbicularis oculi contraction raising the cheeks to form the Duchenne smile.

the eye corners (Ekman & Friesen, 1978). In the sections that follow, we critically review an emerging body of research indicating that when compared to smiles without orbicularis oculi contraction, Duchenne smiles occur in infants during positive interactive events and are associated with self-reported pleasure in adults (Ekman, Davidson, & Friesen, 1990; Fox & Davidson, 1988; Messinger, 1994).

In play smiles, the lip corners are raised and the jaw is dropped, opening the mouth (see Figure 9.2). Play smiles often occur during interaction that involves physical contact (Dickson, 1994; Messinger, 1994) or games (Dedo, 1991). In this chapter, we critically review research suggesting that play smiles emerge from games involving physical contact and tend to occur during boisterous, affiliative play (Dedo, 1991; Dickson, 1994; van Hooff, 1972; Messinger, 1994; Plooij, 1979).

From a Dynamic Systems perspective, we began to think of Duchenne and play smiles as constituted by the co-occurrence of potentially independent facial actions (Messinger, 1994). The co-occurrence of lip corner raising and cheek raising constitutes Duchenne smiling. The co-occurrence of lip corner raising and mouth opening constitutes play smiling. When these smiles are analyzed into their separate actions, several

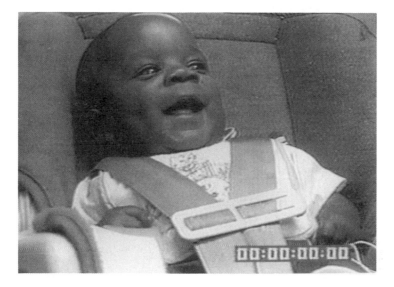

Figure 9.2. Lip corner raising due to zygomatic major contraction co-occurs with a lowered jaw to create a play smile.

questions emerge. Do the co-occurrences that create Duchenne and play smiles occur at greater than chance levels? Do these co-occurrences become more or less probable as infants grow older? Are these smiles more likely to come together during some interactive conditions than during others? To answer such questions, we could not measure the amount of Duchenne and play smiling as whole entities. Instead, we separately coded the three facial constituents – lip corner raiser, cheek raiser, and mouth opening – that co-occurred to form these smiles.[1]

To understand the relationship of Duchenne and play smiles to other co-occurring elements of the interaction, we separately coded (1) the position in which the infant was being held, (2) where the infant was gazing, and (3) whether the mother was smiling. Our data base consisted of observational data on a sample of a dozen middle-class mothers playing with their infants on their laps (Messinger, 1994). Because we were interested in the process of developmental change, mothers and infants were videotaped playing together *weekly* when infants were between 1 month and 6 months of age.

Our primary analysis strategies focused on finding which facial actions and social actions co-occurred for the group as a whole and how those patterns changed with age (Messinger, 1994). This was done with data-driven (hierarchical) loglinear analyses in which only terms that had Z scores significant at the .01 level for analyses by both duration and frequency were interpreted. We are currently replicating and expanding the results reported in different samples and in analyses that examine each mother–infant dyad individually (Messinger, 1995; Messinger, Fogel, & Dickson, in preparation).

Self-organization and mutual influence

From a Dynamic Systems perspective, facial actions are elements of self-organizing processes in which the mutual influence of relevant constituents creates a coherent pattern. In this section, we consider different self-organizing processes in the formation and development of the Duchenne and the play smile. In the following section, we describe what is known about the neural anatomy involved in the formation and development of these facial displays.

Duchenne smiling

Fridlund (1994) suggests that there is no intrinsic affinity between zygomatic and orbicularis oculi contraction. In contrast, we argue that there is a synergistic relationship between the action of the zygomatic major, which produces lip corner raising, and the action of that part of orbicularis oculi (the large orbital portion including pars lateralis) that raises the cheeks. Before 6 months of age, we found that orbicularis oculi contraction was almost 12 times more likely in the presence than in the absence of lip corner raising (Messinger, 1994). The original FACS manual (Ekman & Friesen, 1978) indicated that intense contraction of the zygomatic major necessarily involved contraction of orbicularis oculi because intense smiling is almost invariably associated with orbicularis oculi contraction. Although actions of the two muscles are potentially independent (Friesen & Ekman, 1992), intense contraction of the zygomatic major without orbicularis oculi contraction looks forced and artificial (cf. Blurton-Jones, 1972). Weak contraction of the zygomatic major, on the other hand, is rarely associated with orbicularis oculi contraction and, when it is, may give the impression of wincing (cf. Ekman & Friesen, 1978, exemplar photographs).

How do we account for these patterns? The first potential type of influence involved in the formation of the Duchenne smile is anatomical. As the zygomatic major lifts the corners of the mouth, it raises the cheek, functioning synergistically with (performing some of the same function as) the orbital portion of orbicularis oculi. The *decreased* downward pull on the orbital portion of orbicularis oculi (caused by the raising of the cheek by the zygomatic) may encourage increases in the resting tonus of orbicularis oculi, resulting in noticeable contraction. In addition, zygomatic contraction raises portions of the cheek over and adjacent to the orbital portion of orbicularis oculi surrounding the eye (Williams, Warwick, Dyson, & Bannister, 1989). The sensation of malar tissue (the cheek) rising next to and over the orbital portion of orbicularis oculi may also increase the probability of orbicularis oculi contracting.[2]

The presence of such anatomically based processes suggests several hypotheses. In general, the stronger the intensity of zygomatic contraction, the more likely should be orbicularis oculi contraction. In addition, zygomatic contraction should typically precede, perhaps be coincident with, but not follow, orbicularis oculi contraction. The influence of zygomatic major contraction on the probability of orbicularis oculi contraction would be seen most prototypically when zygomatic contraction slowly increases in intensity and is accompanied by the coordinated contraction of orbicularis oculi. However, this train of events may typically occur quickly, making relatively precise electromyographic or video observation techniques necessary to determine which muscle contracted first.

The physical effects of zygomatic contraction on orbicularis oculi contraction are one source of the coordination evident in Duchenne smiling. Another source involves the motor neurons in the seventh cranial nerve, the facial nerve, which travel from the facial nucleus in the brain stem and form five branches that innervate the face. Orbicularis oculi typically receives inputs from the temporal and zygomatic branches of this nerve, and the zygomatic major typically receives inputs from the upper portion of the buccal branch (Williams et al., 1989). There is, however, a considerable degree of interconnection between all these branches through a network referred to as the *parotid plexus* (Rinn, 1984). In an anatomical study of 100 faces, McCormack, Cauldwell, and Anson (1945) found that in 87 cases there were intersections between the buccal and zygomatic branches of the facial nerve after their initial division. The functions of these connections are unclear. However, they are a potential source of the coordination of the contraction of the zygomatic major and orbicularis oculi that leads to Duchenne smiling.

A coordinative structure is a functional linkage of *potentially* independent muscular actions into a basic motor unit (Thelen, 1995; Thelen & Smith, 1994; Turvey, 1990). Coordinative structures form out of the mutual influence of joints and muscles as they change rates of movement in a gravitational environment. These movements occur in coordination with patterns of neural innervation, but there is no one-to-one correspondence between the firing of effector neurons and a particular movement. The presence of both muscle linkages and overlapping patterns of neural innervation suggest that zygomatic and orbicularis oculi contraction typically function as a coordinative structure. It would be a *mistake*, however, to attempt to *reduce* the coordination of Duchenne smiling to a neuromuscular pattern. The presence of neural and muscular proclivities for co-action does not exhaust the possible explanations of the co-occurrence of zygomatic and orbicularis oculi contraction. Moreover, like the elements of other coordinative structures, zygomatic and orbicularis oculi contraction also occur independently. Links between the component actions of coordinative structures – such as the leg movements involved in taking steps (Thelen & Ulrich, 1991) – typically occur under particular environmental conditions.

Is Duchenne smiling likely in particular social contexts? The issue is theoretically important because Fridlund (1994) argues that the Duchenne smile is caused by zygomatic and orbicularis oculi contraction each being *independently* associated with particular environmental conditions. In our data, there were indeed significant individual associations between gazing at mother and zygomatic contraction on the one hand and orbicularis oculi contraction on the other (Messinger, 1994). However, in addition to these associations, there was a strong tendency for these facial actions to be *co-occurring* during mother smiling ($Z= 8.33$). This suggests that the Duchenne smile is an emergent configuration with properties above and beyond the properties of its constituents (see the later section, "Wholes and Parts").

What are the temporal characteristics of interactions involving Duchenne smiling? Preliminary results of research in progress suggest that half of infant Duchenne smiling at 3 months was accompanied by *maternal* Duchenne smiling (Messinger, 1995). Mothers tended to match infant Duchenne smiles with Duchenne smiles of their own. It is likely that infants become aware of this pattern and that at some point they also begin to match their mothers' Duchenne smiles. Fox and Davidson (1988) found that 10-month-old infants Duchenne smiled when their mothers smiled and approached the infant.

The meaning of infant Duchenne smiles cannot be known with certainty. Ekman et al. (1990) found that adults did more Duchenne smiling than non-Duchenne smiling in response to pleasant stimuli such as films of animals playing. In addition, the duration of Duchenne smiling was significantly associated with self-reported amusement, happiness, excitement, and interest (Ekman et al., 1990). Adult Duchenne smiling may arise from the adult's perception of puppies and gorillas enjoying themselves during play and their engagement with that perceived enjoyment. This process may begin with infants detecting contingencies when their Duchenne smiles are matched by their mothers' Duchenne smiles. Through such a process, Duchenne smiling may become tied to the visual perception of positive experience in one's interactive partner (the smiling mother) or one's imaginative partner (the film clip of the playful puppy, cf. Fridlund, 1994). This process is prototypically mutual, involving the simultaneous visual perception and communication of positive engagement.

This hypothesis underscores the idea that facial configurations are simultaneously experiential and social. It is not compatible with rigidly distinguishing Duchenne smiles as expressions of pleasure from non-Duchenne smiles as social signals (Fridlund, 1994). Such rigid distinctions are also not compatible with the empirical literature, which typically indicates probabilistic rather than deterministic associations between facial muscles, interactive processes, feeling states, and neurophysiological processes. More pointedly, a full account of the significance of Duchenne and non-Duchenne smiles must account for the fact that by contracting and relaxing the orbicularis oculi, infants move smoothly between these configurations. In our data, approximately one-half of Duchenne smiles were immediately preceded by non-Duchenne smiles, and approximately one-quarter of non-Duchenne smiles were immediately preceded by Duchenne smiles (Messinger, 1994; Messinger et al., in preparation). Additional research is clearly needed to determine what types of changes are associated with transitions between these facial configurations.

The development of Duchenne smiling. Despite provisions for social learning, Differential Emotion perspectives often indicate that the development of early emotion expressions is a maturationally controlled phenomenon (e.g., Izard & Malatesta, 1987). If this is the case, one might expect Duchenne smiles – at least insofar as they are a prototypical index of enjoyment (Ekman, 1994) – to emerge fully formed. That is, relevant neural circuitry would emerge at a certain point and coordinate a relatively mature form of the expression.

Data relevant to the development of Duchenne smiling are scarce and somewhat contradictory. Although Oster and Rosenstein (in press) have photographed Duchenne smiles in premature neonates, Duchenne smiling in full-term neonates is rare (Emde & Koenig, 1969). Wolff (1987) first observed the configuration in full-term infants at 3 weeks. Our hypothesis is that in full-term infants, zygomatic major contraction in the form of early smiling coexists with early orbicularis oculi contraction (during crying) without co-occurring. In response to unknown changes, these actions begin to come together as Duchenne smiling around the first month and with increasing strength through the first 6 months. Our data indicate that, comparing the period from 1 to 3 months to the period from 3 to 6 months, the proportion of time spent in Duchenne smiling increased from 6.4% to 10.5% (Messinger, 1994). Expressed differently, the strength of the association between zygomatic and orbicularis oculi contraction increased by almost three times. From a dynamic perspective, developmental changes are characterized by increases and decreases in the stability of certain system configurations. These data suggest that Duchenne smiling forms out of the co-occurrence of independent muscular actions that form an increasingly stable configuration in the first half-year of life.

Play smiling

Just as there are strong associations between the facial actions that constitute Duchenne smiling, there are strong associations between the facial actions that constitute play smiling. We found that infant mouth opening was about four times more likely during infant zygomatic contraction (smiling) than during its absence (Messinger, 1994). Unlike Duchenne smiling, however, there is not likely to be an anatomical explanation for the coordination evident in play smiling. The zygomatic major and the muscles responsible for opening the mouth (e.g., the lateral pterygoid, digrastic) have somewhat antagonistic functions (Williams et al., 1989). In addition, many of the muscles responsible for opening the mouth receive input from the trigeminal as opposed to the facial nerve (which innervates the zygomatic), making intranerve activity a less likely source of coordination. Instead, other concurrent actions of the infant and the infant's partner may be primarily necessary for the association of lip corner raising and mouth opening.

Our data-driven analyses suggested parallels between the independent occurrences of lip corner raising and mouth opening. Infant lip corner raising (smiling) and mouth opening occurred in similar interactive circumstances at similar ages (Messinger, 1994). Like lip corner raising, mouth opening was more likely after 3 months. Like lip corner raising (smiling), mouth opening was more likely while mother was smiling. These results replicate earlier findings of Kaye and Fogel, 1980. In addition, like lip corner raising, mouth opening tended to occur while infants were gazing at mother, particularly when infants were being held by mothers in more supported supine or cradled positions (Messinger, 1994).

What is the meaning of these parallel associations? An important index of the meaning of infant facial actions is how those actions are associated with ongoing interactive processes. As infant mouth opening and lip corner raising occur in conjunction with some of the same social actions, they may have similar functions in face-to-face interaction. Perhaps mouth opening communicates positive engagement in young infants. This challenges the view that culturally recognized "emotional expressions" have a special status as indices of infant affective engagement. That is, smiles may not be unique expressions of positive affect in young infants (Ekman, 1994; Izard et al., 1983b). Similarities between lip corner raising and mouth opening caution against a priori judgments of the emotionality of a given facial action. Open-minded descriptive research is needed to understand how different facial actions are associated with different interactive contexts.

Perhaps the most important aspect of the parallel associations described was a developmental increase of the likelihood of these facial actions coming together as a play smile in particular interactive contexts. Between 3 and 6 months of age, the likelihood of lip corner raising being associated (co-occurring) with jaw dropping increased in two interactive contexts: (1) when infants were being held in lying or reclining positions by mother, and (2) when infants were gazing at mother (Messinger, 1994). That is, relatively intense tactile and visual interchange with a partner became developmentally more strongly associated with the coordination of play smiling. In a separate sample of 12-month-olds, Dickson (1994) found that open-mouthed smiles predominated during play that involved physical contact with the infant's parent. Among nonhuman primates, van Hooff (1972) has reported that open-mouth displays similar in function to human play smiles were associated with social play and mock fighting.

How do play smiles form during interaction? Dickson (1994) hypothesized that infants who are already smiling may open their mouths (creating play smiles) immediately after physical contact with a partner.

Among infant chimpanzees, this reaction may have its roots in mouth opening as a response to perioral contact (Plooij, 1979). With experience, human infants may open their mouths in response not only to actual but to imminent physical contact. This would include infants preparing to suck on an object or on mother's hands; it would also include infants responding to an imminent hug or snuggle by dropping their jaws as if to mouth some part of the partner's body. If this mouth opening occurs when infants are already smiling or about to smile, a play smile would form. Fox and Davidson (1988) have hypothesized that *Duchenne* smiles are differentially associated with a motivation to approach. If physical contact plays a role in the formation of play smiles, it would also suggest investigating indices of approach motivation associated with open-mouthed (play) smiles.

The development of play smiling. How do play smiles develop? This section introduces Edelman's (1987) concept of neural reentry as part of an explanation of how the co-occurrence of *different* facial actions becomes a favored pattern of neural and motor activity. Reentry is a process in which neural information within and between motoric and sensory activities is integrated. How, for example, is neural information from visual and auditory sources integrated into the perception of a single stimulus? How is a unitary perception of smiling constructed from neural activity accompanying the contraction of the zygomatic major and from neural activity accompanying the afferent sensation of the lip corners rising? One clue is that efferent neural activity accompanying contraction of the zygomatic major is temporally synchronized with afferent neural activity stemming from the upward movement of the lip corners. A reentrant structure is a group of neurons that interface with two or more such sources of temporally linked information. Edelman (1987) suggests that neurogenesis is a dynamic process involving selection for populations of neurons that interface with two or more sources of co-ordinated neural activity. The presence of temporally coordinated but separate sources of neural activity strengthens the likelihood of a reentrant structure linking these sources. Through their reciprocal connections, populations of neurons that interface between simultaneously activated muscle groups in turn support the *sources* of neural activation with which they synapse.

Consider the coordination of different facial actions such as those involved in play (open-mouth) smiling. Gazing at mother is associated with both infant zygomatic contraction and mouth opening. Hence, gazing at mother will tend to be associated with co-occurring lip corner raising and mouth opening (i.e., play smiling). This will lead to neural change. There will be selection for reentrant structures that synaptically interface with the sources of neural efference associated with the production of zygomatic contraction and with mouth opening. There will be selection for neural connections associated with the *perception* of the area around the lip corners being raised by lip corner contraction and simultaneously pulled downward as the jaw opens. Patterns of neural activity associated with both production and perception will be integrated into the higher-level perception of play smiling.

How might coordinated facial action become a favored pattern? There would be a strengthening and selection for the activity of neural populations (reentrant structures) that synaptically link these two sources of synchronous neuronal firing. Reentrant structures have reciprocal influences on the neural activity associated with the performance of particular facial actions. They not only respond to synchronous neural activity but make the activity associated with synchronous patterns of movement more likely. We postulate that such interfacing neural groups will make the performance and perception of either zygomatic major contraction or mouth opening more likely to be linked to the performance and perception of the other action.

This scenario fits the data. Initially, play smiling should be dependent on the confluence of environmental events associated with *each* of its muscular constituents. Over the first 6 months of life, zygomatic contraction was associated with gazing at mother. In an independent association, mouth opening was also associated with gazing at mother (Messinger, 1994). Given a history of neural selection through activation of interfacing reentrant structures, the likelihood of the constituents of play smiling co-occurring should increase. This effect would be particularly clear in the interactive context with which each constituent of play smiling was associated. In fact, after 3 months of age, zygomatic contraction and mouth opening became more likely to co-occur as play smiling while infants were gazing at mother (Messinger, 1994).

The possibility that the emerging developmental coordination manifested in play smiling is structured by environmental events is attractive because there is no obvious neural or anatomical basis for the association of the constituents of play smiling. However, neural reentry is a generic process, an element in a more general theory of neurogenesis, that may support many types of coordinated action (see Thelen & Smith, 1994). In the case of the Duchenne smile, we have argued that muscular processes, the structure of the branches of the facial nerve, as well as joint positive visual engagement link the contraction of the zygomatic and orbicularis oculi. This would provide a primary basis for co-occurrence that would be further strengthened by reentry processes.

Alternate (top–down) explanations of facial coordination

The development of FACS (Ekman & Friesen, 1978) was accompanied by interest in the diversity of facial actions associated with zygomatic contraction (Oster, 1978). In order to resolve inconsistencies in the literature, however, empirical and theoretical attention turned first to distinguishing true from false smiles (Ekman & Friesen, 1982). For Ekman and his colleagues, zygomatic major contraction must be accompanied by orbicularis oculi contraction to index enjoyment (Ekman, 1994; Ekman et al., 1990; Ekman & Friesen, 1982). For Izard and his colleagues, the contraction of the zygomatic major alone is sufficient to index enjoyment (Izard, 1983; Izard et. al, 1983a). Both researchers seek to identify that smile which is an unambiguous signal of positive emotion. Mouth opening and other facial actions such as nose wrinkling are ignored (Dedo, 1991). Diversity in the form of smiling is not typically a focus of theoretical interest.

Given this overall perspective, how might a Differential Emotions approach account for the coordination evident in Duchenne smiling or other configurations of facial actions? Differential Emotions approaches have made use of the concept of sensory feedback from the face to the brain in the experience of emotion (Izard, 1981; Izard & Malatesta, 1987). Recent portrayals have steered clear of unidirectional causal accounts (Ekman, 1994) and emphasized nonlinear, systemic relations between emotion constituents (Izard, chapter 3, this volume; Malatesta, Culver, Tesman, & Shepard, 1989). However, a dominant perspective has been that unique patterns of neural activity produce distinctive and prototypical patterns of facial action in a relatively unidirectional fashion (cf. Panksepp, 1994). Izard and Malatesta (1987), for example, emphasize that genetically based neural processes lead to a specific facial expression.

Before examining difficulties with a unidirectional emphasis on facial action, it is helpful to review what is known about the neuroanatomy of such processes. The immediate source of innervation of the facial muscles is the motor nucleus of the facial nerve at the level of the pons in the brain stem (see Rinn, 1984, for a review). The facial nucleus receives inputs from two relatively distinct pathways. Neural activity from the cortical motor strip makes its way to the facial nucleus through the pyramidal system. This activity is thought to be associated with volitional facial actions. The second pathway stems from the extrapyramidal system involving subcortical as well as cortical structures including the basal ganglia and amygdala. Neural activity in these structures is thought to be involved in more spontaneous emotional displays. Although this distinction may not be absolute, it is the generally recognized neurological basis for several types of facial paralysis that affect one but not the other system (Rinn, 1984).

Why *not* conceive of central nervous system activity as a centrally organized plan that unidirectionally coordinates all facial action? One problem is the recognized diversity of neural processes – with cortical and subcortical points of origin – that are involved in the organization of facial activity. To the extent that top–down, relatively spontaneous, neural organizers of facial action exist (as in Differential Emotions approaches), they are one of a plurality of neural processes. During social interaction, more and less "volitional" neural processes may become dynamically related in the coordination of facial actions.

A more pervasive problem for the hypothesis of central organization is complexity. This discussion has focused on only three facial actions – lip corner raising, cheek raising, and mouth opening – whose presence or absence gives rise to eight (2^3) possible facial configurations. In fact, there are dozens of distinct facial actions and virtually no limit to the number of facial actions that can occur simultaneously (Ekman & Friesen, 1978). This potentially enormous set of combinations of facial actions to be coordinated is itself a *simplification* of how the face actually moves. In reality, facial actions are not simply present or not present. The degree of contraction of facial muscles is a continuous, not a categorical, variable.

In general, top–down solutions that hypothesize a central processor responsible for organizing the peripheral components simply displace the problem of complexity to the neurological system. This solution is workable if one attempts to explain only facial action patterns that have been defined a priori as prototypical expressions of discrete emotions. Researchers who confront the descriptive data must ask, for example, if there are separate neural programs for lip corner raising alone, for play smiles, Duchenne smiles, and combination Duchenne–play smiles. When one considers all possible combinations of all possible facial actions at all possible levels of contraction, the explanatory potential of preset neural programs falters.

Wholes and parts: Emergent properties

This section explores how the mutual influence of system constituents gives rise to patterns that are qualitatively different than the properties of their individual constituents. The contention here is that the coordination of facial actions creates emergent properties – social impacts, patterns of neural activity, and, potentially, feeling states – not present in the individual actions. The role of orbicularis oculi in raising the cheeks in a variety of facial configurations is offered as an illustration. For the sake of this argument, we accept Differential Emotions and approach–avoidance perspectives on the meaning of these facial configurations.

Fox and Davidson (1988) coded facial configurations identified as joy and anger by Izard's (1983) MAX in 10-month-old infants. They also coded the presence of orbicularis oculi contraction during smiles (joy expressions) and noted whether infants were crying during anger expressions. The onset of crying during these MAX-identified anger expressions was accompanied by the onset of orbicularis oculi contraction or by its extreme intensification.[3] Fox and Davidson (1988) also recorded frontal cerebral electrical activity during these facial actions.

The contraction of orbicularis oculi transforms a non-Duchenne into a Duchenne smile. In contrast with non-Duchenne smiles, Duchenne smiles are associated with self-reports of pleasurable emotions in adults and situations thought to involve enjoyment in infants (Ekman et al., 1990; Fox & Davidson, 1988). Fox and Davidson (1988) found that smiles with orbicularis oculi contraction (Duchenne smiles) were associated with greater relative left frontal activity than were smiles without. They interpreted this to indicate greater approach motivation during smiles with orbicularis oculi contraction (Fox, 1991; Fox & Davidson, 1984).

Next consider a description of what Differential Emotions perspectives have considered a prototypical anger expression. The brow is lowered, the upper lip is lifted to reveal the teeth, the corners of the mouth are drawn to the side, and the mouth is opened (Izard, 1983; Izard et al., 1983a). If orbicularis oculi now contracts, raising the cheeks and closing the eyes, this becomes a discomfort-pain (Izard, 1983; Izard et al., 1983a) or distress-cry (Camras, Oster, Campos, Miyake, & Bradshaw, 1992) configuration. The contraction of orbicularis oculi increases the negative signal value of anger configurations, transforming them into distress configurations. Fox and Davidson (1988) found that "anger" expressions with strong orbicularis oculi contraction (as indexed by crying) were associated with greater relative right frontal activity than the same anger expressions without orbicularis oculi (as indexed by the absence of crying). They interpret the presence of orbicularis oculi contraction during anger expressions as an indication of greater withdrawal orientation.

Orbicularis oculi contraction by itself has no recognized affective meaning, although Fridlund (1994) posits that it is an occluding response to strong stimuli. One might argue about the particular emotional meaning and motivational valences associated with the facial configurations discussed here. The point is that orbicularis oculi contraction is associated with contrasting patterns, depending on the other facial actions with which it occurs. Specifically, orbicularis oculi contraction may *intensify* the signal value, neurophysiological activity, and possibly affective significance associated with particular facial configurations. It may make positive expressions more positive and make negative expressions more negative.

To generalize, the meaning of facial configurations cannot be deduced by adding up the presumed valences or signal values of their components. The co-occurrence of facial actions reflects the mutual influence of muscular, neural, and interactive constituents. Out of the mutual influences involved in these configurations, *new properties emerge*. It is the task of future research to continue specifying the processes through which novel phenomena emerge from the coordination of facial actions in a neural and interactive milieu.

Conclusion: A metatheoretical framework?

To answer the questions posed at the beginning of the chapter, infant smiles and other facial actions are at once muscular contractions, social signals, and constituents of felt processes. Their meaning depends on interactive context, on the specific facial actions involved, and on how these constituents influence changes in each other over time. A facial action is a dynamic pattern whose meaning emerges out of the mutual influence of involved constituents.

In this conclusion, we attempt to demonstrate that acknowledging the mutual influences involved in the creation of emotional patterns exposes some debated dichotomies as more apparent than real. What, for example, is the association between facial action and feeling? Fridlund (1991, and chapter 5, this volume) argues that prototypical discrete emotion configurations function to alert or deceive a social partner as to one's social goals but do not necessarily reflect emotional states. Izard (chapter 3, this volume) argues, however, for a probabilistic association of infant facial actions and feelings. Our position is a synthesis. We regard infant facial actions not as unmediated expressions of emotions but as potential constituents of emotional processes. Infant facial actions come to function as social displays but are not reducible to social displays.

What is meant by feeling in Izard's account? The Differential Emotions position (see Izard, chapter 3, this volume; Izard & Malatesta, 1987) postulates a set of discrete feeling states. The complexity of emotional experience is thought to stem from links between these feelings and particular cognitions and perceptions. Although the distinction between abstractly defined feeling states and the rest of experience has a heuristic function, it contradicts fundamental systems principles. The mutual influence between an emotional feeling and a particular cognition or perception creates a unique gestalt. Pleasure in Duchenne smiling, the feeling of mutual positive involvement with a partner, and the sensation of tightened cheeks, all are inextricably combined. Each constituent transforms the experience of the other. The infant's experience of his or her embodied facial actions and his or her sensory experience of the partner are important constituents of the infant's emotional feeling (Fogel, 1993).

Broadening our conception of emotional experience has a theoretical advantage in accounting for the development of positive affect. Vygotsky (1978) has proposed that conventional communication develops because infants' gestures are treated as though they were intentional by the infants' social partners. A similar process may occur in the development of smiling. Face-to-face interaction is a social frame in which infants experience the influence of their facial actions on a partner. Mothers treat early infant zygomatic contraction as indices of pleasure. They smile back, comment, and try to elicit more smiles. Some of the feelings associated with zygomatic contraction such as an experience of engagement and mutuality may stem from such experiences. Part of the phenomenological experience of zygomatic contraction may develop from experiences of smiling while engaged with a smiling partner.

It is tempting to argue that infants' feelings are an internal reaction, a subjective summary of the meaning of an infant's actions in an interactive process. The difficulty with this position is that infant feeling ultimately becomes epiphenomenal. Subjective feeling may be a reflection of an ongoing process, but it is also a part of that process. Clearly, feeling states are on a different level of analysis than, say, cerebral activation. But constituents at different levels of analysis are rarely reducible to one another (Oyama, 1985). Like any other constituent of a process, infant feeling influences and is influenced by other constituents such as the infant's facial actions, his or her propensity to react to the social partner, and his or her state of sympathetic nervous system activation.

A recent debate concerns the temporal relationship of feeling to action. Izard (chapter 3, this volume) argues that emotional feelings are prior motivators of action. Campos et al. (1994) argue that emotional experience occurs just as a positive event is perceived. From a Dynamic Systems perspective, it seems unlikely that either possibility is exclusive. Positive feelings may motivate social actions such as gazing at a partner just as positive feelings may arise in the act of gazing at the partner. The principle here is that unidirectional cause–effect relationships between system constituents are unlikely. Mutual influence between infant facial and other actions, subjective feeling, and the response of a partner over the actual time span of an emotional interaction is likely to be a more productive assumption.

In this chapter, we have indicated how Dynamic Systems principles emphasizing the self-organization of complex systems can inform our understanding of facial action. We have identified how the mutual influence of neuromuscular, anatomical, neural, interactive, and affective processes can yield coordinated facial action. Finally, we applied the concept of mutual influence to problematics in emotion theory to achieve a more appropriately balanced understanding of these dynamic phenomena.

Acknowledgment

Research presented in this chapter was supported by an American Psychological Association Science Directorate Dissertation Research Award and a University of Utah Research Committee Graduate Student Fellowship to Daniel Messinger, by a grant to Alan Fogel from the National Institutes of Mental Health (MH 48680), and by a grant to D. K. Oller from the National Institute on Deafness and Other Communication Disorders. The authors would like to thank Alan Fridlund, Carroll Izard, Eli Messinger, and Charles Nelson for insightful comments on previous versions of this chapter. Correspondence should be addressed to the first author at the Department of Pediatrics, University of Miami, P.O. Box 016960 (M-827), Miami, FL 33101.

Notes

1 These three constituents – lip corner raising, cheek raising, and jaw dropping – can all co-occur as a combined Duchenne–play smile. See Messinger (1994) for a discussion of this salient display.
2 These sensations may occur in the skin and connective tissue above the orbital portion of orbicularis oculi. There is much controversy as to whether the facial muscles themselves have sensory neurons that provide information on their movement and contraction (for reviews, see Elliot, 1969; Rinn, 1984).
3 In MAX (Izard, 1983), several configurations of facial actions lead to anger

codes but do not involve cheek raising. In the anger configurations that do involve cheek raising, it is described as "incidental" to a drawn brow and squarish mouth (Izard, 1983, p. 33).

References

Barrett, K. C. (1993). The development of nonverbal communication of emotion: A functionalist perspective. *Journal of Nonverbal Behavior, 17*(3), 145–169.

Blurton-Jones, N. G. (1972). Non-verbal communication in children. In R. A. Hinde (Ed.), *Nonverbal communication*. Cambridge, MA: Cambridge University Press.

Campos, J. J., Mumme, D. L., Kermoian, R., & Campos, R. G. (1994). A functionalist perspective on the nature of emotion. In N. A. Fox (Ed.), *The development of emotion regulation: Biological and behavioral considerations. Monographs of the Society for Research in Child Development, 240, 59*(2–3).

Camras, L. A. (1992). Expressive development and basic emotions. *Cognition and Emotion, 6*(3/4), 269–283.

Camras, L. A., Oster, H., Campos, J. J., Miyake, K., & Bradshaw, D. (1992). Japanese and American infants' responses to arm restraint. *Developmental Psychology, 28*(4), 578–583.

Dedo, J. Y. (1991). *Smiling during later infancy: Relationships among facial expressions, contexts, and other communicative behaviors*. Unpublished doctoral dissertation, Purdue University, IN.

Dickson, K. L. (1994). *The parent–infant communication system: Infant smiles in relation to play type and gaze direction*. Unpublished doctoral dissertation, University of Utah.

Edelman, G. M. (1987). *Neural Darwinism*. New York: Basic Books.

Ekman, P. (1994). All emotions are basic. In P. Ekman & R. J. Davidson (Eds.), *The nature of emotion: Fundamental questions* (pp. 15–19). New York: Oxford University Press.

Ekman, P., Davidson, R. J., & Friesen, W. (1990). The Duchenne smile: Emotional expression and brain physiology II. *Journal of Personality and Social Psychology, 58*, 342–353.

Ekman, P., & Friesen, W. (1978). *The facial action coding system*. Palo Alto, CA: Consulting Psychologists Press.

Ekman, P., & Friesen, W. V. (1982). Felt, false, and miserable smiles. *Journal of Nonverbal Behavior 6*(4), 238–252.

Ekman, P., Friesen, W. V., & Ellsworth, P. (1972). *Emotion in the human face*. New York: Pergamon.

Elliot, H. C. (1969). *Textbook of neuroanatomy* (2nd ed.). Philadelphia: J. B. Lippincott.

Emde, R. N., & Koenig, K. (1969). Neonatal smiling and rapid eye movement states. *Journal of the American Academy of Child Psychiatry, 8*, 57–67.

Fogel, A. (1993). *Developing through relationships: Communication, self, and culture in early infancy*. London: Harvester-Wheatsheaf.

Fogel, A., & Thelen, E. (1987). Development of early expressive and communicative action: Reinterpreting the evidence from a dynamic systems perspective. *Developmental Psychology, 23*, 747–761.

Fox, N. A. (1991). If it's not left, it's right: Electroencephalograph asymmetry and the development of emotion. *American Psychologist, 46*(8) 863–872.

Fox, N. A., & Davidson, R. J. (1984). Hemispheric substrates of affect: A developmental model. In N. A. Fox & R. J. Davidson (Eds.), *The psychobiology of affective development*. Hillsdale, NJ: Erlbaum.

Fox, N. A., & Davidson, R. J. (1988). Patterns of brain electrical activity during facial signs of emotion in 10 month old infants. *Developmental Psychology, 24*(2), 230–236.

Fridlund, A. J. (1991). Evolution and facial action in reflex, social motive, and paralanguage. *Biological Psychology, 32*, 3–100.

Fridlund, A. J. (1994). *Human facial expression: An evolutionary view*. San Diego: Academic Press.

Friesen, W. V., & Ekman, P. (1992). *Changes in FACS scoring. Instruction manual*. San Francisco, CA: Human Interaction Lab.

Hooff, J. A. R. A. M. van (1972). A comparative approach to the phylogeny of laughter and smiling. In R. A. Hinde (Ed.), *Non-verbal communication* (pp. 209–241). Cambridge: Cambridge University Press.

Izard, C. E. (1981). Differential emotions theory and the facial feedback hypothesis of emotion activation: Comments on Tourangeau and Ellsworth's "The role of facial response in the experience of emotion." *Journal of Personality and Social Psychology, 40*, 350–354.

Izard, C. E. (1983). *The maximally discriminative facial coding system* (rev. ed.). Newark, DE: Instructional Resources Center, University of Delaware.

Izard, C. E., Dougherty, L. M., & Hembree, E. A. (1983a). *A system for identifying affect expressions by holistic judgements (AFFEX)*. Newark, DE: Instructional Resources Center, University of Delaware.

Izard, C. E., Hembree, E. A., Dougherty, L. M., & Spizzirri, C. C. (1983b). Changes in facial expressions of 2- to 19-month-old infants following acute pain. *Developmental Psychology, 19*, 418–426.

Izard, C. E., & Malatesta, C. Z. (1987). Perspectives on emotional development I: Differential emotions theory of early emotional development. In J. Osofsky (Ed.), *Handbook of infant development* (2nd ed., 494–554). New York: Wiley & Sons.

Kaye, K., & Fogel, A. (1980). The temporal structure of face-to-face communication between mothers and infants. *Developmental Psychology, 16*, 454–464.

Levenson, R. W., Ekman, P., & Friesen, W. V. (1990). Voluntary facial action generates emotion-specific autonomic nervous system activity. *Psychophysiology, 27*(4), 363–384.

Malatesta, C. Z., Culver, C., Tesman, J. C., & Shepard, B. (1989). The development of emotion expression during the first two years of life. *Monographs of the Society for Research in Child Development, 54*(1–2, Serial No. 219).

McCormack, L. J., Cauldwell, E. W., & Anson, B. J. (1945). The surgical anatomy of the facial nerve with special reference to the parotid gland. *Surgery, Gynecology, and Obstetrics, 80*, 620–630.

Messinger, D. S. (1994). *The development of smiling: A dynamic systems approach*. Unpublished doctoral dissertation, University of Utah.

Messinger, D. S. (1995, April). *How mothers and infants smile*. Poster presented at the biennial meeting of the Society for Research in Child Development, Indianapolis, IN.

Messinger, D., Fogel, A., & Dickson, K. L. *What's in a smile? Individual, morphological, and developmental variability in infant emotional expression*. Manuscript in preparation.

Michel, G. F., Camras, L. A., & Sullivan, J. (1992). Infant interest expressions as coordinative motor structures. *Infant Behavior and Development, 15*(3), 347–358.

Oster, H. (1978). Facial expression and affect development. In M. Lewis & L. A. Rosenblum (Eds.), *The development of affect*. New York: Plenum Press.

Oster, H., & Ekman, P. (1977). Facial behavior in child development. In A. Collins (Ed.), *Minnesota symposia on child psychology* (Vol. 11, pp. 231–276). Hillsdale, NJ: Erlbaum.

Oster, H., & Rosenstein, D. (in press). *Baby FACS: Analyzing facial movement in infants*. Palo Alto, CA: Consulting Psychologists Press.

Oyama, S. (1985). *The ontogeny of information*. New York: Cambridge University Press.

Panksepp, J. (1994). The clearest physiological distinctions between emotions will be found among the circuits of the brain. In P. Ekman & R. J. Davidson (Eds.), *The nature of emotion: Fundamental questions* (pp. 258–260). New York: Oxford University Press.

Plooij, F. (1979). How wild chimpanzee babies trigger the onset of mother–infant play – and what the mother makes of it. In M. Bullowa (Ed.), *Before speech: The beginning of interpersonal communication* (pp. 223–243). London: Cambridge University Press.

Rinn, W. E. (1984). The neuropsychology of facial expression: A review of the neurological and psychological mechanisms for producing facial expressions. *Psychological Bulletin, 95*(1), 52–77.

Thelen, E. (1995). Motor development: A new synthesis. *American Psychologist, 50*(2), 79–95.

Thelen, E., & Smith, E. (1994). *A dynamic systems approach to the development of cognition and action*. Cambridge, MA: MIT Press.

Thelen, E., & Ulrich, B. D. (1991). Hidden skills: A dynamic systems analysis of treadmill stepping during the first year. *Monographs of the Society for Research in Child Development, 223, 56*(1).

Tomkins, S. S. (1962). *Affect, imagery, consciousness: Vol. 1. The positive affects*. New York: Springer-Verlag.

Turvey, M. T. (1990). Coordination. *American Psychologist, 45*(8), 938–953.

Vygotsky, L. (1978). *Mind in society: The development of higher psychological processes* (M. Cole, V. John-Steiner, S. Scribner, & E. Souberman, Eds.). Cambridge, MA: Harvard University Press.

Williams, P. L., Warwick, R., Dyson, M., & Bannister, L. H. (1989). *Gray's anatomy*. Edinburgh: Churchill Livingstone.

Wolff, P. H. (1987). *The development of behavioral states and the expression of emotions in early infancy: New proposals for investigation*. Chicago: The University of Chicago Press.

PART IV

With a psychological and social focus

10. A Componential Approach to the meaning of facial expressions

CRAIG A. SMITH AND HEATHER S. SCOTT

When we want to know what someone is thinking, how they are feeling, or what they might do, the first place we frequently look is to their face. This makes considerable sense because the human face is capable of generating expressions associated with a wide range of affective states; the grimace of pain, the sneer of contempt, the glare of anger, the averted eyes of shame, the wide-eyed look of surprise, the intent stare of interest, the quizzical look of puzzlement, the frozen stare of terror, the radiant smile of joy, the sly grin of mischief, and much more, all emanate from the face. Indeed, it could be argued that the face has the only skeletal muscles of the body that are used, not to move ourselves, but to move others.

Given that the face is an important channel of social communication, among the questions that arise are: What are the major messages that are communicated through this channel, and how are they encoded? Facial actions can clearly be used to communicate information other than an individual's emotional state (see Bavelas, Black, Lemery, & Mullett, 1986; Bavelas & Chovil, chapter 15, this volume; Ekman, 1979; Fridlund, 1994). However, from Darwin (1872/1965) to the present, the main focus of research on facial expression has been on the expression of emotion, and for the bulk of this chapter, we maintain this focus.

There is considerable evidence (reviewed in Ekman, Friesen, & Ellsworth, 1982) indicating distinct, prototypical facial signals that across a variety of cultures can be reliably recognized as corresponding to at least six different emotions (happiness, sadness, surprise, disgust, anger, and fear), and possibly others, including interest, shame (Izard, 1971), and contempt (Ekman & Friesen, 1986; Izard, 1971; Izard & Haynes, 1988). It should be noted, however, that this evidence has relied almost exclusively on having subjects categorize carefully selected photographs of posed facial expressions. Thus, this research most directly concerns how observers *decode* facial expressions, and it is quite limited in what it can directly reveal about the information that senders have *encoded* in the expressions (see Russell, 1994; and Wagner, chapter 2, this volume, for thorough critiques of this research).

Nevertheless, the fact that these expressions are widely recognized strongly suggests that psychologically meaningful information is encoded in them, which increases the importance of systematically examining the nature of the encoded information. Thus, using these widely recognized expressions as a starting point, the questions already posed become: What information is conveyed through these facial expressions, and how is this information organized? More specifically, the question we examine is: Do the facial expressions for various emotions systematically encode information about the person's emotional state beyond the emotion's categorical identity, and if so, how is this information encoded? In pursuing this issue, it is helpful to contrast three models.

The first might be termed the *Purely Categorical Model*. Within this model, emotional facial expressions are conceptualized as comprising a primitive, nonverbal "language" (e.g., Mandler, 1980, 1984) in which individual expressions are the basic units of meaning, analogous to words in spoken language. In this language, the meanings conveyed by facial expressions consist of the categorical identities of the various emotions. Just as most words are arbitrary symbols whose meanings are determined by convention or historical accident, facial expressions are arbitrarily structured symbols that are imbued with meaning through learned cultural conventions governing relationships between specific expressions and the emotions they represent. The fact that expressions for some emotions (e.g., fear and surprise) appear more similar to one another than others (e.g., fear and happiness), and that this similarity is due to shared facial actions (here, raised eyebrows and widely opened eyes; see Ekman & Friesen, 1978; Izard, 1971), is coincidental and noninformative. Taken by themselves, the individual facial actions (or components) that contribute to the expressions are essentially meaningless. This is just as is the case with the fact that the English words *dog* and *door* both start with the letters *d* and *o*. The fact that those particular letters contribute to the spelling of those particular words tells us nothing about what the words mean.

The second model represents the *Componential Model*, which we have adopted. This model, in direct contrast to the purely categorical one, hypothesizes that rather than being arbitrary and meaningless, at least some of the individual components contributing to a given facial expression are inherently meaningful. That is, emotional expressions have a systematic, coherent, and meaningful structure, and consideration of the individual components that contribute to that structure can directly reveal much about the underlying properties of the emotion being expressed. For example, the fact that the prototypical expressions of fear and surprise share raised eyebrows and widely opened eyes indicates something about the properties that these states share – possibly that the person experiencing either emotion is uncertain about some aspect of his or her circumstances and is actively attending to the environment in an attempt to reduce that uncertainty.

Our version of the Componential Model shares the Categorical Model's hypothesis that an emotion's categorical identity is conveyed by the overall facial expression. In our model, as in the purely categorical one, different distinct emotions may be expressed through different distinct configurations of facial muscle activity. We believe that the information conveyed by overall facial configurations need not be entirely redundant with that carried by the individual components. Thus, the overall facial configuration corresponding to fear could convey information about aspects of the person's emotional state that are unique to fear and that are not captured by any individual muscle action – for instance, that the person feels threatened and perceives him- or herself as being in some kind of danger. In other words, the information conveyed by an overall facial expression could represent more than the sum of its parts.

Our model can be contrasted with a third one, which might be termed the *Purely Componential Model*. This model, a version of which has been advanced by Ortony and Turner (1990), takes issue with the idea that facial activity directly encodes an emotion's categorical identity. On this view, all the information conveyed by facial expression is encoded at the level of the individual components. The full facial configuration represents nothing more than the sum of its parts, and assigning a categorical identity to such a configuration is an inference made during decoding rather than something that is directly encoded by the combined muscle actions (see, for example, Russell, chapter 13, this volume). It should be noted that the assumptions underlying our version of the Componential Model are less restrictive than those underlying a purely componential one. In this chapter, in describing the Componential Approach, we are working from our less restrictive model.

Although seldom explicitly discussed as such, some form of componential model has implicitly underlain hypotheses concerning the significance of individual facial actions, such as those advanced by Duchenne (1862/1990), Darwin (1872/1965), and Andrew (1965). It has also been present to varying degrees in general theoretical approaches to emotion advanced by Izard (1971, 1977), Lazarus (1968), Frijda (1969, 1986), and others. Relatively specific componential models have been outlined recently by Scherer (1984, 1992) and Smith (1987, 1989).

In this chapter, we consider the Componential Approach to facial expression in depth. First, we review reasons why one might expect emotional facial expression to have a meaningful componential structure. Next, we review (1) the specific hypotheses that have been advanced regarding the significance of the individual components of facial expression, and (2) the evidence that has been garnered to evaluate these hypotheses. Finally, we consider the potential relevance of the Componential Approach for such issues as the existence of basic or fundamental emotions (e.g., Ortony & Turner, 1990) and the relations of emotional facial expression to other forms of facial communication (e.g., Bavelas et al., 1986; Bavelas and Chovil, chapter 15, this volume; Fridlund, 1994).

Reasons for expecting a meaningful componential structure to facial expressions

Anatomical considerations

Overall, there is considerable agreement on the specific muscle actions that combine to produce the widely recognized expressions of happiness, sadness, surprise, disgust, anger, and fear. Darwin (1872/1965), Frois-Wittmann (1930), Izard (1971), and Ekman and Friesen (1978) have each provided descriptions of these six expressions. In Table 10.1, we list the salient actions that at least two of these sources agree contribute to these expressions. Also listed are the action units (AUs) of the *Facial Action Coding System* (FACS) (Ekman & Friesen, 1978) that correspond to these actions, as well as the major muscles responsible for producing them.

The most important thing to note about this table is that most individual muscle actions are common to multiple expressions. For example, the eyebrow frown is present in expressions of sadness, anger, disgust/contempt, and fear, and the eyebrows are raised in surprise, fear, and sadness. Thus, most emotions are not signaled by the activity of single muscles or muscle groups; there is no single "fear muscle" whose contraction unambiguously signals fear, nor an "anger muscle" to signal anger. Instead, it is the overall *pattern* of activity across the face that is distinct for each emotion (Ekman et al., 1982; Frois-Wittmann, 1930).

Table 10.1. *Important components of some widely recognized facial expressions*

	Facial action						
	Eyebrow frown	Raise eyebrows	Raise upper eyelid	Raise lower eyelid	Lip corners	Open mouth	Raise upper lip
Muscular basis	corrugator supercilii	medial frontalis	levator palpebrae superioris	orbicularis oculi	a	orbicularis oris	levator labii superioris
Action Units	4	1	5	6,7		26,27	9,10
Emotion expressed							
Happiness				X	Raise		
Surprise		X	X			X	
Anger	X		X	X		X	
Disgust/contempt	X			X			X
Fear	X	X	X			X	
Sadness	X	X			Lower		

Note: Descriptions are drawn from Darwin (1872/1965), Ekman and Friesen (1978), Frois-Witmann (1930), and Izard (1971). A facial action is listed as being associated with a particular emotion only in cases where two or more of these sources agree on the association. ᵃRaising the lip corners is due to contraction of the zygomaticus major (AU 12), and lowering them is due to contraction of the depressor anguli oris (AU 15).

Taken alone, the facts that emotional identity is expressed by global patterns of facial muscle activity, and that different patterns often share components, do not speak directly to the Componential Approach. They do, however, make it reasonable to ask the central question addressed by this approach: Are the individual components – especially those shared by multiple expressions – directly meaningful? Stated another way, is reliable information about one's affective state available at a more molecular level than that of the overall facial expression?

Reasons of communication efficiency

An important advantage of a componentially based system is that it allows the face to retain considerable communicative power under conditions where a purely categorical one would likely break down. If the information to be communicated through facial expressions were carried only by global patterns of activity, and the individual components contributing to the patterns were themselves meaningless, then communication would only be successful when a valid, meaningful pattern (or, more precisely, enough of the pattern to allow it to be uniquely identified) had been successfully produced. Short of this, no information about one's emotional state could be communicated through an expression. In contrast, a system in which individual expressive components carried meaning would be much more flexible and resilient. Under such a system, in cases of degraded, partial, or ambiguous expressions that precluded categorization, one could still learn much about the emotional state being expressed through information conveyed by any individual components that were produced. In other words, partial expressions that would be useless in a purely categorical system could still be quite communicative in a componential one.

This advantage becomes important when one considers what little is known about spontaneous emotional expressions produced in naturalistic contexts. It must be emphasized that, as noted by Russell (1994) and Fernández-Dols and Ruiz-Belda (chapter 11, this volume), there is a dearth of empirical evidence examining this issue. However, the available evidence suggests that spontaneous displays of full expressions of single emotions are rare. First, as has often been noted (e.g., Ekman & Friesen, 1969), spontaneous expressions of emotion may be constrained by cultural or personal display rules that prescribe whether and under what conditions certain emotions may be freely expressed. For example, it appears that individuals are generally less expressive in the presence of strangers than when among friends (e.g., Buck, Losow, Murphy, &

Costanzo, 1992; Wagner & Smith, 1991); and there appears to be a pervasive norm, practiced to the extreme by some individuals, to minimize the expression of negative emotion in the presence of others (e.g., Buck et al., 1992; Smith, McHugo, & Lanzetta, 1986).

Second, the idea that each emotion has a single, clearly defined expression associated with it (as suggested by Table 10.1) is an oversimplification. In truth, each emotion can be signaled roughly equally well by several different expressions. The variants for a given emotion share strong family resemblance because they share a number of facial actions, but they are distinguishable (see Ekman & Friesen, 1975, 1978; Izard, 1971). Such multiple expressions reduce the efficiency of a purely categorical system, since each variant represents a different "word" (synonym) to be learned. If, however, the individual components carried meaning, the variant features could represent a degree of fine-tuning, in which the particular components emphasized, deemphasized, added, or omitted from a given expression could provide specific information about the emotion being expressed.

As a further complication, there is considerable evidence suggesting that it is rare for most individuals to experience strong feelings of a single isolated emotion. Instead, across a variety of emotionally evocative contexts, it is common for individuals to report the subjective experience of blends of up to four (or more) emotions (e.g., Ellsworth & Smith, 1988; Folkman & Lazarus, 1985; Schwartz & Weinberger, 1980; Smith & Ellsworth, 1987). Although there have been attempts to describe the facial expressions characteristic of a limited number of emotional blends (e.g., Ekman & Friesen, 1975), the principles by which such blended expressions are produced have not yet been articulated. In any event, it is likely that the resulting composite patterns of facial activity would obscure the identities of the individual emotions contributing to the blends. A categorical system could handle some degree of blending if it treated the expressions characteristic of specific blends as distinct expressive categories. However, such a system would quickly become unwieldy because the number of distinct blends that can be produced by combinations of up to four or more emotions, each at varying levels of intensity, is dauntingly large.

Theoretical reasons

Finally, there is a strong theoretical basis for expecting facial expressions to have a meaningful componential structure. Many contemporary theories of emotion (e.g., Ekman, 1984; Ellsworth, 1991; Frijda, 1986; Izard,

1977; Lazarus, 1991; Plutchik, 1980; Scherer, 1984; Smith & Lazarus, 1990; Tomkins, 1980) posit the existence of an organized, functional emotion system. In these theories, emotion is viewed as a flexible system that mediates between environmental stimulation and behavioral response. Emotions arise in particular contexts and prepare and motivate individuals to respond to these contexts in usually adaptive ways (Ellsworth & Smith, 1988). Each emotion is proposed to serve a particular set of functions. For example, anger prepares and motivates one to remove an irritant or obstacle; fear prepares and motivates one to escape danger; guilt motivates one to adhere to personal and social norms (e.g., Ellsworth & Smith, 1988; Izard, 1977; Lazarus, 1991; Plutchik, 1980).

These theories propose that emotional reactions consist of several distinct but interrelated facets (see especially, Scherer, 1984): a subjective feeling state, a pattern of physiological (both autonomic and somatic) activity, a characteristic facial expression, and a motivational urge (or action tendency) to respond to one's circumstances in a certain way. In a number of *appraisal theories* (e.g., Ellsworth, 1991; Frijda, 1986; Lazarus, 1991; Roseman, 1984; Scherer, 1984; Smith, 1989), a characteristic *appraisal,* or meaning analysis, is hypothesized to trigger the emotional reaction in a context-sensitive manner. Importantly, the individual facets of the emotional response are posited to be organized in a highly interdependent fashion. For instance, physiological activity is hypothesized to prepare the person physically to act in ways motivated by action tendencies, and both the physiological activities and the action tendencies are hypothesized to be organized around the adaptational implications of the appraisals that elicited the emotion (e.g., Frijda, Kuipers, & Terschure, 1989; Lazarus, 1968; Roseman, Wiest, & Swartz, 1994; Scherer, 1984; Smith, 1989).

From such a functionalist perspective, one would expect the individual components of facial expressions to be linked to the various emotions in a highly systematic fashion. For any given emotion, the components of the emotion's overall facial expression should be systematically related to both the other facets of the emotional response and to the adaptational functions served by the emotion. For instance, in describing his attempts to identify the characteristic expressions associated with various emotions, Izard (1971) asserted that consideration of the specific functions theoretically served by a particular emotion could provide important clues as to how that emotion might be expressed both facially and posturally. Similarly, Frijda (1969, 1986; Frijda & Tcherkassof, chapter 4, this volume) has linked the components of facial expression to action tendencies associated with various emotions. Finally, as noted previously, both Scherer (1984, 1992) and Smith (1987, 1989) have hypothesized relations between specific appraisals and specific facial components. It is to such hypotheses, and the evidence supporting them, that we now turn.

Specific componential hypotheses and supporting evidence

Specific hypotheses regarding the potential meanings of individual facial actions can be derived from four main sources: the rich descriptions of emotional facial expressions provided by Darwin (1872/1965), the theoretically based hypotheses of Scherer (1984, 1992), and some indirect empirical evidence provided by both Frijda (1969) and Smith (1989, Pilot Study).[1] The hypotheses that have been derived from these four sources are depicted in Table 10.2. It should be noted that these hypotheses are not meant to be exhaustive. It is very likely that additional facial actions not depicted in the table also carry meaning, and it is possible that some of the depicted actions convey meanings beyond those indicated. Table 10.2 merely presents the major relations that have been proposed to date.

At the most general level, the table suggests two distinct clusters of facial actions, each of which provides information along a broad dimension of meaning. One cluster, which includes the eyebrow frown and a variety of activities involving the mouth, is proposed to encode information about the subjective pleasantness of the emotional state, including related appraisals, such as the perception of goal obstacles or the anticipation of the need to expend effort. The second cluster, which includes raised eyebrows and a variety of activities around the eyes, is proposed to encode information related to the type of attentional activity associated with the emotional state, including the novelty of the situation and one's degree of certainty about one's circumstances. These proposals accord well with the findings of a long tradition of dimensional analyses of the perception of facial expressions (e.g., Frijda & Philipszoon, 1963; Osgood, 1966; Schlosberg, 1952, 1954; see Smith & Ellsworth, 1985, for a review), in which two of the three most commonly recovered dimensions correspond to pleasantness and attentional activity. The third commonly recovered dimension corresponds to "level of activation" or "arousal." This dimension is likely reflected in the overall intensity of the facial expression rather than by the presence or absence of specific facial actions (see Frijda, 1969).

The final set of entries in the table suggests that many of the facial actions proposed to be associated with attentional activity also encode information along an additional dimension corresponding to personal

Table 10.2. *Meanings proposed to be associated with individual facial actions*

	Facial action							
Meaning	Eyebrow frown	Raise eyebrows	Raise upper eyelid	Raise lower eyelid	Lip corners	Open mouth	Tighten mouth	Raise chin
Pleasantness	-(D, F, S)				+(D, S, F)	+(S)	-(S)	-(S)
Goal obstacle/goal discrepancy	+(Sch, D?)							
Anticipated effort	+(S, D?)							
Attentional activity		+(D) -(S)	+(D, F, S)			+(D)		
Certainty		+(Sch)	+(Sch)	+(S)				
Novelty		-(D, S)	-(S, Sch)					
Personal agency/control						-(D, Sch, S)		

Note: A "+" indicates that the facial action is hypothesized to increase with increasing levels of the meaning dimension; a "−" indicates that the facial action increases as the meaning dimension decreases (e.g, low levels of personal agency are associated with raised eyebrows). The "+" sign for lip corners indicates that they are hypothesized to be raised (primarily due to contraction of the *zygomaticus major*) with increasing pleasantness, and to be lowered (primarily due to contraction of the *depressor anguli oris*) with increasing unpleasantness. The letters following the symbols indicate who proposed the hypotheses. "D" indicates Darwin (1872/1965), "F" indicates Frijda (1969), "S" indicates Smith (1989), and "Sch" indicates Scherer (1984).

agency or control. Facial actions associated with high levels of attention are also associated with low levels of agency/control. This proposal also accords well with the existing literature in that a fourth dimension, often labeled "control" or "controllability," has occasionally been recovered (e.g., Frijda, 1969; Osgood, 1966).

In addition, the table contains suggestions that the information encoded by individual facial components may be more specific than implied by a consideration of these relatively broad dimensions. However, there is some disagreement across investigators as to the specific information encoded by several of the components. For instance, the eyebrow frown is hypothesized to be associated with subjective feelings of unpleasantness, but it has been hypothesized to encode something else as well. Specifically, Darwin (1872/1965, p. 220) associated the eyebrow frown with "reflection with an effort, or with the perception of something difficult or disagreeable," and he noted (p. 221) that "a man may be absorbed in the deepest thought, and his brow will remain smooth until he encounters some obstacle in his train of reasoning, or is interrupted by some disturbance, and then a frown passes like a shadow over his brow." Scherer (1984) translated Darwin's observations into a proposal that the eyebrow frown is associated with the perception of some type of discrepancy between one's needs or goals and one's actual circumstances. In contrast, Smith (1989) interpreted Darwin's statements as implying that the frown was associated with anticipating the need to expend effort to cope with one's situation.

Similarly, there is general consensus that raising the eyebrows and raising the upper eyelids are both associated with something related to attentional activity. However, individual investigators differ in the specific meanings they associate with these actions. Darwin (1872/1965) associates both activities with attentional activity, whereas Scherer (1984) associates them with the perception of novelty in the environment. Smith (1989), in contrast, associates raising the upper eyelid with attentional activity and raising the eyebrows with uncertainty about some aspect(s) of one's circumstances. Finally, Frijda (1969) associates raising the upper eyelid with attentional activity but does not address the significance of raised eyebrows.

It is also evident from Table 10.2 that in a number of cases there is not proposed to be a simple one-to-one mapping between single components of facial activity and simple meanings. To the extent to which the hypotheses listed in the table prove to be valid, certain types of information may be encoded by multiple facial actions, and a single facial action may encode several distinct types of information. The first possibility simply implies that there is some redundancy in the communication system. In general, such redundancy increases the system's resiliency because it provides multiple ways for a given piece of information to be communicated.

The latter possibility is, however, potentially problematic because it creates ambiguity as to the meaning of particular facial components when they are viewed in isolation. However, the degree of ambiguity involved is not great because in virtually every instance, the multiple meanings hypothesized to be encoded by a single component are related. Thus, unpleasant experiences often involve goal discrepancies and expenditure of effort. Similarly, uncertainty about one's circumstances, perceptions of novelty, and/or feelings of not being in control, are often associated with attempts to attend closely to one's environment. Nonetheless, given that these related constructs are not identical, to the extent that individual components are found to encode multiple constructs, it is important to investigate the degree to which the specific meaning encoded by a particular component can be disambiguated contextually.

Supporting evidence

Although Table 10.2 suggests a number of hypotheses worth investigating, virtually all of the existing evidence directly relevant to these hypotheses has focused on the potential meanings of two components: the eyebrow frown, produced by contracting the *corrugator supercilii* and related muscles, and the raised lip corners (as in the smile), produced by contracting the *zygomatic major*. A large body of data demonstrates that the eyebrow frown is associated with unpleasant stimuli and emotions (e.g., Cacioppo, Martzke, Petty, & Tassinary, 1988; Cacioppo, Petty, Losch, & Kim, 1986), while raised lip corners are associated with pleasant stimuli and emotions (e.g., Cacioppo et al., 1986; Ekman, Friesen, & Ancoli, 1980). In addition, in accord with Darwin's observations, there have been suggestions that something distinct from unpleasantness, often interpreted as "concentration," is associated with the eyebrow frown (Cacioppo, Petty, & Morris, 1985).

Smith (1989) and Pope and Smith (1994) have built upon this evidence and have conducted two studies designed to examine the significance of the eyebrow frown. Both studies involved monitoring muscle activity in the eyebrow and cheek regions (corresponding to activity of the *corrugator* and *zygomatic* muscles, respectively) using surface EMG while subjects engaged in directed imagery.

The first study (Smith, 1989) focused on pleasant situations. Subjects imagined themselves in hypothetical situations in which the combined appraisals of anticipated effort and perceived goal obstacles (i.e., specific goal discrepancies) were manipulated. In a between-subjects design, subjects imagined themselves in situations that either did or did not involve the presence of a goal obstacle and the expenditure of effort (e.g., trying to beat a friend in a foot race versus having a relaxing picnic lunch with friends in a meadow). In addition, in a within-subject manipulation, subjects first imagined their reactions to the global situation, and then their attention was drawn (in counterbalanced order) to the pleasant aspects of the situation, and, separately, to the aspects of the situation that involved high or low levels of effort and/or goal obstacles.

Consistent with the relevant hypotheses listed in Table 10.2, muscle activity in the eyebrow region, but not the cheek region, was observed to increase significantly with the combined evaluations of anticipated effort and perceived goal obstacles. These increases were largest when subjects' attention was specifically focused on the effort and/or obstacle-related aspects of their imagined situations. Thus, these findings directly support the hypotheses advanced by Darwin (1872/1965), Scherer (1984), and Smith (1989) that the eyebrow frown encodes information distinguishable from subjective pleasantness that concerns individuals' perceptions of goal obstacles and/or anticipated effort.

Moreover, follow-up analyses suggested the eyebrow frown is more closely related to perceived goal obstacles than to anticipated effort, thereby supporting Scherer's (1984) interpretation of the meaning of this component over Smith's (1989). Although the experimental design intentionally confounded evaluations of anticipated effort and perceived goal obstacles, subjects serendipitously dissociated these two evaluations across the experimental scenarios. A series of regression analyses indicated that the relation between goal obstacles and the eyebrow frown was more direct than that between anticipated effort and the eyebrow frown; statistically controlling for the perception of goal obstacles eliminated the observed relation between anticipated effort and the eyebrow frown, but controlling for anticipated effort did not eliminate the relation between the eyebrow frown and the perception of goal obstacles.

This latter finding was conceptually replicated by Pope and Smith (1994). In their study, using a within-subjects design, subjects imagined themselves in a variety of pleasant and unpleasant situations in which goal discrepancies and anticipated effort varied freely (these situations ranged from receiving an "A" on a midterm exam to learning that a friend had been in a serious car accident). In response to the imagined situations, subjects provided self-reports of subjective pleasantness, perceived goal obstacles, the presence of goal discrepancies more generally, and anticipated effort. In this study, no evidence was obtained for a relation between anticipated effort and the eyebrow frown, but brow region activity was found to be positively correlated with perceived goal obstacles and goal discrepancies and negatively correlated with subjective pleasantness. In contrast, cheek region activity was negatively correlated with perceived goal obstacles and goal discrepancies and was positively correlated with subjective pleasantness. Importantly, even though the subjects' self-reports of subjective pleasantness and goal discrepancies were themselves highly correlated (approximately .90, an uncharacteristically high value for this relation; see Pope & Smith, 1994), regression analyses indicated that brow activity (reflecting the eyebrow frown) was most directly related to the perceived presence of goal discrepancies, whereas cheek activity (reflecting the raising of the lip corners in a smile) was most directly related to subjective pleasantness. Thus, the existing evidence suggests that, as most investigators have hypothesized, raising the lip corners primarily encodes feelings of subjective pleasantness, and that, in line with Scherer's (1984) hypothesis, the eyebrow frown most directly encodes appraisals related to the perception of need–goal discrepancies – appraisals that are correlated with subjective unpleasantness but are nonetheless distinguishable from it.

That both the smile and the eyebrow frown have been demonstrated to encode relatively specific information related to one's emotional state augurs well for the validity of the Componential Approach. Nonetheless, it is still the case that only a small subset of the proposed relations between individual components and specific meanings has received direct empirical attention. Obviously, a necessary step in the further development of this approach to understanding facial expression is to test the validity of the additional hypotheses that have been proposed.

Extensions and implications of the Componential Approach to facial expression

The organization of physiological activity in emotion

Although we have limited our consideration thus far to facial expression, we believe that the Componential Approach can be fruitfully used to study the organization of physiological activity in emotion. Lazarus

(1968, p. 206) has asserted that in emotion: "The physiological patterns should be associated with the different adaptive tasks which the appraisals leading to the different emotions seem to require." We resonate to this view and agree with Frijda's (1986, Frijda & Tcherkassof, chapter 4, this volume) observation that numerous facets of the emotional response are likely to be organized to support the specific instrumental actions that are motivated by the emotional state. Emotional response components that likely reflect emotionally motivated demands include patterns of autonomic arousal and somatic muscle tension, aspects of facial expression that contribute directly to instrumental action (such as widening the eyes with increased attentional activity), and certain parameters of vocal expression, such as pitch, that covary with arousal or tension level (see Scherer, 1986).

To the extent that such parameters of emotional response reflect the physiological demands of emotionally motivated actions, the Componential Approach is likely to prove especially valuable in understanding the physiological organization of emotion. This is because, as Frijda and Tcherkassof (chapter 4, this volume) argue, the range of behaviors associated with any particular emotion is diverse and encompasses a broad spectrum of physiological demands. For instance, the behavioral strategies associated with anger can range from active, violent attack to quiet sulking and/or plotting of revenge. Obviously, the physiological demands of such responses are very different.

These considerations make it unrealistic to expect each emotion to have a distinctive prototypical pattern of associated physiological activity, and they could explain why attempts to describe patterns of autonomic activity for various emotions have been notoriously unsuccessful (see also Stemmler, 1989). It is noteworthy that the most successful attempts to produce such patterns (e.g., Levenson, Ekman, & Friesen, 1990; Levenson, Ekman, Heider, & Friesen, 1992) have involved subjects posing precisely defined facial expressions while sitting quietly in a chair. Seemingly minor procedural changes, such as substituting a carefully designed directed-imagery task for the posing task, have resulted in reductions in the distinctiveness of the autonomic patterns observed for the different emotions (e.g., Ekman, Levenson, & Friesen, 1983; for reviews, see Cacioppo, Klein, Berntson, & Hatfield, 1993; Zajonc & McIntosh, 1992).

Instead, the Componential Approach, which considers the physiological functions served by various parameters of physiological response and attempts to link these functions to the specific actions that one is attempting to perform, is likely to prove more productive in understanding the organization of physiological activity in emotion. In fact, the results of initial attempts to explore autonomic activity from this framework have been promising. For instance, cardiovascular activity is thought to operate largely in the service of the metabolic demands associated with expending effort (e.g., Obrist, 1976), whereas skin conductance activity has been closely linked to attentional processes (e.g., Dawson, Schell, & Filion, 1990; Öhman, 1979).

In addition to the EMG findings described previously, Smith (1989) observed that heart rate covaried directly with anticipated effort, and that skin conductance level was correlated with self-reported levels of attentional activity. Moreover, several researchers have linked changes in a number of parameters of cardiovascular activity to the level of effort that a person is exerting, or preparing to exert, during a variety of problem-solving tasks. These parameters have included increases in heart rate and blood pressure (e.g., Wright, Contrada, & Patane, 1986; Wright & Dill, 1993); decreases in peripheral resistance (which reflect the opening of peripheral blood vessels to increase the availability of oxygenated blood to the peripheral muscles; e.g., Tomaka, Blascovich, Kelsey, & Leitten, 1993); and increases in the slope of peripheral skin temperature change (which reflects the increased blood flow resulting from the reduced peripheral resistance; Smith & Pecchinenda, 1995). In addition, Pecchinenda and Smith (1995) observed that changes in spontaneous skin conductance activity were positively correlated with changes in cognitive engagement in a difficult anagram-solving task. Thus, these initial attempts to elucidate the organization of physiological activity associated with emotion indicate that this activity is systematically organized, and that the Componential Approach is useful for exploring its organization.

The existence of basic emotions

A further issue we would like to address concerns the relevance of the Componential Approach to facial expression for questions concerning the existence of discrete, basic emotions, such as have been proposed by Tomkins (1962, 1963), Izard (1977), and Ekman (1984). This issue arises because, working from the Purely Componential Model (which, the reader will recall, we have differentiated from our less restrictive model), Ortony and Turner (1990) have argued against the existence of basic emotions. In making their case, they drew upon some of the evidence that Smith (1989) had collected in support of the Componential Approach, and they argued that the Componential and Discrete-Emotions approaches were generally incompatible.

We believe that the Purely Componential Model as advanced by Ortony and Turner (1990) is a potentially viable one, and it is clear that their model is incompatible with a discrete-emotions account. However, we do not believe that the Componential and Discrete-Emotions approaches are inherently incompatible. Nor do we believe that data supporting the existence of a componential structure for facial expression are necessarily evidence against the existence of basic emotions. Instead, we believe that the Componential Model we have adopted, and the evidence that has been gathered to support it, is neutral with regard to the existence of basic emotions.

In our view, the existence of a componential structure for facial expressions is compatible with the existence of basic emotions unless one requires the basic emotions to be entirely fixed, rigid entities that cannot be further analyzed or decomposed into subcomponents, as Ortony and Turner (1990) appear to have done. However, as previous commentators on the Ortony and Turner (1990) position have noted (e.g., Ekman, 1992a, b; Izard, 1992; Panksepp, 1992), such a conceptualization of basic emotions is untenable and is not what discrete-emotions theorists have proposed. Once one allows for some degree of plasticity within the basic categories of emotional experience (e.g., Ekman, 1979, 1992a), and acknowledges that basic emotions can be decomposed and described in terms of various components such as feeling states, facial expressions, and patterns of physiological activity (e.g., Ekman, 1979, 1992a; Izard, 1971, 1992; Scherer, 1984), there are no inherent conflicts between the Discrete-Emotions view of emotion and the Componential view. A generic componential view of emotion does not require the existence of basic emotions, but the existence of such states would not undermine it.

In fact, we would like to push this issue further and echo the arguments advanced by Plutchik (1980) and Smith and Ellsworth (1985) – that, more generally, the dimensional and categorical approaches to emotion are not inherently incompatible. From a categorical perspective, unless one views basic emotions as a strictly unstructured collection of entities that cannot be meaningfully compared in terms of similarities and differences, then one is tacitly acknowledging that emotions can be described in terms of a dimensional structure that underlies the similarities and differences among the basic categories of emotional experience. From the dimensional perspective, although the dimensions in one's system may define a continuous "emotion space" containing an infinite number of "locations," each corresponding to a distinct hypothetical emotional experience, actual experience need not be uniformly distributed in this space. Instead, it is entirely possible for experiences to cluster densely in certain regions of this space. Such regions would, almost by definition, have "special status" within the space and thus could be considered basic or fundamental categories of emotional experience.

It is noteworthy that at least two models of emotion have profitably integrated categorical and dimensional perspectives. First, Roseman (1984) has long championed an appraisal model of emotion, in which several dimensions of appraisal are combined to produce a finite set of discrete emotions. In a similar vein, Smith and Lazarus (1990, 1993) have advanced an appraisal model of discrete emotions, in which the emotion-eliciting appraisals themselves are described in both dimensional and categorical terms. In this model, emotions are conceptualized as responses to adaptationally significant types of harm and benefit, and each category of emotion corresponds to a different type of harm or benefit. For instance, sadness is evoked by permanent harm or loss, fear by threatened or impending harm, anger by harm or loss caused by someone else, and so on. At a dimensional level, the model identifies six major components of appraisal, which are conceptualized as the specific questions or issues that are evaluated to identify the type of harm or benefit that may be confronting the individual. At a categorical level, the model describes appraisal in terms of a finite number of *relational themes* that correspond to the adaptationally significant kinds of harm and benefit hypothesized to evoke specific emotions. Although not every possible combination of outcomes along the appraisal components results in a relational theme, every relational theme can be described as a specific combination of outcomes along the components. Thus, the relational themes represent the adaptationally significant "answers" to the appraisal "questions" that result in emotion. In other words, the relational themes represent the specific combinations of outcomes along the appraisal components that have "special status" and are associated with basic emotions.

Emotional expression and conversational and other signals

Throughout this chapter, we have confined ourselves to considerations of emotion and emotional expression. In this final section, we consider the relevance of the Componential Approach to understanding communicative facial actions that are not directly emotional.

First, a number of investigators have emphasized that even seemingly emotional expressions often do not indicate the expressive individual's emotional state but instead seem to serve more strictly communicative functions (see Fridlund, 1994). For example, in a study of bowlers, Kraut and Johnston (1979) documented that individuals' smiling behavior was not strongly associated with how the person was bowling (e.g., whether he or she had rolled a spare or a strike) but rather was associated with whether or not the person was socially engaged with (i.e., looking at or talking to) his or her fellow bowlers. In addition, individuals often assume a facial expression that captures their perceptions of an interactional partner's feelings, especially if eye contact has been established. This may represent a way of communicating empathy (Bavelas et al., 1986). It also appears that individuals often imitate expressions that they observe in others (e.g., Dimberg, 1982; Vaughan & Lanzetta, 1980). This imitation is believed to provide a nonverbal basis for the direct communication of feelings from one person to another – to provide a physiological basis for empathy (e.g., Bavelas, Black, Lemery, & Mullett, 1987; Hatfield, Cacioppo, & Rapson, 1994; Vaughan & Lanzetta, 1980, 1981). Finally, as Fridlund (1994) has noted, a person might produce an angry expression without experiencing anger to warn an offending party to alter his or her behavior. Such displays often forestall the necessity of becoming angry. Indeed, as discussed by Fridlund (1994), such seemingly nonemotional displays appear to play important roles in the establishment and maintenance of dominance hierarchies among nonhuman primates.

Building upon such observations, Fridlund (1994) has cogently argued that facial expression has much to do with social communication but essentially nothing to do with emotion. Although we find this position to be somewhat extreme, we strongly resonate to the idea that facial expressions are often produced in the service of communicative functions that transcend simple indications of one's current emotional state. We also agree that, to date, these more purely communicative functions have been relatively neglected.

With regard to the relevance of the Componential Model, we note that in each of the foregoing examples, although facial expressions do not necessarily reflect the expressor's underlying emotional state, they nonetheless have their basis in emotion. For instance, when a parent expresses anger at a mischievous child, even while secretly amused by the cleverness of the mischief, the expression communicated is nonetheless one of anger, and the intent is to convince the child that he or she had best not repeat the mischief. Similarly, in imitating another's emotional expressions, the expressions used are the same as those we have considered in this chapter. Thus, in such instances, we believe the utility of the Componential Approach for understanding the specific information encoded in expressions is directly applicable. The individual components indicate much about the information that the person is trying to communicate, whether or not this information is "felt."

We are also interested in the degree to which the Componential Approach might prove useful for understanding the significance of facial actions that are even further removed from emotion. For instance, Ekman (1979) has distinguished between "emotional" and "conversational" signals. The latter signals consist largely of individual expressive components produced in isolation (e.g., the eyebrow frown, or raised eyebrows), and they appear to facilitate nonverbal communication, emphasize speech, and regulate conversation. Although we recognize both the nonemotional character of these facial actions and the need to distinguish them from more emotion-related actions, we wonder whether these actions are as separate from emotion-related expression as they may first appear. In particular, we are intrigued by the possibility that the information conveyed by expressive components in their roles as conversational signals is related to the information that these same components convey in emotional expressions. In other words, we are interested in whether the meanings that these components encode in their roles in emotional expressions might provide the basis for their use as conversational signals.

Data relevant to this issue are scarce, but existing indications suggest that there may be merit to this hypothesis. For example, the eyebrow frown is a common and effective way for a listener to signal "I'm not following you" or "I doubt it." Such uses seem to derive directly from the relation of the eyebrow frown to the perception of need–goal discrepancies (with the goal here being to understand or agree with the speaker). Similarly, Ekman (1979) has noted that a number of observers, including Darwin (1872/1965) and Eibl-Eibesfeldt (1972), have commented that raised eyebrows are often used to indicate a question. This use, too, seems to derive directly from the proposed relation between raised eyebrows and appraisals of uncertainty about one's situation (see Table 10.2). Finally, Eibl-Eibesfeldt (1972) has reported that raising the eyebrows is also a common form of greeting that is observed across a variety of cultures. Although the derivation is somewhat less direct for this example, it seems plausible that the eyebrow raise may be used in greeting to ask the other party "Do you recognize me?" Thus, the use of this sign may also be rooted in the relation between raised eyebrows and uncertainty (see also Ekman, 1979). Clearly, the degree to which the Componential Approach to emotional expression is also relevant to understanding the information communicated through nonemotional facial actions is an open issue that merits research attention.

Concluding thoughts

In this chapter, we have described a theoretical framework, which we refer to as the Componential Approach, that emphasizes the rich informational structure of emotional facial expression. Central to this approach is the belief that emotional facial expressions, and emotions more generally, are highly organized. The implication drawn from this belief is not only that the expressive patterns of facial muscle activity that correspond to various discrete emotions are informative, but also that the individual components contributing to those patterns carry meaning that supports and enriches the information conveyed by the overall pattern. The net result is a communicative channel that is richer and more powerful than a purely categorical channel would be. In addition to describing this approach and its rationale, we have reviewed the hypotheses that have been proposed regarding the specific meanings conveyed by particular components as well as the existing evidence that examines these hypotheses. We have also explored what we believe are some important extensions and implications of this approach. In this concluding section, we emphasize two themes that have permeated this discussion.

First, we have stressed that our approach complements rather than competes with current categorically oriented conceptualizations of facial expression. We find it noteworthy that both traditions justifiably trace their roots to the rich observations of Darwin (1872/1965). Moreover, although proponents of the Discrete-Emotions Approach have not explicitly developed the componential perspective, they have contributed to its conceptual basis when they have argued that the components contributing to various facial expressions are not random (e.g., Ekman, 1979), and that at least some of them can be derived through a consideration of the functions served by the expressed emotion (e.g., Izard, 1971). In short, we believe that emotional facial expression carries both componential and categorical meaning.

Second, we believe that the core idea underlying this approach – that the various facets of emotional response are highly interdependent and systematically organized to serve adaptational functions – has importance that transcends anything we have said about facial expression. We believe that this idea provides a powerful theoretical lens for studying emotion and emotion-related processes. For instance, initial explorations of the implications of this idea have led both to the Componential Approach to emotional facial expression and to a set of rich hypotheses regarding emotional information communicated through the voice (Scherer, 1986). In addition, early signs are that it will contribute to an improved understanding of the organization of physiological activity in emotion (e.g., Pecchinenda & Smith, 1995; Smith, 1989). Further attempts to appreciate and explore more fully the implications of this conceptualization of emotion should greatly enrich our understanding not only of emotional facial expression but of emotion more generally.

Acknowledgments

Preparation of this chapter was supported, in part, by the Dean's office of Peabody College of Vanderbilt University. We would like to thank Phoebe Ellsworth, José Miguel Fernández-Dols, Nico Frijda, Jerry Ginsburg, Anna Pecchinenda, Jim Russell, and Tom and Bonnie Scott, for their helpful comments on previous versions of this chapter.

Note

1 We are treating the empirical findings reported by Frijda (1969) as well as Smith's (1989) pilot study as hypotheses rather than supporting evidence because the evidence provided by both sources is indirect. In both cases, the investigators related specific meanings to facial actions depicted in voluntarily posed facial expressions. The data reported by Frijda (1969) came from decoding studies, in which viewers' judgments of posed expressions were related to the facial actions present in the poses, whereas Smith's (1989) pilot study was an encoding study in which subjects posed facial expressions to depict their feelings during selected past experiences, and the facial actions present in the poses were related to subjects' ratings of their remembered appraisals during the original experiences. In describing the evidence supporting the hypothesized meanings of individual facial components, we have limited ourselves to considering encoding studies that have attempted to relate specific meanings to more spontaneously generated facial actions.

References

Andrew, R. J. (1965). The origins of facial expressions. *Scientific American, 213*, 88–94.

Bavelas, J. B., Black, A., Lemery, C. R., & Mullett, J. (1986). "I *show* how you feel": Motor mimicry as a communicative act. *Journal of Personality and Social Psychology, 50*, 322–329.

Bavelas, J. B., Black, A., Lemery, C. R., & Mullett, J. (1987). Motor mimicry as primitive empathy. In N. Eisenberg & J. Strayer (Eds.), *Empathy and its development* (pp. 317–338). New York: Cambridge University Press.

Buck, R., Losow, J. I., Murphy, M. M, & Costanzo, P. (1992). Social facilitation and inhibition of emotional expression and communication. *Journal of Personality and Social Psychology, 63*, 962–968.

Cacioppo, J. T., Klein, D. J., Berntson, G. G., & Hatfield, E. (1993). The psychophysiology of emotion. In M. Lewis & J. M. Haviland (Eds.), *Handbook of emotion* (pp. 119–142). New York: Guilford.

Cacioppo, J. T., Martzke, J. S., Petty, R. E., & Tassinary, L. G. (1988). Specific forms of facial EMG response index emotions during an interview: From Darwin to the continuous flow hypothesis of affect-laden information processing. *Journal of Personality and Social Psychology, 54*, 592–604.

Cacioppo, J. T., Petty, R. E., Losch, M. E., & Kim, H. S. (1986). Electromyographic activity over facial muscle regions can differentiate the valence and intensity of affective reactions. *Journal of Personality and Social Psychology, 50*, 260–268.

Cacioppo, J. T., Petty, R. E., & Morris, K. J. (1985). Semantic, evaluative, and self-referent processing: Memory, cognitive effort, and somatovisceral activity. *Psychophysiology, 22*, 371–384.

Darwin, C. (1965). *The expression of the emotions in man and animals.* Chicago: University of Chicago Press. (Original work published 1872)

Dawson, M. E., Schell, A. M., & Filion, D. L. (1990). The electrodermal system. In J. T. Cacioppo & L. G. Tassinary (Eds.), *Principles of psychophysiology: Physical, social, and inferential elements.* New York: Cambridge University Press.

Dimberg, U. (1982). Facial reactions to facial expressions. *Psychophysiology, 19*, 643–647.

Duchenne, G. B. (1990). *The mechanism of human facial expression* (R. A. Cuthbertson, Ed. and Trans.). Cambridge: Cambridge University Press. (Original work published 1862)

Eibl-Eibesfeldt, I. (1972). Similarities and differences between cultures in expressive movements. In R. A. Hinde (Ed.), *Nonverbal communication* (pp. 297–311). Cambridge, England: Cambridge University Press.

Ekman, P. (1979). About brows: Emotional and conversational signals. In M. von Cranach, K. Foppa, W. Lepenies, & D. Ploog (Eds.), *Human ethology* (pp. 169–249). New York: Cambridge University Press.

Ekman, P. (1984). Expression and the nature of emotion. In K. R. Scherer & P. Ekman (Eds.), *Approaches to emotion* (pp. 329–343). Hillsdale, NJ: Erlbaum.

Ekman, P. (1992a). An argument for basic emotions. *Cognition and Emotion, 6*, 169–200.

Ekman, P. (1992b). Are there basic emotions? *Psychological Review, 99*, 550–553.

Ekman, P., & Friesen, W. V. (1969). The repertoire of nonverbal behavior – Categories, origins, usage and coding. *Semiotica, 1*, 49–98.

Ekman, P., & Friesen, W. V. (1975). *Unmasking the face: A guide to recognizing emotions from facial clues.* Englewood Cliffs, NJ: Prentice-Hall.

Ekman, P., & Friesen, W. V. (1978). *Investigator's guide to the Facial Action Coding System.* Palo Alto, CA: Consulting Psychologists Press.

Ekman, P., & Friesen, W. V. (1986). A new pan-cultural facial expression of emotion. *Motivation and Emotion, 10*, 159–168.

Ekman, P., Friesen, W. V., & Ancoli, S. (1980). Facial signs of emotional experience. *Journal of Personality and Social Psychology, 39*, 1125–1134.

Ekman, P., Friesen, W. V., & Ellsworth, P. (1982). Research foundations. In P. Ekman (Ed.), *Emotion in the human face* (2nd ed., pp. 1–143). New York: Cambridge University Press.

Ekman, P., Levenson, R. W., & Friesen, W. V. (1983). Autonomic nervous system activity distinguishes among emotions. *Science, 221*, 1208–1210.

Ellsworth, P. C. (1991). Some implications of cognitive appraisal theories of emotion. In K. T. Strongman (Ed.), *International review of studies of emotion* (Vol 1., pp. 143–161). New York: Wiley.

Ellsworth, P. C., & Smith, C. A. (1988). From appraisal to emotion: Differences among unpleasant feelings. *Motivation and Emotion, 12*, 271–302.

Folkman, S., & Lazarus, R. S. (1985). If it changes it must be a process: Study of emotion and coping during three stages of a college examination. *Journal of Personality and Social Psychology, 48*, 150–170.

Fridlund, A. J. (1994). *Human facial expression: An evolutionary view*. San Diego: Academic Press.

Frijda, N. H. (1969). Recognition of emotion. In L. Berkowitz (Ed.), *Advances in experimental social psychology* (Vol. 4, pp. 167–223). New York: Academic Press.

Frijda, N. H. (1986). *The emotions*. New York: Cambridge University Press.

Frijda, N. H., Kuipers, P., & Terschure, E. (1989) Relations among emotion, appraisal, and emotional action readiness. *Journal of Personality and Social Psychology, 57*, 212–228.

Frijda, N. H., & Philipszoon, E. (1963). Dimensions of recognition of expression. *Journal of Abnormal and Social Psychology, 66*, 45–51.

Frois-Wittmann, J. (1930). The judgment of facial expression. *Journal of Experimental Psychology, 13*, 113–151.

Hatfield, E., Cacioppo, J. T., & Rapson, R. L. (1994). *Emotional contagion*. New York: Cambridge University Press.

Izard, C. E. (1971). *The face of emotion*. New York: Appleton-Century-Crofts.

Izard, C. E. (1977). *Human emotions*. New York: Plenum.

Izard, C. E. (1992). Basic emotions, relations among emotions, and emotion–cognition relations. *Psychological Review, 99*, 561–565.

Izard, C. E., & Haynes, O. M. (1988). On the form and universality of the contempt expression: A challenge to Ekman and Friesen's claim of discovery. *Motivation and Emotion, 12*, 1–16.

Kraut, R. E., & Johnston, R. E. (1979). Social and emotional messages of smiling: An ethological approach. *Journal of Personality and Social Psychology, 37*, 1539–1553.

Lazarus, R. S. (1968). Emotions and adaptation: Conceptual and empirical relations. In W. J. Arnold (Ed.), *Nebraska Symposium on Motivation* (Vol. 16, pp. 175–266). Lincoln: University of Nebraska Press.

Lazarus, R. S. (1991). *Emotion and adaptation*. New York: Oxford University Press.

Levenson, R. W., Ekman, P., & Friesen, W. V. (1990). Voluntary facial action generates emotion-specific nervous system activity. *Psychophysiology, 27*, 363–384.

Levenson, R. W., Ekman, P., Heider, K., & Friesen, W. V. (1992). Emotion and autonomic nervous system activity in the Minangkabu of West Sumatra. *Journal of Personality and Social Psychology, 62*, 972–988.

Mandler, G. (1980). The generation of emotion: A psychological theory. In R. Plutchik & H. Kellerman (Eds.), *Emotion: Theory, research, and experience: Vol. 1. Theories of emotion* (pp. 219–243). New York: Academic Press.

Mandler, G. (1984). *Mind and body*. New York: Norton.

Obrist, P. A. (1976). The cardiovascular-behavioral interaction – as it appears today. *Psychophysiology, 13*, 95–107.

Öhman, A. (1979). The orienting response, attention and learning: An information-processing perspective. In H. D. Kimmel, E. H. van Olst, & J. F. Orlebeke (Eds.), *The orienting reflex in humans* (pp. 443–471). Hillsdale, NJ: Erlbaum.

Ortony, A., & Turner, T. J. (1990). What's basic about basic emotions? *Psychological Review, 97*, 315–331.

Osgood, C. E. (1966). Dimensionality of the semantic space for communication via facial expressions. *Scandinavian Journal of Psychology, 7*, 1–30.

Panksepp, J. (1992). A critical role for "affective neuroscience" in resolving what is basic about basic emotions. *Psychological Review, 99*, 554–560.

Pecchinenda, A., & Smith, C. A. (1995). *The motivational significance of skin conductance activity during a difficult problem-solving task.* Unpublished manuscript, Université Laval, Quebec City, Canada.

Plutchik, R. (1980). *Emotion: A psychoevolutionary synthesis.* New York: Harper & Row.

Pope, L. K., & Smith, C. A. (1994). On the distinct meanings of smiles and frowns. *Cognition and Emotion, 8*, 65–72.

Roseman, I. J. (1984). Cognitive determinants of emotion: A structural theory. In P. Shaver (Ed.), *Review of personality and social psychology: Vol. 5. Emotions, relationships, and health* (pp. 11–36). Beverly Hills, CA: Sage.

Roseman, I. J., Wiest, C., & Swartz, T. S. (1994). Phenomenology, behaviors, and goals differentiate discrete emotions. *Journal of Personality and Social Psychology, 67*, 206–221.

Russell, J. A. (1994). Is there universal recognition of emotion from facial expression? A review of the cross-cultural studies. *Psychological Bulletin, 115*, 102–141.

Scherer, K. R. (1984). On the nature and function of emotion: A component process approach. In K. R. Scherer & P. Ekman (Eds.), *Approaches to emotion* (pp. 293–317). Hillsdale, NJ: Erlbaum.

Scherer, K. R. (1986). Vocal affect expression: A review and a model for future research. *Psychological Bulletin, 99*, 143–165.

Scherer, K. R. (1992). What does a facial expression express? In K. T. Strongman (Ed.), *International review of studies of emotion* (Vol. 2, pp. 139–165). New York: Wiley.

Schlosberg, H. (1952). The description of facial expressions in terms of two dimensions. *Journal of Experimental Psychology, 44* 229–337.

Schlosberg, H. (1954). Three dimensions of emotion. *Psychological Review, 61*, 81–88.

Schwartz, G. E., & Weinberger, D. A. (1980). Patterns of emotional responses to affective situations: Relations among happiness, sadness, anger, fear, depression, and anxiety. *Motivation and Emotion, 4*, 175–191.

Smith, C. A. (1987). The informational structure of the facial expression of emotion. *Dissertation Abstracts International, 47*, 4002B. (University Microfilms No. 87-00, 820)

Smith, C. A. (1989). Dimensions of appraisal and physiological response in emotion. *Journal of Personality and Social Psychology, 56*, 339–353.

Smith, C. A., & Ellsworth, P. C. (1985). Patterns of cognitive appraisal in emotion. *Journal of Personality and Social Psychology, 48*, 813–838.

Smith, C. A., & Ellsworth, P. C. (1987). Patterns of appraisal and emotion related to taking an exam. *Journal of Personality and Social Psychology, 52*, 475–488.

Smith, C. A., & Lazarus, R. S. (1990). Emotion and adaptation. In L. A. Pervin (Ed.), *Handbook of personality: Theory and research* (pp. 609–637). New York: Guilford.

Smith, C. A., & Lazarus, R. S. (1993). Appraisal components, core relational themes, and the emotions. *Cognition and Emotion, 7,* 233–269.

Smith, C. A., McHugo, G. J., & Lanzetta, J. T. (1986). The facial muscle patterning of posed and imagery-induced expressions of emotion by expressive and nonexpressive posers. *Motivation and Emotion, 10,* 133–157.

Smith, C. A., & Pecchinenda, A. (1995). *The dynamics of digit skin temperature during a math problem-solving task.* Manuscript in preparation, Vanderbilt University, Nashville, TN.

Stemmler, G. (1989). The autonomic differentiation of emotions revisited: Convergent and discriminant validation. *Psychophysiology, 26,* 617–632.

Tomaka, J., Blascovich, J., Kelsey, R. M., & Leitten, C. L. (1993). Subjective, physiological, and behavioral effects of threat and challenge appraisal. *Journal of Personality and Social Psychology, 65,* 248–260.

Tomkins, S. S. (1962). *Affect, imagery, consciousness: Vol. 1. The positive affects.* New York: Springer.

Tomkins, S. S. (1963). *Affect, imagery, consciousness: Vol. 2. The negative affects.* New York: Springer.

Tomkins, S. S. (1980). Affect as amplification: Some modifications in theory. In R. Plutchik & H. Kellerman (Eds.), *Emotion: Theory, research, and experience: Vol. 1. Theories of emotion* (pp. 141–164). New York: Academic Press.

Vaughan, K. B., & Lanzetta, J. T. (1980). Vicarious instigation and conditioning of facial expressive and autonomic responses to a model's expressive display of pain. *Journal of Personality and Social Psychology, 38,* 909–923.

Vaughan, K. B., & Lanzetta, J. T. (1981). The effect of modification of expressive displays on vicarious emotional arousal. *Journal of Experimental Social Psychology, 17,* 16–30.

Wagner, H. L., & Smith, J. (1991). Facial expression in the presence of friends and strangers. *Journal of Nonverbal Behavior, 15,* 201–214.

Wright, R. A., Contrada, R. J., & Patane, M. J. (1986). Task difficulty, cardiovascular response, and the magnitude of goal valence. *Journal of Personality and Social Psychology, 51,* 837–843.

Wright, R. A., & Dill, J. C. (1993). Blood pressure responses and incentive appraisals as a function of perceived ability and objective task demand. *Psychophysiology, 30,* 152–160.

Zajonc, R. B., & McIntosh, D. N. (1992). Emotions research: Some promising questions and some questionable promises. *Psychological Science, 3,* 70–74.

11. Spontaneous facial behavior during intense emotional episodes: Artistic truth and optical truth

JOSÉ MIGUEL FERNÁNDEZ-DOLS AND
MARÍA-ANGELES RUIZ-BELDA

In 1872, the pioneer of photography Eadweard Muybridge was given an intriguing commission by Leland Stanford, a California magnate interested in animal locomotion. The commission was to test whether horses really galloped in the way artists had always represented them. For example, are their forelegs actually raised symmetrically (as seen in Figure 11.1)?

With much ingenuity, given the primitive stage of photographic equipment at that time, Muybridge obtained a series of high-speed pictures that showed an unexpected and even disturbing pattern in the way horses galloped. The most characteristic conventions in the artistic representation of a galloping horse (including the symmetrical extended forelegs) did not occur at all. Galloping was actually a complex, asymmetrical pattern of leg movements. Muybridge's results were met with incredulity. The erroneous version of this movement was so strongly believed that Muybridge devised a primitive form of cinematographic projection – the zoopraxiscope, which projected his pictures as if frames of a film – in order to show how the "shocking" still representations fit a credible and smooth pattern of movement (see Figure 11.2).

We now know that laypersons and experts from different cultures – including the most careful and skilled painters – had for centuries been wrong about the movements of an extremely familiar animal that were readily visible in many common situations.

The extended debate among Muybridge's contemporaries over his findings raised an interesting distinction between "optical truth" and "artistic truth" (Mozley, 1979). Muybridge's "optically true" photographs showed the running horse with an asymmetrical, "clumsy" stride. A symmetrical and simpler stride, although fictional, has an "artistic truth" in that it communicates easily to an audience not only the

Figure 11.1. Representation of galloping horses from different cultures and times. *Clockwise from top left*: Assyrian (7th century B.C.), Botticelli's painting (15th century), Degas' painting (19th century), and a contemporary carousel horse.

physical movement but more importantly the beauty and elegance of a moving horse.

In this chapter, we ask a question not unlike that asked by Leland Stanford: What is the actual facial behavior of a happy person, an angry person, and so on? Nothing would seem more obvious than that the answer is smiling, frowning, and so on. Like Muybridge, we suggest that this conventional answer, known to artists, actors, and everyone else throughout the ages, is wrong. Although our suggestion may be met with incredulity, we show that the available evidence raises serious doubts about the conventional answer.

We suggest that smiles, frowns, and other "facial expressions of emotion" do possess an "artistic truth." That is, if a painter, actor, or layperson sets out to convey happiness or anger by a single image, then a smiling or frowning face is the right image to choose. In the absence of words, context, or further explanation, a smiling face conveys "a happy person," just as a cartoon mouse is successful in conveying "mouse," a teddy bear in conveying "bear," or a horse with the conventional stride

Figure 11.2. A sample of Muybridge's photographs of a galloping horse.

in conveying "galloping horse." But the everyday reality of mice, bears, or galloping horses need not coincide with these artistic images.

The study of facial behavior during emotional episodes has been dominated by what was termed in chapter 1 the *Facial Expression Program*. According to theories such as those offered by Tomkins, Izard, and Ekman, emotion triggers certain facial patterns that are recognizable to all. Unlike the galloping of a horse, these facial movements are signals that evolved as part of communication, and there is little chance that everyone is mistaken about the facial behavior of happy, angry, sad, or frightened people. Nature has selected facial behavior to maximize its communicative value. In any case, the hypothesis stemming from such theorizing is clear: The spontaneous facial behavior produced by intense emotions consists of the kinds of prototypical expressions identified by the Facial Expression Program and with which everyone is familiar (see Ekman & Friesen, 1978; Matsumoto & Ekman, 1988).

Much of the evidence offered in support of the Facial Expression Program concerns the recognition (more precisely, the attribution) of emotion from these facial expressions. Observers are typically shown photographs of posed facial behavior (often carefully selected by the experimenter). Although this research is the subject of debate (Ekman, 1994; Izard, 1994; Russell, 1994, 1995), let us assume for the moment that observers consensually and universally attribute the same specific emotions to these facial poses. We would translate such evidence as demonstrating that the poses shown to observers possess an artistic truth. What the evidence would not show is that happy people actually smile, angry people actually frown, and so forth. We therefore need evidence on their actual facial behavior recorded at the very moment in which they are feeling a particular emotion.

The Facial Expression Program would seem to suggest that such evidence would be readily available. And yet very little evidence is available. We next review the evidence on recordings of adults' spontaneous facial behavior during intense emotional episodes (see Camras, Malatesta, & Izard, 1991; Oster, Hegley, & Nagel, 1992, for interesting comments on studies on spontaneous facial behavior in infants). We then describe two studies from our laboratory. Finally, we offer some hypotheses about the nature of spontaneous behavior during emotional episodes.

Landis's challenge

In 1934, Landis's review of the research on emotion concluded that observers can often understand *posed* facial expressions but cannot make much sense of *spontaneous* emotional facial behavior. Characterizing posed expressions as "social," Landis wrote:

> These social expressions may, and probably do, possess certain patterns. It still remains to be demonstrated that such patterns of reaction of facial muscles occur in emotion and if they do occur that they agree with the social expressions of emotions. (1934, p. 320)

Landis himself (Landis, 1924) had carried out probably the first controlled observation of spontaneous facial behavior in intense emotional episodes. He took still photographs of 25 persons who endured a series of 17 emotion-eliciting situations, reporting their feelings during each one. Unfortunately, Landis published only a global analysis of the facial behavior that he photographed, but the overall result was clear: striking variability in different subjects' facial behavior in the same situation, and even in subjects who reported the same feeling. There was little evidence of the expected conventional expressions for each emotion.

Landis's findings were met with the kind of incredulity that Muybridge faced – as were those of Sherman (1927) on the recognition of spontaneous expressions in infants. Admittedly, some of the skepticism stemmed from the primitive and highly obtrusive methods used, but perhaps some of the emphasis on such problems stemmed from the unexpectedness of his findings (Davis, 1934; Ekman, Friesen, & Ellsworth, 1972; Frois-Wittmann, 1930).

After Landis, few authors reported observations of emotional expressions and none with the theoretical relevance of Landis's study. For example, Thompson, (1941), Leventhal and Sharp (1965), and Eibl-Eibesfeldt (1973) obtained interesting but partial descriptions of facial behavior in particular groups (e.g., blind children, women in labor). Landis's data were undoubtedly questionable, but his challenge remained. The principal response was to come from the Facial Expression Program.

Response from the Facial Expression Program

Most of the evidence associating emotions with the prototype facial expressions comes from judgments about posed faces. The assumption that these prototype expressions occur spontaneously (and during clear emotional experiences of the hypothesized sort) rests on a much smaller set of studies. We first discuss the most general of the studies and then focus on evidence of smiles as a sign of happiness.

Ekman (1972)

Universality of spontaneous facial expressions of emotion was tested by a single study, reported by Ekman (1972) and Friesen (1972). As recently as 1994, Ekman cited this study as the support for the application of his neurocultural theory to spontaneous behavior across cultural boundaries.

Ekman and his collaborators asked 25 American and 25 Japanese students to watch a film that included one neutral and three stressful clips. Researchers took two samples of the facial behavior of each subject during the last 3 min of the neutral clip and the entire 3 min of the last stressful clip. These samples were analyzed using an observational code, FAST (Ekman, Friesen, & Tomkins, 1971).

The most frequent facial response to the stress clips was an "expression of surprise" in the Americans, but an "expression of sadness" in the Japanese (Ekman, 1972, Table 2, p. 256). Despite such differences, Ekman interpreted the results as strong evidence of universality, demonstrated by "strikingly high" rank-order correlations between Americans and Japanese in the frequency within categories of facial actions. Ekman (1994) cited one correlation of .97.

Unfortunately, such correlations are difficult to interpret. No evidence was reported of interrater reliability of the facial scoring, but this appears to have been low; Friesen (1972) reported an overall intercoder agreement of 55% during the same experiment. Furthermore, a correlation coefficient varies greatly with the base rates (irrespective of emotion) of the coding categories. Base rates can be influenced by combining heterogeneous coding categories, and, in fact, Ekman calculated correlations across coding categories that included artificially high base rates (combinations of different emotional expressions or miscellaneous unclassifiable behaviors). For example, the aforementioned correlation of .97 cited by Ekman (1994) involved such combined categories (e.g., "sadness and/or fear plus disgust and/or anger" was one category).

Finally, Ekman characterized the emotional state of all subjects as "stress." By his own analysis of facial behavior, different subjects experienced different specific emotions, but Ekman had provided no independent assessments of the specific emotion experienced by each individual, either overall or moment to moment over the course of the 3-min stress film. Nor did Friesen (1972) provide specific data on the interviews that followed the films. Therefore, the study does not provide us with data about how specific emotions are associated with specific facial patterns.

Ekman, Friesen, and Ancoli (1980)

Ekman, Friesen, and Ancoli (1980) carried out a partial replication of the experiment reported by Ekman (1972) but without including a cross-cultural comparison. In this study, 35 Americans watched positive and negative films. Two main improvements were made: Subjects rated their global experience of emotion after seeing the films, and the researchers applied a new and more precise coding of facial expressions, based on the Facial Action Coding System (FACS), Ekman and Friesen's (1976) development of Hjortsjö's (1969) coding system.

We consider the positive films later, but the responses to the negative films were highly interesting. Subjects reported their emotion in terms of eight emotion categories, but the authors did not provide the average intensities of the reports of anger. The most intense of the reported emotions were "arousal," pain, fear, and surprise. The lowest were disgust and sadness (Ekman et al., 1980; Table 3, p. 1130). Nevertheless, the only specific facial expressions analyzed were those hypothesized for disgust "since very few subjects showed action units relevant to any of the other negative emotions [than disgust]" (p. 1131). In other words, apparently, the hypothesized facial expressions of other emotions did not occur. Ekman et al. also found no clear discriminative pattern between the subjects who never showed facial signs of negative emotion and the subjects who did; the subjects with no facial signs of any negative emotion reported more anger and as much disgust as other subjects. In any case, even the occurrence of "disgust expressions" showed an ambiguous and inconclusive pattern of correlations with self-reports of disgust and of other negative emotions.

Rosenberg and Ekman (1994)

Rosenberg and Ekman (1994) also used FACS to code facial behavior and obtained reports of viewers' moment-to-moment emotional feelings during films; this was a significant improvement on Ekman et al.'s (1980) procedure. Facial expressions were recorded while subjects watched a series of six clips; after viewing each film, subjects provided retrospective reports of their emotions while the clip was replayed. Data were reported from two of these films, selected to elicit primarily disgust and secondarily fear and other negative emotions.

In general, reports of disgust did *not* match facial expressions. The researchers then included a new variable – intensity of the reported emotion – as a way of obtaining some coherence. However, the coherence reported for *intense* reports of disgust and facial expressions of disgust is seriously flawed. In one of the films, the researchers themselves reported that the observed coherence could be an artifact because the film elicited only expressions and reports of disgust, and, therefore, any co-occurring measures would by definition agree on category.

Rosenberg and Ekman also portrayed the other film as the main elicitor of disgust, but the highest mean intensity ratings of emotion were of fear rather than disgust; in fact, 65% of the most intense reports of negative emotion for each subject were negative emotions other than disgust. Rosenberg and Ekman found no cases in which the intense reports of nondisgust negative emotions were coincident with intense emotional facial expressions, which, in our view, implies a lack of coherence between clear facial expressions and the reports of intense negative emotions other than disgust.

With respect to the disgust reports, Rosenberg and Ekman (1994) claimed that "75% of the subjects who gave a report at the same location as most intense facial expression reported disgust as the peak emotion" (p. 222), leading the reader to conclude that this sole finding represented strong evidence of the coherence between facial expression and self-reports of emotion at specific moments. Unfortunately, these "specific moments" were, in our view, *too* specific: Rosenberg and Ekman made an a priori selection of *only* the moments in which the most intense expressions and the most intense reports coincided. The claimed coherence seems to apply only to this selected set. No data were provided about how many different kinds of faces (e.g., neutral faces) coincided with reports of intense disgust, and, even more importantly, no data were reported about how many intense expressions of disgust coincided with no reports of emotion at all. We do not know, for example, whether the film elicited a large number of intense expressions of disgust but most of the time paired with no reports of felt emotion.

Smiling and happiness

The relationship between smiling and happiness is particularly illustrative and important. Cross-culturally, observers attribute happiness to smiling with more agreement than when attributing any other emotion to any other expression. The link between happiness and smiles has also received considerable attention from Ekman and his collaborators, who claim a direct connection between smiling, particularly Duchenne smiles, and happiness (Davidson, Ekman, Saron, Senulis, & Friesen, 1990; Ekman, Davidson, & Friesen, 1990; Ekman et al., 1980).

Ekman et al.'s (1980) aforementioned study found a coherence between the action of *zygomatic major* and the positiveness of the affective content of two films, but this finding was considered as provisional by the authors themselves because there was no clear pattern of correlation between the different measures of muscular action (frequency, duration, and intensity) and subjects' reports of happiness: None of the six analyzed patterns of correlation was significant for both films. For example, the correlation between the frequency of the action of the *zygomatic major* and the score of happiness reported during the second film was .60, while the same correlation in the first film was −.08.

In a new version of Ekman et al.'s (1980) experiment, Ekman et al. (1990) reported that the discriminative clue for happiness was the smile produced by the action of both the *zygomatic major* and *orbicularis oculi* (the Duchenne smile). On the basis of this study, Ekman (1992) implicitly criticized Ekman's (1972) and Ekman et al.'s (1980) studies, pointing out that "no account should be taken of studies that . . . treat all smiles as a single category, not separating Duchenne from non-Duchenne smiles" (Ekman, 1992, p. 37).

Unfortunately, no necessary or sufficient link between happiness and Duchenne smiles has been substantiated by other researchers. In a series of detailed observations, Schneider and Unzner (1992) found that preschoolers' spontaneous facial behavior in positive situations involved the *zygomatic* reaction two to three times more often than the *orbicularis oculi* reaction:

> The assumption that only the common appearance of the zygomaticus and the orbicularis oculi reaction is a proper display for true joy . . . seems to be a premature dogmatic assumption. . . . The more parsimonious assumption, therefore, seems to be that most of the time these events triggered only low intensity joy reactions which then became manifest in the *zygomaticus* reaction alone without any visible reaction of the *orbicularis oculi*. (p. 58)

In the same vein, Fridlund (1994, p. 117) argued that wrinkles caused by the *orbicularis oculi* are not specific to smiling. For Fridlund, wincing is an occlusive, protective reflex, and it can be observed in intense facial movements; Duchenne smiles would be intense but not exclusive expressions of happiness.

Furthermore, other research reported by Ekman (1992) as supporting the relationship between happiness and Duchenne smiles confuses emotional states and emotional traits, identifying enjoyment with personal adjustment or mental health. Only one report concerned specific experiences of happiness and Duchenne smiles: Fox and Davidson (1988) found that 10-month-old infants' Duchenne smiles were more frequent in response to their mother's approach, whereas other smiles were more frequent in response to a stranger. Unfortunately, the mother's approach is simultaneously positive and social, which raises an important problem that we discuss in the next section.

Smiles as social signals

The debate about the relationship between smiles and happiness is not restricted to the distinction between Duchenne and non-Duchenne smiles. Some researchers (Fridlund, 1991; Kraut & Johnston, 1979) have raised important questions about the link between happiness and any kind of smile.

In a pioneering and innovative study, Kraut and Johnston (1979) observed facial behavior in natural settings (a bowling alley, a stadium, and the street) when people were presumably happy for different reasons (a good roll at the bowling alley, goals scored by their team at the stadium, and good weather in the street). Smiles were observed mostly during social interaction.

Fridlund (1991) measured facial electromyographic signals for smiling in subjects watching a video in conditions of varying sociality: a nonsocial situation, an implicitly social situation, and an explicitly social situation. Fridlund found that action of the *zygomatic major* was better predicted by the social condition than by subjects' happiness.

Kraut and Johnston's study lacked a precise description of facial expression, and Fridlund did not analyze the action of *orbicularis oculi* in his subjects' smiles. Both of these shortcomings were overcome by Schneider and Josephs (1991), who analyzed the action of *zygomatic major* and *orbiculari oculi* in preschool children playing a competitive game. As had Fridlund, they found that the social situation played a major role in the display of smiles: Children smiled more in interactive than in non-interactive episodes. The coherence between positive emotion and Duchenne smiles was much less clear than the relationship between Duchenne smiles and other social factors: Smiles were more frequent among losers than among winners, and losers' smiles were more often Duchenne smiles and more often intense smiles, as compared with the winners' smiles.

In summary, the relationship between happiness and smiles – plain smiles or Duchenne smiles – is, at the moment, far from clear. The consensual "artistic truth" that smiles convey happiness has not, so far, been shown to correspond to an "optical truth." No clear link between happiness and smiles has been found in research on spontaneous facial behavior.

Two studies of smiling in natural settings

With these problems in mind, we are carrying out a series of studies in which we analyze all the instances of facial expression that occur during intense and natural emotional episodes.

These studies are aimed at answering a misleadingly simple question: To what extent do people display the hypothesized prototypical expressions of an emotion when they are feeling that emotion? Our studies have also been designed to test whether the social aspect of the emotional episode plays a major role in facial behavior. We have tried to keep a balance between ecological relevance and control, looking for intense and natural elicitors of emotion and an explicit assessment of the emotional experience and the facial expression of our subjects.

Gold medalists

Our first study (Fernández-Dols & Ruiz-Belda, 1995a) examined the awards ceremony at the 1992 Olympic Games. This ceremony rigidly included three stages: two noninteractive and one highly interactive. The noninteractive stages were the medalists' waiting time behind the podium while authorities took their positions (Stage A), and the time when athletes turned toward the flag and listened to the national anthem (Stage C). The interactive stage was sandwiched between these two. The medalist stood on the podium interacting with authorities and the public (Stage B).

Winning a gold medal at the Olympic Games is probably one of the happiest events in an athlete's life, and it is hard to imagine a clearer elicitor of one intense emotion. We did not have direct access to the gold medalists whose facial behavior we studied, and therefore no self-reports of their feelings during the ceremony. However, we did ask 10 other gold medalists to rate their own emotional experience during each stage of the awards ceremony. We also asked university students to infer the emotional experience of a gold medalist during each stage. Both the experienced medalists and the lay judges judged the emotional experience of the gold medalists to be intense happiness in each of the three stages of the ceremony. All other emotions were negligible in comparison.

Even though close-ups of faces are frequent on TV and in films, they are almost exclusively of professional actors and actresses; close-up records of nonactors are rare. For the Olympics, exhaustive TV coverage provided us with high-quality records of athletes' facial behavior, which we analyzed with Ekman and Friesen's (1978) FACS. We coded all the available complete records of gold medalists' facial behavior during the three stages. Overall, 22 medalists were recorded for 398 sec in Stage A, 467 sec in Stage B, and 499 sec in Stage C. Figure 11.3 shows typical facial behavior during each of the three stages.

Table 11.1 shows the percentage of time in each of the three stages that included smiling, the hypothesized expressions of other basic emotions (Ekman & Friesen, 1978), neutral faces, and other nonprototypical configurations. A more precise description in terms of Duchenne smiles produced a similar distribution.

Happiness per se was not a sufficient cause for smiling. Stages A and C of the awards ceremony were times of intense happiness but little smiling. Smiling, such as occurred during Stage B, was a means for the medalists to express their happiness to an audience.

Facial behavior of happy people included a surprising number of facial configurations. This finding confirms that smiling might be a good conventional representation of "happiness" (an "artistic truth"), but not a necessary sign of happiness (not an "optical truth").

Stage A

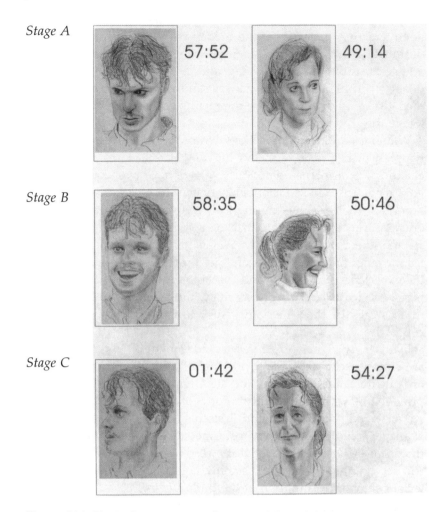

Stage B

Stage C

Figure 11.3. Typical expressions of two medalists during the three stages of the awards ceremony. Medalists displayed Duchenne smiles only during Stage B, whereas other expressions or neutral faces were observed during the noninteractive Stages A and C.

Soccer fans

Our second study examined ardent fans watching soccer matches on TV (Ruiz-Belda, 1995). The simple formal rules of competitive sports provide unambiguous "good" and "bad" events. For example, goals scored by one's own team are a source of instant happiness for any soccer fan.

Table 11.1. *Gold Medalists: Percentage of total time for each facial behavior across stages of the Olympics Awards Ceremony*

Facial behavior	Stage A	Stage B	Stage C
Smiles[a]	4.52	50.96	1.60
Neutral	32.41	7.71	14.43
Other expressions[b]	.50	.21	6.01
Other actions	62.56	41.11	77.96

[a]Prototypical expressions of happiness as described by Ekman and Friesen (1978).
[b]Prototypical expressions of other basic emotions as described by Ekman and Friesen (1978).

The study took place in a private home, familiar to most of the fans. We obtained 30 complete recordings; these involved 20 different fans and 6 different matches during 1994. Four fans were recorded during 3 matches, 2 fans during 2 matches, and 14 fans during 1 match. We also kept a synchronized record of the match itself and obtained fans' reports of their own emotional state. Before the match, subjects had been trained in how to report their emotional state at any time they felt an emotion and at various control points specified by the researcher. We describe here the facial behavior seen in those episodes in which fans stated in their own words that they were happy. The recorded changes of facial appearance observed immediately prior to the subjective reports of happiness were analyzed using Ekman and Friesen's (1978) FACS. We also distinguished those episodes that were clearly interactive (those that involved clear gaze interaction or verbal communication) from those that were not (the remaining episodes).

The results varied strongly according to whether the episode was interactive or noninteractive. We found 51 interactive episodes of happiness (produced by 17 fans). In 32 of these episodes (produced by 16 different fans), we found smiles. In 4 episodes (produced by 3 different fans), we found prototypical expressions of other emotions. In the remaining 15 episodes, we found other facial movements or neutral expressions.

We found 38 noninteractive episodes (from 16 fans). In 3 of these episodes (produced by 3 different fans), we found a smile. Within the category "smiles," we include both Duchenne and non-Duchenne smiles of "happiness" as described by Ekman and Friesen (1978). The scarcity of

Table 11.2. *Soccer fans: Percentage of total time for each facial behavior across interactive and noninteractive stages (Ruiz-Belda, 1995)*

Facial behavior	Noninteraction	Interaction
Smiles[a]	9.52	45.60
Neutral	7.74	8.19
Other expressions[b]	18.64	4.78
Other actions	64.08	41.42

[a]Prototypical expressions of happiness as described by Ekman and Friesen (1978).
[b]Prototypical expressions of other basic emotions as described by Ekman and Friesen (1978).

smiles contrasts with the frequency of other nonexpected expressions. In 13 of these noninteractive episodes of happiness (produced by 9 different fans), we found facial configurations described by Ekman and Friesen as prototypical expressions of surprise, sadness, and fear. In the remaining 22 episodes, we found other facial movements or neutral expressions.

These same data can also be analyzed in terms of duration, producing a direct comparison of the results from the Olympic gold medalists. As shown in Table 11.2, scoring the duration of smiling and other facial behavior confirmed the difference between interactive and noninteractive occasions. A description in terms of Duchenne smiles produced a similar distribution. Once again, smiling was not a necessary sign of happiness.

Furthermore, other data showed that smiling may not be a sufficient sign of happiness. We examined those occasions when basic emotions other than happiness were reported, and we coded the fans' preceding facial behavior. Duchenne and non-Duchenne smiles were not infrequent: Smiles were observed in 3 out of 7 fans who reported a total of 15 episodes of anger, in 1 out of the 7 who reported a total of 11 episodes of fear, 3 out of the 6 who reported a total of 7 episodes of sadness, and 1 out of the 4 who reported a total of 5 episodes of surprise. Overall, 11 out of 26 prototypical expressions observed during nonhappy episodes were smiles.

Conclusions

The inconclusiveness of the research on spontaneous facial behavior is caused, at least in the case of smiling and happiness, by an unexpectedly complex pattern of relationships between facial expression and emotional experience. Our data confirm that there is a clear gap between the complex and varied expression of emotion in the noninteractive periods and the smiles observed in social interaction. This finding leads to some interesting conclusions that, it is hoped, will encourage further research.

A "social audience" effect

The fact that smiling is a joint effect of an emotional experience and an interactive encounter supports Fridlund's hypothesis of an "audience effect" for some facial expressions. Nevertheless, Fridlund's concept of social audience involves subjective levels of sociality (see Buck, 1991; Chovil, 1991; Chovil & Fridlund, 1991; Hess, Banse, & Kappas, 1995), which we did not consider in our studies. Our social audience effect is restricted to actual episodes of social interaction, which makes the concept of "social audience" more straightforward.

Another question is whether the differences between the facial behavior observed during the interactive and the noninteractive periods could be manifestations of the same emotional process. Our data suggest that gold medalists and soccer fans experienced happiness in both the interactive and the noninteractive periods, yet the facial behavior varied.

Happiness as a mere facilitator of smiling

Our main and most robust finding is that happiness does not elicit smiling in all circumstances (for example, in noninteractive circumstances). In our words, our main conclusion is that *happiness is not a sufficient cause of smiling*.

However, our study of soccer fans also hints at a further speculation concerning a more serious chasm between emotion and facial expression. The reported presence of Duchenne and non-Duchenne smiles during negative emotional episodes suggests that in some particular circumstances yet to be specified, spontaneous smiling could be a sign not of happiness but of any positive or negative emotion. In other words, there is evidence that *happiness is not a necessary cause of smiling*.

If happiness is neither necessary nor sufficient for smiling, researchers should explore alternative approaches to the relationship between happiness and smiling, and between emotion and facial expression in general. Gottlieb (1976) suggested an interesting conceptual distinction between inducing and facilitating factors. Our suggestion is that social interaction is the factor that *induces* smiling; the experience of happiness does not induce smiling but rather *facilitates* smiling (causing variations in the amount of smiling, once smiling has been induced).

An expression of nonspecific emotion

Tests of the emotional meaning of facial behavior should be complemented with descriptions of actual facial behavior. For example, what actual facial behavior occurs during noninteractive periods of intense emotion? In the case of happiness, our data point to a complex and rapid succession of facial movements. One possible hypothesis is that this stream of facial behavior is not a sign of any specific emotion but of nonspecific emotion (Fernández-Dols & Ruiz-Belda, 1995b). The stream would be *entrained* into prototypical expressions of specific emotions only when the subject becomes engaged in social interaction. Figure 11.4 shows the expressive pattern of a soccer fan on watching a match. In a sequence of 4 sec, the fan displays a striking set of facial behaviors throughout an episode of clear and intense happiness; a Duchenne smile is clearly observed only when the episode finishes and the fan interacts with other people around him.

Alternatively, we can search for facial patterns related to isolated components of specific emotions (see Smith and Scott, chapter 10, this volume) in the apparently disorganized facial behavior observed during the noninteractive period. This hypothesis suggests that the complexity of the noninteractive period can be disentangled by looking for any possible specific pattern linked to a particular emotion or to any intense emotional episode.

An urgent need to avoid hurry

Our final oxymoron is meant to suggest that launching theoretical models as soon as some evidence seems to suggest them can be dangerous, because doing so might constrain their proponents into searching for ways to confirm that model. In our view, commitment to a premature theoretical framework was what led researchers to focus on studies of recognition (whose "artistic truth" seemed to confirm the theory) rather than on people's actual facial behavior (whose "optical truth" seems not to confirm the theory).

Researchers in the field should gather a substantial descriptive data base *before* any further theoretical development. In fact, our hunch is that our findings are only a first glimpse of an extremely complex and fas-

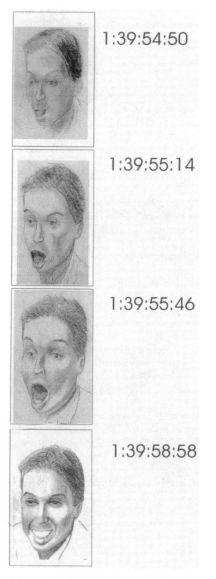

1:39:54:50

1:39:55:14

1:39:55:46

1:39:58:58

Figure 11.4. Typical expressive pattern of a soccer fan in an episode of happiness. In a sequence of 4 seconds, the fan displays a set of unexpected facial behaviors; a Duchenne smile is clearly observed only when the episode finishes and the fan interacts with other people around him (*lower frame*).

cinating "optical truth" whose complete understanding will require us to explore an exciting range of emotions and social variables across and through intense, ecologically valid situations.

References

Buck, R. (1991). Social factors in facial display and communication: A reply to Chovil and others. *Journal of Nonverbal Behavior, 15*, 155–161.

Camras, L. A., Malatesta, C., & Izard, C. E. (1991). The development of facial expressions in infancy. In R. S. Feldman & B. Rimé (Eds.), *Fundamentals of nonverbal behavior* (pp. 73–105). Cambridge, England: Cambridge University Press.

Chovil, N. (1991). Social determinants of facial displays. *Journal of Nonverbal Behavior, 15*, 141–154.

Chovil, N., & Fridlund, A. J. (1991). Why emotionality cannot equal sociality: Reply to Buck. *Journal of Nonverbal Behavior, 15*, 163–167.

Davidson, R. J., Ekman, P., Saron, C. D., Senulis, J. A., & Friesen, W. V. (1990). Approach-withdrawal and cerebral asymmetry: Emotional expression and brain physiology I. *Journal of Personality and Social Psychology, 58*, 330–341.

Davis, R. C. (1934). The specificity of facial expressions. *Journal of General Psychology, 10*, 42–58.

Eibl-Eibesfeldt, I. (1973). The expressive behavior of the deaf-and-blind-born. In M. von Cranach & I. Vine (Eds.), *Social communication and movement* (pp. 163–194). New York: Academic Press.

Ekman, P. (1972). Universals and cultural differences in facial expressions of emotion. In J. K. Cole (Ed.), *Nebraska Symposium on Motivation, 1971* (Vol. 19, pp. 207–283). Lincoln, NE: University of Nebraska Press.

Ekman, P. (1992). Facial expressions of emotion: New findings, new questions. *Psychological Science, 3*, 34–38.

Ekman, P. (1994). Strong evidence for universals in facial expressions: A reply to Russell's mistaken critique. *Psychological Bulletin, 115*, 268–287.

Ekman, P., Davidson, R. J., & Friesen, W. V. (1990). The Duchenne smile: Emotional expression and brain physiology II. *Journal of Personality and Social Psychology, 58*, 342–353.

Ekman, P., & Friesen, W. V. (1976). Measuring facial movement. *Environmental Psychology and Nonverbal Behavior, 1*, 56–75.

Ekman, P., & Friesen, W. V. (1978). *Facial Action Coding System (FACS): A technique for the measurement of facial action*. Palo Alto, CA: Consulting Psychologists Press.

Ekman, P., Friesen, W. V., & Ancoli, S. (1980). Facial signs of emotional experience. *Journal of Personality and Social Psychology, 39*, 1125–1134.

Ekman, P., Friesen, W. V., & Ellsworth, P. (1972). *Emotion in the human face: Guidelines for research and an integration of findings*. New York: Pergamon Press.

Ekman, P., Friesen, W. V., & Tomkins, S. S. (1971). Facial Affect Scoring Technique: A first validity study. *Semiotica, 3*, 37–58.

Fernández-Dols, J. M., & Ruiz-Belda, M.-A. (1995a). Are smiles a sign of happiness? Gold medal winners at the Olympic Games. *Journal of Personality and Social Psychology, 69*, 1113–1119.

Fernández-Dols, J. M., & Ruiz-Belda, M.-A. (1995b). Expression of emotion versus expressions of emotions: Everyday conceptions about spontaneous facial behavior. In J. A. Russell, J. M. Fernández-Dols, A. S. R. Manstead, & J. C. Wellenkamp (Eds.), *Everyday conceptions of emotion* (pp. 505–522) Dordrecht, Netherlands: Kluwer Academic Press.

Fox, N. A., & Davidson, R. J. (1988). Patterns of brain electrical activity during facial signs of emotion in ten-month old infants. *Developmental Psychology, 24*, 230–236.

Fridlund, A. J. (1991). Sociality of solitary smiling: Potentiation by an implicit audience. *Journal of Personality and Social Psychology, 60*, 229–240.

Fridlund, A. J. (1994). *Human facial expression: An evolutionary view.* San Diego, CA: Academic Press.

Friesen, W. V. (1972). *Cultural differences in facial expression in a social situation: An experimental test of the concept of display rules.* Unpublished doctoral dissertation, University of California, San Francisco, CA.

Frois-Wittmann, J. (1930). The judgment of facial expression. *Journal of Experimental Psychology, 13*, 113–151.

Gottlieb, G. (1976). Conceptions of prenatal development: Behavioral embryology. *Psychological Review, 83*, 215–234.

Hess, U., Banse, R., & Kappas, A. (1995). The intensity of facial expression is determined by underlying affective state and social situation. *Journal of Personality and Social Psychology, 69*, 280–288.

Hjortsjö, C. H. (1969). *Man's face and mimic language.* Lund, Sweden: Studentlitteratur.

Izard, C. E. (1994). Innate and universal facial expressions: Evidence from developmental and cross-cultural research. *Psychological Bulletin, 115*, 288–299.

Kraut, R. E., & Johnston, R. E. (1979). Social and emotional messages of smiling: An ethological approach. *Journal of Personality and Social Psychology, 37*, 1539–1553.

Landis, C. (1924). Studies of emotional reaction: General behavior and facial expression. *Journal of Comparative Psychology, 4*, 447–509.

Landis, C. (1934). Emotion: II. The expressions of emotion. In C. Murchinson (Ed.), *Handbook of General Experimental Psychology* (pp. 312–351). Worcester, MA: Clark University Press.

Leventhal, H., & Sharp, E. (1965). Facial expressions as indicators of distress. In S. S. Tomkins & C. E. Izard (Eds.), *Affect, cognition and personality, empirical studies* (pp. 296–318). New York: Springer.

Matsumoto, D., & Ekman, P. (1988). *Japanese and Caucasian facial expressions of emotion (JACFEE) and neutral faces (JACNeuf)* [Slides & brochure]. San Francisco: San Francisco State University.

Mozley, A. V. (1979). Introduction to the Dover Edition. In E. Muybridge, *Muybridge's complete human and animal locomotion: All 781 plates from the 1887 Animal Locomotion* (3 vols., pp. vii–xviii). New York: Dover Publications.

Oster, H., Hegley, D., & Nagel, L. (1992). Adult judgments and fine-grained analysis of infant facial expressions: Testing the validity of a priori coding formulas. *Developmental Psychology, 28*, 1115–1131.

Rosenberg, E. L., & Ekman, P. (1994). Coherence between expressive and experiential systems in emotion. *Cognition and Emotion, 8*, 201–229.

Ruiz-Belda, M. A. (1995). *La coherencia entre comportamiento facial espontaneo y emocion* [The coherence between spontaneous facial behavior and emotion]. Unpublished doctoral dissertation, Universidad Autonoma de Madrid, Madrid, Spain.

Russell, J. A. (1994). Is there universal recognition of emotion from facial expression? A review of cross-cultural studies. *Psychological Bulletin, 115*, 102–141.

Russell, J. A. (1995). Facial expressions of emotion: What lies beyond minimal universality? *Psychological Bulletin, 118*, 379–391.

Schneider, K., & Josephs, I. (1991). The expressive and communicative functions of preschool children's smiles in an achievement-situation. *Journal of Nonverbal Behavior, 15*, 185–198.

Schneider, K., & Unzner, L. (1992). Preschoolers' attention and emotion in an achievement and an effect game: A longitudinal study. *Cognition and Emotion, 6*, 37–63.

Sherman, M. (1927). The differentiation of emotion responses in infants: I. Judgments of emotional responses from motion picture views and from actual observation. *Journal of Comparative Psychology, 7*, 265–284.

Thompson, J. (Ed.). (1941). Development of facial expression of emotion in blind and seeing children. *Archives of Psychology, 37*(264).

12. Is the meaning perceived in facial expression independent of its context?

JOSÉ MIGUEL FERNÁNDEZ-DOLS AND
JAMES M. CARROLL

We see infants smile when they encounter an adult. We see adults smile when they watch a slapstick cartoon. We see people weep at homages and funerals. We see teenagers frown when their computers flash a strange message, and teachers frown when a teenager makes an inappropriate remark. Smiles, frowns, and other facial configurations described as "expressions of emotion" are highly meaningful cues in our perception of others.

This chapter concerns the meaning perceived in such facial expressions, and, specifically, whether that meaning depends on the context in which the expression occurs. (By "context" we mean the situational events that surround the facial movement, and we use the words *situation* and *context* interchangeably.) Common sense suggests *yes*. As with any behavior, facial expressions are embedded in a context; they happen at a particular time (e.g., while gazing at someone) and in a particular place (e.g., at a funeral). Psychological wisdom says that any perception is an interaction between the stimulus and its context (between the figure and its ground), and ethologists have found that animal messages get their specific meaning through context (Hinde, 1982; Smith, 1977).

What, then, are the figure–ground interactions between facial expressions and context? The answer implicit in the mainstream view of facial expression is very simple: There are none. Most research on facial expressions presupposes that they have meaning independent of their context or, in other words, that the context plays no essential role in the recognition of emotions from facial expressions. A specific facial expression means happiness, surprise, fear, or whatever, irrespective of the occasion of its occurrence. Even when feigned, a smile still means happiness, a wrinkled nose disgust.

This view implies that smiling infants and adults are perceived as

Figure 12.1. What emotion is each person feeling? Reproduced by permission of Agencia EFE, S.A. (*left*), and Frank Spooner Pictures (*right*).

happy, crying heroes and widows as sad, and frowning teenagers and teachers as angry, regardless of the context. When their facial expressions are placed back in context, some of these implications seem feasible: A crying widow at a funeral probably is sad, and a teacher frowning at an irreverent student probably is angry. Many pictures display these transparent messages: Figure 12.1 shows two such facial expressions. Who needs context to see grief in the woman and anger in the man?

Other implications are less certain. When a computer flashes a strange message, are teenagers angry or just puzzled? When infants smile to adults, are they happy or just being sociable? Are crying heroes sad in their own homage? Are smiling adults happy because the character of a slapstick cartoon has been crushed? Turn now to Figure 12.2. It is identical to Figure 12.1 except now some contextual information is available. Consider the actual contexts: The woman has just received a gold medal at the Olympics, experiencing one of the happiest moments of her life. The man has just been freed after more than a year in captivity. He is exultant on arriving home. Your first judgments – grief and anger – were feasible, but the second ones – overcome with happiness – seem at least equally feasible.

Knowledge of the context can thus lead us to doubt that a genuine (nonfeigned) smile expresses happiness, a genuine frown anger, or genuine crying sadness. If so, our everyday experience puts us at odds with the conclusion of 65 years of experimental research. How can this be so? In our view, the answer to this sensible question is that, paradoxically, most research on the relationship between facial expression and context has systematically misrepresented the context and its role in creating an emotional message. By "misrepresentation" we do not mean just artificiality. Admittedly, the ecological validity of most of these experiments is negligible; contexts have consisted of short written texts or graphic vignettes in which the smell, sounds, and specific images of the real

Figure 12.2. The woman is an Olympic gold medalist, Gwen Torrance, on the podium, living one of the happiest times of her life. The man is an American soldier kept as an Iranian hostage for 444 days; in the picture he arrives at an American base after being freed. His expression was described by Time-Life (1994) as "an unambiguous expression" of joy. Reproduced by permission of Agencia EFE, S.A. (*top*), and Frank Spooner Pictures (*bottom*)

situation disappear, and the time frame is condensed or divided. Nevertheless, creating artificial stimuli in laboratories is an acceptable way of securing a controlled environment capable of keeping the basic features of a phenomenon.

Researchers' misrepresentation has been deeper. They have mistakenly assumed that expression and context are co-equal competing sources of information and that each transmits its own emotional message. This assumption has been maintained through years of research carried out in the framework of a 65-year-old experimental paradigm, in which observers judge discordant combinations of facial expressions and contexts (i.e., the face and context suggest different emotions) in order to ascertain whether judgments about the emotional content of the combination are more predictable from the judgment of the face alone or from the judgment of the context alone. Most of the time, it has been concluded, they are more predictable from the judgment of the face alone.

In our view, expression and context do not typically compete and do not each convey an emotional message. Rather, they interact in complex and almost unknown ways. The relation of face to context is more figure to ground. Consider the way the ground generally influences the perception of a figure. For example, consider how a white background influences the perception of a gray target. It is not that the gray suggests "gray," while white suggests "white," and the observer then chooses between two competing color suggestions. Rather, the white ground makes the gray figure seem darker.

Admittedly, some contexts do convey a clear emotional message: A funeral is a sad event, and winning a gold medal is a happy one. But most contexts do not convey a self-contained message independent of the expression. A casual encounter between a baby and an adult suggests no strong emotion. The flashing, puzzling message from the computer is, by definition, an enigma. A smashed cartoon character can amuse but, even though happiness and amusement are positive emotions, we would not be willing to accept the inference that if we smile the annihilation of the character makes us happy (assuming we are not sadists).

In this chapter, we describe representative studies in this field and their main conclusions. We then describe alternative approaches that explore the nature of context and its interaction with facial expression and that show how interpretation of facial expressions depends on context. Finally, we discuss the implications of this evidence for research on facial expression.

The Goodenough–Tinker paradigm

Historical antecedents

In 1931, Goodenough and Tinker published a paper entitled "The relative potency of facial expression and verbal description of stimulus in the judgment of emotion." Their title aptly captures their assumption of two independent sources of emotional information. Their method has become the most popular in research on the relationship between expression and situation. Goodenough and Tinker asked observers to judge what emotion was felt by a hypothetical character simultaneously experiencing a described situation (e.g., finding a dead rat in the kitchen) and displaying the facial expression depicted in a photograph (e.g., a smile). Their goal was to determine whether judgments of such discordant combinations would match the emotional message of the situation or that of the facial expression. They examined all possible combinations created through a factorial design. Their results were equivocal: neither the face nor the context was consistently dominant. However, their methodological assumptions were to guide research in this field decades later.

Goodenough and Tinker's approach was not immediately influential. In the 1940s, Munn (1940), Hanawalt (1944), and Vinacke (1949) analyzed candid photographs of persons in real situations in an attempt to find out whether isolated expressions on characters' faces (face alone) transmitted their emotional message as well as did the whole photograph (face + situation). Munn presented observers with pictures of live scenes cut from magazines such as *Time* and *Life*. He was not concerned about whether face and situation, judged alone, were concordant or discordant. Rather, he chose stimuli based on their emotional content as a whole. Although Munn's approach was more a description than an experimental test, it was, in many ways, more interesting than that of Goodenough and Tinker because the contextual and the expressive information were both visual and both natural events. More important is Munn's attempt to examine whether placing the face (figure) back into its natural context (ground) would affect judgments of the facial expression. As such, facial expression and context were considered complementary rather than competing sources of information. Unfortunately, recent replications of Munn's paradigm have consisted of visual versions of the Goodenough–Tinker experiment, in which most of the exploratory characteristics of Munn's study were replaced by experimental methods in order to compare the influence of face versus context (Spignesi & Shor, 1981; Wallbott, 1988a).

Goldberg (1951) similarly provided an alternative to the Goodenough–Tinker approach. He showed subjects two short films in which the middle scenes were different, suggesting a different context for the last scene (a woman screaming). Unfortunately, this line of research has been replicated only once, in a study by Wallbott (1988b). Both Goldberg (1951) and Wallbott (1988b) found that context influenced the meaning of the facial expression.

Reviewers at the time were quite aware that Goodenough and Tinker's, Munn's, and Goldberg's research provided little evidence on the actual role played by context in the recognition of emotion. Tagiuri's review (1969), probably representative of researchers' thinking at the end of the 1960s, included a paragraph on emotion perception from face and context. Tagiuri cited the study by Munn (1940) and recalled Hebb's (1946) observation of the influence of a previously observed facial expression on the judgment of a given expression (for example, a smile after a frown might be judged as relief). Tagiuri concluded that the context was an important influence on the interpretation of facial expressions but emphasized that there was a need for more data on the processing and integration of expressive and contextual pieces of information.

The Facial Expression Program

Tagiuri's cautious approach fell out of favor when authors like Tomkins (1962, 1963), Izard (1971), and Ekman (1972) initiated what was termed in chapter 1 the *Facial Expression Program*. This program emphasized the importance of facial behavior as an independent and self-sufficient source of emotional information. The single most influential contribution of their Facial Expression Program to the question of context was a review by Ekman, Friesen, and Ellsworth (1972, 1982). Ekman et al. considered the Goodenough–Tinker study "exemplary" (Ekman et al., 1972; p. 147) and criticized all other approaches. They argued that Munn and Goldberg should have compared, as had Goodenough and Tinker, the context alone with the face-and-context combination. Only then could Munn and Goldberg have examined the relative influence of face versus situation.

Especially influential for subsequent research were Ekman et al.'s methodological guidelines. In effect, they suggested an improved version of Goodenough and Tinker's method with larger samples of faces, contexts, and observers. Their focus of improvement was equating the *clarity* of facial expressions and contexts. Equating the clarity of both facial and contextual information would allow researchers to compare *equivalent* sources of information. Combining faces and contexts in a factorial design would make face and context independent of one another. "Clarity" was not defined theoretically, but in procedural terms, and it consisted of three factors: Clarity was diminished by ambiguity (disagreement among observers), complexity (number of attributed emotions), and lack of strength (lack of intensity of the attributed emotions).

Table 12.1 shows a representative sample of those studies that have compared the relative influence of facial and contextual information in the perception of emotion. Their chronological order shows how Goodenough and Tinker's (1931) method has come to dominate this field. All studies listed since 1960 have used some variation of the Goodenough–Tinker paradigm. Researchers have, however, introduced changes to the original design. Frijda (1969) and Wallbott (1988a) introduced new procedures for analyzing the results, and Nakamura, Buck, and Kenny's (1990) procedure included dynamic facial stimuli rather than posed still photographs.

Replications of the Goodenough–Tinker paradigm that included Ekman et al.'s recommendations on clarity found a dominance of expressive over contextual information (Watson, 1972; Knudsen & Muzeraki, 1983; Wallbott, 1988a; Mallo, Fernández-Dols, & Wallbott, 1989; Nakamura et al., 1990). Similar experiments have been carried out with children (Gnepp, 1983; Camras, 1986). Facial dominance was crucial for the Facial Expression Program because it seemed to confirm that the recognition of emotions through faces is independent of the context in which the expression is produced. This premise justified the mushrooming of studies on the recognition of emotions from facial expressions "in vacuum" – freed from any context.

The limits of the Goodenough–Tinker paradigm

Ekman et al.'s chief recommendation was that in pitting expressions against contexts, researchers should make sure that both sources convey one clear and intense emotion. This might seem to be a fair way of selecting the key features of both stimuli. After all, if context and expression are to compete for the emotional tone of the perceiver's judgment, which criterion is better than this?

Table 12.1. *Studies of facial and contextual information in emotion perception*

Author and date	Research question	Facial stimuli	Contextual stimuli	Conclusion made by researcher
Goodenough and Tinker (1931)	What are the relative influences of context and facial expression in the perception of emotion?	Posed still photographs	Verbal descriptions	Both context and facial expression play a role in the perception of emotion.
Munn (1940)	Does context affect judgments of emotion from facial expression?	Candid camera still photographs	Picture surrounding facial expression with caption	Context influences the perception of emotion from facial expressions.
Goldberg (1951)	Does the context preceding the scene of an emotional reaction affect judges' interpretations of that emotional reaction?	Motion picture of actress acting	Movie clips prior to facial reaction	Both context and facial expression play a role in the perception of emotion.
Frijda (1958)	What are the relative influences of context and facial expression in the perception of emotion?	Posed still photographs	Verbal description	Both context and facial expression play a role in the perception of emotion.
Frijda (Warries study; 1969)	Does facial or contextual information dominate judgments of attentiveness?	Posed still photographs	Verbal description	Facial expression dominates in the perception of attentiveness.
Frijda (Janus study; 1969)	Does facial or contextual information dominate judgments of pleasure?	Posed still photographs	Verbal description	Facial expression dominates in the perception of pleasure.
Watson (1972)	Does facial or contextual information dominate in the perception of emotion?	Posed still photographs	Verbal description	Facial expression dominates in the perception of basic emotions.

Study	Question	Facial information	Contextual information	Conclusion
Spignesi and Shor (1981)	Does facial or contextual information dominate judgments of pleasure?	Candid camera still photographs	Picture surrounding facial expression with caption	Neither the facial expression nor the context dominates in the perception of pleasure.
Knudsen and Muzekari (1983)	Does contextual information affect judgments of emotion from facial expression?	Posed still photographs	Verbal description	Context influences the perception of emotion from facial expressions.
Wallbott (1988a, study 1)	Does facial or contextual information dominate in the perception of emotion?	Posed still photographs	Verbal descriptions	Facial expression dominates context in the perception of emotion.
Wallbott (1988a, study 2)	Does facial or contextual information dominate in the perception of emotion?	Candid camera still photographs	Picture surrounding facial expression	Neither the facial expression nor the context dominates in the perception of emotion.
Wallbott (1988b)	Does facial or contextual information dominate in the perception of emotion?	Motion picture of actors acting	Movie clips prior to facial expression	Neither the facial expression nor the context dominates in the perception of emotion.
Nakamura, Buck, and Kenny (1990)	Does facial or contextual information dominate in the perception of emotion?	Video recording of spontaneous facial expressions	Slide that presumably elicited the facial expression.	Facial expression dominates context in the perception of basic emotions.
Fernández-Dols, Wallbott, Sanchez (1991, Study 1)	Does facial or contextual information dominate when subjects have previously experienced the experimental context?	Posed still photographs	Verbal descriptions	Facial expression dominates a verbally presented context in the perception of emotion.

Table 12.1 (cont.)

Author and date	Research question	Facial stimuli	Contextual stimuli	Conclusion made by researcher
Fernández-Dols, Wallbott, and Sanchez (1991, Study 2)	Does facial or contextual information dominate when subjects are familiarized with categorizing situations in terms of emotions?	Posed still photo-graphs	Verbal descriptions	Judgments are equally influenced by facial expression and context.
Fernández-Dols, Wallbott, and Sanchez (1991, Study 3)	Does facial or contextual information dominate when the face is presented before context and vice versa?	Posed still photo-graphs	Verbal descriptions	Facial expression dominates a verbally presented context in the perception of basic emotions.
Fernández-Dols, Sierra, and Ruiz-Belda (1993)	Does facial or contextual information dominate when particular selection criteria are used?	Posed still photo-graphs	Verbal descriptions	Judgments are equally influenced by facial expression and context.
Carroll and Russell (1996)	For certain theoretically chosen combinations, does context dominate face?	Posed still photo-graphs	Verbal descriptions	Context can dominate facial expressions of basic emotion.

Unfortunately, source clarity fails to account for another much more important source of inequity between expression and context: their radical differences in nature. Notice, first, that the requirement of source clarity forces the researcher to examine only those contexts that convey a single clear emotional message. Moreover, this requirement limits our understanding to those instances where face and context are equally clear. We have no guarantee that the face and context are ever equal in clarity in everyday life.

Setting ecology aside, notice that the control imposed by source clarity is based on the way people categorize faces, but it is probably irrelevant, or at least insufficient, for detecting the key factors that enable situations to shape our interpretation of facial expressions. Simply put, what is good for selecting faces may not be as good for selecting situations. Researchers do not know the specific features of situations in which we see facial expressions, and how these features shape our recognition of emotions. Equating source clarity presupposes that contexts and facial expressions are equally categorized in terms of specific emotions, with only quantitative differences in the "strength" of the message.

In the following paragraphs, we describe two lines of research that expose limitations in the Goodenough–Tinker paradigm. The first line focuses on the specific features that make a context "clear." This line of research maintains the assumption of the independence of facial expression and context. The second line examines this assumption, suggesting that the relationship between expressions and contexts is not just a confrontation between sources of equal clarity, but, as early researchers suggested, a more complex interactive process related to other subtle factors, such as the susceptibility to reinterpretations of each source. In both lines, minimal modifications in the Goodenough–Tinker paradigm produce unexpected results.

The clarity of the contexts

Ekman et al. assumed that the way in which context influences emotion perception is parallel to the way the face influences emotion perception. We suggest that this assumption is very unlikely. As evidence, we present a series of studies conducted by Fernández-Dols and his colleagues that suggest that face and context are indeed dissimilar sources of information.

Fernández-Dols, Wallbott, and Sanchez (1991) hypothesized that the usual dominance of facial expressions found in the Goodenough–Tinker paradigm could be an artifact of the different modes of presentation used in these experiments: Emotions could be a more accessible category for pictures of faces than for written descriptions of situations. If so, judgments of the combinations of the two sources of information would be biased toward the visual source. And, indeed, training in categorizing situational information in terms of emotion ("anger," "sadness," etc.) increased the influence of the contextual information.

Furthermore, Fernández-Dols, Sierra, and Ruiz-Belda (1991) found that the amount of time required to categorize situations in terms of emotion varied across situations: Texts describing more unusual situations required less time. If we assume that categorization of faces is rapid, this finding suggests that the accessibility of an emotion category might be a key factor in judging face–context combinations and in the dominance of the face.

Based on these previous findings, Fernández-Dols, Sierra, and Ruiz-Belda (1993) suggested alternative criteria for the selection of contextual stimuli. They selected contexts that described highly prototypical, yet unusual, social situations. Empirically, contexts so selected were found to be as influential as the facial information in the judgment of discordant combinations.

In another study using the Goodenough–Tinker paradigm, Carrera and Fernández-Dols (1994) showed that facial dominance was not due to the face's emotional content. They hypothesized that facial expressions that lacked emotional content would also dominate. Replicating findings previously reported by Frijda (1969) and by Watson (1972), they found that neutral expressions (i.e., faces that lack emotional content when judged alone) were at least as dominant, over situational information, as clear and intense prototypical expressions. Subjects tended to ignore the emotional message of the situation and rated the combination in terms of the neutrality of the nonemotional facial expression.

Altogether, such findings suggest that the usual dominance of facial expression over context in the Goodenough–Tinker paradigm was not due to the nature of facial expressions but rather to experimental artifacts related to stimulus selection. Once a minimum of control is applied to the features of the context, the Goodenough–Tinker paradigm provides unexpected findings for the study of the recognition of emotions (i.e., no facial dominance) but rather unsurprising and commonplace findings for the study of perception: The salience of the messages and accessibility of the categories shape our interpretations.

Vulnerability to reinterpretation

When observers judge combinations of facial and contextual sources of information, as in the Goodenough–Tinker paradigm, how do they come to a decision? Attempts to answer this question have assumed that the observer "will try to infer an emotion from person [facial expression] and context information separately" (Wallbott, 1988a; for a similar discussion, see Frijda, 1969). So for concordant sources of information, both sources indicate the same emotion and the observer infers a single emotion. But what about discordant combinations? Wallbott (1988a) describes several possible strategies that the observer might use. The observer might create a possible list of the emotional meanings of each source, ordered in descending likelihood. The observer would then compare these lists for the most probable emotion. Alternatively, observers might disregard facial expression by inferring that the person is masking or hiding the true emotion, or the observer might disregard the contextual information by inferring that the person is responding atypically or inappropriately to the given context.

Here we provide an alternative account. The observer's main goal might be to *integrate* the information given before judging any emotions, rather than judging each source separately. Carroll and Russell (1996) provide some preliminary evidence for an integrative process. For example, in one condition, observers were presented with a facial expression typically recognized as anger (staring eyes, furrowed eyebrows, and lips pressed tightly together) and were read the following story intended to suggest puzzlement:

> This is a story of a woman who went to McDonald's for lunch. After a short wait in line, it is her turn to order. The cashier says, "May I help you please?" The woman acknowledges the cashier and returns her attention to the menu. What is the woman feeling?

Apart from the occasional "disgust" interpretation, observers reported the woman to be "puzzled," even more so than for the context alone. The staring eyes matched that of someone peering at a menu. The furrowed eyebrows and pressed lips matched that of someone having difficulty in making up his or her mind. Combined, the two discordant sources of information resulted in a single consensual judgment.

The process of integration, however, may only be possible if the face and context fit together subjectively. Indeed, if the face and context fail to fit together subjectively, regardless of whether the face and context are extremely discordant or simply awkwardly matched, observers would probably ask themselves why the person is looking a particular way given the context.

If an observer is indeed trying to integrate the two sources of information, then the degree to which the interpretation of one source is influenced by the other becomes central. We introduce the term *vulnerability to reinterpretation* to refer to the extent to which the interpretation of one source of information changes when presented with a second. In our earlier example, the facial stimulus, which is typically judged as anger when presented alone, was interpreted differently when presented with a particular context. Depending on the specific pieces of information, one source may more likely be interpreted as consistent with the second source – thus appearing to reflect the dominance of one source of information over the other.

Ekman et al.'s (1982) notion of clarity does not take vulnerability to reinterpretation into account. This is because reinterpretation is a relational phenomenon between particular facial and contextual information. As such, vulnerability to reinterpretation could not be assessed for each source alone: A particular situation may be vulnerable to reinterpretation when paired with one facial expression but not when paired with another. No index of vulnerability to reinterpretation is therefore possible without knowledge of the other source with which it is paired.

It is likely that in past experiments of the Goodenough–Tinker type, contextual information, not facial information, has been vulnerable to reinterpretation. Consider, for example, a contextual description created by Watson (1972) to convey sadness: "He is told that a close friend, stricken with leukemia, has died." Although the situational description can be easily associated with sadness, it may also be relatively vulnerable to reinterpretation in terms of anger (e.g., thinking that medical care was inadequate), surprise (e.g., being surprised by the unexpected notification of a friend's death), or even a positive emotion such as relief (e.g., relieved that his friend will no longer suffer). The one-line sentence is clear but may easily be interpreted in terms of the set of implicit biographical and cultural assumptions included in this short piece of information. In contrast, the highly complex facial expressions used by Watson were impervious to such simple descriptions of context.

The studies by Carroll and Russell (1996), an example from which was presented previously, suggest that decreasing the vulnerability to reinterpretation of contextual information reverses the usual facial dominance found in replications of the Goodenough–Tinker paradigm. Contextual dominance was easily attained when combinations were selected according to certain rules of feasibility rather than achieved factorially. Carroll and Russell reduced the contexts' vulnerability to reinterpretation by creating situational stories (contexts) that matched specific facial expressions of basic emotion on quasi-physical features (i.e., eyes staring, tense mouth) and pleasure and arousal, but which nonetheless differed in terms of the emotion category attributed to the stimuli judged alone. For 22 of 22 combinations, judgments of the emotion label of the facial expression and situational story combined were consistent with the situational story judged alone rather than facial expression judged alone.

The results of Carroll and Russell show more than just context dominance. They were able in one study to demonstrate that certain combinations of face and context resulted in judgments that could not be predicted by a linear combination of the judgments of each source alone. In one case, observers agreed more on the combination than on either source alone. For example, a face judged as expressing "anger" by 64% of observers combined with a context judged to elicit "determination" by 40% of observers yielded a combination that was judged as an example of "determination" by 84% of observers. More telling was a case in which observers agreed to a qualitatively different emotion for the combination than for either source alone. In this case, the modal response to the face was "fear," the modal response to the context was "anger," and the modal response to their combination was "pain." These results suggest that facial and contextual sources of information are not used independently in the perception of emotion. They are integrated.

Conclusions

As our opening examples with infants, teenagers, and adults suggested, an observer can recognize not only sadness in crying but also happiness, not only anger in frowns but also puzzlement, and not only happiness in smiles but also amusement or social invitation. Selection of one from these multiple, variable meanings of the face depends on the context. Those investigations that supported the assumption of the self-sufficiency of facial expressions were based on an experimental paradigm that misrepresented the contextual sources of information. The recognition of emotions from face is, as is any other perceptual process, no exception to the principles relating figure to ground.

Facial expressions were found to dominate context in the Good-enough–Tinker paradigm because the categories of emotion are more accessible for faces than for situations, because pictures of faces are more salient and vivid than written descriptions of situations, and because the situational stimuli used in previous studies were particularly vulnerable to reinterpretation. The Goodenough–Tinker paradigm is less an experiment on emotion, expression, and context than an experiment in which an isolated visual message and an isolated verbal message (with a rather remote and arbitrary connection to real faces and situations) are paired for some judges who have to make very specific and artificial ratings on this complex aggregate. A verbal description of the situation and a still picture of a face can be a good target of research in, for example, some advertising strategies but can barely reproduce the enfolding array of factual and psychological features that constitute the context of facial expressions. Even when improvements are made to this procedure, such as a successive presentation of two video clips (one for the context and another for the face; Wallbott, 1988b), the faulty assumption of a confrontation between two sources of information remains fatal.

Our studies were critical of the Goodenough–Tinker paradigm but do no more than hint at a more enlightened theoretical approach. Our studies on the importance of context were an unavoidable chore, and they expose rather than answer the basic question. These studies showed that 65 years of experimentation carried a burden of flawed assumptions. Our findings are enlightening mainly in terms of method, but they were as limited in ecological validity as the paradigm they criticize. Like the Goodenough–Tinker paradigm, these findings say little about how spontaneous facial expressions occurring in natural contexts are perceived in everyday life. Current knowledge on the relationship between expression and context is extremely limited and coincides with ordinary psychological wisdom: As with any other stimulus, the interpretation of facial expressions depends on the context. However banal, this conclusion has two important practical corollaries.

The first corollary concerns research on the recognition of emotion from facial expressions alone, the backbone of the Facial Expression Program. This research is based on the assumption that the meaning of the facial expression is perceived independently of context. Observers were presented facial expressions that, theoretically, were "context-proof." If the message of a facial expression is actually a joint product of the facial expression and its context, then current evidence on the universal recognition of emotions has left uncontrolled a major factor. Each face was actually presented in a context: Observers are given a series of faces, and this quite unecological context has been found to exert a powerful influence on the emotion seen (Russell & Fehr, 1987; Tanaka-Matsumi, Attivissimo, Nelson, & D'Urso, 1995). Moreover, observers are free to imagine whatever situation they choose for each person whose face is shown.

The second corollary is also a desideratum: Researchers must question the theoretical assumptions and must look for alternatives to the Good-enough–Tinker paradigm. The degree to which recent research (Table 12.1) has followed the lead of Goodenough and Tinker is unhealthy from any point of view. We need to know what happens in other kinds of research designs. Where might we find new sources of inspiration for such studies? Much of value can be found in those sophisticated and open-minded authors who, 50 years ago, emphasized the complexity of the relationship between expression and context (e.g., Frijda, 1958; Gold-berg, 1951; Munn, 1940; Tagiuri, 1969). In this chapter, we do not pro-mote a particular experimental paradigm, but we do suggest that future research should pursue certain basic goals, as follows.

A better description of the context. Serious study of the situations that elicit facial expressions is long overdue. This deficiency impairs the study of the production of facial expressions (Fridlund, 1994) as well as the study of the recognition of emotion from facial expression. As a source of information, context is much more complex than the face. A face can make thousands of movements, but there is an infinite variety of situa-tions, including an overwhelming amount of sensory information that must be filtered, categorized, and stored in its own way. A context con-sists not only of the actual events encountered but also of our memories of former similar experiences, and so on. A misleadingly simple story (e.g., my dog died) requires an amazing number of implicit assumptions about a long time frame (e.g., the dog's life), cultural expectations about dogs (e.g., you don't eat dogs, you love dogs), the current time of the action (e.g., it died a short time ago, not 40 years ago), and so on.

More ecological procedures. A second task is to use more natural sources of expressive and contextual information. The usual study in this field included blatantly different and artificial stories of a situation and a photograph of a posed facial expression. Neither source of information bears much resemblance to everyday life. New procedures should obviously include visual and dynamic representations of persons and situations (Fernández-Dols & Ruiz-Belda, 1995). But more importantly, future researchers must solve conceptual problems as well. For example, the perception of emotion rarely involves just one face and one situation but rather is based on temporal changes in faces and events (Tagiuri, 1969). When considered more closely, the very distinctions among context, face, and emotion begin to blur. The context is not just a concomitant of an emotional expression but is the sequence of events that includes the (sometimes implicit) causes and consequences of the emotion itself.

New approaches to the dependent variable. Exclusive focus on a few verbal categories (such as "happiness," "fear," and so on) as the criteria of recognition creates methodological and theoretical problems. At the methodological level, a closed list of mutually exclusive categories of alleged basic emotions could provide a misleading impression of uniform recognition among observers (Russell, 1994). At the theoretical level, spontaneous response to face–context combinations might not consist simply of ascribing verbally labeled emotion categories. It is doubtful whether observers even have much experience in this type of categorization (Fernández-Dols, Wallbott, & Sanchez, 1991). Alternative accounts of the lay understanding of emotions, and the way in which people understand the emotional message of the face need to be explored. For example, Frijda (1969; Frijda & Tcherkassof, chapter 4, this volume) pointed out that an observer might use the face to guess another person's emotion (e.g., she looks scared) but also to guess the situation (e.g., she looks as if she is looking at a small child), and to guess other persons' actions (e.g., we expect friendly behavior from a smiling person).

New approaches to the processing of expressive and contextual information. There is a need for hypotheses and evidence on the *process* of interpreting emotion from face and context. We have criticized the implicit assumption that, given a combination of face and a situation, the process of interpretation is additive and noninteractive. We have also provided evidence that face and context are integrated, suggesting, as Tagiuri (1969) did, a higher-order interaction. Others, however, have offered accounts that adhere to the assumption of linearity (Frijda, 1969; Wallbott, 1988a). Before progress is possible, we need to clarify this issue.

References

Camras, L. A. (1986). Judgments of emotion from facial expression and situational context. In C. E. Izard & P. B. Read (Eds.), *Measuring emotions in infants and children* (pp. 75–89). Cambridge, England: Cambridge University Press.

Carrera, P., & Fernández-Dols, J. M. (1994). Neutral faces in context: Their emotional meaning and their function. *Journal of Nonverbal Behavior, 18,* 281–299.

Carroll, J. M., & Russell, J. A. (1996). Do facial expressions signal specific emotions? Judging emotion from the face in context. *Journal of Personality and Social Psychology, 70,* 205–218.

Ekman, P. (1972). Universals and cultural differences in facial expressions of emotion. In J. K. Cole (Ed.), *Nebraska Symposium on Motivation, 1971* (Vol. 19, pp. 207–283). Lincoln, NE: University of Nebraska Press.

Ekman, P., Friesen, W. V., & Ellsworth, P. (1972). *Emotion in the human face: Guidelines for research and an integration of findings.* New York: Pergamon Press.

Ekman, P., Friesen, W. V., & Ellsworth, P. (1982). What are the relative contributions of facial behavior and contextual information to the judgment of emotion? In P. Ekman (Ed.), *Emotion in the human face* (2nd. ed., pp. 111–127). Cambridge, England: Cambridge University Press.

Fernández-Dols, J. M., & Ruiz-Belda, M. A. (1995). Are smiles a sign of happiness? Gold medal winners at the Olympic Games. *Journal of Personality and Social Psychology, 69,* 1113–1119.

Fernández-Dols, J. M., Sierra, B. & Ruiz-Belda, M. A. (1991). Reconnaissance et catégorisation des situations émotionnelles et leur interaction avec l'expression: nouvelles perspectives méthodologiques [Recognition and categorization of emotion situations and their interaction with expression: New methodological approaches]. *Les Cahiers Internationaux de Psychologie Sociale, 11,* 37–49.

Fernández-Dols, J. M., Sierra, B., & Ruiz-Belda, M. A. (1993). On the clarity of expressive and contextual information in the recognition of emotions: A methodological critique. *European Journal of Social Psychology, 23,* 195–202.

Fernández-Dols, J. M., Wallbott, H., & Sanchez, F. (1991). Emotion category accessibility and the decoding of emotion from facial expression and context. *Journal of Nonverbal Behavior, 15,* 107–123.

Fridlund, A. J. (1994). *Human facial expression: An evolutionary view.* San Diego, CA: Academic Press.

Frijda, N. H. (1958). Facial expressions and situational cues. *Journal of Abnormal and Social Psychology, 57,* 149–153.

Frijda, N. H. (1969). Recognition of emotion. In L. Berkowitz (Ed.), *Advances in experimental social psychology* (Vol. 4, pp. 167–223). New York: Academic Press.

Gnepp, J. (1983). Children's social sensitivity: Inferring emotions from conflicting cues. *Developmental Psychology, 19,* 805–814.

Goldberg, H. D. (1951). The role of "cutting" in the perception of motion pictures. *Journal of Applied Psychology, 35,* 70–71.

Goodenough, F. L., & Tinker, M. A. (1931). The relative potency of facial expression and verbal description of stimulus in the judgment of emotion. *Comparative Psychology, 12,* 365–370.

Hanawalt, N. G. (1944). The role of the upper and the lower parts of the face as the basis for judging facial expressions: II. In posed expressions and "candid camera" pictures. *Journal of General Psychology, 31,* 23–36.

Hebb, D. O. (1946). Emotion in man and animal: An analysis of the intuitive processes of recognition. *Psychological Review, 53,* 88–106.

Hinde, R. A. (1982). *Ethology: Its nature and relations with other sciences.* Glasgow, Scotland: Fontana.

Izard, C. E. (1971). *The face of emotion.* New York: Appleton-Century-Crofts.

Knudsen, H. R., & Muzeraki, L. H. (1983). The effects of verbal statements of context on facial expressions of emotion. *Journal of Nonverbal Behavior, 7,* 202–212.

Mallo, M. J., Fernández-Dols, J. M., & Wallbott, H. (1989). Reconocimiento de emociones a partir de la expresion facial y el contexto [Recognition of emotions from facial expression and context]. *Revista de Psicologia Social, 4,* 303–310.

Munn, N. L. (1940). The effect of knowledge of the situation upon judgment of emotion from facial expressions. *Journal of Abnormal and Social Psychology, 35,* 324–338.

Nakamura, M., Buck, R., & Kenny, D. A. (1990). Relative contributions of expressive behavior and contextual information to the judgment of the emotional state of another. *Journal of Personality and Social Psychology, 59,* 1032–1039.

Russell, J. A. (1994). Is there universal recognition of emotion from facial expression? A review of the cross-cultural studies. *Psychological Bulletin, 115,* 102–141.

Russell, J. A. & Fehr, B. (1987). Relativity in the perception of emotion in facial expressions. *Journal of Experimental Psychology: General, 116,* 223–237.

Smith, W. J. (1977). *The behavior of communicating.* Cambridge, MA: Harvard University Press.

Spignesi, J., & Shor, S. (1981). The judgment of emotion from facial expressions, contexts, and their combination. *The Journal of General Psychology, 104,* 41–58.

Tagiuri, R. (1969). Person perception. In G. Lindzey & E. Aronson (Eds.), *Handbook of social psychology* (Vol. 3, pp. 395–449). Reading, MA: Addison-Wesley.

Tanaka-Matsumi, J., Attivissimo, D., Nelson, S., & D'Urso, T. (1995). Context effects on the judgment of basic emotions in the face. *Motivation and Emotion, 19,* 139–155.

Time-Life (1994). Emotions: *Journey through the mind and body.* Richmond, VA: Time-Life.

Tomkins, S. S. (1962). *Affect, imagery, consciousness: The positive affects.* New York: Springer-Verlag.

Tomkins, S. S. (1963). *Affect, imagery, consciousness: The negative affects.* New York: Springer-Verlag.

Vinacke, W. E. (1949). The judgment of facial expressions by three national-racial groups in Hawaii: Caucasian faces. *Journal of Personality, 17,* 407–429.

Wallbott, H. G. (1988a). Faces in context: The relative importance of facial expression and context information in determining emotion attributions. In K. R. Scherer (Ed.), *Facets of emotion* (pp. 139–160). Hillsdale, NJ: Erlbaum.

Wallbott, H. G. (1988b). In and out of context: Influences of facial expression and context information on emotion attributions. *British Journal of Social Psychology, 27,* 357–369.

Watson, S. G. (1972). Judgment of emotion from facial and contextual cue combinations. *Journal of Personality and Social Psychology, 24,* 334–342.

13. Reading emotions from and into faces: Resurrecting a dimensional-contextual perspective

JAMES A. RUSSELL

Students of film study an experiment conducted in the great Russian director Lev Kuleshov's experimental workshop just after the 1917 revolution (Cook, 1981). With students including Eisenstein and Pudovkin, Kuleshov created three silent film strips each ending with the same footage of a deliberately deadpan face of the actor Ivan Mozhukhin. In one strip Mozhukhin's face was preceded by a bowl of hot soup, in the second by a dead woman lying in a coffin, and in the third by a young girl playing with a teddy bear. The result was an illusion: Audiences saw emotions expressed in Mozhukhin's expressionless face. Pudovkin (1929/1970) recalled, "The public raved about the acting of the artist. They pointed out the heavy pensiveness of his mood over the forgotten soup, were touched and moved by the deep sorrow with which he looked on the dead woman, and admired the light, happy smile with which he surveyed the girl at play. But we knew that in all three cases the face was exactly the same" (p. 168).

Students of psychology study an experiment conducted by Paul Ekman and Wallace Friesen (1971) in the highlands of Papua New Guinea among the Fore tribe, then living in Stone Age isolation. Members of the tribe were shown still photographs of Americans posing various theorized facial signals of emotion. They were also told stories suggesting specific emotions and asked to select the most appropriate photograph for each story protagonist. Ekman (1975) recalled, "Isolated from Western culture, the New Guinea Fore were able to match the photographs with the appropriate stories" (p. 38). "The subtle creases of a grimace tell the same story around the world, to preliterate New Guinea tribesmen, Japanese and American college students alike" (p. 35). The implication? "If you meet a native in New Guinea or your old boss in a Manhattan bar, you will be able to interpret their facial expressions easily, knowing how they feel – or how they want you to think they feel.

295

You'll be able to do this from the particular pattern of facial wrinkles and movements that evolution has associated with the primary emotions" (p. 35).

Which of these two experiments best captures what typically happens when one person "sees" pensiveness or sorrow or happiness or some other emotion in the face of another? Are people reading emotion *into* a person's face, based on its surrounding context? Or are people accurately reading biologically given emotion signals *from* the face? Is the perception of emotion in faces more like the misperception of hearing melancholy in the baying of wolves, or is it more like the detection of rain from water hitting your face? Is it illusion or accurate detection? Both experiments could be right, in different ways or under different circumstances, but, if so, when? Which captures the typical case? How could the two perspectives be reconciled? In this chapter, I offer an account of the perception of emotion in faces that seeks to reconcile these seeming opposites.

Scientific opinion has moved from the accurate detection theory toward the illusion theory and then back again. From the time Homer wrote the *Iliad*, tradition has it that we can accurately read emotions from faces, and 19th-century naturalists, including the greatest, Charles Darwin (1872/1965), shared this view. Early experimental psychologists tried to test such deeply held beliefs in the laboratory. When genuine rather than posed emotions were studied, the resulting facial expression did not seem to reveal that emotion (Landis, 1924). Different observers gave different emotion labels to the same expression when isolated from its surrounding context (Buzby, 1924; Feleky, 1914). Indeed, the emotion seen in a face depended more on knowing the expresser's situation than on the actual facial behavior (Sherman, 1927). Controlled research seemed to support Kuleshov on the hidden role of contextual information. But after the 1920s, scientific opinion swung steadily back toward the accurate detection end of the continuum.

In 1938, Robert Woodworth offered evidence for a compromise position: Perception was neither an illusion nor the detection of a specific emotion. The information read from the face suggests a family of possible emotions similar in broad terms such as pleasant or unpleasant, attending or rejecting, and activated or relaxed (Woodworth & Schlosberg, 1954). Woodworth's students and colleagues found evidence of similarity across cultures in such qualities as pleasant or unpleasant (Klineberg, 1938, 1940; Osgood, 1966; Schlosberg, 1941, 1952, 1954; Triandis & Lambert, 1958; Vinacke, 1949; Woodworth, 1938; Woodworth & Schlosberg, 1954).

Then, in 1962, Silvan Tomkins began a project that would put the more traditional accurate detection view back into the textbooks. Especially through the research, literature reviews, and theorizing of Izard (1971) and Ekman (1972), Tomkins's vision has since dominated the study of not only the face but emotion. Theirs is today's standard account. There are seven (plus or minus two) basic human emotions (happiness, surprise, fear, anger, disgust, contempt, and sadness), and when one of them occurs, a "facial signal" of that emotion also occurs – unless hidden or masked, and even then the expression can leak out. All emotions consist of one or more of the basic emotions, and we are always in some emotional state. Therefore, unless successfully masked or inhibited, a person's emotional state is always available on the face for anyone to read. What's more, whatever their culture or language or age, observers easily recognize these facial expressions; they are part of an innate signaling system.

The approach to be described here contrasts with that taken by Tomkins, Izard, and Ekman; it reemphasizes the role of context and has much in common with the attempt at reconciliation proposed by Woodworth and his students. If an account along the lines I propose is successful, then seeing an emotion in a face is typically neither an illusion (à la Kuleshov) nor simple detection (à la Tomkins); it is not necessary to postulate an emotion signaling system. Here, I outline my account and point to evidence that favors it and to areas where there is a lack of evidence favoring Tomkins's account. I also set out testable hypotheses even where evidence is now lacking.

A dimensional-contextual perspective on the perception of emotion in faces

Whatever the cause of the expresser's facial behavior, each of us monitors the other's face and sometimes sees emotion there. Of course, we see in faces much besides emotion. A man wrinkles his nose in order to ask "do you smell something?" and the observer gets the intended question. Such nonemotional interpretations are beyond the scope of this chapter. I also consider only cases where the observer perceives the expresser as actually having an emotion, not miming it.

On the account proposed here, the face does not signal specific emotions, but the observer does infer much about the expresser from the face that is relevant to emotion. The observer easily and automatically obtains two kinds of information: First, the observer obtains nonemotional, quasi-physical information from the face: The observer sees that the expresser is staring or looking away, remaining silent or shouting, listening, smelling, or tasting, and so forth. The observer sees what the expresser is doing and how much attention the expresser is paying to it. Second, the observer judges the expresser's overall level of pleasure (pleased vs. displeased) and arousal (agitated vs. sleepy). Judgments about quasi-physical happenings and about pleasure and arousal are made quickly and automatically by all human beings, whatever their culture or language. This primary information, combined with situational and other information about the expresser, determines which, if any, specific emotions the observer may attribute to the expresser.

Quasi-physical features

The head nods, turns, and tilts; the eyes open, close, wink, squint, blink, and change in direction of gaze; the mouth opens and closes, shouts, talks, eats. Movement of the eyes reveals visual attention, movement of the nose olfactory attention. The observer can see from the eyes whether the expresser is weeping, winking, looking down or up, staring at something, or looking away. The mouth shows whether the expresser is talking, shouting, screaming, yawning, laughing, smiling, or grimacing. Note that *smiling, laughing,* and *weeping* are included here as "quasi-physical" in their literal, descriptive meaning with no indication whether the smiling is from pleasure or embarrassment, the weeping is from joy or grief, or the laughing is in merriment or derision.

Equally important, in all but the most contrived situations, the observer sees whom the expresser is smiling at, or what the expresser is looking at. Looking down has a different meaning when it is looking away from something than when it is looking toward something.

Pleasure and arousal

In our face-to-face encounters, each of us monitors the current psychological state of the other. We inevitably judge how happy or unhappy and how sleepy or agitated the other appears. I call these two ubiquitous dimensions *pleasure* and *arousal*, although they might be called evaluation and activity, hedonic tone and activation, valence and energy, or something else. These two dimensions represent not specific emotions but

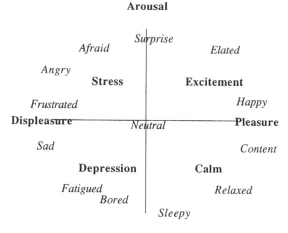

Figure 13.1. A Pleasure-Arousal judgment space for affective feelings.

general features common to many different emotions, some of which are mentioned in Figure 13.1.

Pleasure and arousal describe a "psychological judgment space." As with all stimuli, the observer must make sense of the stimulus. When the stimuli vary in temperature, the psychological judgment space consists of a single dimension ranging from cold to hot. When the stimuli are colors, the psychological judgment space consists of the dimensions of brightness, saturation, and hue. When the stimuli are auditory, the psychological judgment space includes loudness and pitch dimensions. When the stimuli are persons, the psychological judgment space includes dimensions of pleasure and arousal. As with temperature, colors, and tones, the full story is more complicated, but these two dimensions are essential to understanding the observer's perception of another person. Other dimensions might be involved; something like potency, power, or control seems a likely candidate.

When the two dimensions of pleasure and arousal are treated as axes of a Cartesian space, Figure 13.1 results. The horizontal dimension ranges from displeasure (misery, unhappiness) at one end through a neutral point to pleasure (happiness, contentment) at the other end. The vertical dimension ranges from sleep (drowsiness, lethargy) through the same neutral point to extreme arousal (agitation, frenzy). The pleasure and arousal dimensions are thus bipolar, in the same sense that most perceptual dimensions are. The neutral point is established at a point of central tendency, the adaptation level (Helson, 1964). A parallel would be hot and cold, which has a neutral point at its center, with increasing cold to one side and increasing hot to the other. The arousal dimension also has a natural interpretation where sleep corresponds to zero, and with degrees of arousal increasing from that point. Alternatively, arousal could as well be described as bipolar, with the neutral point corresponding to an average wakeful state, with increasing arousal to one side and increasing sleepiness to the other. The parallel is to loudness, a psychological dimension that can be described either as having a natural zero point (silence) with increasing degrees of loudness, or, alternatively, as having an adaptation level with degrees of quietness on one side and loudness on the other. An instrument for the judgment of pleasure and arousal is available (Russell, Weiss, & Mendelsohn, 1989).

These two dimensions describe primitive and universal aspects of person perception found across a range of cultural and language backgrounds (Russell, 1991b). If pleasure and arousal are related to the evaluation and activity dimensions of the semantic differential (Osgood, 1966), then the universality of these dimensions is firmly established. Moreover, pleasure and arousal dimensions can be found in the study of facial expressions (Adolphs, Tranel, Damasio, & Damasio, 1994, 1995; Kring & Sloan, 1991; Manstead & Edwards, 1992; Russell & Bullock, 1986; Russell & Fehr, 1987). For example, these two dimensions account for the judgments of similarity made by 2-year-olds shown facial expressions of emotion (Russell & Bullock, 1986). At two years of age, these children do not yet know the labels for the so-called basic emotions.

Any emotional stimulus – faces, words, tones of voice, postures, emotion-eliciting situations, actions (fight or flight) – can be placed in (given a value in) the pleasure-arousal space. Like all perceptual judgments, placement in the space of Figure 13.1 is not absolute but relative. Thus, the same face appears happier alongside a "sad" expression, sadder alongside a "happy" expression (Russell & Fehr, 1987; Russell, 1991a). This is not to say that any stimulus face can take on any value but to acknowledge that facial expressions do not come with a single value.

Facial Action Units in pleasure-arousal space

What emotional meaning does the observer attribute to specific facial movements? Snodgrass (1992) approached this question by combining the description of facial movement provided by Ekman and Friesen's

Table 13.1 *Pleasure and Arousal scores for single Action Units*

AU	Description	Pleasure	Arousal
1	Inner brow raised	−1.92	−0.85
2	Outer brow raised	1.85	2.11
4	Brow furrowed	−2.00	1.23
5	Upper eyelid raised	−1.19	3.04
6	Cheek raised	1.46	.73
7	Lower eyelid raised	−1.85	.58
9	Nose wrinkled	−2.33	2.33
10	Upper lip raised	−3.67	1.97
15	Lip corner depressed	−2.26	−.63
17	Chin raised	−.93	.60
46	Wink	1.19	.54

Note. Values shown are those obtained for a face with the Action Unit minus the same face with no Action Unit. Each scale is numbered 1 to 9. Thus, the potential range of the difference would be −8 to +8. In practice, the neutral face falls near the middle of the scale; thus, the effective range of the difference is −4 to +4.

(1978) Facial Action Coding System (FACS) with the dimensional approach to emotional meaning just outlined. Thus, she chose as her stimuli not the seven prototype facial configurations featured in the standard view but the entire set of possible muscle movements. Specifically, she used what in FACS are the basic units, individual facial movements ("Action Units" or AUs), each of which is numbered and objectively described. Second, she chose as her response space not the labels for prototypic "basic" emotions featured in the standard view but the dimensional approach described previously. In this way, Snodgrass began to compile a dictionary of the meaning of elemental facial movements.

Some representative results are shown in Table 13.1. Each row corresponds to a different AU. For example, the first row concerns AU 1, which is the raising of the inner sections of the brow. The pleasure score shown is the mean rating (on a 9-point scale) of a face showing AU 1 minus the mean rating of the same face showing no AUs. In other words, the pleasure score shown is relative to the rating of the same face with a neutral expression. The arousal score is similarly defined relative to the same neutral face. The third row shows her results for AU 4, which is a furrowing of the brows: Subjects rated the expresser as 2 points less pleasant and as 1 point more aroused with this expression than without. The fourth row shows the results for AU 5, which is a raising of the upper eyelids: Subjects rated the expresser as 1 point less pleasant and

Table 13.2 *Pleasure and Arousal scores for combinations of Action Units*

AU	Description	Pleasure	Arousal
1 + 2	Whole brow raised	.85	2.85
1 + 4	Inner brow raised and furrowed	−2.58	.12
1 + 2 + 4	Whole brow raised and furrowed	−1.39	.61
1 + 2 + 5	Whole brow raised + upper eyelid raised	.27	3.58
4 + 5	Brow furrowed + upper eyelid raised	−.66	1.16
5 + 7	Upper and lower eyelids raised	−2.04	2.73

Note. Value given is the difference between the face showing the configuration minus the rating of the same face showing no visible Action Units.

3 points more aroused. Both AU4 and AU5 thus resulted in the expresser appearing more distressed (the combination of displeasure and arousal; Figure 13.1) but with a difference: The major change with AU 4 lies on the pleasure dimension, whereas the major change with AU 5 lies on the arousal dimension.

Action Units sometimes occur in combination. Table 13.2 shows some preliminary results for combinations. In this way, we approach the full prototype configurations, the "facial expressions of emotion." Figure 13.2 shows how eight facial configurations can be placed in the pleasure-arousal space. Thus, the emotion words of Figure 13.1 label the corresponding faces of Figure 13.2.

Snodgrass's results for single Action Units are illustrated when Figure 13.2 is thought of as consisting of rows and columns. In the left column, the downturned mouths and furrowed brows are interpreted as signs of displeasure. In the right column, smooth brows and upturned mouths (smiles) are the signs of pleasure. (Recall Darwin's principle of Antithesis: Opposite states of mind result in expressions opposite in appearance.) Within each column, arousal rises from the bottom to the top. In the bottom row, lowered eyelids and lowered muscle tone convey lower arousal. In the topmost row, widened eyes, raised brows, and increased muscle activity generally convey increasing arousal. (Figure 13.2 suggests that the jaw might convey two very different messages depending on the rest of the face. When the face conveys low arousal, a jaw drop would probably convey even lower arousal – presumably a loss of normal control that occurs in drowsiness or sleep. When the face conveys at least moderate arousal, then dropping the jaw conveys even higher arousal – presumably excess arousal produces a temporary loss of normal control.)

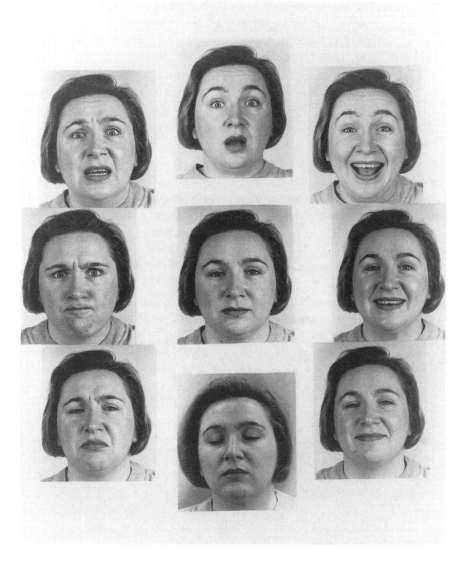

Figure 13.2. Eight facial expressions in the Pleasure-Arousal space of Figure 13.1.

Judgments of emotion categories from faces

Judgments of quasi-physical information, pleasure, and arousal are automatic, effortless inferences that our perceptual system imposes on a facial pattern. But the cognitive processing of the face does not stop at this first stage. The observer can, with more effort and attention, attempt to make further inferences from the facial information. The observer can ask, for example, is the facial expression spontaneous or deliberate? Am I being deceived or manipulated? What is the expresser about to do? What is she thinking? What does she want? What emotion is she feeling? What is the state of her mental and physical health? What kind of person is she? It is at this second stage that categories of emotion (*anger, fear, jealousy, shame, hope, embarrassment*) enter the story.

In the psychology of emotion, a traditional debate has pitted categories of emotion against dimensions. Actually, both sides acknowledge the other, and the debate is not headed toward an either/or solution. My account is dimensional in the sense that dimensions are basic and primary, categories secondary and derived. Dimensions are automatic, elemental (they cannot be further decomposed), and universal; categories of emotion require effort, are complex (they can be analyzed into features), and are, to some degree, variable with language and culture (Russell, 1991b; Wierzbicka, 1992). Dimensions are fundamental, being presupposed by categories such as *anger* and *fear*. Categories such as *anger* and *fear* are not fundamental but depend on prior perception of dimensions. (See Russell & Bullock, 1986, for an elaboration of this point of view.)

Return to Figure 13.1. The regions of the space (combinations of pleasure and arousal) can be named, and they reveal the relevance of this space to emotion. Indeed, under various names and with slightly different interpretations, these two ubiquitous dimensions are key concepts in various accounts of emotion (Lang, 1995; Mandler, 1984; Watson & Tellegen, 1985). Each category of emotion has a prototypical value on pleasure and arousal but actually covers a fairly large region. As with color names, so with emotion names: The applicability of any name spreads in a circle from a focal point as do ripples from a pebble dropped in a pond. In the specific version of the two-dimensional model used here, known as the *circumplex*, categories of emotions and emotion-related states fall in a roughly circular order around the perimeter of the Cartesian space. In this way, the circumplex specifies the similarity between any two emotion categories. There are many such categories. Tomkins's "basic" emotion categories hold no privileged status; *jealous, excited, frustrated, distress, embarrassed,* and *fatigued* are just as applicable to faces. Rather, categories vary one from another and across individuals in availability.

Now return to Figure 13.2 and examine the quasi-physical information in the faces there. Most faces look as if the woman is looking at something, even staring in some cases. In the unpleasant, moderately aroused face at 9 o'clock, the lips are pressed together, as if in preparation for determined action. Given this additional information, the observer is close to an inference of a hostile emotion. In contrast, suppose that instead of the pressed lips, the same face showed a wrinkling of the nose as if she were smelling or tasting something. Given this information, the observer would be close to an inference of an emotion such as disgust. Or, instead, add to the same face bared teeth as if she is about to bite. The observer would be back to a hostile emotion.

The observer also typically has information about the expresser and the expresser's immediate situation to help infer a specific emotion. Such information determines whether a smile is judged as sincere or faked, friendly or hostile, a sign of embarrassment, nervousness, or sympathy; I return to the role of context further on. Concepts such as *anger* and *fear* are not defined solely in terms of feelings (displeasure and arousal) and behavior (fight and flight). Rather, *anger, fear,* and the like presuppose certain situational antecedents. Shame, guilt, fear, and anger could all be equal in displeasure and arousal but differ in the situations in which these terms are appropriate. One way to think of the meaning of such terms is as a script (a prototype) containing information about the entire sequence of events involved (Fehr & Russell, 1984; Russell, 1991c). Thus, a specific category of emotion is attributed to the expresser on the basis of all the information obtained about the expresser and how well that information matches a prototype for that emotion.

Do faces signal basic emotions?

The last section outlined what I think is a reasonable account of what happens when an observer finds emotional meaning in the face of another. No one would deny that the observer perceives from the face quasi-physical information such as shouting or staring. I doubt that anyone would want to deny that the observer perceives faces in terms of pleasure and arousal. Moreover, my account includes occasions when the observer infers such specific categories of emotion as anger and fear. I have tried for an account that is parsimonious in its assumptions. But is it perhaps too parsimonious?

Proponents of the standard view might well accept the positive assertions made so far but balk at the suggestion that such an account is complete. Perhaps they might even concede that my account suffices for most single Action Units, and even for some combinations about which their account is silent. (If they would concede these points, I would be quite pleased because I believe that, except when we are pretending, single Action Units and small combinations are pretty much all that occur in daily life.) Proponents of the standard view would nevertheless insist that certain specific "facial expressions of emotion" are special. They are signals. Faced with one of the hypothesized facial signals, observers see more than just quasi-physical information and pleasure and arousal – they recognize (directly according to Buck, innately according to Izard, universally according to Ekman) the specific emotion signaled. The special power of these signals, the notion that in them observers see more, is precisely what separated the Tomkins–Ekman–Izard account from its historical predecessors. Ekman, Friesen, and Ellsworth (1972) and Izard (1971) contrasted their emotion-signaling account explicitly with the dimensional account that had been formulated by the Woodworth school and with the contextualist views of Landis and Sherman.

Most readers are probably convinced that the proponent of the standard view has a point here. Why not, you might be asking, allow that some special facial patterns signal specific emotions? I am not convinced, and here I explain why. I begin by quickly summarizing six reasons. I then elaborate on a seventh.

Six objections to the standard account

First, producing faces. Do happy people smile, or angry people frown, unless they deliberately mask or inhibit the facial movement? I can find no evidence showing that the answer is *yes*, that human beings spontaneously produce facial patterns that reliably indicate specific discrete emotions. I realize that most readers will be skeptical of my assertion. If you are among them, then even if you read nothing else in this book, read chapter 11, this volume, by Fernández-Dols & Ruiz-Belda. This is one aspect of facial production (encoding) that must affect our analysis of perception (decoding). The observer may not have the benefit of a facial signal that reliably marks the expresser's specific emotion.

Second, emotion categories. Universal and innate recognition of basic emotions from facial signals presupposes that all human beings recognize the same categories of emotion. *Happiness, fear, anger, jealousy,* and the other categories of emotion named in the English language seem so natural and so obvious that it might seem that all people must divide the emotions as English speakers do – many of psychology's major theorists of emotion (including Tomkins and Izard) assumed so. On this presupposition, *happiness, fear,* and so on are natural kinds.

Yet anthropologists and linguists have offered examples that appear to violate this assumption (Briggs, 1970; Howell, 1981; Levy, 1973; Lutz, 1982; Rosaldo, 1980; see Russell, 1991b, and Wierzbicka, 1992, for reviews). For instance, Briggs (1970) spent 17 months in the Canadian Arctic studying an Inuit band, the Utku. She concluded, "Utku do not classify the emotions exactly as English speakers do; their words for various feelings cannot in every case be tidily subsumed under our words" (p. 311). For example, fear is not one category of emotion for the Utku, for they distinguish *iqhi* (feelings of present physical danger) from *kappia* (anticipation of future physical injury) from *ilira* (fear of social problems). There is no reason to believe that *iqhi, kappia,* and *ilira* are thought of by the Utku as one type of emotion. Similarly, love is not one category of emotion for the Utku, for they distinguish *niviuq* (the romantic feeling between lovers) from *naklik* (love for a baby or small animal, or God's love for humanity). *Niviuq* and *naklik* are not thought of as the same emotion.

Third, single-emotion signals. Tomkins theorized that each facial signal codes precisely one emotion. Yet observers see more than one emotion in the same face. Given the opportunity, observers indicate that each face expresses various emotions to various degrees (Russell & Bullock, 1986).

Fourth, ecology. We have no evidence on how often and in what circumstances the seven prototype facial expressions offered by Ekman and Friesen (1976) or Matsumoto and Ekman (1988) actually occur. When Izard (1977) writes that humans are always in some emotional state, one might anticipate that the corresponding prototype facial expressions would be common. Yet with the exception of the smile, researchers have rarely studied the perception of naturally occurring expressions; the facial expressions studied have been posed. Again, other than the smile, in my experience, the kinds of expressions seen in Ekman and Friesen's (1976) photographs are rare (Carroll & Russell, in press) – with one exception. They are seen in the theater, as poses or pantomimes, created to convey without words. Marcel Marceau can mime a marvelous range of actions, emotions, thoughts, intentions, and beliefs without uttering a word. However powerful, Marceau's performances do not show that his actions actually occur outside the theater. Rather, they are stylized movements created for the purpose of conveying meaning to an audience. (You could mime hunger by rubbing your belly, but that does not mean that hungry people rub their bellies.) All of us engage in amateur drama when we tell stories to each other, and even when we listen to stories (Bavelas & Chovil, chapter 15, this volume). My guess is that the seven "facial expressions of emotion" that have been studied so extensively are melodramatic poses used largely as mimes as we tell each other stories during our daily conversations.

More generally, we must ask a series of ecological questions. In what frequency and in what circumstances does each hypothesized "facial expression of emotion" occur? In what frequency and in what circumstances does other facial behavior occur? What information is available to observers when they attribute emotions to others? These are simple empirical questions, but I suspect that answers will not suggest the postulation of an innate, highly functional emotion signaling system.

Fifth, universality. The evidence that is purported to show universal recognition of basic emotions from facial expressions is in dispute. The technical issues involved have been discussed at length (Ekman, 1994; Izard, 1994; Russell, 1994, 1995), and I do not repeat that discussion here, except to say that I do not believe that the evidence favors the Tomkins–Izard–Ekman account over various alternatives. (Indeed, Ekman, 1994, seems now to acknowledge that universality demonstrated so far is a statistical trend.) Although many writers cite the evidence on universality as favoring Tomkins's account, they do not specify how the evidence supports Tomkins's account over any of the alternatives, including the one outlined in this chapter. Frijda and Tcherkassof (chapter 4, this volume) write that facial configurations have an *affinity* (and no more than an affinity) with emotion categories. Such an affinity, I suggest, can be accounted for through the mediation of quasi-physical information, pleasure, and arousal.

To illustrate, return to Ekman and Friesen's (1971) study of the Fore society in Papua New Guinea. One story told to the Fore was about someone who sees a dangerous wild pig. The Fore were then asked to find the picture of the protagonist. Recognition of emotion was said to occur because the Fore selected the "facial expression of fear" more often than predicted by chance. One problem is that the Fore might have selected the "fear" photograph simply because it showed someone highly aroused staring at something. Consistent with this interpretation, the Fore were as likely to select the "facial expression of surprise" (which also includes high arousal and a stare) as that of "fear." Although wild pigs are dangerous, they are not very surprising to the Fore.

Sixth, children. Although babies can discriminate different patterns of facial movement (Nelson & deHaan, chapter 8, this volume), I believe that the emotional meaning that they perceive in faces can be described in terms of pleasure and arousal rather than discrete emotions. It is not until 3 or 4 years of age that children begin to infer adultlike discrete emotions from faces (Russell & Bullock, 1986).

Context

My seventh objection concerns the meaning attributed to even the prototype "facial expressions of emotions" even by adult observers even in our own culture. I challenge the assumption that such facial expressions are constant in meaning. Observers attribute different emotions – even different so-called basic emotions – to one and the same facial configuration, depending on context.

I distinguish two kinds of context: the expresser's and the observer's. From the point of view of the observer, the *expresser's context* consists of the expresser and events in the expresser's life surrounding the particular facial movement in question: what sort of person the expresser is, what the expresser is doing or saying, what the expresser did and said in the immediate past, what situation the expresser is in, and so on. The *observer's context* consists of the events surrounding the act of observation: what other faces the observer has seen, what question is asked, what has been seen before. In research, the observer's context is strictly controlled by the experimenter and includes all aspects of the method through which the observations are gathered. In everyday situations, the expresser's and the observer's context are typically confounded. In experi-

The face	The standard interpretation	My interpretation

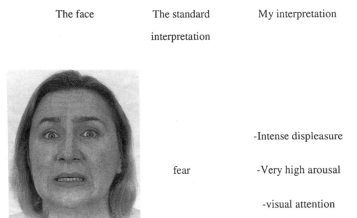

		-Intense displeasure
	fear	-Very high arousal
		-visual attention

Figure 13.3. Two interpretations for the "facial expressions of fear."

mental situations, the two are generally kept quite separate through photographs and other means of control.

The expresser's context

Consider the facial expression shown in Figure 13.3. According to Ekman and Friesen, this is an "expression of fear." Our human ancestors, if they saw this configuration at all, would have seen it embedded in some naturally occurring context. They would almost always have some additional information about the situation in which it occurred. Tomkins, Izard, and Ekman would presumably predict that this facial signal would be recognized as "fear" across a reasonable range of such natural contexts. This prediction is necessary for the hypothesized communication function of facial signals, for the hypothesized evolutionary origin of those signals (Izard, chapter 3, this volume), and for Ekman and Friesen's (1975) hypothesized learning mechanism whereby children acquire the ability to recognize facial expressions by seeing them in the right context.

Other considerations lead to the same prediction – provided that the face actually signals fear. In the logical inference of emotion from facial and situational information, facial information should have a normative precedence over situational information because the facial reaction is part of the very reaction being judged, whereas the situation is not. The situation provides the observer with only a generalized guidepost as to how most people might react, but, of course, different individuals can react differently to the same situation. Their reactions depend on their expectations, construals, and so on. So, if the face signals fear, then, given the normative precedence of facial information, the observer should infer fear whatever the situation might suggest.

On my interpretation, in contrast, it is the woman's pleasure, arousal, and quasi-physical information that takes normative precedence over any expectations derived from the woman's situation. But because the face does not signal a specific emotion, the face does not take normative precedence as to the specific emotion inferred. The displeasure, high arousal, and staring of Figure 13.3 should be compatible with a range (although a limited range) of individual emotions (those from about 9 to 12 o'clock in the circumplex of Figure 13.1).

Now consider a small study (Carroll & Russell, 1996) that put these contrasting predictions to the test. The observer is given a story, such as the following:

> This is a story of a woman who wanted to treat her sister to the most expensive, exclusive restaurant in their city. Months ahead, she made a reservation. When she and her sister arrived, they were told by the maitre d' that their table would be ready in 45 minutes. Still, an hour passed, and no table. Other groups arrived and were seated after a short wait. The woman went to the maitre d' and reminded him of her reservation. He said that he'd do his best. Ten minutes later, a local celebrity and his date arrived and were immediately shown to a table. Another couple arrived and were seated immediately. The woman went to the maitre d', who said that all the tables were now full, and that it might be another hour before anything was available.

The observer is then shown a photograph of a woman, supposedly the protagonist as she appeared at the end of the story. The expression shown is similar to that seen in Figure 13.3. The actual photograph used was one published by Matsumoto and Ekman (1988) as an "expression of fear." The observer is told to look carefully at the woman in the photograph and is asked, "What emotion is the woman feeling? Please choose one term from the following list: *anger, disgust, fear, happiness, sadness, surprise.*"

The control group saw the same face, but did not hear the story; as expected, they chose *fear*. But the experimental group, which heard the story, did not. Instead, 60% chose *anger*; 0% chose *fear*. Note that although the story suggested anger, it did not exclude fear, and so, if the face really signaled fear, this result would be baffling.

Carroll and Russell also examined cases when the face was paired with a situation judged to elicit a non–basic emotion, and the observer was allowed to select a term for a non–basic emotion. The result was an even

The face	The standard interpretation	My interpretation

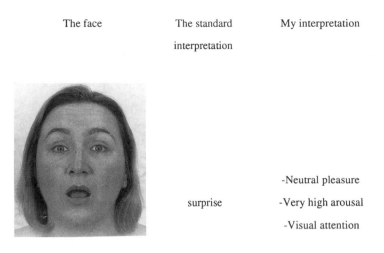

| | surprise | -Neutral pleasure
-Very high arousal
-Visual attention |

Figure 13.4. Two interpretations for the "facial expression of surprise."

stronger influence of the situation. Situational dominance remained even when the situation was described more ambiguously so that the face alone was the far clearer source of information. To illustrate, Figure 13.4 shows a facial expression thought on the standard view to signal "surprise." My interpretation is that it conveys high arousal, a neutral value on pleasantness–unpleasantness, and very high attention. This face, paired with an appropriate situation, would therefore be interpreted as conveying any specific emotion consistent with high arousal, neutral valence, and high attention (an arc on the top of the circumplex of Figure 13.1). Carroll and Russell asked whether it would convey hope. Observers were told the following story:

> This is a story of a woman who went to the horse races to bet five hundred dollars. She bet it all on horse number 7. For her to win, the horse has to finish first or second. She is now watching the horses make the final turn down the stretch to the finish line. Horse number 7 is in second place.

The actual photograph was one published by Ekman as a "facial expression of surprise." The modal response was *hope*. Again, the story did not exclude surprise, and this result too would be baffling if the face of Figure 13.4 really signaled surprise.

The full study (Carroll & Russell, 1996) included 22 replications of this effect with different facial expressions and stories. In every case, the modal emotion chosen coincided with the prediction based on the situation rather than on the face. The situational dominance found consistently in this study contrasts with the general finding of facial dominance found in previous studies on this topic, although this literature is subject to a variety of deep problems (see Fernández-Dols & Carroll, chapter 12, this volume).

In summary, given the normative precedence of facial over situational information, if facial expressions actually signaled one specific emotion, then the observer can be predicted to recognize that specific emotion, whatever other emotion is suggested by the situation. This prediction provides a means of testing the standard theory, because the present account makes a different prediction. If the facial expression does not signal any specific emotion but rather provides quasi-physical information, pleasure, and arousal, then situational information would determine the specific emotion inferred by the observer. Carroll and Russell's (1996) data supported the present account.

The observer's context

In response to the results just presented, it might be argued that the standard account is nevertheless true for a facial expression seen *alone*. And indeed, almost all research on the hypothesized "facial expressions of emotions" have presented faces with no information whatsoever about the expresser's context. Of course, until the invention of the camera, few ever saw a facial expression alone. In the low-tech world of our ancestors, the observer saw a facial expression embedded in some context. Think how rare it would be that an observer could catch a glimpse of a stranger's face just at the moment of a facial expression but see nothing before or after, see nothing else of the stranger's body or behavior, and know nothing at all about the stranger's circumstances.

In any case, Izard (chapter 3, this volume) argues that we need to study judgments of the face alone in order to examine "the independent signal value of the facial signals." In this way, we can understand how the observer combines facial information with situational information in arriving at a final emotion judgment. This argument assumes that before being combined, facial and situational information are each independently judged as to the emotion implied. I doubt that, but for the sake of argument, let us accept the idea that we should study judgments of the face alone.

The extensive research on judgments of the face alone is widely cited as showing that each of the seven prototypical facial expressions signals one specific emotion. I argue that the meaning attributed to a given facial stimulus even when seen alone still depends on context – in this case, the observer's context. Even if we can technically strip the facial expression from every aspect of the expresser's context, we cannot strip observers from theirs.

The notion that the face alone has but one specific meaning (a specific basic emotion, on the standard account) presupposes that the meaning attributed to that face is invariant across a reasonable range of observational contexts – invariant, for example, across a range of appropriate methods. Recent evidence shows that the meaning attributed to a face alone varies with method.

The relativity of judgment. Judgments of a particular face are not absolute but relative to what other faces the observer happens to see. For example, emotion judgments depend on faces seen previously during the experiment. A relatively neutral face seems sad alongside someone else's happier face but happy alongside someone else's sadder face. This relativity effect is not limited to neutral faces: Judgments of even prototypical facial expressions of emotion are relative to what other faces are seen. Such relativity effects have now been reported by a number of different investigators (Manis, 1967, 1971; Russell, 1991a; Russell & Fehr, 1987; Tanaka-Matsumi, Nelson, Attivissimo, & D'Urso, 1995; Thayer, 1980a, b).

A corollary of this relativity effect correctly predicts that different results can be found in a within-subject than in a between-subjects design. For example, Ekman and Friesen's "facial expression of contempt" was judged as contempt in a within-subject design (when the "contempt" expression was judged relative to six previously seen facial stimuli), but it was judged as disgust in a between-subjects design (when no prior facial expressions were available for comparison) (Russell, 1993). Russell (1994) reported follow-up data showing a small but reliable general difference between within- and between-subjects designs.

Response format. Much of the evidence that observers recognize one basic emotion from each facial expression was gathered with a response format in which observers were given little choice: They are required to select one basic emotion. When observers are allowed to respond in any manner they want, they sometimes tell stories, anticipate behaviors, or describe a situation (Frijda, 1953). For example, on seeing one face, the observer said, "as if looking at something with fixed attention, a game or something tense, two cars which almost get into collision, but nothing happens" (Frijda, 1953, p. 314). In most cases, no specific emotion was mentioned at all.

In chapter 4 of this volume, Frijda and Tcherkassof interpret this evidence as nevertheless consistent with the observer's having made an emotional interpretation of the expresser's face. The question, of course, is exactly what is meant by "emotional." My interpretation is that the observer focused on the quasi-physical information, the hedonic value, and degree of arousal conveyed by the face; the observer did not spontaneously perceive a specific emotion in the face. My guess is that Frijda's method exposed a part of the natural sequence in which facial information is interpreted. First and very quickly, quasi-physical information is perceived. Second, pleasantness and arousal are perceived. Next, a story is constructed that builds on and explains the quasi-physical, pleasure, arousal information (if the face is staring, then the story might be "as if looking at something with fixed attention, a game or something tense"). (Ordinarily, of course, the observer knows something of the expresser and his or her context, and the story is built upon that information as well.) Next, and especially if asked, the observer attributes a specific emotion to the expresser on the basis of the story constructed.

Even with a forced-choice response format, small changes in the list of options can result in dramatic changes in the apparent judgment. For example, consider one of Ekman's "anger" expressions included in Carroll and Russell's (1996) study, described earlier. In developing this photograph, Ekman and Friesen had found that a majority of observers chose *anger* when given the choice of *happy, surprised, afraid, angry, sad,* or *disgusted*. Carroll and Russell added four more options: *puzzled, determined, in pain,* and *hope*. The percentage of observers who chose *anger* for this particular "facial expression of anger" dropped to 0. Earlier, Russell (1993) provided examples showing that such effects are common and systematic. And when observers make quantitative ratings, they indicate that the face expresses not one emotion but rather various emotions to various degrees (Russell & Bullock, 1986).

Conclusion. Past research has generally been conducted under the influence of a theory in which certain facial expressions were thought to have but one precoded interpretation. Accumulating evidence challenges that assumption. The meaning attributed to even the seven "facial expressions of emotion" varies with observational context. My guess is that the meaning attributed to naturally occurring facial expressions is even more context-dependent. If so, you might be wondering, how have researchers found consensus in studies with which everyone is familiar?

The conclusion that to each prototype facial expression is attributed one basic emotion stems from a research tradition in which the face is typically seen in one context: The observer is given no information about the expresser's context, sees a specific set of other still photographs with which he or she can compare the target face, and is forced to choose one from a list of 7 ± 2 "basic" emotions. These features of the experimental method channel different interpretations of a given face into one specific category. Justification for using such a method would require evidence that a single interpretation emerges across a variety of methods. In fact, the opposite has occurred; the more you change methods, the more you change the results.

Conclusion

Each of us naturally monitors the faces of those around us, and we derive valuable information by doing so. None of us, however, scientist or non-scientist, knows exactly why people move their faces as they do. It is a matter of interpretation. As observers, we consider the available information and form a hypothesis or two that best accounts for that information. The meaning seen in a face is thus not determined by the face alone but by how the features of the face are related to everything else known about the expresser. In this way, sometimes, we accurately detect the emotion of another, *and*, sometimes, we project an emotion onto the face of another. But in most cases, we are between these extremes, making a reasonable guess.

The observer is in an epistemological position analogous to that of a scientist, who must consider all the information available on a particular topic and then form a hypothesis that best accounts for that information. The hypothesis is not fixed by the data, and different scientists often disagree on the best interpretation. For instance, scientists have disagreed about what and how emotional meaning is attributed to facial expressions.

In the attempt to bring the perception of emotion from facial patterns into the laboratory, psychologists have understandably used still photographs, posed melodramatic expressions, and simple paper-and-pencil judgment tasks. In the 1970s, a research program offered a coherent account of facial behavior and emotions, together with dramatic evidence supporting the account. The methods used to gather that evidence have their place but cannot tell the whole story and are capable of providing a distorted image of what happens in natural settings. I believe that when scientists study people's natural interpretation of the spontaneous facial movements seen in daily life, a very different picture will emerge.

Spontaneous facial movements to be found in daily settings are mild, often single Action Units, sometimes two units combined, but very rarely the types of extreme configurations published by Ekman and Friesen (1976). Their interpretation depends on the context.

I have offered my reasons for being skeptical of the standard account and outlined an alternative to it. I realize that most readers will be reluctant to abandon the idea that to each facial expression corresponds one specific precoded emotion. In our cultural traditions, smiling, glaring, and crying faces are symbols (*emblems* in Efron's, 1941, terms) for happiness, anger, and grief. Our most revered writers from Aristotle to Darwin wrote about facial expressions of emotion. The appeal of the idea does not derive from these authorities, but these historical endorsements do underscore how plausible we find the idea. No matter how plausible an idea seems, evidence is still required. In offering my own account, I do not mean to imply that the jury is in or that all the needed evidence is in. No definitive experiments have been carried out, and in critical areas, evidence is largely lacking. I do believe that, on balance, the available evidence is more encouraging to my account than to Tomkins's.

Still, the most useful message to find in my words would not be faith in my account but skepticism about any one account. Faced with skeptics, those who find merit in an idea will be motivated to gather the evidence needed. I hope that my skeptical questioning of the standard view stimulates believers and nonbelievers alike to undertake a thorough study of natural facial expressions and their natural interpretation. Those who are skeptical of any one account will pay closer attention to all the alternative views proposed throughout this volume and elsewhere. Common wisdom is that old ideas are accepted until better ones come along. In some cases, however, better ideas might be ignored because old ones are assumed true.

Acknowledgments

I thank Deborah von Lipinski and Lorraine Russell for lending me their talents as model and artist. I thank the series editors and the authors of other chapters for their comments on a draft of this chapter and Lisa Ferguson for her help in everything. This work was facilitated by a grant from the Social Sciences and Humanities Research Council of Canada.

References

Adolphs, R., Tranel, D., Damasio, H., & Damasio, A. (1994). Impaired recognition of emotion in facial expressions following bilateral damage to the human amygdala. *Nature, 372*, 669–672.

Adolphs, R., Tranel, D., Damasio, H., & Damasio, A. (1995). Fear and the human amygdala. *Journal of Neuroscience, 15,* 5879–5891.

Briggs, J. L. (1970). *Never in anger: Portrait of an Eskimo family.* Cambridge, MA: Harvard University Press.

Bruner, J. S., & Tagiuri, R. (1954). The perception of people. In G. Lindzey (Ed.), *Handbook of social psychology* (Vol. 2). Cambridge, MA: Addison-Wesley.

Buzby, D. E. (1924). The interpretation of facial expressions. *American Journal of Psychology, 35,* 602–604.

Carroll, J. M., & Russell, J. A. (1996). Do facial expressions signal specific emotions? Judging the face in context. *Journal of Personality and Social Psychology, 70,* 205–218.

Carroll, J. M., & Russell, J. A. (in press). Facial expressions in Hollywood's portrayal of emotion. *Journal of Personality and Social Psychology.*

Cook, D. A. (1981). *A history of narrative film.* New York: Norton.

Darwin, C. (1965). *The expression of the emotions in man and animals.* Chicago: University of Chicago Press. (Original work published 1872)

Efron, D. (1941). *Gesture and environment.* New York: King's Crown Press.

Ekman, P. (1972). Universal and cultural differences in facial expressions of emotions. In J. K. Cole (Ed.), *Nebraska symposium on motivation,* 1971 (pp. 207–283). Lincoln: University of Nebraska Press.

Ekman, P. (1975, Sept.). Face muscles talk every language. *Psychology Today,* 35–39.

Ekman, P. (1994). Strong evidence for universals in facial expressions: A reply to Russell's mistaken critique. *Psychological Bulletin, 115,* 268–287.

Ekman, P., & Friesen, W. V. (1971). Constants across cultures in the face and emotion. *Journal of Personality and Social Psychology, 17,* 124–129.

Ekman, P., & Friesen, W. V. (1975). *Unmasking the face.* Englewood Cliffs, NJ: Prentice-Hall.

Ekman, P., & Friesen, W. V. (1976). *Pictures of facial affect.* Palo Alto, CA: Consulting Psychologists Press.

Ekman, P., & Friesen, W. V. (1978). *The Facial Action Coding System.* Palo Alto, CA: Consulting Psychologists Press.

Ekman, P., & Friesen, W. V. (1978). A new pan-cultural expression of emotion. *Motivation and Emotion, 10,* 159–168.

Ekman, P., & Friesen, W. V., & Ellsworth, P. (1972). *Emotion in the human face.* New York: Pergamon.

Fehr, B., & Russell, J. A. (1984). Concept of emotion viewed from a prototype perspective. *Journal of Experimental Psychology: General, 113,* 464–486.

Feleky, A. M. (1914). The expression of the emotions. *Psychological Review, 21,* 33–41.

Frijda, N. H. (1953). The understanding of facial expression of emotion. *Acta Psychologica, 9,* 294–362.

Helson, H. (1964). *Adaptation-level theory.* New York: Harper & Row.

Howell, S. (1981). Rules not words. In P. Heelas & A. Lock (Eds.), *Indigenous psychologies: The anthropology of the self* (pp. 133–143). San Diego, CA: Academic Press.

Izard, C. E. (1971). *The face of emotion.* New York: Appleton-Century-Crofts.

Izard, C. E. (1977). *Human emotions.* New York: Plenum.

Izard, C. E. (1994). Innate and universal facial expressions: Evidence from developmental and cross-cultural research. *Psychological Bulletin, 115,* 288–299.

Klineberg, O. (1938). Emotional expression in Chinese literature. *Journal of Abnormal and Social Psychology, 33,* 517–520.

Klineberg, O. (1940). *Social psychology.* New York: Holt.

Kring, A. M., & Sloan, D. (1991). *The facial expression coding system (FACES): A user's guide.* Unpublished manuscript.

Landis, C. (1924). Studies of emotional reactions: II. General behavior and facial expression. *Journal of Comparative Psychology, 4,* 447–509.

Lang, P. J. (1995). The emotion probe. *American Psychologist, 50,* 372–385.

Levy, R. I. (1973). *Tahitians.* Chicago: University of Chicago Press.

Lutz, C. (1982). The domain of emotion words in Ifaluk. *American Ethnologist, 9,* 113–128.

Mandler, G. (1984). *Mind and body: Psychology of emotion and stress.* New York: Norton.

Manis, M. (1967). Context effects in communication. *Journal of Personality and Social Psychology, 5,* 326–334.

Manis, M. (1971). Context effects in communication. In M. H. Appley (Ed.), *Adaptation level theory* (pp. 237–255). New York: Academic Press.

Manstead, A. S. R., & Edwards, R. (1992). Communicative aspects of children's emotional competence. In K. T. Strongman (Ed.), *International review of studies on emotion* (Vol. 2). Chichester: Wiley.

Matsumoto, D., & Ekman, P. (1988). *Japanese and Caucasian facial expressions of emotion (JACFEE)* [Slide set and brochure]. Available from first author, San Francisco State University.

Osgood, C. E. (1966). Dimensionality of the semantic space for communication via facial expressions. *Scandinavian Journal of Psychology, 7,* 1–30.

Pudovkin, V. I. (1970). *Film technique and film acting.* New York: Grove. (Original work published 1929)

Rosaldo, M. Z. (1980). *Knowledge and passion: Ilongot notions of self and social life.* Cambridge, England: Cambridge University Press.

Russell, J. A. (1991a). The contempt expression and the relativity thesis. *Motivation and Emotion, 15,* 149–168.

Russell, J. A. (1991b). Culture and the categorization of emotions. *Psychological Bulletin, 110,* 426–450.

Russell, J. A. (1991c). In defense of a prototype approach to emotion concepts. *Journal of Personality and Social Psychology, 60,* 425–438.

Russell, J. A. (1993). Forced-choice response format in the study of facial expression. *Motivation and Emotion, 17,* 41–51.

Russell, J. A. (1994). Is there universal recognition of emotion from facial expression? *Psychological Bulletin, 115,* 102–141.

Russell, J. A. (1995). Facial expressions of emotion: What lies beyond minimal universality? *Psychological Bulletin, 118,* 379–391.

Russell, J. A., & Bullock, M. (1986). Fuzzy concepts and the perception of emotion in facial expressions. *Social Cognition, 4,* 309–341.

Russell, J. A., & Fehr, B. (1987). Relativity in the perception of emotion in facial expressions. *Journal of Experimental Psychology: General, 116,* 223–237.

Russell, J. A., Weiss, A., & Mendelsohn, G. A. (1989). The Affect Grid: A single-item scale of pleasure and arousal. *Journal of Personality and Social Psychology, 57,* 493–502.

Schlosberg, H. (1941). A scale for judgment of facial expressions. *Journal of Experimental Psychology, 29,* 497–510.

Schlosberg, H. (1952). The description of facial expressions in terms of two dimensions. *Journal of Experimental Psychology, 44,* 229–237.

Schlosberg, H. (1954). Three dimensions of emotion. *Psychological Review, 61,* 81–88.

Sherman, M. (1927). The differentiation of emotional responses in infants: II. The ability of observers to judge the emotional characteristics of the crying of infants and of the voice of an adult. *Journal of Comparative Psychology, 7*, 335–351.

Snodgrass, J. (1992). *Judgment of feeling states from facial behavior: A bottom–up approach.* Unpublished doctoral dissertation, University of British Columbia.

Tanaka-Matsumi, J., Nelson, S., Attivissimo, D., D'Urso, T. (1995). Context effects on the judgment of basic emotions in the face. *Motivation and Emotion, 19*, 139–156.

Thayer, S. (1980a). The effect of facial expression sequence upon judgments of emotion. *Journal of Nonverbal Behavior, 5*, 71–79.

Thayer, S. (1980b). The effect of facial expression sequence upon judgments of emotion. *Journal of Social Psychology, 111*, 305–306.

Tomkins, S. S. (1962). *Affect, imagery, consciousness: Vol. 1. The positive affects.* New York: Springer.

Triandis, H. C., & Lambert, W. W. (1958). A restatement and test of Schlosberg's Theory of Emotion with two kinds of subjects from Greece. *Journal of Abnormal and Social Psychology, 56*, 321–328.

Vinacke, W. E. (1949). The judgment of facial expressions by three national-racial groups in Hawaii: I. Caucasian faces. *Journal of Personality, 17*, 407–429.

Watson, D., & Tellegen, A. (1985). Toward a consensual structure of mood. *Psychological Bulletin, 98*, 219–235.

Wierzbicka, A. (1992). *Semantics, culture, and cognition.* New York: Oxford University Press.

Woodworth, R. S. (1938). *Experimental psychology.* New York: Holt.

Woodworth, R. S., & Schlosberg, H. (1954). *Experimental psychology.* New York: Holt, Rinehart, & Winston.

14. Facing others: A social communicative perspective on facial displays

NICOLE CHOVIL

Within the study of human facial displays, there has been considerable interest in their relationship to emotion. There is, however, an emerging view that emphasizes the social nature and communicative functions of facial displays. This approach begins with the assumption that facial displays are expressive *to* another person rather than expressive *of* an underlying state. Instead of examining facial displays as a route into psychological processes, they are followed outward into the social interaction. In this approach, facial displays are analyzed in terms of the messages they convey to others in communicative situations. The display may convey a message by itself (e.g., a smile) or work in conjunction with other communicative acts (e.g., words, gestures, intonation) to convey a more complex message.

In this chapter, I have attempted to bring together the models and empirical data for a social communicative view of human facial displays. In the first section, the differences between the Emotional Expression Approach and the Social Communicative Approach are presented. In the next two sections, empirical studies that approached the study of facial displays from the Social Communicative Perspective are discussed. Although we are far from fully understanding how facial displays function as communicative acts, there are two themes that have received considerable attention: (1) the influence of sender–receiver variables (e.g., eye contact), and (2) the communicative functions of facial displays. In the final section, the implications of this approach are addressed and directions for future investigations are suggested. Readers who are interested in how facial movement conveys meaning in dialogue are referred to chapter 15, by Bavelas and Chovil, this volume.

Differences between the Emotional Expression Approach and the Social Communicative Approach to study of facial displays

The Social Communicative Approach provides an alternative to the Emotional Expression Approach for understanding and studying facial displays. This approach does not deny that facial actions may convey information about emotional reactions but assumes there is a broad domain of information that is conveyed through our displays. Facial expressions of emotion are regarded as a subset of facial displays.

The Emotional Expression and Social Communicative approaches complement each other by providing information about two quite different aspects of facial displays. The Emotional Expression Approach (hereafter referred to as the Emotion Approach) focuses on individual and psychological processes. Facial displays are viewed as "expressions of" underlying emotions. The relationship between the internal emotion and the overt facial behavior is the primary focus of emotion researchers. Social factors are considered important but are viewed as altering the "spontaneous" expression of emotion. For this reason, researchers interested in a better understanding of emotion have often attempted to minimize any social influences.

Within a Communicative Approach, the facial display is regarded as a communicative act that provides information to another party. The social interaction is essential to understanding the occurrence of facial displays. The focus of study also includes the effect of the facial display on the recipient of that display. No assumptions are made about the relationship between the facial display and an underlying emotion.

The two approaches also differ in the hypothesized mechanisms that are proposed to underlie the display's occurrence. Within the emotion perspective, an emotion is set off by a stimulus, and this emotion leads to the facial expression. The communicative value of facial expressions is not the primary explanation underlying the display's occurrence. Spontaneous facial expressions would occur regardless of whether there is a receiver there to see them and are thus assumed to be quite different from other communicative acts (e.g., speech) that are specifically directed to other individuals. Within the Emotion Approach, the facial expression has communicative value only in the sense that it can be used by others as a *sign* of someone's emotional state (i.e., an inference about an emotion is made from the behavior).

Within a communicative approach, facial displays are hypothesized to be *symbolic representations* of a wide variety of meaning. They occur for the benefit of others and enable individuals to communicate effectively and efficiently with others on a variety of topics (i.e., not just emotion). Thus, the sender–receiver relationship is viewed as essential for understanding why facial displays occur. Verbal and nonverbal communicative acts are not regarded as distinct from each other but rather as parts of the same process. The importance of nonverbal elements (including facial displays) in face-to-face communication has been emphasized by many researchers from a variety of disciplines – for example, Birdwhistell (1968, 1970), Blurton-Jones (1972), Duncan and Fiske (1977, 1985), Pike (1972), Poyatos (1980), Sanders (1987), Scherer (1980), and Weiner, Devoe, Rubinow, and Geller (1972).

Various researchers have attempted to develop models of communication that include nonverbal acts. Birdwhistell (1968, 1970), Sanders (1987), and Scherer (1980) characterized communication as a multichannel process. Bavelas and Chovil (1995) and Slama-Cazacu (1976) proposed that face-to-face communication is an integrated set of verbal and nonverbal acts. In much of our face-to-face communication, the various verbal and nonverbal acts appear congruent and work in concert to produce the discourse exchange. To some degree, the acts are specialized in terms of the kinds of information that they are best suited to convey, but at the same time, there is much flexibility in how we express ourselves. Our communication system is also adaptive to the requirements of the situation.

Importance of social factors

Until the late 1970s, there were few studies on facial displays in social settings. In order to observe spontaneous emotion displays unaffected by social factors, investigators attempted to elicit facial expressions of emotion in essentially nonsocial settings. Kraut and Johnston (1979) criticized the field, arguing that

> although workers in this tradition have emphasized the importance of facial expressions in communication and social behaviour, they have rarely studied such communication in natural settings by studying the causes and consequences of [for example] smiling; rather, they have focused on the recognition and verbal labelling of emotions in facial expressions, generally in still photographs. (p. 1540)

Kraut and Johnston's study was a landmark in establishing that adults' facial displays were sensitive to the presence of an available receiver. In four field studies, smiles were observed to occur more frequently when individuals were in social contact with others than when they were not facing or interacting with others. Bowlers were more likely to smile when they were looking at or interacting with others than when they had scored or were facing the pins. Fans at a hockey game were more likely to smile when they were interacting with others than when they were watching the game. People walking outside were more likely to smile if they were talking with or greeting another than if they were not interacting. Overall, the results showed that people smiled more often *to* other people than as a result of some pleasurable experience. Even when there was a pleasurable experience, the smile was directed to other people.

Kraut and Johnston's findings were recently replicated by Fernández-Dols and Ruiz-Belda (1995; chapter 11, this volume). In this study, the researchers analyzed Olympic games gold medalists during different stages of their awards ceremony. Smiles occurred overwhelmingly more often in the social interactive stage than in the two nonsocial stages of the ceremony.

Other types of facial displays also appear to be sensitive to the sociality of the situation. For example, in Brightman, Segal, Werther, and Steiner's (1975) study, subjects were observed as they ate sandwiches containing various levels of sucrose (17, 51, 85, and 136%) or salt (22, 44, 66, and 110%). In the group condition (triads), subjects exhibited heightened facial displays to both types of taste stimuli. There was "no change" in the facial displays of subjects who ate alone, even for the highest levels of sucrose or salt. Brightman et al. concluded that communication was an important factor in the production of facial displays in response to various taste sensations.

Two experimental studies have demonstrated that facial displays were affected by eye contact. In other words, facial displays were more likely to be exhibited if there was a receiver *to see the display* than if there was no receiver available. Bavelas, Black, Lemery, and Mullett (1986) showed that observers' motor mimicry displays (e.g., wincing at someone else's injury) are affected by visual availability of a receiver. These displays were differentially affected depending on whether or not the "victim" made eye contact with the observer. When no eye contact was made, these displays were less likely to occur or were shorter in duration than when eye contact was made.

Schneider and Josephs (1991) found that the frequency of smiles by preschoolers (aged 3½ to almost 6) increased with the possibility of eye contact by the experimenter. Children who played a game while the experimenter sat turned away exhibited fewer smiles than children who played the game while the experimenter sat beside them.

In an attempt to define more precisely the components that make up sociality of communicative situations, Chovil (1991) demonstrated that the likelihood of facial displays was affected by communicative parameters of the situation. Subjects were videotaped as they listened to another subject tell them about a personal close-call experience. There were four conditions: face-to-face, separated by a partition, over the telephone, or alone (listening to a tape recording). Frequency of listeners' motor mimicry displays varied monotonically with the sociality of the four conditions. The highest frequency of listener facial displays was found in the face-to-face condition. Listener facial displays sharply decreased in frequency as the communicative situation became more removed from a full face-to-face interaction.

Within the developmental field, there is evidence that the presence of an available receiver is also important in understanding infants' facial displays. Jones and Raag (1989) examined the attentiveness of mothers and strangers and smiling by 18-month-old infants. They found that the majority of smiles were directed to the mother rather than to a toy they were playing with, and the frequency of smiles directed to her was considerably higher when the mother was attentive rather than inattentive. Although mothers appeared to be preferred targets of smiles, attentive friendly strangers were also used when mothers were not attending. The authors concluded that the smiles of infants "appear to be produced as social signalling behaviours rather than as the obligatory expressive components of emotions" (p. 817).

Jones, Collins, and Hong (1991, 1992) have shown that smiling by 10-month-old and 8-month-old infants was similarly affected by the presence of an audience (mother). These findings are particularly important, as they suggest that even infants at this relatively young age use facial acts as communicative messages to their mother.

In addition, there is some suggestion that infants may learn very early on to direct these messages to specific others. Spitz and Wolf (1946) found that infants under 6 months of age smiled indiscriminately to any adult whereas the older infants were more discriminating about who they smiled to. Early communicative development would also appear to involve learning to direct messages to certain individuals. Stenberg, Campos, and Emde (1983) found that "anger" faces of 7-month-old infants directed toward the mothers were more intense than those directed toward a stranger. The authors suggested that the infant may have expected the mother to put a stop to the frustrating task. A study by Stenberg and Campos, discussed in Campos, Campos, and Barrett (1989), found that 4-month-old infants directed "anger communicating movements" toward the source of the irritation (in this case, the hands restraining the infant's arm). Seven-month-old infants, however, directed these movements toward their mother (who could presumably help rid them of the irritant). Together, these two studies suggest that around 7 months of age, infants begin to direct their communications to specific others – people they know. These findings suggest an interesting direction for future research into understanding how communication develops during infancy and childhood.

The foregoing studies have helped to provide a good foundation for a social communicative theory by showing that (1) facial displays such as smiling generally occur more frequently in social situations than in nonsocial situations, (2) availability of a receiver increases the likelihood of a facial display, and (3) facial displays occur more often in face-to-face interactions than in nonvisual interactions.

Communicative functions of facial displays

In addition to establishing the importance of social factors in eliciting facial displays, there has been interest in uncovering the functions that facial displays serve in social interactions. The idea that facial displays convey other types of information, in addition to emotion, is supported by Ekman and Friesen's findings that of 6,000 facial displays, less than one-third could be classified as emotional expressions (unpublished data; see Ekman & Fridlund, 1987).

Various general functions have been hypothesized. Mandler (1975) proposed that facial displays are social communicative acts that convey information about evaluations of the situation. More recently, Fridlund (1991, 1992) proposed that facial displays of both animals and humans serve as signals to others and serve social motives.

Facial displays have been hypothesized to play specific roles in discourse. Birdwhistell (1970) was one of the first to propose that facial displays serve linguistic functions. He discussed their role in marking emphasis and other aspects of linguistic structure, how they serve as supplements to speech, and their role as listener commentaries. Fridlund and Gilbert (1985) and Fridlund (1991) also proposed that most facial actions serve a paralinguistic function.

There is some empirical research on the use of facial displays by both speakers and listeners. In an exploratory study, Ekman (1979) investigated the use of eyebrow movements as speaker and listener conversational signals. He observed that speakers' brow movements emphasized speech, functioned as punctuation, and indicated questions and word searches. Listeners' brow movements also provided contributions to the conversation by indicating agreement and calls for information.

Brunner (1979) found that listener smiles were used as auditor "back-channels" (feedback by the listener). He suggested that back channels can serve to indicate listener involvement, level of listener understanding, and listener's reactions (e.g., agreement) to the content of the conversation. His analysis revealed that smiles occurred at specific points in relation to the speaker's behaviors. Ekman (1979) also suggested that facial displays can be used to provide information such as disbelief or a surprise reaction of the listener.

More recently, Chovil (1989, 1991/92) analyzed the various functions that facial displays other than smiles play in conversation. (For a more detailed discussion of this study, see chapter 15, by Bavelas and Chovil, this volume.) Subjects' faces were videotaped while they discussed various conversational topics with their partners. Facial displays (excluding smiles) made by speakers were found to contribute both syntactic and semantic information to the conversation. As in Ekman's (1979) study, facial actions, particularly brow movements, were observed to serve a number of syntactic functions. Other facial actions made by speakers were found to provide semantic information (e.g., conveying dislike or difficulty in recalling an event). The semantic information conveyed by the facial display was often also conveyed in the spoken words, although in a significant proportion, the information was solely conveyed through the display. Listeners' facial displays also conveyed a variety of information, such as indicating understanding as well as various types of reactions such as disbelief, confusion, empathy, and so on.

The linguistic functions of facial actions in American Sign Language have been noted by Corina (1989). Facial displays were found to help mark introduction of topic, clauses, questions, and other syntactic construction. For example, a *yes/no* question is conveyed by a forward head tilt and raised eyebrows.

Several researchers have noted that a particular facial action or display often serves a variety of different functions (e.g., Chovil, 1991/92; Ekman, 1979) or can convey various meanings (e.g., Birdwhistell, 1970; Ekman, 1985). Bavelas and Chovil (1995) and Chovil (1991/92) argued that in most if not all cases, the meaning or function of the display can only be derived when the display is viewed in its conversational context. An example of context-dependent meanings has been provided by Sherzer (1973), who discussed how the "pointed lip gesture" of the San Cuna Indians had a number of different meanings that were discernible only from the syntactic context and co-occurring discourse.

Other research has provided support for the communicative function of facial displays by demonstrating that facial displays have an effect on a receiver's behavior. Sorce, Emde, Klinnert, and Campos (cited in Klinnert, Campos, Sorce, Emde, & Svejda, 1983) investigated infants' willingness to cross a visual cliff as a function of the mother's posed facial expression. When the mothers smiled, 14 out of 19 infants crossed over the deep side. When mothers displayed a "fear" face, none of the 17 infants crossed the deep side. The facial expressions made by each mother clearly affected her child's behavior.

Camras (1977) examined the effect of aggressive facial displays by one child on another child's behavior in conflict over a desirable object. She found that children who observed an aggressive facial response from a playmate were less likely to try to obtain the object than were those children who observed a benign facial response.

Smith, Chase, and Lieblich (1974) conducted numerous observational studies with regard to the "tongue show display" and hypothesized that it conveys a message that the individual is "unwilling to interact." Dolgin and Sabini (1982) devised a study to test this hypothesis. Subjects were asked to fill out a questionnaire in which one page was missing, so they had to ask the experimenter for another booklet. Subjects took significantly longer to approach the experimenter when he performed a tongue-show display than when he did not exhibit the tongue-show display. Even though subjects reported that they did not notice this display, it had an effect on their behavior that was consistent with the hypothesized message.

In summary, there has been considerable interest in identifying the communicative functions of facial displays in face-to-face interactions. Analyses of conversations have revealed a variety of discourse functions. The communicative function of facial displays is supported by evidence that they have an effect on the behavior of others.

Implications of social communicative theory of facial displays and directions for future research

The results of the research presented in this chapter offer some initial insights into the communicative role that facial displays play in our interactions with others. The hypothesis that facial displays are communicative acts is supported by evidence that they are more likely to occur when there are others present, particularly others who are facing the person and can see the displays. It is important to note, though, that a communicative approach does not argue that social factors will always be potentiating. As Chovil and Fridlund (1991) have suggested, facial displays are more likely to be emitted when there is an available receiver, when they are useful in conveying the particular information, and when that information is pertinent or appropriate to the social interaction.

Several studies suggest that facial displays are used by others as information about the situation and that they have an effect on another person's behavior. Young children appear to use their mothers' displays as information about the situation. Facial displays also have been shown to affect differentially the behavior of the recipient. One area for future research might be to explore other types of messages conveyed by facial displays by examining the effect that these messages have on the recipient. Reactions to the facial display can be used to help determine the specific message. For example, if the facial expression exhibited by the mother in the visual cliff experiment is decoded by the infant as a message of "fear," then one prediction might be that the infant should move closer to the mother (seeking safety). Suppose, however, that the mother's facial display is perceived by the infant as a message of warning or "danger." This message would be consistent with the behavioral reluctance of infants to cross the visual cliff.

Examination of facial displays in interpersonal and conversational settings has revealed a broad domain of information that can be conveyed through facial displays. Within discourse, facial displays serve a variety of linguistic functions and enable us to communicate effectively and precisely with the other person. Through facial displays, we can convey information not only about a current reaction to an event or stimulus but also to illustrate reactions that occurred in the past (or are anticipated in the future) or the reactions of another person (e.g., "he looked at me like I was crazy"). Facial displays often appear to work in conjunction with spoken words as well as other nonverbal acts. One task for researchers will be to uncover the ways in which the various communicative acts combine and the roles that they play in face-to-face communication and social interaction. Furthermore, although it seems clear that facial displays convey important information, there has been virtually no work on how these displays are interpreted by others in social interaction.

The evidence demonstrating the close link of facial displays to speech also suggests that they are indeed part of our communication system, and it may be inaccurate to treat them as a distinct form of communication. Limiting the focus to facial expressions that occur in response to emotion-provoking stimuli (e.g., films) may have led many researchers to regard facial expressions as distinct from other kinds of communicative acts that occur in face-to-face interactions. Moreover, studying facial displays in situations where individuals are alone creates a situation where communicative processes are minimized. The resulting facial displays may simply be the equivalent of muttering to ourselves. This raises the issue of whether monadic data can adequately capture aspects of a social behavior.

The findings discussed in this chapter have implications for research both on communicative exchanges between individuals and on the link between facial displays and emotion. Analysts of face-to-face discourse need to take into account processes by which facial displays convey information as well as help to regulate interaction. The importance of social processes in determining the likelihood of facial displays has implications for using facial displays as an index of emotion. As Fridlund (1992) noted, there has been a confounding of social and emotional factors in emotion studies of individuals. In order to understand fully facial displays, we need to learn more about the situations in which they are exhibited. Findings that facial displays do not always coincide with an emotional experience suggest that their connection to emotion may be more of an overlap between two systems – communication and emotion – rather than part of the emotion system. Although we undoubtedly do use facial displays to convey information about our reactions to events, the studies reviewed here suggest that these displays are primarily socially directed rather than emotionally determined.

Research discussed here, as well as other work on nonverbal communicative acts, has revealed that the meaning or function of the display may not be apparent when the display is viewed out of context. The same action(s) may serve several different functions. Understanding how facial displays contribute to conversation and social interactions requires that we take into consideration the context in determining what the display is doing.

Although the developmental literature has made definite contributions to our knowledge regarding the communicative nature of displays by both infants and their caregivers, we still know relatively little about the kinds of spontaneous displays that are produced by children and the messages that they convey. Historically, infants' facial displays have been regarded as involuntary signs of emotion; however, the studies reviewed here suggest that they are social acts – messages to others. From very early in infancy, they are *directed* to others and responded to by the receiver. The messages conveyed by these infant displays are not limited to emotional reactions; it appears that even very young infants use smiles as social messages. There is also little known about the process by which children move from relying predominantly on facial displays and vocalizations to communicate with others to using combinations of speech, gestures, and facial information to produce messages. McNeill (1985) reviewed research demonstrating how the development of the use of speech-oriented gestures (illustrators) coincides with the development of spoken language. How facial displays continue to be used as other means of communicating develop is a question for future investigations.

Taking a social approach to the study of behaviors such as facial displays enables us to increase our knowledge about the role that these actions play in our lives. Given that much of our behavior takes place in the presence of others, it is difficult to imagine how it would not be shaped in part by others present. This chapter is intended to provide a starting point for others interested in the role that facial displays play in face-to-face interactions. It is hoped that this review will encourage others to take a closer look at this relatively uncharted domain.

References

Bavelas, J. B., Black, A., Lemery, C. R., & Mullett, J. (1986). "I show how you feel." Motor mimicry as a communicative act. *Journal of Personality and Social Psychology, 50,* 322–329.

Bavelas, J. B., & Chovil, N. (1995). *Redefining language. An integrated message model of language in face-to-face dialogue.* Unpublished manuscript.

Birdwhistell, R. L. (1968). Communication. In D. L. Sills (Ed.), *International Encyclopedia of the Social Sciences* (Vol. 3. pp. 24–28). New York: Macmillan Company and the Free Press.

Birdwhistell, R. L. (1970). *Kinesics and context: Essays on body motion communication.* Philadelphia: University of Pennsylvania.

Blurton-Jones, N. G. (1972). Criteria for use in describing facial expressions of children. In N. G. Blurton-Jones (Ed.), *Ethological studies of child behavior* (pp. 365–413). London: Cambridge University Press.

Brightman, V., Segal, A., Werther, P., & Steiner, J. (1975). Ethological study of facial expression in response to taste stimuli. *Journal of Dental Research, 54,* L141.

Brunner, L. J. (1979). Smiles can be back channels. *Journal of Personality and Social Psychology, 37,* 728–734.

Campos, J. J., Campos, R. G., & Barrett, K. C. (1989). Emergent themes in the study of emotional development and emotion regulation. *Developmental Psychology, 25,* 394–402.

Camras, L. A. (1977). Facial expressions used by children in a conflict situation. *Child Development, 48,* 1431–1435.

Chovil, N. (1991/92). Discourse-oriented facial displays in conversation. *Research on Language and Social Interaction, 25,* 163–164.

Chovil, N. (1991). Social determinants of facial displays. *Journal of Nonverbal Behavior, 15,* 141–154.

Chovil, N. (1989). Communicative functions of facial displays in conversation. *Dissertation Abstracts International, 51–04B,* 2111.

Chovil, N., & Fridlund, A. J. (1991). Why emotionality cannot equal sociality: Reply to Buck. *Journal of Nonverbal Behavior, 15,* 163–167.

Corina, D. P. (1989). Recognition of affective and noncanonical linguistic facial expressions in hearing and deaf subjects. *Brain and Cognition, 9,* 227–237.

Dolgin, K., & Sabini, J. (1982). Experimental manipulation of a human non-verbal display: The tongue-show affects an observer's willingness to interact. *Animal Behaviour, 30,* 935–936.

Duncan, S. D., & Fiske, D. W. (1977). *Face-to-face interactions. Research, methods, and theory.* New York: Erlbaum.

Duncan, S. D., & Fiske, D. W. (1985). *Interaction strategy and structure.* Cambridge: Cambridge University Press.

Ekman, P. (1979). About brows: Emotional and conversational signals. In J. Aschoof, M. von Cranach, K. Foppa, W. Lepenies, & D. Ploog (Eds.), *Human ethology* (pp. 169–202). Cambridge: Cambridge University Press.

Ekman, P. (1985). *Telling lies.* New York: Berkeley Books.

Ekman, P., & Fridlund, A. J. (1987). Assessment of facial behavior in affective disorders. In J. D. Maser (Ed.), *Depression and expressive behavior.* Hillsdale, NJ: Erlbaum.

Fernández-Dols, J., & Ruiz-Belda, M. (1995). Are smiles a sign of happiness? Gold medal winners at the Olympic Games. *Journal of Personality and Social Psychology, 69,* 1113–1119.

Fridlund, A. J. (1991). Evolution and facial action in reflex, social motive, and paralanguage. *Biological Psychology, 32,* 3–100.

Fridlund, A. J. (1992). The behavioral ecology and sociality of human faces. *Review of Personality and Social Psychology, Vol. 13,* 90–121.

Fridlund, A. J., & Gilbert, A. N. (1985). Emotions and facial expressions. *Science, 230,* 607–608.

Jones, S. S., & Raag, T. (1989). Smile production in older infants: The importance of a social recipient for the facial signal. *Child Development, 60,* 811–818.

Jones, S. S., Collins, K., & Hong, H. (1991). An audience effect on smile production in 10-month-old infants. *Psychological Science, 2,* 45–49.

Jones, S. S., Collins, K. & Hong, H. (1992). *Early social context effects on facial expression production: An audience effect on 8-month-old infants' smiles.* Unpublished manuscript.

Klinnert, M. D., Campos, J. J., Sorce, J. F., Emde, R. N., & Svejda, M. (1983). Emotions as behavior regulators: Social referencing in infancy. In R. Plutchik & H. Kellerman (Eds.), *Emotion, theory, research, and experience: Vol. 2. Emotions in early development* (pp. 57–86). New York: Academic Press.

Kraut, R. E., & Johnston, R. E. (1979). Social and emotional messages of smiling: An ethological approach. *Journal of Personality and Social Psychology, 42,* 853–863.

Mandler, G. (1975). *Mind and emotion.* New York: John Wiley & Sons.

McNeill, D. (1985). So you think gestures are nonverbal? *Psychological Bulletin, 92,* 350–371.

Pike, K. L. (1972). Towards a theory of the structure of human behavior. *General Systems Yearbook, 2,* 135–141.

Poyatos, F. (1980). Interactive functions and limitations of verbal and nonverbal behaviors in natural conversation. *Semiotica, 30,* 211–244.

Sanders, R. E. (1987). The interconnection of utterances and nonverbal displays. *Research on Language and Social Interaction, 20,* 141–170.

Scherer, K. R. (1980). The functions of nonverbal signs in conversation. In R. N. St. Clair & H. Giles (Eds.), *The social and psychological contexts of language* (pp. 225–244). Hillsdale, NJ: Lawrence Erlbaum.

Schneider, K., & Josephs, I. (1991). The expressive and communicative functions of preschool children's smiles in an achievement-situation. *Journal of Nonverbal Behavior, 15,* 185–198.

Sherzer, J. (1973). Verbal and nonverbal deixis: The pointed lip gesture among the San Blas Cuna. *Language in Society, 2,* 117–131.

Slama-Cazacu, T. (1976). Nonverbal components in message sequence: "Mixed syntax." In W. C. McCormack & S. A. Wurm (Eds.), *Language and man: Anthropological issues* (pp. 217–227). The Hague: Mouton.

Smith, W. J., Chase, J., & Lieblich, A. K. (1974). Tongue showing: A facial display of humans and other primate species. *Semiotica, 11,* 201–246.

Spitz, R., & Wolf, K. (1946). The smiling response: A contribution to the ontogenesis of social relations. *Genetic Psychology Monographs, 34,* 57–125.

Stenberg, C. R., Campos, J. J., & Emde, R. N. (1983). The facial expression of anger in seven-month-old infants. *Child Development, 54,* 178–184.

Weiner, M., Devoe, S., Rubinow, S., & Geller, J. (1972). Nonverbal behavior and nonverbal communication. *Psychological Review, 79,* 185–214.

15. Faces in dialogue

JANET BEAVIN BAVELAS AND NICOLE CHOVIL

Most of our communication with other people occurs in ordinary conversation – that is, in spontaneous face-to-face dialogue. Whether we are talking at home, at work, or in a public place, the format is most likely to be face-to-face conversation. Many scholars treat conversation as "among the most pervasive forms of human interaction" (Goodwin, 1981, p. 12; see also Clark & Wilkes-Gibbs, 1986, p. 1; Levinson, 1983, p. 284). Because of the ubiquity of conversation, any serious examination of the communicative functions of faces must consider what our faces are doing during dialogue. Yet until very recently, the literature contained almost no empirical or theoretical resources. This chapter is a prospectus for this new area of research: the study of facial action in dialogue. We propose that the facial displays of conversants are *active, symbolic* components of *integrated* messages (including words, intonations, and gestures; see Bavelas & Chovil, 1994).[1] After elaborating on these features, we describe the methodological implications of our theoretical framework and some preliminary findings.

The mobile face

One of the most striking aspects of the face in actual dialogue is the rapidity and precision of movement and change. In contrast to other primates, humans' faces are flexible, with an extraordinary number of highly enervated, independent muscle groups. In one experiment (Bavelas, Black, Lemery, & Mullett, 1986a), we microanalyzed videotapes of our subjects' faces for 3 or 4 sec immediately after they had witnessed an apparent injury, and we found that in those few seconds,

> our observers' faces were often kaleidoscopic and typically included a rapid succession of expressions and components of expressions. (p. 324)

334

In conversation, a speaker[2] can shift quickly from raising a single, quizzical eyebrow over a wry smile, to flashing both brows for emphasis on a particular word or phrase, to furrowing the brows and pursing the lips in disbelief or suspicion. Indeed, an immobile face is unusual; even apparently impassive listeners make subtle changes in their faces as they follow the speaker's narrative. (It would be ideal if, as a supplement to this chapter, the reader could view a segment of videotape in which two people have been filmed, close up, in spontaneous conversation; all of our examples come from these kinds of data.)

We are emphasizing the mobility of the face because the literature on facial expression is full of *still photographs* of people with fixed, unmoving expressions. Obviously, such photographs are currently the only means available for publishing facial displays, but we can speculate whether our field's traditional focus on a limited number of fixed displays may have been shaped, in part, by the fact that publication technology has permitted only the transmission of static, two-dimensional faces. A precise but fleeting expression becomes something very different when frozen in time; for example:

(1) A woman is explaining that, while she likes a food that the listener dislikes, she doesn't eat it often. As she says the last phrase, she enacts, very quickly, an asymmetrical "disgust" expression (wrinkling one side of her nose with the *caninus* muscle). Remember that she likes the food, so she is not indicating disgust; instead, she is using the metaphor of rejection that is implicit in disgust to indicate abstract negation, "I *don't* eat it very often." (Bavelas, 1992, p. 23)

A still photograph of her face at that moment would freeze it forever as literal disgust.

Facial signifiers

We propose that with the exception of adaptors such as licking the lips or reflexive blinking, most facial actions in dialogue are *symbolic* acts. Like words, they depict information that one person is communicating to the other. Like words, there is the classical relationship of signifier to signified – in this case, of the facial configuration to the concept it signifies (de Saussure, 1915/1966).

In more modern terms, Clark and Gerrig (1990, p. 765) explained that people face to face have three basic methods of conveying meaning to others: They can simply *indicate*, or point at the object or event that they wish to draw to the other person's attention. They can *describe* the information, usually in words. Or they can *demonstrate* their meaning by performing actions that depict selected aspects of what they want to convey. Clark and Gerrig's goal was to develop the principles of demonstration and to apply them to verbal quotations in particular (e.g., "and he tells her 'no I can't guarantee these ones' "; p. 771). However, they also applied their principles to other, nonverbal actions:

> People can demonstrate a cough, the rhythm of part of a Chopin prelude, the sound of a car engine, the sound and action of a jackhammer, the length of a fish, the size and shape of a platter, the speed of a snail, or the appearance of a chimpanzee [or] palace guard. . . . The referents of these demonstrations may be events (e.g., the cough), states (the length of the fish), processes (the working of the jackhammer), or objects (the chimp [or] guard . . .).

Note that all of these demonstrations have referents; they are symbolic acts. Here, we illustrate how facial displays in conversation fit Clark and Gerrig's criteria for demonstrations – that is, they are nonliteral, selective depictions of meaning. For example:

(2)   A woman is telling about a close call she had as a child, when she nearly fell off a barn roof. In her story, she is emphasizing the humorous as well as horrifying aspects of the event. At the climax of the story, she says, *"[I] just managed to catch the, ah, the beam, the supporting beam, with the tips of my fingers. It was so funny, I was yelling 'Dad! Dad! Dad!' . . . My dad's yelling 'Hang on! Hang on!' and comes running over, pulls me up. . . ."* She depicts herself mockingly, with a wide-eyed, childlike expression. When depicting her dad, she shows what his face might have looked like at that moment by raising her eyebrows, looking deeply concerned, and moving her head emphatically in time with his words. Throughout, she is also smiling slightly, which conveys the humorous perspective she is now putting on the story.

Recall that demonstrations are not literal actions. Our speaker was not literally being childish during her narrative, nor was she claiming to feel as her father had felt at that moment; she is not necessarily even claiming that her father actually looked as she is now portraying him. These are, to use Goffman's (1974) term, *nonserious* or make-believe actions. (*Nonserious* here does not mean playful, although in this particular example, the tone was humorous.) The speaker is not feeling frightened or concerned; she is *depicting* being frightened or concerned. Her face, along with her words and manner, is a signifier of the events as she wants to convey them now. (Note that her use of present tense when describing her father's actions is also nonserious; obviously, his actions are not occurring as she tells them.)

Because demonstrations are not literal, they can be partial and selective; they are intended not as faithful reproductions but as stylized depictions of key, selected features. In the few seconds of her narrative, our speaker necessarily left out most of the actual events and economically portrayed only the fleeting suggestions required to create the scene as she wished to convey it. Some of these features, such as her mockery, are even inaccurate in the sense of being anachronistic; she was obviously not laughing or mocking at the time.

We have demonstrated that not only speakers but also listeners or observers engage in symbolic facial displays (Bavelas et al., 1986a; Bavelas, Black, MacInnis, Lemery, & Mullett, 1986b; Chovil, 1991). Allport (1968) used the term *motor mimicry* to describe actions by an observer that are appropriate to the situation of the person being observed rather than to the observer's own situation (for example, wincing at another's injury). In one study (Bavelas et al., 1986a), we demonstrated that facial mimicry such as showing pain in response to an apparent accident was not a byproduct of vicarious emotion (which would be literal and nonsymbolic) but a symbolic representation of the observer's empathy. Motor mimicry is not a literal expression of pain; rather, it conveys "It is *as if* I am you, feeling your pain." These facial displays are highly stylized and easily decoded; they are selective demonstrations of key features of a pain response, and they are significantly more likely to occur when the victim can see them (Bavelas et al., 1986a; Chovil, 1991; see chapter 14, by Chovil, this volume, for a review of other studies on the importance of a receiver).

In sum, facial displays in dialogue are symbolic acts selected to convey meaning to a recipient. Although they often depict emotional reactions by self or other, they are not emotional expressions; they signify rather than reveal.

Integrated messages

In the aforementioned close call (Example 2), the speaker's facial actions were precisely timed to coincide with the appropriate words (the reported statements of her father and herself). At the same time as she was depicting their facial and head actions, she also depicted their vocal style, mocking versions of her fear and her dad's encouragement. When she described catching the beam with the tips of her fingers, she gestured the horizontal beam and then curled her fingers to grab this imaginary beam where she had located it. While enacting her dad telling her to

"*Hang on!*", she also moved her arms slightly, as if in a running motion. Thus, she integrated her words, intonation, facial actions, gestures, and other movements into a unitary depiction of the scene for the other person.

The simultaneous integration of words, face, gestures, and prosody is an important feature of conversational language. Speakers do not say something and then demonstrate it facially; the facial action is timed to occur with precisely those words that it illustrates or supplements. Conversational hand gestures, too, are synchronized with speech (McNeill, 1985). Slama-Cazacu (1976) illustrated how words and gestures can work together to create a sentence, a phenomenon she called *mixed syntax*; we propose that facial action can also be part of this mixed syntax. For example, in the close-call story excerpted earlier, the other person interrupted to ask, "*How high up were ya?*" and the narrator responded with

(3)   *Um!* [flashes her eyebrows, then stops smiling, and looks serious for a
          moment, as if looking for something; then she resumes smiling and says:]
          I'm really not too sure [pauses, then laughs and resumes her narrative]

Her stylized display of trying to remember the exact height not only explains her brief silence (while still holding the speaking turn); it also shows that she is treating his question seriously, even though she does not, in the end, provide an answer. It is as if she had said, in mixed syntax,

Um! Let me think about that for a minute; sorry, I'm really not too sure.

Note that we are treating her facial action as a demonstration or depiction of trying to remember, for the asker's benefit, and not as an involuntary byproduct of her effort to remember. The facial display need not be veridical; that is, she may not have been trying to remember but may have been depicting (nonserious) remembering in order to be polite before resuming her story.

Like hand gestures, facial actions are an efficient means of illustrating information that may be difficult or time-consuming to put into words. Although one facial depiction may not be worth a thousand words, it may well take the place of at least a full phrase. Moreover, a facial depiction can occur simultaneously with the words so that an entire adverbial or adjectival phrase often occurs at the same time as the verbal component, rather than in linear sequence as would be necessary for words. Finally, facial action is particularly well suited to work with words because it is the only communicative act that can match the speed of the spoken word. For example, the rapidity of eyebrow movements makes them uniquely useful for stressing individual syllables (e.g., Chovil, 1991/92; Ekman, 1979).

Methodological implications

In brief, our theory is that faces in dialogue move rapidly to convey meaning in conjunction with other, simultaneous symbolic acts. It should be apparent that this is not a theory that can be investigated by physical descriptions of still photographs or by study of only the isolated video track of a videotape. To us, such methods would be like describing music as amplitude and frequency or studying only the woodwind part of a symphony. We analyze facial displays as they occur in actual social interaction, with the goal of understanding their meaning in context. Like words, facial signifiers only have meaning in context. Just as with words, there are two important contexts to consider: First, we must locate the facial display in the ongoing development of the dialogue, which includes the topic of conversation, preceding utterances and displays, and what is happening at that moment (e.g., presenting new information, repairing an error, confirming understanding, or answering a question). In addition to the cumulative context, there is the simultaneous context of other symbolic acts – that is, the words, gestures, and intonation that accompany the facial action. As emphasized earlier, we assume that symbolic acts are integrated with each other and work together to create meaning.

Our insistence on analyzing behaviors as meaningful wholes rather than as molecular parts is similar to that of Wright and Barker (1950), who pointed out that a person

> does not sweat or salivate, nor does he often bend his knees in walking, manipulate his tongue in talking, move his eyeballs in reading, or bend at the waist in sitting down. He *walks, talks, reads,* or *sits down,* leaving his glandular and motor apparatus to take care of the sweating, salivating, bending, manipulating and all such molecular units of behavior which, as molecular, are lost to the person in what he actually does. (p. 50; italics added)

Many researchers believe that only the molecular level of physical description is objective and reliable, because meaning requires interpretation and is therefore in the domain of the ephemeral and subjective. We disagree:

> Objectivity is merely intersubjective agreement; there are no inherently ob-
> jective facts, only those on which observers' perceptions (always subjective)
> are obviously likely to be aligned. The question becomes whether we [can]
> achieve high levels of independent agreement for our interpretations. . . .
> (Bavelas, 1994, p. 212)

Our research (e.g., Chovil, 1991/92) has shown that reliability for assessing the meaning of a facial display in context can be as high or higher
than systems of physical description.

Besides the importance of context, there are two further principles that
guide our analyses: First, we assume that it is natural for people, including our analysts, to approach dialogue at the level of meaning. In our
spontaneous interactions with others, we are attending to meaning and
not to physical movements or configurations. We see surprise or skepticism, not facial movements, just as we hear the meaning of words and
not their physical properties, such as fricatives. So when we analyze
videotapes of facial signifiers, we can easily watch and listen at the level
of what one person is conveying to another, just as we do in everyday
life. Second, it follows that our training is mostly metalinguistic – that
is, teaching people to articulate the meaning that they have already understood and to attend to how that meaning was conveyed. The best
way to achieve this is a clearly structured protocol that guides the analyst
from step to step, requiring him or her to make relatively broad and easy
decisions first and then move to more specific or difficult ones. The next
section illustrates the first such analysis of faces in dialogue.

Functions of speakers' and listeners' faces

Apart from Ekman's (1979) description of the conversational functions
of eyebrows, there have been almost no studies of faces in dialogue. As
far as we know, Chovil's (1989, 1991/92) was the first systematic study
of the faces of two people in spontaneous conversation (i.e., not one
person alone or with an interviewer or confederate). Chovil studied the
faces of 12 conversational dyads (4 female, 4 male, and 4 mixed pairs),
who had been given three topics chosen to elicit a broad range of conversation: They told each other about a close call or near miss that each
person had had or heard about; they told each other about a minor conflict or argument with another person; and they planned a nutritional
meal together out of foods they both disliked.

Both participants were videotaped, close up, in split screen, on high-
quality color video; the goal was to capture their faces as they looked at

each other during the conversation. These videotapes were later analyzed using a large monitor and an industrial-quality VCR with stable freeze frame and slow motion. It is also useful to have a sound track that will stay on during slow motion; this sound track, however distorted, keeps the audible and visible actions together and makes their intimate synchrony apparent. An on-screen time signal accurate to tenths of seconds is invaluable for locating the individual displays.

Chovil's goal was to look for and understand the function of the conversants' meaningful facial actions. So, first, facial movements that were byproducts of other actions (e.g., blinking, swallowing, or talking) were ignored. Facial adaptors such as biting or licking the lips were identified and set aside. Then, all meaningful facial actions except smiles were located and analyzed. Smiles were omitted for purely economic reasons, because their sheer frequency would have overwhelmed all of the other less obvious displays. As it was, the data yielded 880 meaningful displays, 301 adaptors, and only 3 that could not be analyzed. We focus here on the 880 meaningful displays, which are summarized in Table 15.1.

Instead of imposing an a priori categorization, Chovil's approach was both inductive and functional. She asked: What is this display doing at this point in the conversation? How is it conveying meaning in the context in which it occurs? Three broad linguistic functions emerged, each with many subsets of functions. A second analyst scored a large sample of the data independently, with reliabilities of 82% to 97%.

The largest group of meaningful facial actions consisted of *semantic* displays by the speaker – that is, facial actions that conveyed a meaning directly relevant to the speaker's narrative. For example, the speaker raised her eyebrows and one side of her upper lip and then squinted her eyes to illustrate her personal distaste, while saying

(4)   *I hate, I hate desserts with alcohol in them.* (p. 180)[3]

Speakers also portrayed or reenacted past reactions, both of themselves and of others; for example, the speaker demonstrated someone's odd look at him by reenacting it:

(5)   *and the guy just sort of looked* [pause] *you know, sorta looked down at me.* (p. 182)

During his brief pause, the speaker tilted his head down, lowered his eyes, and formed a straight mouth. His facial portrayal made specific

Table 15.1. *Functions of conversational facial actions*

Function	Frequency[a]			
Meaningful Displays by speakers[b]	720			
Semantic		405		
Redundant			243	
Personal reaction				87
Portrayal				83
Thinking/remembering				20
Facial shrug				17
Yes				15
+ six other functions				21
Nonredundant			162	
Personal reaction				73
Thinking/remembering				43
Facial shrug				31
+ five other functions				15
Syntactic		315		
Grammatical markers			286	
Emphasizer (word)				156
Underliner (phrase)				57
Question marker				45
+ four other functions				28
Organization of story			27	
Story continuation				18
+ three other functions				9
Speech corrections			2	
Meaningful displays by listeners[b]	160			
Back channel			84	
Personal reaction			48	
Motor mimicry			21	
+ three other functions			7	

[a]Frequencies are nested in the same format as the function names, with successively finer breakdowns as one moves to the right. Thus, each column adds up to the figure that is above it and to its left (e.g., 87 + 83 + 20 + 17 + 15 +21 = 243).
[b]Except smiles.
Source: Adapted with permission from Chovil (1989).

and vivid exactly *how* the other person looked down at him, acting as the visual equivalent of an unspoken adverbial phrase.

A surprising 40% of the speakers' semantic displays went well beyond their verbal descriptions and conveyed information that was completely *nonredundant* with their words – for instance, in Example 3 (earlier) or

(6)   *That was only a couple of days ago but ah* [pause] (p. 186)

During the pause, the speaker pushed out his bottom lip and raised his eyebrows, as if to say, "That's about it; the rest doesn't matter." Based on the words alone, we would expect the speaker to continue, but his face conveyed that he was finished.

Another major function of the speakers' facial displays was to act as *syntactic* markers; these were usually eyebrow actions. Most served as grammatical markers, especially to emphasize a particular word or to underline a whole phrase. In Example 3, the speaker stressed her *"Um"* prosodically and also marked it with an eyebrow flash. When a longer grammatical unit was being emphasized, the brows remained up over the entire phrase; in Example 2, she marked her Dad's yelling *"Hang on! Hang on!"* by raising her eyebrows precisely over that phrase. Another common grammatical function was to mark a question; for example,

(7)   *We were up, uh, nailing on boards, for the roof?*

She said the last three words in a "Do you know what I mean?" tone of voice and also raised her brows and held them up until the listener nodded and said *"Mhm."* Both her intonation contour and her brows marked this as a question rather than the declarative sentence that it would appear to be verbally.

Altogether, the speaker of the moment accounted for over 80% of the meaningful facial displays in Chovil's data. Listeners, though, were not impassive. The third major group of facial displays, *listener responses*, consisted primarily of back-channel responses, which are indications that he or she is listening and following the narrative. These were often miniature in scale, mere components of other displays – for example, turning the corners of the lips down in appreciation of something serious, pressing the lips together in concern or suspense, closing the eyes briefly ("I don't want to see this"), and raising the brows in alarm or disbelief. Other listener displays went beyond simple back channels and portrayed a more pronounced or exaggerated reaction to what the speaker was saying; for example:

(8)   The speaker is telling about a conflict with her father, whose reaction to her getting a grade of 92% on a test was to say, *"Why didn't you get a hundred?"* The listener portrayed surprise and disbelief at the father's statement by dropping his jaw, widening his eyes, and raising his brows. (p. 188)

Another listener response that particularly interested us was motor mimicry, in which the listener portrayed a reaction appropriate to the speaker's situation (e.g., fear or pain during a close-call story). Our previous research (Bavelas et al., 1986a; Bavelas, Black, Chovil, Lemery, & Mullett, 1988) had established that this is not a vicarious emotional reaction but a communicative act. In those studies, however, we had limited the data to a fixed eliciting stimulus and response. In spontaneous conversational data (Chovil, 1991, 1991/92, we found the true home of mimetic displays: They are a significant part of the listener's conversational repertoire, a brief and eloquent way for the listener to participate briefly in the speaker's narrative. With motor mimicry, the listener not only indicates appreciation of the speaker's point but becomes a co-narrator for a moment, illustrating the speaker's point with his or her own face. Our recent research (Bavelas, Coates, & Johnson, 1995) has shown that mimetic responses by the listener are a distinct and important part of dialogue.

The reader may have noticed that each of the semantic response categories (speaker-redundant, speaker-nonredundant, and listener responses) had a group of *personal reaction* displays (e.g., Table 15.1 and Examples 4 and 8). In our view, the conversational display of a personal reaction is entirely different from a classic emotional display. There is no doubt that these facial actions often draw on the familiar code of emotion displays (e.g., enacting disgust), but they are not evidence of an emotional reaction in the individual making the display, for several reasons: First, these facial actions are partial and selective (i.e., symbolic, nonserious). Second, they are extremely rapid – often 1 sec or less, which is too rapid to assume that a corresponding emotion has come and gone during the display. Third, they are precisely timed to the accompanying words, so that they are shaped by linguistic rather than affective forces.

Our interpretation of the frequency of these displays is that they take advantage of the unique ability of the face to encode people's internal reactions vividly, which words can do only abstractly. This is supported by the frequent use of facial action to encode *other people's* reactions as well – for example, the speaker's semantic portrayals and the listener's motor mimicry. We postulate that there is a division of labor among words, gestures, and facial actions so that material is encoded in the most suitable form – for example, personal reactions in faces, shapes and movements in gestures, and abstract categories and syntax in words.

We hope that this chapter has engaged the interest of researchers who have previously not looked closely at faces in dialogue. Our goal is to free the face from its historically exclusive relationship with emotion so that we can begin to see other functions of faces in everyday social life.

Acknowledgments

We would like to acknowledge the financial support of the Social Sciences and Humanities Research Council of Canada, in the form of standard research grants to J.B.B. and pre- and postdoctoral fellowships to N.C.

Notes

1 Our theoretical position is very similar to colleagues such as Adam Kendon, David McNeill, and Jurgen Streeck, especially their analyses of hand gestures (see, for example, their articles in Kendon, 1994).
2 We use the traditional terms *speaker* and *listener* for convenience, even though they tend to obscure our thesis that the speaker's meaning is visual as well as auditory and that the listener is also a viewer.
3 Hereafter, examples with page numbers indicated are from Chovil (1991/92); all others are from previously unpublished data.

References

Allport, G. W. (1968). The historical background of modern social psychology. In G. Lindzey & E. Aronson (Eds.), *Handbook of social psychology* (2nd ed.) (Vol. 1, pp. 1–80). Reading, MA: Addison-Wesley.

Bavelas, J. B. (1992). Research into the *Pragmatics of human communication. Journal of Strategic and Systemic Therapy, 11* (2), 15–29.

Bavelas, J. B. (1994). Gestures as part of speech: Methodological implications. *Research on Language and Social Interaction, 27*, 201–221.

Bavelas, J. B., Black, A., Chovil, N., Lemery, C. R., & Mullett, J. (1988). Form and function in motor mimicry: Topographic evidence that the primary function is communicative. *Human Communication Research, 14*, 275–299.

Bavelas, J. B., Black, A., Lemery, C. R., & Mullett, J. (1986a). "I *show* how you feel": Motor mimicry as a communicative act. *Journal of Personality and Social Psychology, 50*, 322–329.

Bavelas, J. B., Black, A., MacInnis, S., Lemery, C. R., & Mullett, J. (1986b). Experimental methods for studying "elementary motor mimicry." *Journal of Nonverbal Behavior, 10*, 102–119.

Bavelas, J. B., & Chovil, N. (1994). *Redefining language. An integrated message model of language in face-to-face dialogue.* Unpublished manuscript.

Bavelas, J. B., Coates, L., & Johnson, T. (1995, May). *Listeners as co-narrators.* Paper presented at the annual meeting of the International Communication Association, Albuquerque, NM.

Chovil, N. (1989). *Communicative functions of facial displays in conversation.* Unpublished doctoral dissertation, University of Victoria, BC, Canada.

Chovil, N. (1991). Social determinants of facial displays. *Journal of Nonverbal Behavior, 15*, 141–154.

Chovil, N. (1991/92). Discourse-oriented facial displays in conversation. *Research on Language and Social Interaction, 25*, 163–194.

Clark, H. H., & Gerrig, R. J. (1990). Quotations as demonstrations. *Language, 66*, 764–805.

Clark, H. H., & Wilkes-Gibbs, D. (1986). Referring as a collaborative process. *Cognition, 22*, 1–39.

Ekman, P. (1979). About brows: Emotional and conversational signals. In J. Aschoof, M. von Cranach, K. Foppa, W. Lepenies, & D. Ploog (Eds.), *Human ethology* (pp. 169–202). Cambridge: Cambridge University Press.

Goffman, E. (1974). *Frame analysis.* New York: Harper & Row.

Goodwin, C. (1981). *Conversational organization. Interaction between speakers and hearers.* New York: Academic Press.

Kendon, A. (1994). Special issue: Gesture and understanding in social interaction. *Research on Language and Social Interaction, 27,* 171–267.

Levinson, S. C. (1983). *Pragmatics.* Cambridge: Cambridge University Press.

McNeill, D. (1985). So you think gestures are nonverbal? *Psychological Bulletin, 92,* 350–371.

Saussure, F. de (1966). *Course in general linguistics* (C. Bally & A. Sechehaye, Eds., in collaboration with A. Riedlinger; W. Baskin, Trans.). New York: McGraw-Hill. (Original work published 1915)

Slama-Cazacu, T. (1976). Nonverbal components in message sequence: "Mixed syntax." In W. C. McCormack & S. A. Wurm (Eds.), *Language and man: Anthropological issues.* The Hague: Mouton.

Wright, H. F., & Barker, R. G. (1950). *Methods in psychological ecology.* Lawrence: University of Kansas Press.

PART V

Integrative summary

16. Faces: An epilogue and reconceptualization

G. P. GINSBURG

It is both a pleasure and a challenge to write an epilogue for this volume. The editors have laid out the major issues and have placed them in historical and conceptual context; and the reading of each chapter draft by other contributors has minimized errors of interpretation, clarified commonalities, and sharpened differences. In this epilogue, I review the chapters, extract certain themes from them, and propose an integration in which the construct "emotion" is narrowed, the expressions of the face are freed from the claim of tight linkage to that construct, and the situated line of activity in which facial displays occur is emphasized. I believe this will facilitate our understanding of facial displays and indicate some change in our research efforts.

The chapters: Contrasts and similarities

Russell and Fernández-Dols

The importance of facial expressions in human affairs is aptly stressed by Russell and Fernández-Dols in their introduction. Throughout recorded history, faces have been depicted as indicators of internal states. This tradition has been maintained through the present day and is reflected in the interpretation of much of our current research. But there are problems with this conception – people do not always reveal what is presumed to be their internal states, and people who display a certain expression are not necessarily in the state conventionally implied by the expression. Moreover, the concept of emotion is ambiguous, making it difficult to ascertain what if any linkage there is between facial movements and emotional states. It is widely presumed that faces and emotions are tightly linked, except as masked or otherwise wittingly disguised by the displayer; and it is presumed by many that emotions cause facial displays, and by some that facial displays produce feedback that cause conscious feelings of specific emotions. Data are cited in support of each of these presumptions, as are personal experiences that make each plausible. But as Russell and Fernández-Dols point out, the ambiguity of the concept of emotion and the diversity of empirical results make each of these presumptions questionable. Perhaps the linkage of faces and emotions is a myth.

Russell and Fernández-Dols pursue several other matters as well. One is universality, both of facial displays and emotions, which they note is not well supported by the data. Another is the *meanings* of facial displays. They propose that we examine the meaning that a given expression has for the recipient or observer, although it is not clear what they mean by "meaning."

Finally, Russell and Fernández-Dols distinguish between facial expressions performed in the course of an emotional episode (first-order displays) and facial expressions performed in the process of telling about that emotional episode, or by an actor (second-order displays). The linkage with internal states might differ for the two kinds of facial expressions. We return to this matter later.

Izard

The chapter by Carroll Izard is largely an elaboration of Differential Emotions Theory (DET). Emotions are construed by Izard as a major subsystem of a more general personality system; they are held to be discrete and serve as the primary motivational system for human behavior. Expressions, including but not limited to facial expressions, constitute a component of the emotion subsystem. They are genetically influenced but modifiable, so that both personal experience and local cultural conventions are reflected. Observable expression is not a necessary component of emotion, and there is no prototypical expression for each basic emotion. Instead, there are many elements, such as oblique brows, any one of which could signal a particular emotion. There also is wide variation in the intensity of emotions, and we should not assume that an instance of weak anger looks like or functions like an instance of strong anger.

Considerable attention is given to emotional experience, which Izard characterizes as "a feeling/motivational state." Feelings are construed as both a source of facial expression and a consequent of facial expression.

The latter aspect is compatible with the facial feedback model of Laird (1984; Laird & Bresler, 1992), although for neither model is such feedback a necessary condition for emotion. Both models also construe expressive behavior as playing an important role in emotion regulation, as have others in this field (e.g., Bell, 1824, p. 141).

Izard distinguishes between basic emotions, or "core feelings," of which there are relatively few, and emotional experiences. Core feelings can be fleeting, can follow each other rapidly, and can even mix (not blend) with each other; and core feelings can become associated with an infinite variety of thoughts, beliefs, and actions. Given the variety of intensities, sequences, and mixes of core feelings, and the variety of events with which they can become associated, the variety of emotional experiences, Izard contends, is infinite. Furthermore, congruence between a facial expression and a feeling is unlikely, since facial displays often are very brief and occur as part of what Izard calls "emotion activation." Therefore, congruence is likely to occur only at the beginning of an emotional episode. Furthermore, facial displays not only are often brief; they also are frequently of low amplitude. The result is that a person does not necessarily know what he is showing or what he is feeling. These points undercut the presumption that a person is necessarily a privileged source of information about his or her state of feeling, and they lessen the import of disjunctions between avowed or inferred feelings and the facial display. On the other hand, they make it difficult to disconfirm the underlying theory.

Izard also discusses universality and distinguishes it from the issue of innateness. Universality has generally been supported, albeit by language-based procedures about which Izard expresses some reservations (see chapters 2, 5, 12, and 13, by Wagner, Fridlund, Fernández-Dols & Carroll, and Russell, respectively, this volume, for critical discussion of the language-based recognition procedures commonly used in universality studies). Innateness, on the other hand, has proven more difficult to investigate, since it requires intensive longitudinal studies and detailed, time-consuming, nonattributional coding. An example cited in the chapter (Izard et al., 1995) involved coding nearly 20,000 codable (by MAX and AFFEX) facial configurations of roughly 100 infants of ages 2.5 to 9.0 months interacting with their mothers. The study indicated some developmental changes in facial display components, demonstrated that infants produced "spontaneous" facial displays that were congruent with different mother–infant interactions, and yielded data that Izard sees as compatible with the notion of innate facial movements linked to specific feeling states. The study is an important contribution to the literature, but there are ambiguities.

First, Izard et al. (1995) report a high frequency of complete facial displays – e.g., complete expressions of anger, or of joy, in contrast to partial expressions. However, this is discrepant with reports by others (see Messinger et al., chapter 9, this volume) who have found infant expressions to be highly fragmented. The discrepancy might in part be due to MAX coding rules (for joy); and a close examination of the Izard et al. report reveals that half of the "anger" and "sadness" displays, taken together, were either partial displays or blends of "anger" or "sad" features and features of other discrete emotion displays.

Another ambiguity concerns differential responses by the infants to affectively different displays by their mothers. Infants did react differently to the mother's anger displays from the way they did to her sadness displays. But the differential responses did not necessarily match the display, and the patterns varied with age. The lack of match leaves unclear the emotional meaning of the infant display and raises some question about Izard's inference of congruence between expression and feeling (see Ginsburg & Harrington, 1996, for further discussion of Izard et al., 1995).

The linkage between feeling and facial expression also arises in Izard's discussion of feeling rather than "intention" (as developed in Fridlund, chapter 5, this volume, as well as 1994) as the basis of facial expressions. He raises critical questions about the use of "social motives" and "intentions" in the causal explanation of facial expression and notes that a model that explains displays on the basis of intentions or social motives is as readily criticized as one that explains expressions on the basis of feelings. Both models attempt to specify causes of facial displays, and both rely upon mental states as the generative mechanism. Fridlund denies that his particular use of the term *intention* construes it mentally, but that is debatable, and Izard's point is well taken.

Izard's chapter offers a model in which emotion is part of a larger system of personality functioning, and in which facial displays are contingently linked to emotions and to emotional experience by means of feelings. Specific facial displays are not necessary or necessarily sufficient for a specific emotion or emotional experience; and a specific emotion is not necessary or necessarily sufficient for a specific facial expression. Full-face configurations do contain specified elements, but a particular configuration is not the only possible display of a particular emotion.

Although Izard adheres to a categorical view of a limited set of discrete basic emotions, emotional experience is infinite. This is a different conception of emotion from other discrete models in which secondary emotions are construed as blends of discrete, basic (primary) emotions.

The loose linkage between facial displays and emotional experience is also raised in chapter 4, by Frijda and Tcherkassof. They explicitly question the view that facial expressions express emotional feelings; and they question the related view that facial expressions exist for the sake of communication with others. Facial expression, they suggest, is facial behavior that implies emotional meanings to perceivers of the facial display. But what does facial expression express?

Frijda and Tcherkassof

Frijda and Tcherkassof argue that facial expressions express the displayer's readiness to act with respect to the environment, and that state of action readiness is inferred (or recognized?) by observers or interaction partners from the expression. The condition for use of emotion terms in ordinary discourse is the recognition of states of action readiness or variations in those states, and facial expressions therefore express what is referred to in ordinary discourse as emotions. This point is extremely important, for it directs explanatory attention not to the relationship between facial patterns and emotions, but to the tie between facial patterns and the conditions under which emotion words are legitimately and comprehensibly used in ordinary discourse. It is not clear whether Frijda and Tcherkassof recognize the importance of their position on this matter, nor whether they would agree with it when stated so baldly, but we return to it later. Facial expressions can be used for detecting or otherwise ascertaining states of action readiness, and with additional cues, for states of emotion. Sufficient cues for the latter include the behavioral context, time course, and information indicative of the event that elicited the readiness state. This implies that emotions exist as real entities and that they are not identical to states of action readiness, despite discussion earlier in the chapter that held them to be at least a subset of states of action readiness. In any case, the relationship between facial expressions and emotions is a loose one, regardless of the specific definition of emotion. It is loose in the same sense that Izard contends it to be variable – the occurrence of a specific instance of one is neither necessary nor necessarily sufficient for the occurrence, or the nonoccurrence, of the other; and yet, the two classes of phenomena are linked in both models. Frijda and Tcherkassof share with Russell and Fernández-Dols a recognition of the importance of the perception of facial expressions and the detection of their meaning by the perceivers. They add to this a concern with the conditions under which we use emotion terms in ordinary discourse to refer to people's states.

Fridlund

Alan Fridlund recognizes the same loose linkage between facial movements and emotion as do Izard and Frijda and Tcherkassof, but he offers a qualitatively different theoretical framework to account for it. Facial movements, Fridlund argues, should be seen as signals that have evolved. As signaling behaviors subject to selection pressures, they must serve functions that facilitate the interactions of the members of the species among themselves and with the larger environment. In particular, they have to serve social functions, especially as indicators of the line of action that the organism is ready to pursue in the given setting; and conspecifics must be vigilant for such signals and responsive to them. To be selected, signaling behaviors must co-evolve with vigilance for and responsivity to those signals. This perspective effectively rules out both readout and spillover views of facial displays, in which expressions are construed as involuntary (but somewhat controllable) displays caused by internal states. From an evolutionary framework, this would put the organism at a selective disadvantage since it would reveal information that could be injurious to the displayer. Therefore, only displays that implicate actions will evolve, and interaction partners will attend selectively to displays that imply the displayer's situated line of action. Information about the displayer's internal states is irrelevant to the co-evolution of displays and vigilance for them, even though such states might be correlated with lines of action. Thus, Fridlund concludes that neither the concept of "feelings" nor the concept of "emotion" is necessary for scientific understanding of facial displays. He also contends that displays are necessarily and primordially social. The social is present even when an individual is alone; others are "present psychologically," a position Fridlund has labeled "sociality." People talk to themselves, interact with imagined others, replay prior interactions, and play out anticipated interactions. There is no "solitary," asocial circumstance in which a facial display will uniquely and without distortion express "true feelings." The circumstances are always and unavoidably social. On this matter, Fridlund is in the company of William James (1950/1890, Vol. 1, especially pp. 309–310) and George Herbert Mead (1934), as well as many current writers (see Hermans, 1996).

In sum, Fridlund shares with Izard and with Frijda and Tcherkassof a sense of importance of motivation – where they write of the motivational importance of emotions (or states of readiness), he writes of social motives and intentions. In all three cases, an objective is to specify the causes of facial displays, and for Izard and for Frijda and Tcherkassof, the causal consequences of facial displays. And all three refer to inner states – Izard to emotions and feelings, Frijda and Tcherkassof to states of readiness and perhaps to emotions, and Fridlund, much as he wishes to deny it, to intentions and goals. Fridlund considers neither the construct of "feeling" nor that of "emotion" to be necessary or helpful in understanding the occurrence of facial displays. He also notes that emotion is still not consensually defined, and many of the definitions offered are so broad as to be useless. There are no specifications of the criteria by which an event will be accepted or rejected as an instance of emotion. He almost but not quite rejects "emotion" as a technical construct (see Russell, 1991, for an explicit discussion of this issue). This, too, is a point to which we return later.

These three chapters lay out very distinct views of facial displays and emotions; and yet there is considerable overlap, both explicit and implicit. Importantly, all three have come to a relational stance, in which facial displays cannot be understood independently of the context of their occurrence and the environmentally related activities in which they are embedded. They also share a concern with the reliance on linguistic data as evidence about the emotional meanings of facial expressions. But they differ in their commitments to internal states and the assumption of a causal linkage between internal states and facial displays.

Smith and Scott

Smith and Scott also conceive of a link between facial movements and internal states, but the linkage involves molecular facial Action Units rather than full "basic emotion" configurations. Smith and Scott make explicit the componential nature of facial displays and point out that most of the facial Action Units, such as raised lip corners, occur in more than one recognizable facial expression (as does Darwin, 1965/1872, p. 149). Patterns of such component actions are distinct for each emotion, but individual facial components can be meaningful – that is, they can make available reliable information about the displayer's affective state.

Partial expressions are common and potentially meaningful. A given emotional state can be signaled by a variety of expressions, although the different expressions usually have sufficient similarity to be considered reflections of an "emotion family" (see Ekman, 1994, as one example) but differ in fine tuning. Mixes and blends of emotions are often experienced and entail various components of different full-face canonical expressions.

Smith and Scott propose four dimensions of meaning on which facial components cluster, organized in part by adaptive functions: pleasantness of the emotional state (e.g., eyebrow frown), the attentional activity associated with the emotional state (e.g., raised eyebrows), arousal (general intensity of the set of facial components), and personal agency or control. The hedonic dimension is associated with the perception of goal obstacles and anticipated effort; the attentional components reflect the novelty of the situation and the degree of certainty of the displayer about the circumstances. Personal agency is not well elaborated, and its hypothesized role is negative – its components (e.g., raised eyebrows, raised upper eyelid, open mouth) are related to *low* levels of personal agency or control. Smith and Scott caution that context must be taken into account when examining the meanings of specific components, since a given facial movement can have very different meanings in different contexts.

Smith and Scott also make an important point about physiological patterns and their relationship to emotions. Specifically, emotional physiological patterns are associated with the adaptive task called into play by the appraisal that led to the emotional state. Appraisals of circumstances can generate emotional states, which in turn motivate specific instrumental actions afforded within the situation, and these actions will be supported by a variety of facets of the emotional response. It is unclear whether the evoked emotional state *is* the set of emotional response components or is a state that leads to those response components. The response components include autonomic patterns, somatic muscle tonus, eye widening, vocal pitch changes, and so on. We should not expect a fixed physiological pattern for all instances of a given emotion, because the pattern depends on the actions that the person undertakes in the situation at hand. This point is consistent with findings and reviews of others as well (Ginsburg & Harrington, 1996; Stemmler, 1989; Zajonc & McIntosh, 1992).

The componential model of Smith and Scott is neutral with respect to the existence of a small set of basic emotions, provided fuzzy "emotion family" sets are allowed. Moreover, the model is presented as a bridge that allows for both categorical and dimensional models of emotion. Emotional experiences, for example, would be expected to cluster in the dimensionally structured space, thereby creating emotion families; and in each family, there would be overlapping sets of components.

If emotions are responses to adaptively significant appraisals of potential harm and benefit, then each category of emotion corresponds to a different type of harm or benefit. This is a functional perspective, and because all action is necessarily situated, actions will always be related to features of the environment – and emotionally motivated actions will necessarily be related to the potential harms and benefits of the environment. Thus, the Smith and Scott model is similar on this matter to the functional model of Fridlund and its reliance on "social motives" for the explanation of facial displays. Smith and Scott also note that facial displays may have communicative function and provide a basis for contagion, imitative empathy, and other interpersonal influences. But they still have a basis in emotion – even if they are used for other purposes, they still are the same display components as those that indicate emotion. This line of argument presumes the existence of emotions as internal states that facial display components indicate; but those same components also can serve as modifiers and intensifiers in communicative activity. Smith and Scott construe facial components as being consequent to emotional states, as demonstrated by their interpretation of the Pope and Smith (1994) directed imagination study. That is, they interpret the data as indicating that feelings lead to facial displays (the displays "encode" feelings); however, the data do not require that construction. They are equally consistent with a claim that (for example) smiles appear in situated acts of approach, politeness, and pleasurable interaction, and feelings are subsequently *reported* as appropriate for those situated acts. This difference in conceptualization has important consequences.

Russell

The final broad perspective to be considered is the chapter by Russell, elaborating on his dimensional perspective and strongly emphasizing context. Russell's concern is with the perceiver's responses to facial displays, especially classificatory responses, rather than with the production of those displays. Russell's criticisms of the basic emotions models of facial expression are well known in the field (Russell, 1994, 1995; also see Ekman, 1994; Izard, 1994), and his chapter both summarizes and elaborates upon them. Facial displays are not signals of specific emotions, but an observer does either detect or infer information about what the displayer is doing (the line of action in which the displayer is engaged), the displayer's attentiveness, and the pleasantness and degree of arousal characterizing the displayer's state. Russell holds that the observer "judges" these matters, but this may be a looseness of phrase, since he also refers to the automaticity of the pickup of these kinds of information. These two types of facial display information – the "quasi-physical features" and "pleasure and arousal" – are combined with contextual information, and with historical and personal information if available, and jointly constitute the basis for any specific emotions that the observer "attributes" to the displayer.

Situational factors include two contexts – that of the displayer (and of the displayed stimulus material, in a controlled experiment) and that of the perceiver or judge. This is an important distinction, and we return to it shortly.

Pleasantness and arousal are construed as two orthogonal dimensions of a psychological judgment space within which emotion labels are locatable. Regions of the two-dimensional space correspond to major classes of emotions and are organized in a circumplex pattern. The dimensions of the space are similar to the Evaluative and Activity dimensions generated in semantic differential work (see Osgood, 1966, for application to face judgments). A somewhat more complex, spiral space is used by Heise (Heise & Calhan, 1995), in which a third dimension of power or control (versus vulnerability) is added, and it, too, is based on the Osgood dimensions of meaning.

The Osgood Model, it should be noted, deals with connotative, not denotative, meaning; the dimensions refer to the *responses of the perceiver* to the object of judgment, and not to the qualities of the object itself (see Osgood, 1952; Osgood, Suci, & Tannenbaum, 1957). It is important to recognize this, since it differs from an interest in the semantics – the *referential meaning* – of judgments of facial displays. Using people's judgments of facial displays to construct a space of the implications that such displays have for perceivers is very different from using those judgments as evidence for the nature of the stimuli themselves. It is my impression that Russell is interested primarily in the connotative rather than referential meaning of facial displays.

Russell proposes the following sequence for the perception and classification of facial displays. An observer first perceives the quasi-physical information of the facial display, and then its pleasantness and degree of arousal; the observer then constructs a story that builds on and explains the preceding perceptions, using available contextual information. The observer then attributes an emotion to the displayer, especially if the observer is explicitly or implicitly asked to do so. In essence, the observer provides an explanation for the actor's display; but explanations are a particular lexical device, the use of which typically is in response to an explicit or implicit claim that a puzzle of human behavior exists and calls for a resolution (see Abelson & Lalljee, 1988; Harré, 1988; Turnbull & Slugoski, 1988, pp. 75–79 and 87–88). If the later, emotional classification stage of the process proposed by Russell does entail an explanation, then Russell's model construes emotion classification as a linguistic act, so that it will be governed by conversational maxims and will not occur in species that do not have language or language-like capacity. By implication, the model also construes research involving classificatory judgments of facial displays as an analog of conversation, in which implicit questions are put to the judges and explanatory answers are given. The data, then, would have no necessary tie to ordinary emotional processes, including perception of emotions. Russell might not agree with this; nevertheless, a similar case has been made for the role of conversational implicatures in research on reasoning and rational judgment (Hilton, 1995). Judgments about emotional categories are no less social than those about base rates and probabilities.

The proposed sequence has another important implication: The perceiver does not directly detect the emotion of a displayer. Instead, the "emotion" of the displayer is an act of attribution by the perceiver. As noted previously, that act may be automatic or deliberate and reflective.

Russell also questions whether facial expressions signal basic emotions. He answers this in the negative, on several grounds: anthropological evidence; relative infrequency of full-face configurations (except for smiling); the likelihood that they are melodramatic poses as part of narratives (Bavelas & Chovil, chapter 15, this volume; Sarbin, 1995); evidence that common spontaneous expressions do not necessarily match the basic prototypes (Fernández-Dols & Ruiz Belda, chapter 11, this volume); the loose linkage between internal emotion states and facial displays (as "affinity" in Frijda and Tcherkassof's chapter 4) implied by evidence on recognition and classification of facial expressions; and the great strength of context effects with respect to both the displayer's context and the observer's context (Fernández-Dols & Carroll, chapter 12, this volume). If the face were tightly linked to internal, emotional states, the influence of facial displays on observers' judgments should override that of contextual factors, but just the opposite occurs. Russell finds this compatible with his proposed sequential process, and he also makes a trenchant methodological point: Judgments of emotion that are based on facial displays will vary across methods and across observational contexts. That being the case, the putative constancy of the meaning of a facial expression of emotion is likely to be a constancy of method. This cries out for a multimethod-multitrait experimental design (as Stemmler, 1989).

In sum, the meaning of a facial display to a perceiver is partly a function of how the facial features are related to other features of the displayer and the displayer's context, and also to the observer's context. Facial displays occur in context and are detected and interpreted in context. Emotions, along with intentions, motives, desires, and beliefs, may then be judged and attributed by the observer to the displayer. The perception of emotion, by this model, is more an act of attribution that comes toward the end of a sequence, and it is a contingent rather than necessary or automatic act. These implications are important and deserve to be pursued. Other chapters give indirect support to their plausibility.

The ethological chapters

The two ethological chapters offer a different perspective on displays and are interesting not only because of the information each offers but because of the contrast between them. Both Provine and Marler and Evans emphasize description, especially *in situ*, and both urge careful description of the activities under examination and of the conditions under which they occur. But Provine explicitly avoids a priori assumptions about emotional states and of any linkage between such states and the target social activity. His chapter is not atheoretical, since he does assume that certain behaviors (such as smiling and yawning) evolved as mechanisms by which the behaviors of other organisms are altered. But Marler and Evans look for internal states that can be construed as causing (jointly with contextual factors) observed differences in target behaviors. For example, an audience of conspecifics can serve to modulate the behavioral outputs of endogenous motivational and emotional processes that are set into motion directly by an exogenous event such as the sound or sight of a predator. The emotion produces an alarm call, the form of which is modulated by the presence or absence of an audience. So the ethological chapters differ in their reliance on notions of internal states, but they share a concern with careful description of behaviors in context. A closer examination of each is worthwhile.

Marler and Evans. The empirical substance of the Marler and Evans chapter does not concern faces; yet the implications of the findings for facial displays, their conditions of occurrence, and their linkage to internal states are considerable. The findings clearly reveal a variety of compound communicative behaviors in the presence of species-specific evocative events and stimuli (predators, food, unfamiliar females) and demonstrate that some elements of the behavioral compounds are differentially sensitive to the presence or absence of an audience whereas other elements remain invariant in the presence of the evocative stimulus (the autonomic features, for example). At the same time, Marler and Evans prefer to explain their findings by means of motivational and emotional causes of the observed behaviors. They subscribe to a linkage between internal states, especially those produced by endogenous programs that run off automatically and observable behaviors caused by those states, albeit subject to considerable modulation.

Provine. Provine largely eschews any explanatory reliance on internal states and causal mechanisms but instead stresses careful observation of social motor acts, preferably in natural settings. This, he argues, will allow linkages between our species and other animals. Provine approaches laughing, talking, and smiling as motor acts distributed in time, thereby allowing for cross-species comparisons. In his chapter, he focuses primarily on laughter, yawning, and smiling. The former two are both contagious (constitute a circumstance under which the same behavior erupts in others), only partially under volitional control, and yet are contextually contingent. We first consider laughter, then yawns, then smiles.

Laughter is highly stereotyped, although its structure varies across species. Laughter can be triggered by laughter, but repeated laughter loses its evocative capacity. Laughter, as a class, has dual valences – it can be part of a bonding activity, as in the predicate, "to laugh *with* someone," but it also can have a very negative connotation, as in the predicate, "to laugh *at* someone." Jeering can lead to violence, a sequence that Provine speculates might be akin to mobbing in some birds and mammals. The vocalization pattern of laughing co-evolved, Provine suggests, with the perception of it, in accord with Fridlund's point about the co-evolution of a signaling behavior and vigilance for it. Laughter occurs commonly in speech and relatively infrequently in structured humor. In speech, laughter very seldom interrupts the phrase structure, and it seems to operate more like punctuation. There are gender differences and audience effects – speakers laugh more than hearers, particularly if the speaker is a woman and the hearer is a man. It is much more likely to be performed in social than in solitary settings. Provine also muses that laughter may be closely tied to tickling, which is a social, interpersonal act, not an individual phenomenon, and can function to establish bonds. It also can serve to facilitate mother–infant interactions, again part of a process of bonding and acquisition of interactional coordination. These are characteristics of laughter as well, and Provine notes that in chimpanzees, most laughter occurs during physical contact or under the threat of it.

Yawning, too, is a highly stereotyped and contagious social act. It is not a function of oxygen or carbon dioxide concentrations, nor is it a simple reflex. It may occur in transition phases between acts, and it might serve to facilitate the transition. It does occur often when one is bored, but it is not clear whether it is a component of a state of boredom or through its occurrence (for whatever reason) helps to bring about a state of boredom. A yawn is reliably evoked by a yawning face and by a yawning face with the gaping mouth occluded, but it is not dependent on a face-to-face orientation.

Smiling is much more under voluntary control than either laughing or yawning, and it is more readily subject to deliberate modulation. From self-report records, Provine notes that smiles are six times more likely to be performed in social than solitary settings and that they are a common element in morning soliloquies (in the first postwaking hour). In stressing the social nature of smiling, as well as talking and laughing, Provine claims that people seldom perform those behaviors to inanimate objects. However, Fridlund and Duchaine (1996) report that people frequently talk, smile, laugh, and frown at alarm clocks, food, computers, and other inanimate objects, in accord with an extension of Fridlund's sociality concept. But this does not contradict the basic point made by Provine – that these acts are all highly social. In fact, they may all be akin to grooming in other primates, in which the content may be less important than the bonding function.

Provine closes his chapter by noting that an ethological approach to human behavior, in its typical and natural settings, but as though we were studying another species, might permit us to see familiar events in new ways.

The communication chapters – Bavelas and Chovil

At first glance, the communicative chapter by Bavelas and Chovil (chapter 15) and the other by Chovil (chapter 14) alone appear very different from the ethological chapters; but on closer examination, they have some strong similarity. They both emphasize the importance of careful observation of facial displays in natural contexts, especially in social situations, for those are the most common contexts for our species. Moreover, they stress the value of examining a wide array of facial displays, even those that are not apparently emotional. They note that facial displays can be used as nonverbal components of communicative interchanges, as part of the symbolic communication process. From that perspective, facial displays are expressive *to* another person rather than expressive *of* an internal state. The two chapters do assume the existence of internal states of emotion and the expression of those states in facial displays, but they conceive of facial expressions of emotion as a subset of facial displays more generally. People can draw on their skills as emotions displayers ("the familiar code of emotion displays," Bavelas & Chovil, chapter 15, this volume) to express a nonverbal, meaningful nuance or modifier of an utterance in a dialogue. However, such displays are not to be construed as revealing an emotional reaction of the displayer. The displays are fragmentary, too rapid to allow for the emergence and dissipation of an emotional state, clearly symbolic, and precisely timed to the flow of words in the dialogue. Their production is linguistic, not affective.

Regardless of the viability of the distinction between emotionally caused facial displays and those generated as part of a linguistic, interactional process, the emphasis on facial actions as part of the flow of dialogue is refreshing. Facial displays are more frequent in social than nonsocial situations, and they are more likely if a recipient is present. They also are more frequent in face-to-face than in nonvisible interactions. They clearly are part of the social process, and they first appear to be used as such at about 7 months of age. In fact, it is argued that facial displays are primarily socially directed rather than emotionally determined.

Both chapters stress the influence of context and urge that our methods of study should take context into account. Context is presented as pertaining both to the ongoing dialogue and to the other symbolic acts that co-occur with the facial display (e.g., intonations, gestures). The former context is progressively cumulative, much like Clark's (1985) notion of common ground, the progressive accumulation of which constitutes a conversation. It is a temporally extensive, linear context. In contrast, the other context mentioned is momentary, simultaneous. We might add a third aspect of context – that of the larger act being accomplished by the performance of the utterances of dialogue, such as an argument, or a contract, or a greeting. The meaning of any communicative gesture, including any facial display, is dependent upon all three of these aspects of context – the dialogue that has gone before, the other symbolic actions that co-occur with it, and the larger act of which the display is a component. The analysis of facial displays requires analysis of their embedding contexts.

These two chapters jointly provide a reminder of the larger, communicative context of facial displays. When faces are observed on living people, during relatively natural, informal interactions, much of what occurs on the face is clearly part of the communicative process. The admonitions of Bavelas and Chovil to examine facial displays in context, and to do so with careful attention to the details and timing of the displays, are well worth keeping in mind. There should no longer be any question about the social nature of facial displays, both evolutionarily and behaviorally. They contain information that is detectable by interacting partners and other observers, and they are among the communicative constituents of dialogue.

Fernández-Dols and Ruiz-Belda

The communicative nature of facial expressions is brought to the fore again in the chapter by Fernández-Dols and Ruiz-Belda. The two empirical studies described demonstrate smiles occur primarily during *interactional* happy times. In the Olympic gold medalist analyses, smiles were a much more common type of facial action when the medalists were free to exchange gaze and expressions with the audience than when interaction was constrained (these results are presented in more detail in Fernández-Dols & Ruiz-Belda, 1995). In the soccer fan study, smiles made up a much larger proportion of facial actions when the fans reported happy emotions but were either gazing at or speaking directly to another fan than when fans reported happy emotions but were not interacting. The self-indicated emotional episodes in which the facial actions were embedded were usually brief (2 to 9 sec), coming and going in the flow of the situated interaction. Fernández-Dols and Ruiz-Belda suggest that the experience of a happy state would facilitate the occurrence of a smile but would not be either a necessary or sufficient cause of it. They propose that the causes of smiling are the interactive encounters (presumably, the content of the actions in the interaction) and the presence of *any* emotion. The latter point is based on the report by Schneider and Josephs (1991) that smiles of preschool children in a competitive game were more frequent among losers than winners and were more often Duchenne smiles and more intense smiles than was true of winners' smiles. Thus, the linkage between internal states and facial displays is seen by the authors as loose and as potentially nonspecific.

The authors also make a useful distinction between "artistic truth" and "optical truth," as illustrated by the experience of Muybridge and the photographs of galloping horses. The conventionalization of "artistic truth" is as readily applied to ordinary emotional experience and talk about it as to the appearance of galloping horses. The possible conventionalization of emotion talk and display – and even of emotion enactment – creates extreme difficulty for research, since we and our human research subjects share the same conventionalizations. Even the use of "experts" as independent judges of the emotional quality of an event is subject to this criticism. The ethological perspective recommended by Provine might be of help, but at the cost of eschewing personal experience – necessarily conventionalized – as a source of insight.

In the process of criticizing earlier studies, Fernández-Dols and Ruiz-Belda imply that insufficient care has been given to the types of conditional probabilities by which hypotheses about facial displays are evaluated. This is a very important issue. Using smiling as an example, there is a difference between the probability of smiling if one is happy and the probability of being happy if one is smiling. The research issue is often phrased as the former (e.g., Ekman, Friesen, & Ancoli, 1980), but the test is almost always of the second form – the probability of being happy if one is smiling (the number of happy people among the smilers or the average happiness rating of people who were smiling, relative to those who were not smiling). To assess the linkages between facial displays and putative internal states, it is necessary to know (1) how often people who aren't happy smile, and (2) what other facial displays, besides smiling, are produced by people who are happy. Such information cannot be estimated directly from how often people who are smiling claim to be happy (or how happy they claim to be). This logic also can be applied to Duchenne smiles and the possibility that they are an artifact of intensity of display.

Fernández-Dols and Carroll

The Fernández-Dols and Carroll chapter brings us back to the issue of context. The authors take strong issue with the claim that emotion judgments are determined primarily by facial information – that is, by facial expressions – and only weakly by contextual information. The designs of studies on which that claim is based are susceptible to serious methodological and conceptual criticism, and research that is free of the criticized features does not show the dominance of facial expression in the creation of emotion impressions. Fernández-Dols and Carroll also take issue with the idea that visually presented facial displays and textually presented contextual information can be combined additively. A facial display in one context may be part of a very different emotional episode – and have different emotional meaning – from a similar facial display in another context. Fernández-Dols and Carroll suggest that a multiplicative (interaction) relationship must be sought. But their point can be taken further on theoretical grounds. The very identity of the phenomenon being investigated – the emotional reaction – cannot be decomposed into contextual and noncontextual elements without changing the identity of the phenomenon. This point was made years ago by Rom Harré (1977) when he distinguished between structural sciences, such as biochemistry and social psychology, and paradigmatic sciences, such as physics. In structural sciences, decomposition of an entity destroys its identity, as when the decomposition of water into its two constituent gasses destroys the identity of the water molecule. The same concern can be raised about emotional episodes and facial displays; asking people to judge the emotional nature of a decontextualized facial display, or a brief situational description without any expressive information, is qualitatively different from asking them to judge or otherwise react to an emotional episode. Neither of the component presentations has the identity of an emotional episode.

Nelson and de Haan

The developmental neurology of facial display detection and recognition is examined in the comprehensive chapter by Nelson and de Haan (chapter 8). Their objective is to produce a biologically plausible model of the neurological processes entailed in the recognition of facial expressions. The chapter reviews the behavioral literature on the development of the ability to recognize facial expressions; it then turns to the neurophysiological literature on adults and on infants, both humans and other primates. Nelson and de Haan do not construe the facial displays used as stimuli in the research they review as emotion displays, which if recognized by infants would imply that the infants realized the emotional significance of the display, but rather as facial feature configurations. Their focus is on the developing ability of infants to discriminate the configurations and on the correlated neurological development.

There are brain areas, especially in the temporal lobe and in the frontal and prefrontal cortex that are involved in the perception, discrimination, and probably recognition of facial expressions. The involvement is reflected in selectively higher firing rates of subsets of cells to facial stimuli. Discrimination starts as early as 3 months of age, but recognition of some negative expressions may not occur reliably until well into the second year. The ability to respond to categories of expressions, rather than isolated features or single presentations, is present by 6 to 7 months. The development of these abilities may parallel the differential maturation of brain structures, including the amygdala, which implies that the bases of emotion expression recognition will change during infancy and early childhood. How much of this is due to accumulated experience, how much to evolved genetic expression independent of experience, and how much to a combination in which experience facilitates genetic expression, is simply unknown. However, it is clear that the discrimination and recognition of facial expressions does entail identifiable patterns of activity in the brain. It is not *caused by* those patterns of activity; instead, the patterns are the neurological substrate of activity and the acts of recognition are what occur behaviorally. Both are aspects of the same situated accomplishment; neither is causal of the other. We see more of this perspective in the chapter by Messinger, Fogel, and Dickson.

Messinger, Fogel, and Dickson

Chapter 9, by Messinger, Fogel, and Dickson, also addresses the issue of development, but with two important differences from Nelson and de Haan's chapter 8. First, Messinger et al. focus on the development of certain infant facial actions rather than the ability to recognize facial expressions. Second, they make very explicit use of a noncausal, Dynamic Systems perspective. In doing so, they differentiate themselves from all of the preceding chapters. They disagree with explanations of facial actions that construe them as products of internal emotions states and with explanations that construe them as evolved communicative devices that are produced in the service of social motives and intentions. Their conception of facial actions incorporates neurophysiological, muscular, attentional, experiential, and dyadic interaction patterns as interdependent constituents of a situated emotional interchange. The quality of the instance is given by all of those constituents – and they are deliberately construed as *constituents*, not as causes or consequences. Although a facial action is part of the flow of interaction, it is considered by Messinger et al. to be a "collective variable" in that it is an index of changes in the dynamic system of which it also is a constituent. Furthermore, the organization of the system is held to emerge from the mutual interdependencies among its constituents. There is no central executive – cognition, brain, or other – that creates or directs the state of the system. This perspective is applied to the analysis of two types of smiles – Duchenne smiles (D smiles henceforth) and open-mouth play smiles (O smiles henceforth) – using detailed coding of videotapes of weekly playful interactions between mothers and their infants.

For D smiles, Messinger et al. examined the joint occurrence of upward lip corner retraction and eye crinkle with cheek raise, respectively indicative of contraction of *zygomatic major* and *orbicularis oculi*. They found that D smiles emerge and disappear in the rapid flow of interaction, are often preceded by non-D smiles, and fairly often precede non-D smiles, all of which implies smooth transitions between "types" of smiles. In addition, D smiles by the infants were often the occasion for D smiling by the mothers, implying some sort of mutual engagement. Messinger et al. interpret this as periods of mutual pleasure. The smooth and rapid transitions imply that the D and non-D smiles are not so much qualitatively different as quantitatively so. If they differ quantitatively – that is, in terms of intensity – that would explain some of the findings by Ekman and his colleagues (Ekman, Davidson, & Friesen, 1990) linking D smiles and ratings of pleasantness or happiness. Also, the high proportion of overlapping occurrences of mother and infant D smiles implies that these are jointly produced constituents of the situated line of action.

The authors speculate that the high likelihood of joint occurrence of lip corner raise and eye crinkle is partly a consequence of neural reentrant processes, a notion very similar to Hebbian cell assemblies (Hebb, 1949), except that the formation of an assemblage of frequently coactivated sets of cells is made possible by a mediating set that has synaptic ties with the two (or more) independent sets. The independent but coactivated clusters of neurons can be those activated during motor acts, reafferentation, inputs through sensory modalities, thinking, and so on

– all of the cell sets activated during the performance of the action. Messinger et al. provide a useful description of the neural and somatic anatomy involved in the two facial actions (lip corner raise and eye crinkle) of the D smile, and they make a plausible case for shared neural activation (through the buccal and zygomatic branches of the facial nerve) and muscular interdependencies as bases of the co-occurrence, especially under conditions of high intensity. Thus, there is some anatomical basis for construing the D smile as a "coordinative structure."

The open-mouth play smile (O smile) is different, since dropping of the jaw and lifting of the lip corners are partially antagonistic muscle actions and do not share neural innervation (facial nerve for the smile, trigeminal for the jaw drop). Nevertheless, mouth opening by the infants was four times more likely if the infant was smiling than if it was not. Messinger et al. propose that the joint occurrence is due in part to concurrent actions of the mother and infant. Both lip corner raise and mouth open increased in frequency after 3 months, and both were more likely if the mother was smiling, if the baby was gazing at the mother, and especially if the mother was holding the baby in a cradled or supported supine position. Joint occurrence, then, was most likely in interaction contexts that involved close physical contact with mutual engagement. Messinger et al. speculate that the mouth opening occurred during (or later, in anticipation of) physical contact, and if the baby was already smiling by virtue of the nature of the interaction, then mouth opening as part of the physical contact (e.g., to take the nipple or the mother's hand into the mouth) would lead to an open-mouth smile. Over time, by the operation of reentrant or other associative processes, the O smile would become a routinized and coherent facial action. The emergence of that facial action would be a function of increased interdependencies among interactional, muscular, and neural processes, which over time would become the interdependent constituents of the O smile action. This is in contrast to the D smile, the emergence of which was based on an interdependency among muscular and neural activation patterns. In neither case, though, was the smile caused by the activation of an internal state, and in neither case was it produced in order to achieve a social goal.

The details of the mechanisms proposed by Messinger et al. might be wrong, but the basic points of the argument are important and worthy of note. Patterned facial actions are to be understood in terms of their status as constituents in the flow of joint action. Their emergence as temporally and spatially coordinated muscle contractions carries with it emergent properties in all of the constituents of the action – the neural patterns, the social impacts, the feeling states. The emergence of a co-ordinated pattern entails not only coordinated motor outputs but per-ceptual and reafferent information – not as consequences or antecedents of the pattern but as interdependent constituents of it. Messinger et al. emphasize mutual interdependence among the constituents, including perceptions, feelings, thoughts, and partner behaviors during the real-time course of an emotional interchange. Infant smiles are muscular con-tractions, social signals, aspects of feelings, all at the same time. A facial action is a dynamic pattern, with a real-time history of emergence and dissipation; its meaning emerges, according to Messinger et al., out of the mutual influence of the involved constituents. Any action within an interaction episode is an instance of *joint* action, including a facial action. Its meaning is to be understood in terms of its constituents, its context of occurrence, and what it affords in the situated line of action underway. A methodological implication is that the reactions of individual subjects to a standardized, evocative stimulus are an *analog* of the real object of analysis. Whether that analog has any ecological validity is seldom ad-dressed.

Wagner

A number of the chapters reviewed so far made methodological points, but the chapter by Hugh Wagner (chapter 2) is devoted to that topic. He begins with the basic reminder that the methods we use should corre-spond to the questions being asked, which in facial expression research are of two basic sorts. There are questions about the components and structure of facial displays, and there are questions about the information available in facial displays. These two sorts of questions require different kinds of methods, and data generated by the methods appropriate to one sort do not afford inferences about the other sort.

The primary focus of Wagner's chapter is on judgment procedures. These typically are used to answer questions about the information avail-able in facial displays. There are two types of judgment procedures in facial expression research: category judgments and rating methods. Cat-egory judgments can use a forced-choice or free-response format and can require answers in terms of emotion labels (the most common approach) or brief situation descriptors (the latter is not mentioned by Wagner). Both ratings and category judgments are widely used, and they have been used by proponents of both discrete and dimensional views of emotion. Guidelines and standards for the use of judgment procedures were set forth by Ekman, Friesen, and Ellsworth (1972) and are still applicable.

First, we should not exclude people who do not show the expected facial displays unless the coder's task is restricted to the components of those particular displays. (See Bruner & Tagiuri, 1954, pp. 638–639, for a classical discussion of this matter.) Second, selection of segments from the record, usually from a videotape or film, must be done carefully since any selection increases the chance of missing important information. Third, over- and underrepresentation of emotions in a set of facial displays can bias the outcomes of both measurement and judgment studies (also see Bruner & Tagiuri, 1954). Unequal numbers of instances of different emotion categories can lead to statistical biases, especially if the categories differ in their ease of recognition.

Fourth, the sampling of emotion categories and dimension terms is very important in both free-response and forced-choice judgment studies, and judges preferably should be allowed to note more than one emotion as characterizing a display. Forced-choice and related formats pose a number of problems: Specification of categories can alert the judges to the required responses; agreement might occur because the displays represent universally recognized intentions to act rather than universally recognized emotion states; judges are unable to use categories not included in the response set; and accuracy in applying an emotion label will depend on how many other positive or negative labels there are in the set (with 2 positive and 4 negative labels, the probability of an accurate judgment will be .50 and .25, respectively). But free-response formats also have problems: They usually are not fully free, since judges are usually required to provide descriptions of *emotions*. Coding also is a problem, particularly with respect to matters of synonymity, and this is especially an issue in cross-cultural research.

Fifth, since a judge's judgment will be in part a function of the judgments already made, Wagner recommends between-subject designs. However, this raises a conceptual issue. One type of cue in detecting and inferring emotional states is the contrast between the current facial display and either a prior display or a display norm (see Bruner & Tagiuri, 1954). Hebb (1946), for example, upon spending a few months observing chimpanzees in the Yerkes laboratory, noted that the "primary emotion pattern is essentially a deviation from a baseline" (p. 97). Therefore, we might wish to include a within-judge design factor.

Wagner also discusses accuracy of measurement, especially in judgment studies, and particularly criticizes hit rate (true positive) as a measure. False positive rates as well as true positives must be taken into account, and so must marginal distributions (Fernández-Dols & Ruiz-Belda, chapter 11, this volume, discuss the effects of skewed marginals on accuracy measures). We should not use the number of categories of the stimuli as the probability base but rather should calculate the products of the marginals (as in chi-square calculations) to take into account judge bias (the preference for one category vs. the others). Bakeman and Gottman (1986) recommend the use of Cohen's kappa (Cohen, 1960); and repeated-measures ANOVA procedures also can be used (Winer, 1962). Wagner recommends the examination of a full confusion matrix, with the stimulus categories as specified by the experimenter as the rows, and with the categories as used by the judge as the columns. This is equivalent to a comparison of the judgments of one judge (the experimenter) with the judgments of another (the actual judge) and is identical to the structure of a kappa matrix (Cohen, 1960). Both kappa and the unbiased hit rate proposed by Wagner yield a measure of accuracy that either takes the marginal distributions into account (Wagner's measure) or gives an estimate of accuracy over and above that which would be expected to occur by chance (kappa). Wagner's unbiased hit rate can be used as a dependent variable after an arcsin transformation, and it can be applied to judges, stimulus persons, or sender–judge pairs.

Wagner's suggestions should be followed routinely in facial judgment studies, along with the design guidelines reviewed in his chapter. But Wagner's presumption that we are restricted to judgment methods for questions about the information available in facial behavior should be qualified. Other techniques can be used, depending on the specific question being asked. For example, the habituation/dishabituation paradigm commonly used with infants (see Nelson & de Haan, chapter 8, this volume) can be applied to adults as well; and other nonverbal designs also can be found in the infant, comparative, and ecological perception literatures. In fact, verbal judgment methods make the questionable assumption that the judgment is a direct reflection of a categorical impression that the stimulus "made" on the judge, and it is not a reflective, thoughtful act of inference by the judge. Moreover, in the verbal lexicon of a culture, there is likely to be a set of emotion norms – norms about how one *should* react to an evocative event, and how people usually *do* react to an evocative event (Heise & Calhan, 1995) – and these norms are likely to play a role in the judgments made by subjects in facial judgment studies. Other than this qualification, the guidance provided by Wagner's chapter will facilitate research on facial displays and will lead to more defensible inferences and greater understanding.

Themes and admonitions: A selective discussion

There are several striking themes that run through the chapters of this volume, despite the differences in perspective. One concerns methodology, and others bear on the roles of facial displays and their relationship to emotion and feelings, the construct of emotion itself, and the importance of context.

The utility of judgment data

The methodological theme concerns judgment studies. Such studies yield information about judgment processes made in response to requests to explain a puzzle. The puzzle is the noncontextualized facial display of another person, usually a stranger, and the task is to explain it by selecting one from a limited set of prescribed emotion labels. This is only an *analog* of emotion perception processes; we do not know whether such judging actually occurs in natural interaction episodes. Further, the judgment procedures do not assess the structure of emotional reactions, and the judgment data cannot be used to infer the form of emotional responses. That is, we cannot use the typical judgment data either to claim or deny the existence of a small set of basic emotions.

The utility of emotion constructs

Two conceptual themes running through the volume are (1) the looseness of the tie between facial displays and emotion, and (2) the acceptance of emotions as states internal to the individual. The concept of emotion is central in the discussions of facial displays, even for those who claim it is not the only basis for such displays. But the construct of emotion is hardly a technical construct (Russell, 1991; also Ginsburg & Harrington, 1996) except in a very restricted sense, and a lawful tie between its instantiations and facial displays should not be expected. A review of emotions and bodily states (Ginsburg & Harrington, 1996) indicated (1) that there are no bodily states that are uniquely and reliably tied to specific emotional states and only to them, and (2) that bodily instantiations of what we refer to as *emotions* appear to be variable and unreliable. Moreover, physiological changes during emotional episodes are likely to reflect the line of action undertaken rather than an internal emotion state; and similarity of physiological changes across instances of a given "emotion" will be a function of similarity in the situated lines of action (Smith & Scott, chapter 10, this volume). Nevertheless, "emotion" remains an important concept in human affairs.

The reason appears to lie in the social and personal functions served by emotion talk and emotion display, including facial displays (Averill, 1974). The use of emotion terms in speech and text is as a claim that an action or series of actions is not fully under control of the actor. The actor is claimed to be less than fully responsible for his actions or their consequences, and the actions are claimed not to have been performed to achieve some end. Any situated behavior or action is a candidate for a claim of emotion to the extent that (1) it can be construed to imply a reduced responsibility on the part of the actor, (2) the actor is not under exogenous influences such as drugs, injury, or physical disease, and (3) the actor is responding to some finite event, whether external or internal (otherwise, the action would be an expression of enduring temperament). An emotion claim can take the form of speech or of culturally recognized canonical displays. Thus, a facial display can constitute an emotion claim.

A culturally competent person usually can choose to be emotional by performing those movements and expressions and thinking those thoughts that constitute a particular emotion. We are guided in these accomplishments by situated emotion norms (Heise & Calhan, 1995), rules of emotion work (Hochschild, 1979), and culturally ingrained narratives, complete with moral plots and characters (Sarbin, 1995). Our engagement in such plots can be full and deep, even to the point of violence (Sarbin, 1995). Once an action is accepted as emotional, it has interpersonal force (as in emotional contagion; Hatfield, Cacioppo, & Rapson, 1992) and sincerity implications (Harré, 1986). There is not necessarily anything common to all emotions, or even to all instances of a particular emotion, although there may be prototypical instances of particular emotions that have a common and unique set of features (features common only to all prototypical instances of an emotion). It is unlikely that prewired emotion programs exist at any level of analysis or that facial displays are causally related to some coherent internal entity to which emotion terms purportedly refer. However, although facial displays are not caused by emotional states, they often are components of situated lines of action that can be given ordinary-language emotion labels.

Contextual grounding of facial displays

All events and processes are embedded in contexts, and any event or process constitutes a context for embedded events and processes. Moreover, an event or process occurs at the end of whatever has occurred to that point, and it also occurs as a component of some larger process or event that its occurrence is helping to bring about. A smile may occur after a smile by a partner, and its occurrence may help to accomplish a greeting. Thus, facial displays have both linear and hierarchical contexts. Furthermore, any event, upon its occurrence, serves as part of the context for what is yet to occur. The smile that follows a partner's smile might set the stage for a kiss and therefore is part of the historical, linear context of the kiss. When viewed in this fashion, it is clear that contexts are cumulative, even the internal context. For example, the physiological status of the body at a point in time is a cumulative function of prior activity, but it also is part of the context for current and future reactions. The hierarchical and linear aspects of context apply across all levels of analysis, and their basic operating principle is a feedforward mechanism – they set the stage for the subsequent actions of the system. Facial expressions, then, necessarily occur in *and are perceived in* their linear and hierarchical context. Their meaning is a contextualized one, in terms of *what preceded them, what they are part of,* and *what they are setting the stage for.*

Feelings and feeling talk. The issue of context also is relevant to the constructs of "feeling" and "felt experience." Discussions of facial expressions usually include feelings as causal precursors of the facial displays (and sometimes as consequents of them). However, it is more likely that they are part of the context of facial displays. In considering this, a distinction must first be made between feelings and talk about feelings. The measurement of feelings through self-report scaling procedures is a form of talk and must be distinguished from the experience to which the talk refers and which we seem to experience directly (to "have"). Talk about one's feelings should not be taken as referring denotatively to extant entities but rather as a conversational claim that has implications for what else one might sensibly say in the discourse. Feeling talk should not be treated as technical references to denotable internal entities.

Felt experience. Felt experience, apart from talk about it, stands in complex relationship to facial displays. Felt experience necessitates some degree of reflection by the experiencer on what is occurring, and it is important to distinguish between a situated bodily phenomenon and the experience of it. LeDoux (1995) draws a distinction between conditioned fear and the experience or feeling of fear – the phenomena are not the same. The importance of reflection has been noted by others as well (e.g., Rolls, 1995, treats feelings as entailing reflective appraisal and as requiring language-like processing abilities; Cacioppo, Berntson, & Klein, 1992, implicitly assume reflective appraisal in their proposal that people reflect on inherently ambiguous somatovisceral feedback as a step in their experience of feelings). Bull (1951) demonstrated that the feeling which we take to characterize a particular emotional state occurs only during a pause in the sequence from a "motor attitude" to the instrumental action. The feelings, she held, are spinoffs of patterns of bodily response – they are frequent concomitants of situated sequences but not central components since the sequence could run off without the pauses necessary for feeling. When the pause and a feeling do occur, though, the feeling is part of the context of subsequent actions.

In sum, feelings are relevant to bodily patterns, including facial displays, but as interdependent phenomena rather than as causes or effects. The relationships are best viewed as contextual – an experienced feeling, and talk about a feeling, can serve as context for a facial display, and a facial display can also serve as part of the context for talk about a feeling or the experience of a feeling. But if facial actions are not linked tightly to "emotions" or "feelings" as internal states, why are they so important? If they do not reveal our innermost desires and passions, why have they persisted? The answer to this may lie in their implications for action.

A conception of facial actions

Facial expressions as implicatures

As a species, we are very attentive to faces and their expressions (Fridlund, and others, this volume) and appear to have some neurological sensitivity to both facial identity and facial displays (Nelson & de Haan, chapter 8, this volume). It is not clear whether we are particularly attentive to facial displays in contrast to postural and vocal displays, but all such displays carry information about what acts the displayer is embarked upon or is prepared to undertake. The neural and muscular anatomy of the human face, especially those parts innervated by the seventh (facial) nerve, affords exceptionally fine variation of feature movement and therefore extremely high resolution of configurations. Nuances of both quality and intensity are readily produced, readily controlled, and readily perceived. The arguments presented in this volume suggest that the function of facial actions is interpersonal and implicative – they imply what is about to occur or could occur. Certainly, facial displays can be indicative of bodily states, just as can posture. Posture, for example, can indicate high or low energy, comfort or discomfort, attentiveness or inattentiveness. Nevertheless, the informational value of such indications is implicational – the indicators carry action implications, and that is their utility and the source of their evolutionary selection. Facial displays can carry the same implicative information, but much more finely tuned.

Integration: Facial displays in situated lines of action

Facial displays form and dissipate in real time in the flow of interaction as components of the situated line of action. Temporal as well as spatial characteristics of the display are discriminable and help establish the meaning of the act under way. Any facial display is part of an embedding larger act and contains interdependent components. These include physiological and motor components. Facial movements are among the motor activities helping to constitute the continuing line of action; they are not caused by internal events, nor do they cause internal events, but rather co-occur at a different level of organization from the "underlying" physiological changes. The actor's experience during any brief interval of time is constituted by – not caused by – all of the interdependent components, including the performed and perceived facial displays. A state of "experiencing," though, is unlikely to be automatic; rather, it requires some degree of reflection (cf. the earlier discussion of feeling). However, when a particular state *is* experienced, that experience itself becomes an element of context and can be a basis of subsequent action. Thus, a scientific understanding of facial displays must take into account not only biological, situational, and interactional factors constituting the display, the conditions of its occurrence, and its perception, but also the consequences of its being *noticed and considered* by the parties to the interaction. That is, facial displays are potential occasions for attribution by participants.

Attributions. There is a large social psychological literature on attributions, but the aspects of it most relevant to an understanding of facial displays concern (1) the conditions under which attributions are made (Hilton & Slugoski, 1986; Turnbull & Slugoski, 1988), and (2) conversational maxims that guide the performance of attributions in discourse (Hilton, 1995). From a conversational perspective, facial displays will become topics for attribution when they are atypical or nonnormative, or otherwise disruptive of the smooth flow of the interaction, since that is when they will become a focus of attention. It is to such focal instances that the results of facial judgment studies will most directly and usefully apply.

Universality. The form and the perceptually detectable meanings of facial displays are likely to be universal to the extent that the problems and affordances of the social and physical environments available to the species are universal. The notion of affordances – opportunities for action – necessarily and jointly takes into account both the characteristics of the context of action and the capacities of the actor with regard to those characteristics. Human infants, for example, mouth objects, including nipples, and are prepared to do so at birth (cf. the rooting reflex). In addition, mothers and infants bond, and they engage in intense interactions as part of the bonding process. Facial actions performed by infants during intimate contact, such as mouthing, rooting, and suckling, and readiness to engage in such actions, are likely to be attended to and capitalized upon by the mother as part of the process of bonding. The co-occurrence of an open mouth and a rudimentary smile in a bonding context is likely to occur universally, so that the open-mouth smile discussed by Messinger et al. (chapter 9, this volume) is a strong candidate for universality – both in production and in vigilant responsiveness by recipients. The mechanisms by which such coherent configurations emerge is subject to speculation at present but is certainly an important topic of investigation. Messinger et al. proposed two mechanisms by which an assembly of constituents can come into being – one through temporal contiguity and the other through shared neuroanatomical elements (as in the D smile).

The structure of the body also imposes functional requirements that can generate universal displays, as described by Darwin (1965/1872, pp. 157f) and Bell (1824): When a baby screams or cries vigorously, or when a person sneezes hard or vomits, the eyes are squeezed tightly shut, and often the face turns red. The tightly shut eyes and the reddened face are an expression that carry implications about the intensity and sincerity as well as the valence of the activity underway. All of the actions described entail vigorous expulsion of air or other contents from the thoracic or abdominal cavity, achieved by rapid and powerful contraction of the musculature. Bell and Darwin both note (1) that a consequence of the contraction is a great restriction of venous return from the head and neck, and (2) that in the absence of tightly closed eyelids, the delicate vasculature of the eyes would probably be damaged by the increased volume and pressure of blood in the local vessels. Such expressions, their conditions of occurrence, and their meanings, are universal, thanks to the functional anatomy of our bodies and the ubiquitous presence of poisons, nasal irritants, and various elicitors of infant crying.

Darwin (pp. 148–149) also gives an example of a crying episode that demonstrates the value of careful, detailed description. The brow muscle begins to contract first, with the orbiculars following almost immediately and with considerable strength, and then the nasal pyramidal muscles. These contractions produce the frown, eye shutting, nose wrinkle, and nostril-widening characteristic of crying, but they also can raise the upper lip and thereby draw the upper parts of the cheeks upward, creating a naso-labial fold on each cheek, running from nostrils to below the mouth corners. Meantime, the mouth is kept open by contraction of the depressor muscles in order to allow full sound to be produced, which gives the mouth the open squarish appearance of the crying child. This, too, is very likely to be a universally produced and recognized facial expression. In neither this case nor the preceding example of tightly shut eyes is our understanding of the expression enhanced by making reference to internal states – whether of anger or sadness or pain or fright.

Future

This volume makes clear that greater attention must be given to context, reflecting the recognition by all contributors that (1) the meaning of facial displays is indeterminate in the absence of context, and (2) subjects given acontextualized facial stimuli will create contexts for the displays. I hope the more extreme form of this point also will be recognized – that the object of analysis for us is the contextualized facial display. There is no such thing as an acontextualized display.

Furthermore, more stress should be given to careful, ethological description, and we should make what use we can of comparative data from different cultures and from different species. Provine's work (chapter 7, this volume) on laughter and the work by Marler and Evans (chapter 6, this volume) on audience effects both elucidate the form and the possible origins of expressive behaviors in our species through interspecies comparisons. The description should trace the natural history of the display – its emergence and dissipation – as well as the linear and hierarchical context of its occurrence. For our species, one ubiquitous context is conversation, and an ethological approach must also take that into account. The contributions of Bavelas and Chovil (chapter 15, this volume) demonstrate that the study of facial displays in discourse will facilitate our understanding of both. It is striking how little those analyses need to rely on emotions, feelings, or other internal states in generating an understanding of the occurrence and functions of facial displays.

Finally, and consistent with the emphasis on an ethological orientation, perhaps readers will be persuaded to eschew a reliance on causal models. The Dynamic System perspective of Messinger and his colleagues (chapter 9, this volume) shows clearly that causal talk is not necessary for a scientific understanding and might even shut off research prematurely by reliance on a hypothetical "causal mechanism." The dynamic system of interest, however, is not simply the face of one person. It is instead the face in context, and that context will include recipients of the facial display, including the displayer. Awareness of this was explicit in the chapters by Frijda and Tcherkassof, Fridlund, and Russell, and it was implicit in several of the other chapters. Facial displays occur in a flow of situated action and can only be understood as features of that flow.

This volume had the objective of reconsidering from a variety of perspectives the underlying assumption of much work on facial displays – that human faces express our internal states. The volume has succeeded admirably in achieving that objective. It is a reflection of what may be a sea change in emotion research.

References

Abelson, R. P., & Lalljee, M. (1988). Knowledge structures and causal explanation. In D. Hilton (Ed.), *Contemporary science and natural explanation: Commonsense conceptions of causality* (pp. 175–203). New York: New York University Press.

Averill, J. R. (1974). An analysis of psychophysiological symbolism and its influence on theories of emotion. *Journal for Theory of Social Behavior, 4* (22), 147–190.

Bakeman, R., & Gottman, J. M. (1986). *Observing interaction: An introduction to sequential analysis.* New York: Cambridge University Press.

Bell, Sir Charles. (1824). *Essays on the anatomy and philosophy of expression* (2nd ed.). London: John Murray, Albemarle-Street.

Bruner, J. S., & Tagiuri, R. (1954). The perception of people. In G. Lindzey (Ed.), *Handbook of social psychology* (Vol. 2). Reading, MA: Addison-Wesley.

Bull, N. (1951). The attitude theory of emotion. *Nervous and Mental Disease Monographs, No. 81.*

Cacioppo, J. T., Berntson, G. G., & Klein, D. J. (1992). What is an emotion? The role of somatovisceral afference, with special emphasis on somatovisceral "illusions." In M. S. Clark (Ed.), *Emotion* (Vol. 14, pp. 63–98). London: Sage Publications.

Clark, H. H. (1985). Language use and language users. In G. Lindzey & E. Aronson (Eds.), *Handbook of social psychology* (Vol. 2, 3rd ed., pp. 179–232). New York: Random House.

Cohen, J. (1960). A coefficient of agreement for nominal scales. *Educational and Psychological Measurement, 20,* 37–46.

Darwin, C. (1965). *The expression of emotions in man and animals.* Chicago: University of Chicago Press. (Original work published 1872)

Ekman, P. (1994). All emotions are basic. In P. Ekman & R. J. Davidson (Eds.), *The nature of emotion: Fundamental questions* (pp. 1–19). New York: Oxford University Press.

Ekman, P., Davidson, R. J., & Friesen, W. V. (1990). The Duchenne smile: Emotional expression and brain physiology II. *Journal of Personality and Social Psychology, 58* (2), 342–353.

Ekman, P., Friesen, W. V., & Ancoli, S. (1980). Facial signs of emotional experience. *Journal of Personality and Social Psychology, 39,* 1125–1134.

Ekman, P., Friesen, W. V., & Ellsworth, P. (1972). *Emotion in the human face: Guidelines for research and an integration of findings.* New York: Pergamon Press.

Fernández-Dols, J-M., & Ruiz-Belda, M-A. (1995). Are smiles a sign of happiness? Gold medal winners at the Olympic Games. *Journal of Personality and Social Psychology, 69,* 1113–1119.

Fridlund, A. J. (1994). *Human facial expression: An evolutionary view.* San Diego, CA: Academic Press.

Fridlund, A. J., & Duchaine, B. (1996). "Facial expressions of emotion" and the delusion of the hermetic self. In R. Harré & W. G. Parrott (Eds.), *The emotions: Social, cultural and physical dimensions.* London: Sage.

Ginsburg, G. P., & Harrington, M. E. (1996). The nature of emotions: Bodily states and context in situated lines of action. In R. Harré & W. G. Parrott (Eds.), *The emotions: Social, cultural and physical dimensions.* London: Sage.

Harré, R. (1977). The ethogenic approach: Theory and practice. In L. Berkowitz (Ed.), *Advances in experimental social psychology* (Vol. 10, pp. 284–314). New York: Academic Press.

Harré, R. (1986). An outline of the social constructionist viewpoint. In R. Harré (Ed.), *The social construction of emotions.* Oxford: Basil Blackwell.

Harré, R. (1988). Modes of explanation. In D. Hilton (Ed.), *Contemporary science and natural explanation: Commonsense conceptions of causality* (pp. 129–144). New York: New York University Press.

Hatfield, E., Cacioppo, J. T., & Rapson, R. L. (1992). Primitive emotional contagion. In M. S. Clark (Ed.), *Emotion* (Vol. 14, pp. 151–177). London: Sage Publications.

Hebb, D. O. (1946). Emotion in man and animal: An analysis of the intuitive processes of recognition. *Psychological Review, 53,* 88–106.

Hebb, D. O. (1949). *The organization of behavior.* New York: Wiley.

Heise, D. R., & Calhan, C. (1995). Emotion norms in interpersonal events. *Social Psychology Quarterly, 58,* 223–240.

Hermans, H. J. M. (1996). Voicing the self: From information processing to dialogical interchange. *Psychological Bulletin, 119,* 31–50.

Hilton, D. J. (1995). The social context of reasoning: Conversational inference and rational judgment. *Psychological Bulletin, 118,* 248–271.

Hilton, D. J., & Slugoski, B. R. (1986). Knowledge-based causal attribution: The abnormal conditions focus model. *Psychological Review, 93,* 75–88.

Hochschild, A. R. (1979). Emotion work, feeling rules and social structure. *American Journal of Sociology, 85,* 551–575.

Izard, C. E. (1994). Innate and universal facial expressions: Evidence from developmental and cross-cultural research. *Psychological Bulletin, 115,* 288–299.

Izard, C. E., Fantauzzo, C. A., Castle, J. M., Haynes, O. M., Rayias, M. F., & Putnam, P. H. (1995). The ontogeny and significance of infants' facial expressions in the first 9 months of life. *Developmental Psychology, 31,* 997–1013.

James, W. (1950). *The principles of psychology* (Vol 1.) New York: Dover. (Original work published 1890)

Laird, J. D. (1984). The real role of facial response in the experience of emotion: A reply to Tourangeau and Ellsworth, and others. *Journal of Personality and Social Psychology, 47* (4), 909–917.

Laird, J. D., & Bresler, C. (1992). The process of emotional experience: A self-perception theory. In M. S. Clark (Ed.), *Emotion* (Vol. 13, pp. 213–234). London: Sage Publications.

LeDoux, J. E. (1995). Emotion: Clues from the brain. *Annual Review of Psychology, 46,* 209–235.

Mead, G. H. (1934). *Mind, self and society.* Chicago: University of Chicago Press.

Osgood, C. E. (1952). The nature and measurement of meaning. *Psychological Bulletin, 49,* 197–237.

Osgood, C. E. (1966). Dimensionality of the semantic space for communication via facial expressions. *Scandinavian Journal of Psychology, 7,* 1–30.

Osgood, C. E., Suci, G. J., & Tannenbaum, P. H. (1957). *The measurement of meaning.* Urbana: University of Illinois Press.

Pope, L. K., & Smith, C. A. (1994). On the distinct meanings of smiles and frowns. *Cognition and Emotion, 8,* 65–72.

Rolls, E. T. (1995). A theory of emotions and consciousness, and its application to understanding the neural basis of emotion. In M. S. Gazzaniga (Ed.), *The cognitive neurosciences.* Cambridge, MA: MIT Press.

Russell, J. A. (1991). Natural language concepts of emotion. In D. Ozer, J. M. Healy, Jr., A. J. Stewart, & R. Hogan (Eds.), *Perspectives in personality: A research annual: Self and emotion* (Vol. 3, pp. 119–138). London: Jessica Kingsley.

Russell, J. A. (1994). Is there universal recognition of emotion from facial expression? *Psychological Bulletin, 115,* 102–141.

Russell, J. A. (1995). Facial expressions of emotion: What lies beyond minimal universality? *Psychological Bulletin, 118,* 379–391.

Sarbin, T. R. (1995). Emotional life, rhetoric and roles. *Journal of Narrative and Personal History, 5,* 213–220.

Schneider, K., & Josephs, I. (1991). The expressive and communicative functions of preschool children's smiles in an achievement-situation. *Journal of Nonverbal Behavior, 15,* 185–198.

Stemmler, G. (1989). The autonomic differentiation of emotions revisited: Convergent and discriminant validation. *Psychophysiology, 26,* 617–632.

Turnbull, W., & Slugoski, B. (1988). Conversational and linguistic processes in causal attribution. In D. Hilton (Ed.), *Contemporary science and natural explanation: Commonsense conceptions of causality* (pp. 66–93). New York: New York University Press.

Winer, B. J. (1962). *Statistical principles in experimental design.* New York: McGraw-Hill.

Zajonc, R. B., & McIntosh, D. N. (1992). Emotions research: Some promising questions and some questionable promises. *Psychological Science, 3* (1), 70–74.

Author index

383

Subject index

Studies in Emotion and Social Interaction

First Series
Editors: Paul Ekman and Klaus R. Scherer